Premiere Elements 8

Chris Grover

POGUE PRESS™
O'REILLY®

Beijing · Cambridge · Farnham · Köln · Sebastopol · Taipei · Tokyo

Premiere Elements 8: The Missing Manual
by Chris Grover

Published by O'Reilly Media, Inc., 1005 Gravenstein Highway North, Sebastopol, CA 95472.

O'Reilly books may be purchased for educational, business, or sales promotional use. Online editions are also available for most titles (*safari.oreilly.com*). For more information, contact our corporate/institutional sales department: (800) 998-9938 or *corporate@oreilly.com*.

Printing History:

October 2009:   First Edition.

 This book uses RepKover™, a durable and flexible lay-flat binding.

ISBN: 978-0-596-80336-0

[M]

Table of Contents

Part Two: Create Your Movie

The Missing Credits

About the Author

 Chris Grover is a veteran of the San Francisco Bay Area advertising and design community. He has degrees in film and creative writing from Emerson College in Boston, Massachusetts. For more than 30 years, Chris has worked on film and video projects in a variety of capacities, including editor, sound recordist, writer, and producer. Chris is the owner of Bolinas Road Creative (*http://BolinasRoad. com*), an agency that helps small businesses promote their products and services. He's also the author of *Word 2007: The Missing Manual; Flash CS4: The Missing Manual;* and *Google SketchUp: The Missing Manual.*

About the Creative Team

Peter McKie (editor) is an editor at Missing Manuals. He graduated from Boston University's School of Journalism and lives in New York, where he researches the history of old houses, and, every once in a while, sneaks into abandoned buildings. Email: *pmckie@gmail.com.*

Nellie McKesson (production editor) currently lives in Brighton, Mass., where she devotes all her free time to her burgeoning t-shirt business (*www.endplasticdesigns. com*). Email: *nellie@oreilly.com.*

Marcia Simmons (copy editor) is a writer and editor living in the San Francisco Bay Area. In addition to covering technology and cocktail culture, she has a personal blog at *www.smartkitty.org.*

Lucie Haskins (indexer) lives in Woodland Park, Colorado. She became an indexer in 2000, after a long career in corporate America, with roles that ranged from computer programmer to management consultant. She specializes in embedded indexing for books on computer- and business-related topics. She loves to share her passion for indexing by talking about it to whoever will listen! Visit her site at *luciehaskins. com* for more information about indexing.

Lori Grunin (technical reviewer) has been using, testing, and reviewing digital imaging products for major print and online publications since before there were any online publications. She's currently a senior editor for CNET Reviews, where she spends her days putting digital SLR cameras and high-definition camcorders through their paces.

Don Willmott (technical reviewer) has been covering computer, technology, and Internet topics for more than 20 years, first as an editor at *PC Magazine* and *Yahoo! Internet Life,* and currently as a freelance writer whose work appears online at such sites as The Weather Channel and ForbesTraveler.com. He is also the author of the book *PC Magazine Best of the Internet* (Wiley, 2004).

Acknowledgements

It takes a team to move a Missing Manual from concept to publication, and I want to thank all the pros who helped with *Premiere Elements 8: The Missing Manual.* Many thanks to my editor Peter McKie for his skill in sharpening up the text and keeping us close to our hectic schedule. Thanks also to Marcia Simmons for copyediting, to Lucie Haskins for indexing, to Karen Shaner for coordinating figures and documents, and to Dawn Frausto for help with the appendixes.

A special thanks to Lori Grunin and Don Willmott for lending their expertise as technical reviewers. And once again, thanks to Peter Meyers for signing me up to the Missing Manuals team. Thanks, as always, to my beautiful wife, Joyce, and my wonderful filmmaking daughters Mary and Amy.

—*Chris Grover*

The Missing Manual Series

Missing Manuals are witty, superbly written guides to computer products that don't come with printed manuals (which is just about all of them). Each book features a handcrafted index; cross-references to specific pages (not just chapters); and RepKover, a detached-spine binding that lets the book lie perfectly flat without the assistance of weights or cinder blocks.

Recent and upcoming titles include:

Access 2007: The Missing Manual by Matthew MacDonald

AppleScript: The Missing Manual by Adam Goldstein

AppleWorks 6: The Missing Manual by Jim Elferdink and David Reynolds

CSS: The Missing Manual, Second Edition by David Sawyer McFarland

Creating a Web Site: The Missing Manual by Matthew MacDonald

David Pogue's Digital Photography: The Missing Manual by David Pogue

Dreamweaver 8: The Missing Manual by David Sawyer McFarland

Dreamweaver CS3: The Missing Manual by David Sawyer McFarland

Dreamweaver CS4: The Missing Manual by David Sawyer McFarland

eBay: The Missing Manual by Nancy Conner

Introduction

Film will only become art when its materials are
as inexpensive as pencil and paper.
——Jean Cocteau, poet and filmmaker

Armed with a camcorder and Premiere Elements video-editing software, you can create art. Or, if your goals are little less lofty, you can chronicle family events, show off on YouTube, or produce a video project for school. Making motion pictures still costs more than pencil and paper, but it gets cheaper every day. If you're a hungry poet or a 12-year-old who wants to break into Hollywood, it doesn't cost much to get started. Somewhere, Jean Cocteau is smiling.

For many, video is a communication tool just like pencil and paper—or like a word processor. Computers and the Internet make communicating via video quick and easy. You don't have to splice and glue bits of film together or work with a production house to turn your raw clips into a finished product. Today's video projects go directly from camcorder to computer to audience, and the entire journey can take just a few hours or, in some cases, minutes. Premiere Elements is the tool you use to do everything except capture the pictures. It moves videos from your camcorder to your computer, helps you find the best shots, and assembles them into a story. When your movie's ready for an audience, Premiere helps you deliver it via disc or the Web, too.

About This Book

Premiere Elements 8: The Missing Manual is divided into four parts, each containing several chapters. In addition, to help you practice your budding skills as a video editor, you'll find free, downloadable video clips for the exercises in this book at the Missing Manuals website (see "Living Examples" on page 8 for instructions).

Here's a little more information about each section in *Premiere Elements 8: The Missing Manual*:

- **Part One: Start a New Project** shows you how to gather all the elements you need for your movie—video clips, songs, sound effects, and still photos. You'll learn how to use Elements Organizer as an efficient organizational tool for all the movie clips and media files you import. You can attach keywords and rank clips by quality and content, along with several other sanity-saving strategies.

- **Part Two: Create Your Movie** focuses on what most people think of as video editing. You learn how to trim your raw footage to just the parts that tell your story and then build your movie clip by clip. You'll add cool transitions between clips and include any of dozens of special effects to spice up your footage.

  Unless you're Charlie Chaplin, you'll want to add a soundtrack and sound effects, too, so you'll learn how to build a multi-layered audio track. Need background music or the sound of a car crash? You'll get tips on finding royalty-free music and sound effects.

- **Part Three: Share Your Movie** is all about showing your movie to an audience. It starts off with a brief background on video formats and then tells you how to use presets to export your finished film. All the details are here for uploading your movies to YouTube or any other website, saving them to DVD or Blu-ray disc, or putting them on your iPod Touch, iPhone, or other handheld gadget.

- **Part Four: Appendixes** are reference guides. You don't have to read them from start to finish, but they're there when you need them, all neatly arranged. You'll find help on installation and finding support, along with each and every menu command in Premiere Elements and Elements Organizer.

Why Premiere Elements?

If you shot still photos when you were on vacation in Greece, you wouldn't come home and show your friends and family every picture you took. No, you'd go through them and get rid of that accidental shot of the ground, the overexposed Parthenon, and the dinner table where the food looks great but everyone's eyes are closed. Video editing is a lot like that. It's not unusual to use about 10 percent of the video you shoot. So, job number one for Premiere Elements is to help you find your good shots. Its next job is to make the good shots look even better. That includes everything from correcting picture problems to adding transitions, special effects, and titles. Last and certainly not least, there's distribution. Any Hollywood big shot will tell you it doesn't do any good to produce a movie if you can't deliver it to an audience. Premiere Elements handles that, too.

If you've got a PC, you probably already have a video-editing program. It may be Windows Movie Maker, or it may have come on a disc with your camcorder. These programs are kind of like bikes with training wheels—they get you where you want to go, but you feel a little hobbled along the way.

At the other end of the spectrum are professional video-editing programs like Final Cut Pro for the Mac and Premiere Elements' big brother, Premiere Pro, for Windows PCs. Pro programs cost a fortune, require serious computer horsepower, and come with a steep learning curve.

Premiere Elements sits comfortably between the two. It doesn't cost much—in fact, you could easily spend more money taking someone to dinner. And you don't have to be a video technician to tap into the editing power it offers: Premiere Elements has a split personality. Use one set of tools, like InstantMovie or sceneline editing, and you can whip a movie together in no time. It's not just a bunch of clips strung together, either. We're talking about a movie with slick transitions, major eye candy, DVD menus with theme-based graphics, and soundtracks with balanced music and effects.

Use another set of tools, timeline editing, and you're a lot closer to the professional video-editing suite. You build your own effects with multiple layers of video and sound, and use keyframes to control the exact timing of special effects, motion effects, sound effects, and the soundtrack. It takes more time, but that's how you create art.

What You Can Do with Premiere Elements

Using the aforementioned pencil and paper, you can create documents as diverse as a play, a financial report, and a shopping list. You get the same diversity with video and Premiere Elements. Someone in your family may capture weddings and birthday parties, while another family member might carry on video correspondence with far-flung friends. Aspiring actors and stand-up comics can create video portfolios (archaically called "reels"). Musicians can capture rehearsals and concerts and then, with Premiere Elements, turn them into their own MTV-style music videos. Training videos, podcasts, school projects—video communication can take an unlimited number of forms.

These days, a video-editing program does a whole lot more than assemble video clips in sequence. Here are a few of the chores Premiere Elements handles for you:

- **Move video clips from your camcorder to your computer.** In the past, this very first step often resulted in computer-crash frustration.

- **Collect and import still photos, graphic art, music, and other media.** Movies are made up of more than just raw video clips.

- **Organize your media clips.** After two or three years of shooting video and making movies, keeping track of all that stuff becomes a major job. Premiere Elements gives you the tools to find that needle in the haystack.

- **Protect your media clips.** Your raw video clips are like a still photographer's negatives. You don't want them sliced, diced, damaged, or lost. No matter how you use clips, Premiere Elements protects your originals.

- **Analyze video clips to separate the good parts from the bad.** Premiere Elements can identify footage that's shaky, over-exposed, lacks contrast, and has bad sound. Oh yeah, it can point out some of the good stuff, too.

- **Find video with people.** Is there a face in that clip? If so, Premiere Elements can tag it, which means you can find it faster.

- **Assemble video clips into a single movie.** Finally, the basic "video-editing" task.

- **Add transitions.** You can apply dozens of different transitions to your movies. Your audience may wish you didn't have so many choices.

- **Add special video and audio effects.** Some effects fix less-than-perfect media clips; others are there to dazzle the senses.

- **Create picture-in-picture video.** Sometimes, one picture isn't enough to tell a story. Just ask the producers of the TV drama *24*.

- **Add and balance music, narration, and sound effects.** Premiere Elements can automatically balance the sounds you add to your movie, or you can go in and fine-tune it yourself.

- **Convert your movie to different video formats.** It seems that every website, handheld device, and disc format wants a different type of video file.

- **Share your movie with the world.** From inside Premiere Elements, you can send your video to DVDs, Blu-ray discs, computer files, or websites.

What's New in Version 8

Even before Premiere Elements got to version 8, it had a bunch of modern features, including support for high-definition camcorders and a video stabilizer to help minimize shaky handheld shots. When it was time to show your masterpiece to the world, you could export to DVDs, Blu-ray discs, or YouTube.

Here are some of Premiere Elements' newer features:

- **Elements Organizer.** In the past, you organized your media clips on a panel inside of Premiere Elements. Now, you use Elements Organizer. It's the same standalone program that Photoshop Elements uses. The idea is you can manage, tag, and organize all your media—video, audio, and stills—with a single program.

- **Auto-Analyzer.** A clever little tool that looks at your video clips frame-by-frame and tags them, so you know what parts are good and what parts aren't so good. The Auto-Analyzer also divides long clips into scenes. You can have this utility run in the background—a sort of set-it-and-forget-it option—or you can run it manually when you need it.

- **Auto Rendering.** Premiere Elements imports a variety of video formats. Some of them don't provide flawless video playback as you work in the editor. In those cases, Premiere Elements smoothes them out without any effort on your part.

- **Effects Masking.** You have lots of options when it comes to special effects. The latest gee-whiz feature is the ability to apply a special effect to just a portion of a video image.

- **Face Tracking.** Want to identify someone in a picture by name? You can create a label and have that label follow the person around your video as you edit.

- **Smart Mixing.** Movies often have several tracks of audio—there's the sound on the video clips, there's narration, and there's music. With Smart Mixing, all you have to do is tell Premiere Elements what should be in the foreground and what should be in the background. Smart Mixing controls the audio levels so that all the sounds are balanced.

- **Additional Project and Sharing Presets.** You don't have to worry about the different file formats in the video universe. Why? Because Adobe has done your homework for you. A single preset takes care of all the settings for frame sizes, frame rates, aspect ratios, codec selection, and a bunch of other technical details. Presets have been in Premiere Elements for a while. Version 8 includes new ones for some of the newer camcorders and sharing options.

The Photoshop Elements Connection

The Adobe software family is huge, but Premiere Elements' closest relative is Photoshop Elements. These two programs are both consumer versions of professional products. That means they cost a lot less, and they're a whole lot easier to use than their hoity-toity brethren. If your video project uses still photos that need a little tweaking and retouching, Photoshop Elements is the perfect tool for the job. There's a copy on your Premiere Elements DVD that you can use for 30 days—to use it longer, the folks at Adobe will gladly accept credit card payment. Seriously, Photoshop Elements is pretty smart when it comes to your video projects. It can create images that fit your video frame size, for example, so you don't have to do the math or wrestle with aspect ratios.

Both Elements programs use Elements Organizer to manage video, audio, and photos. That makes for one-stop shopping when you're looking for media to pop into your movie.

The Premiere Pro Connection

If Photoshop Elements is a sibling to Premiere Elements, then Premiere Pro is a venerable ancestor. The very first version of Adobe Premiere arrived for the Macintosh in 1991. Comparing that early version to today's Adobe Premiere Pro CS4 is like comparing a Stone Age hammer to the space shuttle (with apologies to Stanley Kubrick and Arthur C. Clarke).

In contrast, Premiere Elements first appeared in 2004. From the beginning, it was designed to repackage Premiere Pro for consumers. Each year, Adobe releases a new version of Premiere Elements that adds features to keep pace with the ever-changing video landscape. (If you're doing the math, you may wonder how Adobe got to version 8 so quickly. They skipped versions 5 and 6, so that Premiere Elements could numerically get in step with its older sibling, Photoshop Elements.) Features such as the ability to handle new video formats, analyze video clips, and work with audio, tend to appear first in Premiere Pro. Once they're modified to make them easy to use, they appear in Premiere Elements.

The Very Basics

You'll find very little jargon or nerd terminology in this book. You will, however, encounter a few terms and concepts you'll see frequently in your computing life:

- **Clicking.** This book gives you three kinds of instructions that require you to use your computer's mouse or trackpad. To *click* means to point the arrow cursor at something on the screen and then—without moving the cursor—to press and release the left clicker button on the mouse (or laptop trackpad). To *double-click,* of course, means to click twice in rapid succession, again without moving the cursor. And to *drag* means to press the left button continuously on an object and then move the cursor.

- **Keyboard shortcuts.** Every time you take your hand off the keyboard to move your mouse, you lose time and potentially disrupt your creative flow. That's why many experienced computer fans use keystroke combinations instead of menu commands wherever possible. Ctrl+C, for example, is a keyboard shortcut for Copy in Premiere Elements (and most other programs).

  When you see a shortcut like Ctrl+S (which saves changes to the current project), it's telling you to hold down the Ctrl key, and, while it's down, type the letter S, and then release both keys.

- **Choice is good.** Premiere Elements frequently gives you several ways to trigger a particular command—a menu command *or* clicking a toolbar button *or* pressing a key combination, for example. Some people prefer the speed of keyboard shortcuts; others like the satisfaction of a visual command available in menus or toolbars. This book lists all the alternatives, but by no means are you expected to memorize all of them.

About The Missing Manual Series

Despite the many improvements in software over the years, one feature has grown consistently worse: documentation. With the purchase of most software programs these days, you don't get a single page of printed instructions. To learn about the hundreds of features in a program, you're expected to use online help.

But even if you're comfortable reading a help screen in one window as you try to work in another, something is still missing. At times, the terse electronic help screens assume you already understand the discussion at hand and hurriedly skip over important topics that require an in-depth description. In addition, you don't always get an objective evaluation of the program's features. (Engineers often add technically sophisticated features to a program because they *can*, not because you need them.) You shouldn't have to waste your time learning features that don't help you get your work done.

The purpose of this book, then, is to serve as the manual that should have been in the box along with your program. In this book's pages, you'll find step-by-step instructions for every Premiere Elements feature, including those you may not even quite understand yet, let alone mastered, such as mask effects, timeline key-frames, and video codecs. In addition, you'll find clear evaluations of each feature that help you determine which ones are useful to you, as well as how and when to use them.

Note: This book periodically recommends *other* books, covering topics that are too specialized or tangential for a manual about Premiere Elements. Careful readers may notice that not every one of these titles may be published by the Missing Manual Series' parent, O'Reilly Media. While we're happy to mention other Missing Manuals and books in the O'Reilly family, if there's a great book out there that doesn't happen to be published by O'Reilly, we'll still let you know about it.

Premiere Elements 8: The Missing Manual is designed to accommodate readers at every technical level. The primary discussions are written for advanced-beginner or intermediate computer users. But if you're a first-timer, special sidebars called Up to Speed provide the introductory information you need to understand the topic at hand. If you're an advanced user, on the other hand, keep your eye out for similarly shaded boxes called Power Users' Clinic. They offer more technical tips, tricks, and shortcuts for the experienced computer fan. If you're a fan of film as art, watch for the Famous Movie Moments—quick notes about techniques used by the medium's auteurs.

Macintosh and Windows

While many of Adobe's software products are available on both Windows and Macs, Premiere Elements is not—it's a Windows PC program. It's a little tough competing with Apple's iMovie video editor. If you're of the Mac persuasion and interested in video editing, check out David Pogue's *iMovie '09: The Missing Manual*.

About → These → Arrows

Throughout this book, and throughout the Missing Manual series, you'll find sentences like this one: "Open the Documents → Adobe → Premiere folder." That's shorthand for a much longer instruction that directs you to open three nested folders in sequence, like this: "On your hard drive, you'll find a folder called Documents. Open that. Inside the Documents window is a folder called Adobe; double-click it to open it. Inside that folder is yet another one called Premiere. Double-click to open it, too."

Similarly, this kind of arrow shorthand helps to simplify the business of choosing commands in menus, as shown in Figure I-1.

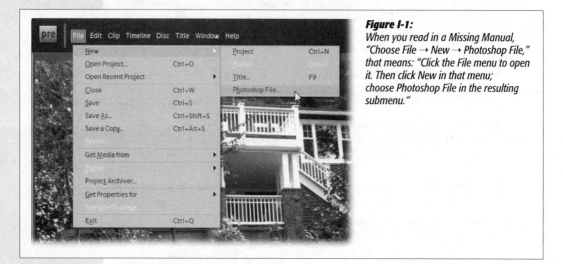

Figure I-1:
When you read in a Missing Manual, "Choose File → New → Photoshop File," that means: "Click the File menu to open it. Then click New in that menu; choose Photoshop File in the resulting submenu."

Living Examples

As you read this book, you'll encounter a number of *living examples*—step-by-step tutorials that show you how to put together a practice movie using raw materials like media clips and a half-completed project. You can download that raw material from the Missing Manuals site. To get there, go to the Missing Manuals home page (*www.missingmanuals.com*), then click the Missing CD link, then scroll down to *Premiere Elements 8: The Missing Manual*, and then click the link labeled Missing CD.

Throughout *Premiere Elements 8: The Missing Manual*, you'll find references to websites that offer additional information and resources for media clips. You'll find a neat, chapter-by-chapter list of these sites on the same Missing CD page.

While you're on the Missing CD page, you can find updates to this book; click the link at the top of the page labeled "View errata for this book." You're invited and encouraged to submit corrections and updates, too. To do so, click the link "Submit your own errata" on the same page.

To keep the book as up-to-date and accurate as possible, each time we print more copies, we'll include any confirmed corrections you've suggested. We'll also note all the changes to the book on the Missing CD page, so you can mark important corrections in your own copy of the book, if you like.

About MissingManuals.com

At *www.missingmanuals.com*, you'll find articles, tips, and updates to *Premiere Elements 8: The Missing Manual*.

We invite (and encourage) you to submit updates (and corrections) yourself. To keep the book as up to date and accurate as possible, each time we print more copies, we'll make any confirmed corrections you suggest. We'll also note such changes on the website, so you can mark important corrections in your own copy of the book if you like. (Go to *http://missingmanuals.com/feedback*, choose the book's name from the pop-up menu, and then click Go to see the changes.)

Also on our Feedback page, you can get expert answers to questions that come to you while reading this book, you can write a book review, and you can find groups for folks who share your interest in Premiere Elements.

We'd love to hear your suggestions for new books in the Missing Manual line. There's a place for that on missingmanuals.com, too. And while you're online, you can register this book at *www.oreilly.com* (you can jump directly to the registration page by going here: *http://tinyurl.com/yo82k3*). Registering means we can send you updates about this book, and you'll be eligible for special offers like discounts on future editions of *Premiere Elements 8: The Missing Manual*.

Safari® Books Online

Safari® Books Online is an on-demand digital library that lets you easily search over 7,500 technology and creative reference books and videos to find the answers you need quickly.

With a subscription, you can read any page and watch any video from our library online. Read books on your cell phone and mobile devices. Access new titles before they are available for print, and get exclusive access to manuscripts in development and post feedback for the authors. Copy and paste code samples, organize your favorites, download chapters, bookmark key sections, create notes, print out pages, and benefit from tons of other time-saving features.

O'Reilly Media has uploaded this book to the Safari® Books Online service. To have full digital access to this book and others on similar topics from O'Reilly and other publishers, sign up for free at *http://my.safaribooksonline.com*.

Part One:
Start a New Project

1

Set Up a New Project

Premiere Elements calls the videos you create *projects* because, more likely than not, you'll include several types of media in your movies. Sure, your project will include video clips, but you might also add narration, background music, still images, text, and title screens. And when you export your video, you might want to add a DVD menu to make navigating the final product easy. So, unlike a word processing document or spreadsheet, your finished video comprises more than just a single PC file—it's a collection of different files sewn together into a whole.

In this chapter, you'll learn how to start a new project (as well as how to open an existing one). Along the way, you'll tour the Premiere Elements workspace—the multifaceted screen where you organize clips, assemble videos, and add sound, transitions, and special effects. At the end of the chapter, you'll look at Premiere Elements' Instant-Movie feature—a tool that let's you quickly turn video clips into finished movies, perfect for YouTube aficionados. In addition, you'll see how InstantMovie gives you a great introduction to the basic steps of editing any video project.

Note: As you're probably aware, this book is about *Premiere Elements*. In an effort to save a tree or two (not to mention your patience as a reader), these pages will refer to the program simply as *Premiere*.

Start Premiere Elements

You start Premiere just as you would any other Windows program—which also means you can do so in a couple of ways. Installing the program (a process described on page 385) puts an Adobe Premiere Elements 8.0 shortcut on your desktop, so the easiest way to start Premiere is to double-click that shortcut. That's

---

fine the first few times you run the program, but you may not want the shortcut on your desktop forever. An alternative way to launch the program is to add its shortcut to Windows' Quick Launch bar. Drag the shortcut from your desktop onto the bar, and a purple "pre" icon appears there. Click it once to start Premiere.

Here are some other ways to start the program:

- From the Vista or Windows 7 Start menu, choose Windows → All Programs → Adobe Premiere Elements 8.0.

- For Windows XP, go to Start → All Programs → Adobe → Adobe Premiere Elements 8.0

- If you're a keyboard enthusiast, press the Windows key and begin to type *premiere*. Before you finish typing, Windows searches for a match and displays a list with programs at the top. Most likely, Premiere is at the top of the list and already selected, so just press the enter key. Otherwise, use your mouse or arrow keys to select and start the program.

Note: Adobe stores Premiere and all its supporting files with your other Windows programs. On most computers, that location is *C:\Program Files\Adobe\Adobe Premiere Elements 8.0*.

Every time you start Premiere, the program displays an introductory screen called a "splash screen" (see Figure 1-1). It includes a "Create Adobe ID" web link to Photoshop.com (see Figure 1-2). Click the link and enter your name and email address to register your copy of Premiere, access Adobe's online support, and get some free storage space for your videos and photos (see the box on page 16 for the details).

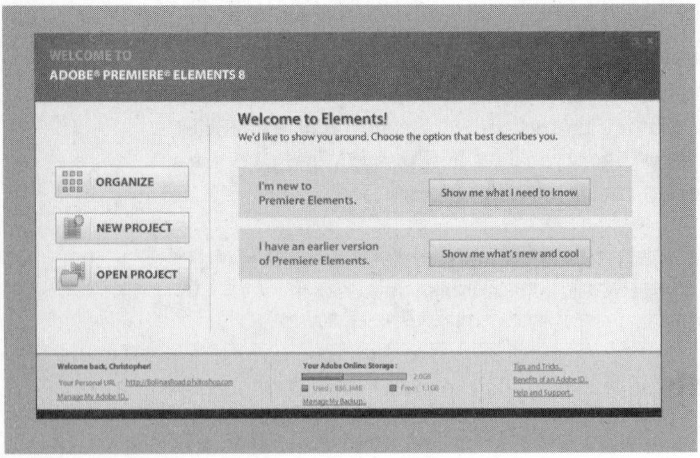

Figure 1-1:
Premiere Elements' splash screen offers help for new comers and links to Adobe web-based resources. There are only three buttons that actually lead to the Premiere Elements program.

Figure 1-2:
Photoshop.com is Adobe's website for photographers and video producers. You don't have to own an Elements program to sign up for it and use some of the basic services, but it's designed to work hand-in-hand with Photoshop Elements and Premiere Elements.

If you're connected to the Internet, don't be surprised if the content in the main part of the splash screen changes. From time to time, Adobe may put different messages here, usually feeding you mini-tours of Premiere features or directing you to Photoshop.com.

Note: Photoshop Elements is a program used to edit and retouch still photos. If you bought the DVD version of Premiere Elements, Adobe included a trial version of Photoshop Elements on the disc. Both programs use a third program, called Elements Organizer, to share photos and videos. Like any product that tries to do two things, the Organizer has its quirks. For a full discussion of it, see page 99.

Once you get used to the splash screen's layout, you soon realize that all the action for video projects is in the three buttons on the left—they open Premiere and let you start editing. Here's the rundown:

- **Organize.** Opens Elements Organizer, which is a separate program you use to keep track of all your videos and other media clips.

• **New Project.** Just back from vacation with a camera full of beach scenes? Click this button to start a new project.

• **Open Project.** Want to edit or add new clips to a project you already started? Click here for a list of your saved projects.

The first time you start Premiere, New Project is probably your best choice, because it lets you explore the program and import video clips (see page 37).

Should I Sign Up for Photoshop.com?

Whenever you fire up Premiere, its opening screen includes links to Adobe's Photoshop.com web services (see Figure 1-2). Adobe provides a free basic membership with 2 gigabytes of storage for videos (about 20 minutes' worth) and photos, but its not-so-hidden agenda is to get you to upgrade to a more robust membership, one with an annual fee. So what do you get from Photoshop.com, and is it worth any extra investment?

Adobe bases its subscription price on how much storage you want. Here's what you get with your free membership and some notes on the additional benefits of a paid subscription:

• Online storage and sharing for your photos and videos. Free membership: 2 gigabytes. Upgrade to one of the paid memberships and, for $49 per year, you get 20 gigabytes of storage. For $69, you get 40 gigabytes, and for $129, you get 100 gigabytes.

• Automatic back-up and synchronization. If you worry about losing your digital photos and videos but never get around to making back-ups, this is an appealing feature. Photoshop.com automatically backs up your files so you never have to worry about them. The downside is that if you need more than 2 gigabytes of space, you have to pay for the storage. The $49 20-gigabyte membership lets you store about four hours of DVD-quality video. As you can tell by the prices listed above, if you shoot a lot of video, storage can get expensive.

• Online management of photos for other websites, such as Facebook, Flickr, Picasa, and Photobucket. If you're a member of one of these photo-sharing sites,

this feature works great. You can move photos from Photoshop.com directly to any of those services. It gives you a central place to manage your online photo albums.

• Basic online training and tutorials. With a paid subscription, you also get advanced tutorials. Online training and tutorials are great, but if that's all you'll use the site for, it probably doesn't justify Photoshop.com's annual fee. You can find free tutorials on AdobeTV and even on YouTube. And you can find professional-quality tutorials on sites such as O'Reilly Media (*www.oreilly.com*) and Lynda.com.

• The free subscription includes some Premiere templates and themes. With a pay-to-play account, Adobe makes even more themes and templates available. Adobe automatically downloads these resources to your PC.

The Bottom Line: For most Premiere Elements users, it makes sense to sign up for the free, basic membership. Explore the services and see if they're valuable to you. As the name Photoshop.com implies, the service was originally created for still photographers (Adobe Photoshop is the tool of choice for editing still images) and, at this point, still photographers are likely to see more benefits. Keep in mind that the 2-gigabyte limit won't get you, the video producer, very far. After all, that's equal to or less than the storage provided by many tapeless video cameras. If you don't mind being responsible for your own backups, you could put the $49 to $129 you'd spend on Photoshop.com toward an external hard drive. Very good 500GB external hard drives are available for well under $100.

A Brief Tour of Premiere Elements

Start Premiere and click the New Project button. Premiere asks you to name your project and address a few other details, but for now, as you learn the layout of the program, simply accept the project name that Adobe assigns (*My Project.prel*) and click the OK button. That takes you to Premiere's workspace, the place where you edit your videos. It's divided into three main areas, as shown in Figure 1-3.

- The **Monitor** panel plays back your video clips. Use the DVD-style buttons below it to control playback.

- Think of the **Tasks** panel, to the right of the monitor, as your video-editing toolbox. Select the task you want to tackle by clicking one of the tabs at the top of the panel (Organize, Edit, Disc Menus, and Share). You'll learn about each of these a little later in this chapter.

- The **My Project** panel displays your movie-in-progress—the video and audio assets you've assembled to create your movie. My Project offers two viewing modes: the *Sceneline* view lets you assemble your movie by dragging clips into a series of boxes, each of which displays a still image of the clip; and the *Timeline* view looks more like a traditional video-editing tool, with a time scale along the top and separate video and audio tracks below.

Monitor panel

Tasks panel

My Project panel

Figure 1-3:
*Premiere is divided into
three main panels: the
Monitor panel, the Tasks
panel, and the My
Project panel. This
chapter introduces
all three.*

As you work in Premiere, you'll find yourself jumping back and forth among these panels. For example, to put together a video of a day in the Caribbean, go to the Tasks panel and click on the Organize tab to review your clips. Select the clips you want in your video, drag them to the My Project panel, and arrange them in the order in which you want them to play back. Preview your draft movie in the Monitor panel. Then move on to the other tabs in the Task panel to fine-tune your video, add special effects, and create a disc or export it to a website.

The Monitor Panel

Think of the monitor as a TV screen where you play your clips as you assemble your movie. No matter how great a cameraperson you are, you won't use every frame of every clip you shoot. Instead, you select the best shots using the monitor's controls (for details on editing clips, see page 141). Move back and forth within a clip using the buttons and controls at the bottom of the panel (Figure 1-4).

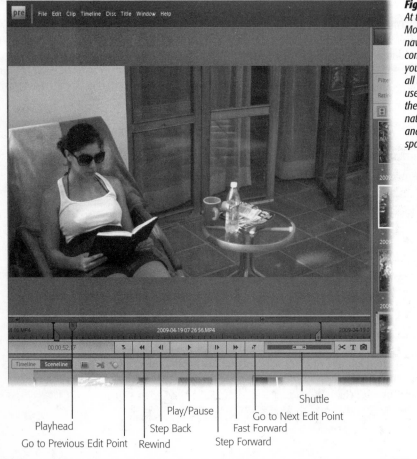

Figure 1-4:
At the bottom of the Monitor panel, you see navigation and playback control buttons. At first, you may not recognize all the buttons and their uses, but soon using them becomes second nature as you jump back and forth to different spots in your video clips.

The Play button actually handles two tasks: Click it once to play back a clip, and click it again to pause playback. As you play your video, the playhead tells you exactly where you are. If, as you edit, you know where you want to be in a clip, you can drag the playhead right to that spot.

The Step Back and Step Forward buttons move you forward and backward through your video a frame at a time—a great way to find the exact frame at which you want to cut to another scene, add a transition, or select a single frame of your video to export as a still image (to use as a DVD cover, for example).

The Rewind and Fast Forward buttons work just as they do on your DVD player.

Video projects are made up of more than just a single clip, of course. The point where one clip meets another is called an "edit point." Premiere uses these edit points as navigational aids to help you move through your movie quickly. The "Go to Previous Edit Point" and "Go to Next Edit Point" buttons move you along each of the edit points in your movie.

The first 20 times you see a clip, you may be patient enough to watch it at normal speed while you admire its cinematic beauty. Later, with a deadline looming, you're eager to zip to a particular point for editing. That's when Premiere's "shuttle" control comes in handy. Shuttle lets you navigate through your video at variable speeds—a favorite trick of experienced video editors. Drag the shuttle to the right to move forward and to the left to move back. The further you drag the control off-center, the faster you move through your video.

Tasks Panel

The Tasks panel is a bit of a chameleon—it looks different depending on which of the four tabs—Organize, Edit, Disc Menus, or Share—you click (see Figure 1-5). When you click a tab, a related set of tools appears in the panel below it. For most video projects, you move from left to right across the tabs as you work toward a finished product. Here's a look at each of the tabs and their tools:

- **Organize** (click the tab itself or, from Premiere's menu bar, choose Window → Organize) is the natural first step for any project. Here, you transfer video clips from your camera to your computer. It's also where you first view your clips and organize them by quality and content. You can drag video clips from here to the sceneline, putting them into sequence, a process described in detail on page 160.

- The **Edit** tab (Window → Effects) is usually the next step for your project. Once you decide on your basic sequence of clips, it's time to add special effects, transitions, and titles. Premiere also provides themes—predesigned visuals and background music ("Road Trip," "Outdoor Wedding"). Themes give you an easy way to apply professionally designed wrappings to your project.

• Use the **Disc Menus** tab (Window → Disc Menus) to create an opening screen and chapter divisions for movies destined for DVD or Blu-Ray discs. Again, Adobe provides visuals, all you need to do is mark the scenes and chapters in your movie. The end result is a slick, fool-proof menu and navigation system.

• Use the **Share** tab (Window → Share) to export your finished project. Premiere makes it easy to burn videos and their menus onto a disc. If your video is headed for the web, the Share tab streamlines the process of meeting the video requirements for sites like YouTube and Photoshop.com.

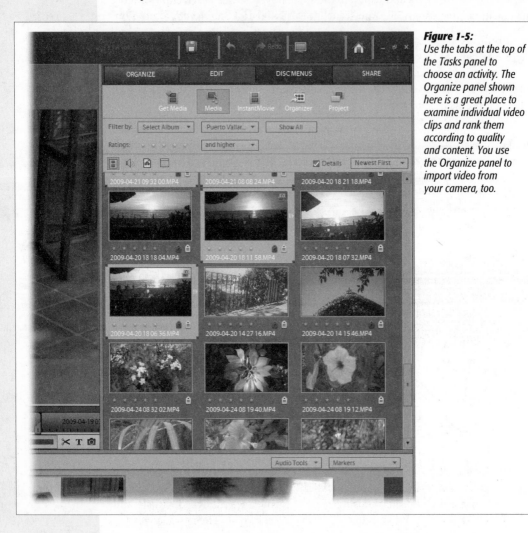

Figure 1-5:
Use the tabs at the top of the Tasks panel to choose an activity. The Organize panel shown here is a great place to examine individual video clips and rank them according to quality and content. You use the Organize panel to import video from your camera, too.

My Project Panel

The **My Project** panel stretches across the bottom of Premiere's workspace. It gives you two distinct views of your project: Sceneline and Timeline. The Sceneline view lets you quickly piece together a video and work on it in broad strokes. The Timeline view gives you granular control over your movie, letting you fine-tune every frame.

Sceneline mode (Figure 1-6, top) looks like a series of boxes. You drop video clips into the boxes in the correct order to turn individual clips into a movie. You apply transitions, like dissolves and wipes, in the small boxes between each clip (for more on transitions, see page 175). The sceneline is similar to a *storyboard*, a tool filmmakers use to visualize their movies before they shoot any film. Typically, a storyboard is a series of drawings, where each drawing represents a scene or some important shot in the movie.

Timeline mode (Figure 1-6, bottom) looks familiar if you've used other video-editing programs. At the top of the panel, the timeline measures the length of your movie and the position of the playhead, using a video "frame" as the basic unit of measurement. Below that, horizontal bands hold video and audio tracks. You can have multiples of each, giving you the ability to superimpose both images and sounds. For example, the soundtrack for your movie might combine the audio you recorded as you shot your video, along with narration, music, and sound effects. You can put each of these components on separate tracks, giving you control over their timing, volume, and other properties.

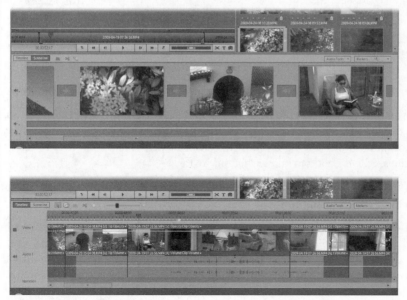

Figure 1-6:
Top: Use the Sceneline panel to organize your video in broad strokes. Drop clips in the big boxes and drop transitions, like wipes and dissolves, in the small boxes.

Bottom: Use the Timeline panel when you want to fine-tune the elements in your video. The timeline looks like a more traditional video-editing workspace.

Create a New Project

Now that you've had a chance to noodle around Premiere's workspace, it's time to officially start a new project. Here are the steps you take:

1. **Click the Premiere icon in Windows' Quick Launch bar or use the Windows Start menu to launch the program.**

Tip: Page 13 explains some of the different ways to start Premiere.

---

2. **On the splash screen, click New Project.**

   Premiere displays a New Project window with boxes for the project's name and file location (Figure 1-7). Below that, "Project Settings" describes the project's video format, with the option to change it via the Change Settings button.

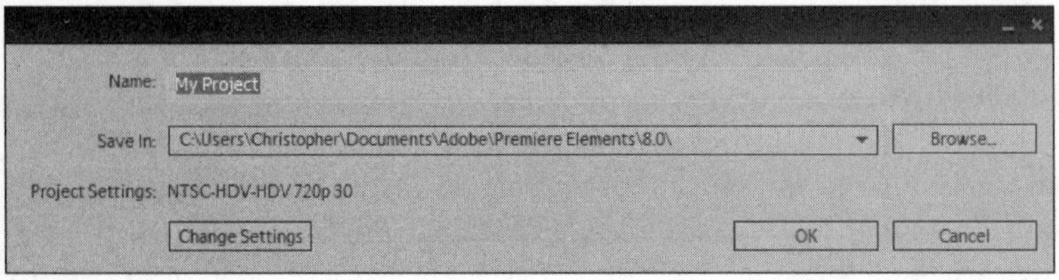

Figure 1-7:
The most important details when you create a new project are the name of your project and where Premiere will store the project. Once you get rolling with video projects, you may not have to change the settings that determine the video size and quality. You're likely to use the same settings most of the time.

3. **In the Name box, type a name for your project, such as *My First Classic Movie*.**

   You have to give each project a unique name. For most projects, this is the only change you'll ever make in the New Project window. You may never specify the location of your saved projects or the technical details related to the Project Settings. Still, it's good to know what they're for.

4. **(Optional) To save your project to a new location, click the Browse button beside the "Save In" box.**

   Initially, Premiere saves your projects in the folder the program itself resides in, *C:\Users\yourname\My Documents\Adobe\Premiere Elements\8.0*. That's fine if you have enough room on your hard drive. But if you want to store your videos elsewhere, such as a dedicated hard drive, click the Browse button and navigate to the new location. Then click OK and you're all set.

5. (Optional) To change the format of the movie you create—say from a standard-resolution video using the 4:3 aspect ratio of TV sets to a high-definition wide-screen format—click the Change Settings button.

A new window opens (see Figure 1-8) where you make a couple of technical decisions based primarily on the type of video camera you use. If you don't know the answers to these questions off the top of your head, it's a good time to pull out the camera's manual. It's not missing, is it?

The first thing you need to figure out is whether your camera and TV set use the NTSC or PAL video system. (In the U.S., nearly all video systems use the NTSC format.)

Once you do that, you need to find out the video format your camera uses. Your choices include an arcane alphabet soup of options like AVCHD, DV, and HDV. Who needs that? The good news is that you should be able to find these details on the cover or within the first few pages of your camera's manual. (If you need more help or want to dig a little deeper, see the box "Choosing Project Settings" on page 25) After you change the settings to match your camera, click OK to close the Project Settings window.

6. **In the New Project panel, click OK.**

The New Project window closes and you see the Premiere workspace, with the three panels described on page 17.

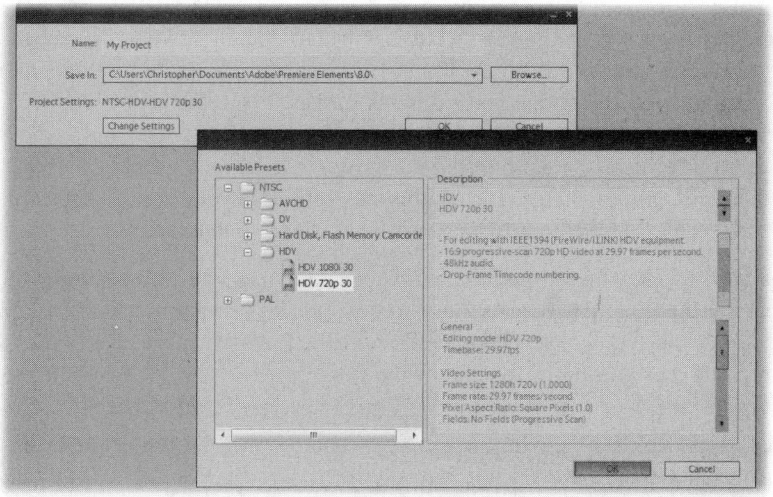

Figure 1-8:
The first time you use Premiere, you need to make sure the project settings match your video camera and your TV. There's a certain amount of video jargon involved, but once it's set up, you don't need to mess with it again unless your equipment changes.

Once you create a new project, you want to add clips to it. You do that from the Organize tab in the Tasks panel. Under that tab, click the Get Media button. The details of importing files for your video project appear in Chapter 2, but because you probably can't wait to get started, click on one of the sources listed and import a file or two so you see the process in action (if you don't have a camera hooked up to your PC just yet, browse to the folder that holds Premiere and click Clip Arts → Common → Nature and double-click the file named Palm Tree.png).

Save and Back Up a Project

Once you create a project, you need to know how to save it. As with most PC projects, it's wise to save early and often. That way, you won't lose any of your hard work if your PC freezes up mid-project. If your work is especially important (or if you're a chronic worrier), you may want to save duplicate or back-up copies of your project.

Saving a video project is about the same as saving a word processing document. Go to File → Save or press Ctrl+S. After a little hard disk action, Premiere saves your file. To save a back-up copy, choose File → Save a Copy. The Save Project window opens, where you can give your project a different name and navigate to a new save location.

Note: Premiere projects are saved with the *.prel* file extension. So, for example, if you double click a file in Windows Explorer that ends in *.prel,* Windows automatically starts Premiere and opens the project file you clicked.

While the mechanics of saving a Premiere file are the same as those for a Word document, the practical aspects are notably different. Here's why: When you save a Word document, you save everything associated with that document—words, embedded pictures, graphs, and so on. When you save a Premiere file, you don't save all the video clips and sound files that make up your movie. If you did, your hard drive, no matter how capacious, would fill up after a couple of movies—video and audio files are notoriously huge. So Premiere, like most video-editing programs, creates a project file that simply *points to* the appropriate sections of your original clips. A Premiere project file, in other words, is essentially a collection of pointers.

By the same token, when you edit one of your video clips, you aren't actually chopping up the clip. You're telling Premiere something like, "I want to use frame 122 to frame 875 of the clip named *mydayatthebeach.mp4*. Premiere takes note of that and displays only that portion of the clip in the Monitor panel. And, when you export your finished movie, it copies just that portion of the clip to your movie file.

Because all the projects you create point to your raw video clips, you don't want to move, rename, or delete those original files. If you do, Premiere won't be able to find them the next time you open a project. For more details on the location of your video files and projects, see the box on page 27.

Choosing Project Settings

If Premiere's alphabet soup of project settings confuses you, here are some tips to help you make the right choices. The good news is, once you choose the project settings for your video equipment, you probably won't have to mess with them again.

When you choose settings, you select them from the Available Presets box on the left side of the Setup box (Figure 1-8). You first choose a video standard, then you choose a video *preset* (settings that tell Premiere how to turn videos into the 1s and 0s of a movie file). When you click one of the purple preset icons to do so, Premiere displays the technical details in the text boxes on the right.

Choose NTSC or PAL. Traditionally, the world is divided into two major video camps. If you live in the Americas, Japan, South Korea, Taiwan, and many other countries, you're on the NTSC team (NTSC stands for National Television System Committee). If you live in Europe, Australia, Russia, China, India, the Middle East, or Africa, your TV probably uses the PAL (Phase-Alternating Line) system. The two systems create color TV images in different ways, making them incompatible with each other. Premiere can work with either system, but you need to select the one that's compatible with your video camera and TV. In the Setup window, under each of these systems, you see several standard-definition and high-definition video formats.

Choose a video preset. It seems that electronics manufacturers create new video formats with each new lunar cycle. Fortunately, you don't have to understand all of them, you just need to know which preset works with your camera and TV. One of the main things the preset defines is the quality, or *resolution,* of the video image. Video images, like those on your computer screen, are made up of pixels (short for *picture elements*).

People often refer to pixels as dots, but they're actually rectangular or square. Resolution is defined as the number of horizontal pixels by the number of vertical pixels. For example a hi-def TV might have a resolution of 1920 × 1080.

There's not enough room in this book for a complete description of all the video formats, but below is a quick rundown of those you can use with Premiere. Adobe tries to make it easy for you to choose the right format by roughly grouping them by type of camera. So you should be able to match your camera specs (like HDV 720p) with the format names listed under "Description" in the Setup window:

- AVCHD. A trademarked high-definition video format developed by Panasonic and Sony and used by other companies as well. The format produces a 1080i-pixel image compatible with today's high-definition TVs. There are two widescreen formats with different resolutions: Full HD measures 1920 × 1080i pixels; HD is 1440 × 1080i. AVCHD supports two audio standards. One is called "better than CD quality stereo;" the other is the traditional 5.1 format. The 5.1 format refers to how many speakers (the number before the dot) and subwoofers (the number after the dot) make up the compatible sound system. The 5.1 standard includes a center speaker, two front and two back speakers, and one subwoofer.

- DV. An earlier digital video format developed by Sony, JVC, and Panasonic for their digital video cameras. DV cameras store video on a variety of media, but the MiniDV tapes developed for consumer and pro camcorders are the most popular. Easy to shoot and edit, DV video produces DVD-quality video. DV resolution is 720 × 480 pixels. You can produce either standard or widescreen video by changing the DV camera's aspect ratio.

- Hard Disk, Flash Memory Camcorder. Tapeless camcorders store video on hard drives or memory chips. The actual video file formats are similar to some of the other choices. For example, HD 1080i 30 is similar to AVCHD 1080i 30. The Standard and Widescreen formats are similar to the DV options.

- HDV. This is another high-definition format used to record HD video on miniDV tapes. There are two image formats: HDV 720p and HDV 1080i.

Tip: If you want to make back-ups of your raw video clips, you need to make copies using Elements Organizer (page 136) or use traditional Windows back-up or file-copying techniques. Just make sure you don't move, delete, or rename the files your projects point to.

Avoid Disaster with Auto Save

Like a lot of programs, Premiere can automatically save your project on a regular basis. That way, if the power goes out due to natural-, child-, or dog-borne disasters, you've got a back-up. Premiere turns Auto Save on when you first install the program. To review or adjust the settings, choose Edit → Preferences. In the list of topics on the left side of the window that pops up, click Auto Save to tweak the settings. Make sure the "Automatically Save Projects" box is checked and then, in the "Automatically Save Every _ minutes" box, type in a number that matches your comfort level. Premiere uses 20 minutes as the default. You may want to change that to, say, 10 or 15 minutes if you're feeling disaster-prone. Just underneath that setting, the Maximum Project box refers to how many versions you want to back up. Five is a good number for most situations.

This way, if your computer crashes, the next time you start Premiere, it asks if you want to open the last auto-saved version of your project.

Tip: While you have your Preferences window open, you may want to take a look at the Scratch Disk preferences. Premiere stores temporary files, called scratch files, on your computer's hard drive. You can manage disk space and maybe get a little better video performance by tweaking these settings. For details, see the box on page 28.

Open an Existing Project

After you create a project, you can open it from Premiere's splash screen or from the File command in Premiere's menu bar at the top of the screen.

- To open a project from the splash screen (shown earlier in Figure 1-1), click on the Open Project button. A list of recent projects appears under your cursor. Click the name of the project you want to open.

- To open a project from Premiere's File menu, choose File → Open Project. A window named Open Project appears displaying the files in your Premiere Elements 8.0 folder. If you want, you can navigate to a different location to open a project file.

- To open a project you recently worked on, choose File → Open Recent Projects. Premiere displays a submenu with your last five projects listed. Click the name of the project you want to open.

FREQUENTLY ASKED QUESTION

Premiere and File Storage

Where Does Premiere Store Imported Files?

It's not hard to figure out where Premiere saves your project files because you can use File → Save As to see the current location. (When you first install Premiere, it saves your files in the *Documents\Adobe\Premiere Elements\8.0* folder, though you can change that; see page 22.)

But what about the video clips that you *import into* Premiere? Where does it stash those files? At first, Premiere also saves them in your Documents folder, usually in sub-folders named after the date you imported the clip. So you're likely to see a folder with a name like *2009 12 15.*

You don't have to settle for that location, however. You may want to keep your clips on a different hard drive, where you have plenty of room for big video files.

To change the save location of your imported Premiere files (or if you just want to check where Premiere stores them), go to Edit → Preferences and in the left-hand column click "Scratch Disks". Premiere displays a list of each type of file in your project ("Video Previews", "Disc Encoding", and so on) and its location, as you can see in Figure 1-9. The top item: "Captured Video", shows you where Premiere stores your imported video clips. The second entry tells you where Premiere saves your imported audio clips. The other items in this list are work files that Premiere makes as you edit. To change any of these locations, click the Browse button and choose a new folder.

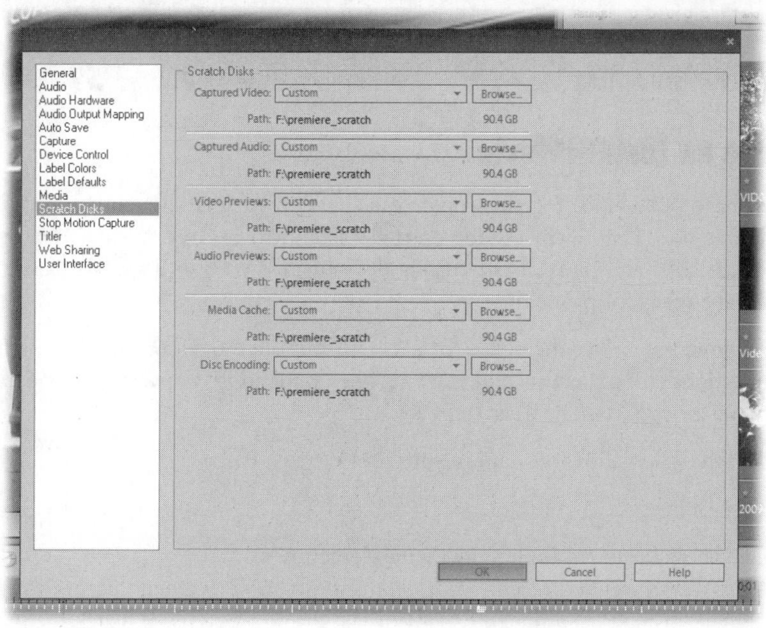

Figure 1-9:
You can tell Premiere where you want it to save certain types of files, such as your raw video clips and some of the work files it creates while you're editing.

No matter which method you use, Premiere opens your project and displays its media files in the Organize tab of the Tasks panel. You can only have one project open at a time. The My Project panel displays your video clips arranged the way you last saved them. Now you're ready to continue editing your project.

The Tale of Scratch Disks

What's a Scratch Disk and Why Do I Care?

As mentioned earlier, video files are big. No, they're really, really big, and that means they're sometimes a challenge for computers to handle. You're jumping around choosing video and audio clips here and there and you expect your computer to keep pace with your snap decisions and to show you accurate previews of your work. One way your computer keeps track of your editing decisions is to create temporary copies of a project's files in an area on your hard drive called a *scratch disk*. Usually, Premiere stores scratch files in the same place it stores your project files, but that may not always be your best choice, especially if you're running out of disk space. For that reason, you can tell Premiere exactly where you want it to store scratch files using the Preferences window. Choose Edit → Preferences → Scratch Disks to see a list of the different types of scratch files Premiere uses. You have three location choices for each file:

My Documents saves scratch files in your Documents folder (usually on your C drive).

Same As Project saves scratch files in the same folder as your Project files. Again, this is usually within your Documents or My Documents folder, unless you changed the location.

Custom saves your scratch files in whatever location you choose. This is a good choice if you have a second or third hard drive with lots of room on it. Here's why: You can store the large scratch files on a disk that's independent of the drive that holds Premiere's files. That way, Premiere doesn't have to compete for disk time to access both its program files and the scratch files.

Speed tips: If you know that one of your hard drives is faster than the others, store your captured video and scratch files on the fastest drive. You can use slower drives for project files and audio files. Try to use discs that are directly attached to your computer. The connections to network discs are sometimes too slow for video-editing projects.

Create an InstantMovie

Impatient to put a video together so you can show off your family reunion or vacation highlights? That's why Adobe created InstantMovie. InstantMovie analyzes your video clips and makes basic editing decisions for you, so it's a fast path to a video that's ready for prime time.

InstantMovie assembles the pieces for a 4- to 6-minute movie by asking you a few easy questions along the way, and you have the opportunity to tweak your video at the end of the process. The basic steps are:

- Select the video clips you want in your movie.

- Choose a theme.

- Decide how Premiere applies the theme elements.

- Premiere analyzes and "smart tags" the clips.

- Premiere assembles the clips.

- Premiere applies the theme elements.

- You preview the movie.

- You tweak the movie.

• Premiere saves the movie as a finished product.

Just for fun, and because you're probably dying to dive into the program, collect some of your favorite movie clips and follow these steps to make an InstantMovie:

Note: For the complete details on importing video clips into Premiere, see page 37.

1. **Click InstantMovie in the Organize tab of the Tasks panel.**

   The Organize tab displays the InstantMovie tools with text prompts in the upper-left corner that lead you, step by step, through the InstantMovie process (Figure 1-10).

InstantMovie instructions

Figure 1-10:
Instructions for InstantMovie appear in the upper-left corner of the Organize panel. Here, the selected movie clips show a blue highlight. Click the Next button to move to the next step.

Selected clips   Next button

2. **Ctrl-click the video clips or assets you want in your InstantMovie.**

   Ctrl-click works like a toggle; it selects and deselects a clip with each click. Try it; put your cursor on a clip and Ctrl-click. The perimeter of the clip turns blue to indicate that it's selected. Now Ctrl-click the clip again, and you deselect it— the blue border disappears.

   Shift-click selects all the clips between two clip selections. Shift-click on the first clip in a sequence, then move your cursor to the last clip in the sequence, and then shift-click again—you select all the clips between the first and last clip.

   Ctrl+A selects all the assets in the Organize window.

3. **In the lower-right corner of the Tasks panel, click the Next button.**

   The Tasks panel changes to the Edit tab, displaying Themes.

4. **Select a theme.**

   You may need to use the scroll bar on the right to see all the themes. You can also use the drop-down menu to display themes by category, such as Style, Events, or Slideshow (see Figure 1-11). One of the Style themes, for example, makes your movie look like a music video.

5. **Click Next.**

   As shown in Figure 1-12, the Edit tab lists the components that make up Premiere's themes: Opening Titles, Closing Titles, Music, Speed and Intensity, Duration, Sequence, Theme Content, and Render Preview. You can edit each of them to fine-tune the way Premiere applies your chosen theme.

6. **Premiere suggests an opening and closing title in the relevant boxes, but you can edit it to say anything you want. You might, for example, change the Opening Title box to read** *My First Classic, Directed by Sheer Genius.*

7. **Under Music, choose Theme Music.**

   If you like the music Premiere pairs with the theme, you don't need to change anything. If not, you have only two options: You can go without music, or you can select a song from your own music files (Premiere doesn't offer an alternative from its own music archive). To use a track stored on your computer, click the Browse button to locate it.

   Below the music choices, the Music/Sound FX slider balances the volume between the music and the sounds recorded in your video clip. Drag the slider to the left to make the music louder and the video clip softer.

8. **Under Duration, choose Match Music.**

   When you choose Match Music, Premiere automatically makes the length of the InstantMovie match the length of the music you selected. (If you chose No Music, the Match Music option isn't available.) If you choose Specify Duration, you dictate the length of the movie. If you choose Use All Clips, the aggregate length of the clips determines the length of your movie.

Figure 1-11:
Use the scroll bar to view all the available themes. Click on a theme to preview the theme elements, including the music. Premiere comes with themes for several different types of events. If you're a Photoshop.com member, you can find addition themes online.

9. Under Sequence, choose Theme Order.

Adobe gives themes their own built-in rules for selecting and ordering video clips. For example, when a theme wants to increase the level of excitement, it may use lots of close-ups, with rapid cutting between clips. When you choose Theme Order, you let Premiere use those pre-set rules. You can override them by choosing Time/Date, which orders the clips temporally. For example, you might want to choose the Time/Date option for a wedding video. That way, the sequence of clips follows the sequence of events: groom arrives, bride walks down aisle, vows taken….

10. Under Theme Content, you can include or exclude certain theme elements, such as the Intro/Closing Movie, Transitions, Titles, and menus. Just check the boxes you want to include.

11. Under Render Preview, click Yes.

   After Premiere creates a video based on its and your choices, you get to preview the results in the monitor. If a movie and its theme include lots of transitions and special effects, the playback may be choppy. That's because your computer is trying to perform all the calculations necessary to coordinate the movie and its soundtrack, transitions, and effects at the same time as it plays back your video. When you "render" the preview, Premiere takes the time to perform all those calculations up front. The result is smoother playback, with the rendered preview looking like the final version of your movie. If you render the preview, a progress bar appears to show the status of the rendering process.

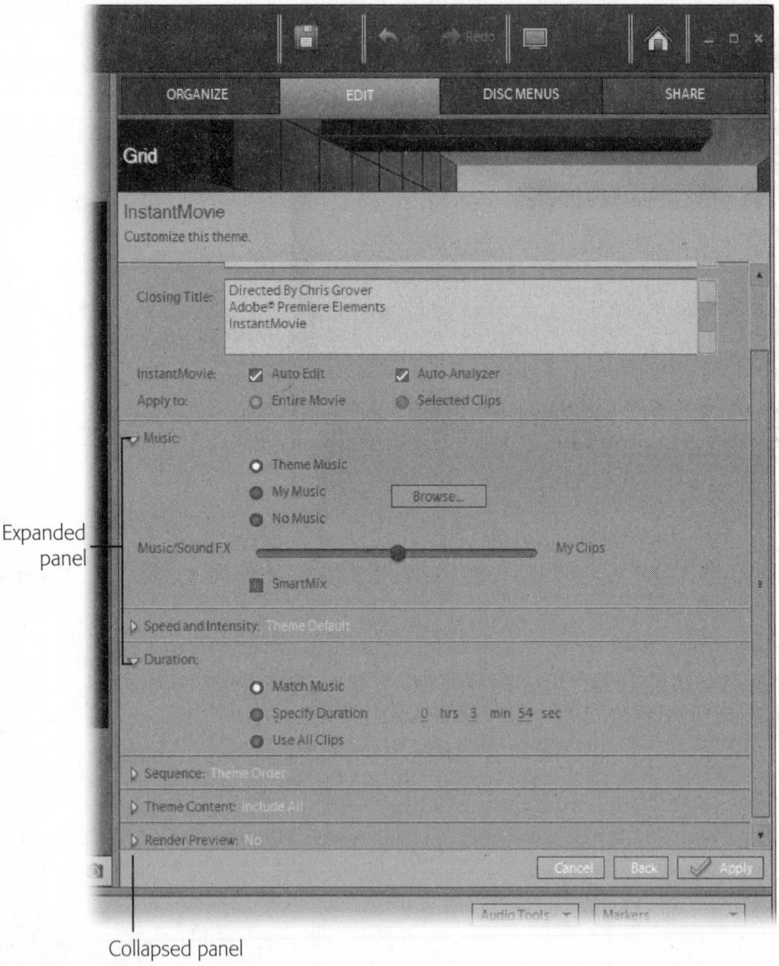

Figure 1-12:
You can customize a theme using the controls in the Edit panel. Click the triangle buttons to expand and collapse the subpanels. As shown here, instead of using the default theme music, a different song was selected.

12. **Click the Apply button.**

Premiere goes to work assembling your video and applying the theme elements you specified. This can take a few minutes, depending on the length of the movie and how powerful your computer is. First, Premiere analyzes the selected clips using its Smart Tags feature (see page 120). This process helps Premiere identify the best parts of a clip. When all the work is done, you see a movie in the Monitor panel and a clip in the sceneline or timeline.

13. **In the Monitor panel, click the Play button.**

Your movie plays as shown in Figure 1-13. If you're happy with it, go ahead with the rest of the steps in this exercise. If you want to make changes, see "Edit Your InstantMovie" on page 34.

Figure 1-13:
After Premiere assembles your movie and applies theme elements, you can preview it in the Monitor panel. Use the monitor controls, including the shuffle tool, to navigate back and forth through your movie.

14. **Click the Share tab.**

It displays several ways to share your video, including posting it online and saving it to disc, to your PC, to your mobile device, or to tape.

15. **Click Personal Computer.**

    You can choose any of the options, but Personal Computer lets you create video files that play back on PCs using Windows Media Player, Adobe's Media Player, or Apple's QuickTime media player.

16. **Choose MPEG and then click NTSC DVD Widescreen.**

    If your video clips aren't in the widescreen format, you can choose the NTSC DVD Standard or another format that suits your movie. You can find more details about video formats on page 40.

17. **In the File Name box, type in a name such as** *My First Classic* **and click the Browse button to choose a save location.**

    Premiere automatically saves your videos in your Documents folder unless you tell it otherwise.

18. **Click Save.**

    Premiere renders your movie, creating a video file in the format you chose. A progress bar shows you how far along the process is. Rendering a movie can take some time, so you may want to grab a beverage of choice or check your email while Premiere does its work.

Edit Your InstantMovie

The mark of a powerful Hollywood director is having "final cut" approval, the last word on every aspect of a film. Premiere gives you that privilege right away, even in InstantMovie. After all, directors and studio heads don't always agree when it comes to editing, and neither will you and Premiere. It's good to be the studio big shot.

When Premiere creates an InstantMovie, it produces a single clip. If you want to make changes, such as swapping a clip here or there, you need to break that clip into pieces. Fortunately, Premiere automates the process.

Right-click the InstantMovie clip in the timeline or the sceneline and then choose Break Apart InstantMovie in the shortcut menu. Premiere breaks the movie into its basic parts, showing clips and special effects in the My Project panel.

Replace any of the clips by right-clicking on them in the timeline and choosing Replace Clip From Media or Project. If the replacement clip is longer than the original, Premiere trims it to fit. If the clip is shorter, a message warns you that the clip's too short.

Tip: The Replace Clip command is only available when you're working in the timeline. It's not available in the sceneline.

It's a Wrap

The steps Premiere goes through to create an InstantMovie are similar to those you take when you create your own movie. In fact, InstantMovie teaches you a lot about assembling a movie and applying transitions and effects. For example, consider the timing and video clip choices Premiere makes in assembling an InstantMovie. Study the way it creates the opening and closing titles. Examine how Premiere applies transitions and special effects to your clips.

In the following chapters, this book expands on each of these movie-making steps and shows how you can add your own personal touches to your movies.

Hooray for Hollywood!

Famous Movie Moment: In 1878, photographer Eadweard Muybridge helped former California Governor Leland Stanford win a bet that when a horse gallops, all four hooves leave the ground at the same time. He used 12 stereoscopic cameras placed 21 inches apart to completely capture a horse's stride. Even though it's more like time-lapse photography, this project is considered one of the stepping stones to the invention of motion pictures. Think of what Muybridge could have done with your camcorder.

CHAPTER 2

Import Your Clips

Before you can create a movie that will entertain friends and family, you need to move your raw video clips from your video recorder to your computer. These days, you shoot video with a slew of gadgets, including camcorders, digital cameras, and cellphones. The technique for transferring raw footage to your computer varies by device, but fortunately Premiere simplifies the process. Best of all, after you import video a few times, it becomes second nature. This chapter is your roadmap to importing clips.

Chances are your finished masterpiece will include more than just video clips. You may add music, narration, still photos, and other images. You need to import *all* these media "assets," but this chapter focuses on video. For details on importing other media, see Chapter 3.

Video Camera Storage Methods

Digital video files are big, so big that storage and processing power have always been issues when it comes to editing video on a PC. The good news is that personal computers keep improving, sporting bigger hard drives and faster processors. If you bought a computer in the last five years (stripped-down netbooks aside), odds are it'll run Premiere (see page 385 for Premiere's system requirements).

At the same time, camcorders have evolved, too. Like all electronic gadgets, the trend is toward smaller devices that hold more. New camcorders benefit from better memory chips and advanced hard drive technology. As a result, video cameras are smaller but hold more than ever before. But the best trend of all is in price: It costs less to buy a camera that captures great-looking video than it ever has.

Tip: You can find links to all the websites mentioned in these pages on this book's Missing CD page at *www.missingmanuals.com*.

Depending on their size and capabilities, video recorders use different storage methods. Larger camcorders store digital video on tape cassettes. Camcorders that fit in your hand store video on little hard disks, like the ones in laptop computers or iPods. Minicamcorders, digital cameras, and cellphones store video on memory chips. Look Ma, no moving parts! Depending on the device, these chips are either permanently fixed in the device or removable (you can take the latter out and replace them with a fresh memory card, perfect for vacations).

Here are the details of each of the storage methods:

• **DV cassettes.** Digital video cassettes come in different shapes and sizes, but the two most popular are MiniDV cassettes and Digital8 cassettes. Not to be confused with the ancient analog video cameras, these camcorders are 100 percent digital. About the size of a matchbox, MiniDV cassettes are popular in pro and consumer camcorders because they're reliable, relatively cheap, and high-quality—they give you a crisp video image. Depending on your camcorder, the cassettes can store standard digital video (DVD quality) or high-definition video, called HDV, which means its quality is similar to that of hi-def TVs and Blu-ray discs.

• **Hard drives.** Today's hard drives are small enough to fit in a tiny camcorder, yet store hours of digital video. And, with the hard drive built into the camera, you won't have to shell out more money to buy media, as you do with MiniDV cameras.

With hard-drive-based cameras, you transfer video files directly from the camera to your computer via a cable. These days it's usually a USB cable, like the one you use to connect most gadgets to your PC. The only issue is making sure that Premiere and your PC can read the type of video files your camera stores. (For more details on digital video formats, see the box on page 40.)

• **Mini-DVDs.** Some camcorders record directly to miniature digital video discs (3-inchers, about the size of a drink coaster). The concept is that you pop the disc out of your camcorder and into your DVD player or computer to view your raw footage. But you should double-check your equipment for compatibility before you buy a mini-DVD camera. If your computer's DVD drive has a tray that pops out, it most likely can handle these little discs—the tray that holds standard-size DVDs usually has a depression in it that accommodates the smaller-size discs. If, on the other hand, you load your DVDs by pushing them into a slot, as is the case with most Macs, small discs may not work (and they may jam the drive). Bottom line: Check before you buy.

Note that before you can play a disc in your TV's DVD player, you have to "finalize" it, a process you can do in your camcorder. In addition, high-definition AVCHD DVDs will only play in a Blu-ray disc drive.

- **Internal memory.** There are lots of examples of video cameras that store digital video directly onto memory chips inside the camera. In some cases, these cameras also have slots for memory *cards,* as described below. Many web-friendly minicamcorders (like the Flip line of cameras) plug directly into your computer's USB port, no cables necessary.

- **Memory cards.** Today, the most popular memory cards for still and video cameras are SD (Secure Digital) cards and their higher-capacity siblings, SDHC (Secure Digital High Capacity) and SDXC (Secure Digital Extended Capacity). You may find tape- or hard-drive-based cameras that have slots for these cards.

- **Your computer's hard drive.** You may have video clips stored on your hard drive from previous projects, from friends, or from a webcam. Premiere can snag these clips for your projects, too.

You can see examples of various camcorders in Figure 2-1. In addition to the media type your camera records on, you need to consider the video *format* it records in. For example, some hard-disk camcorders store video in the AVCHD format, while others use MPEG-2. When you're buying equipment, you want to make sure everything works together. These pages won't bore you with a technical dissertation on the differences between video formats, but if you're interested in more info on the video formats Premiere uses, see the box on page 40.

Figure 2-1:
Camcorders come in a variety of shapes and sizes. Their features and capabilities vary, too. Shown here from left to right, an AVCHD hard disk camcorder, a MiniDV camcorder and MiniDV cassette, and a web-friendly minicamcorder.

Video Format Alphabet Soup

Camcorders come in a bewildering number of digital video formats as manufacturers try to outdo each other by squeezing the best quality video into less space. Some formats are more popular than others, but the important thing to know is what format you're buying. Sometimes the video format's name is written in big letters on the camera; other times you have to dig out the manual to look up the specifications. Manufacturers' websites and sites like *www.bhphotovideo.com* and *www.crutchfield.com* are also great sources for technical specs. Just go to the site and search for a specific camcorder model number.

These days, you can divide digital video into two camps: standard and high-definition. Each format has a particular resolution—the number of pixels used to create an image. DV resolution is similar to what you see on DVDs, while HDV's is closer to HDTV's resolution. Table 2-1 shows the resolution for some of the most popular standards and devices.

In addition to resolution, each video format determines how the digital video file handles audio, how it translates video information into the 1s and 0s of a digital file for the PC, and how it compresses everything into smaller files. But you don't need to worry about that. You just need to make sure that Premiere can import the video format your device records, be it a camcorder, still camera, webcam, cellphone, electronic keychain, pen-cam, or dog collar-cam.

Here's a list with brief descriptions of the video formats Premiere understands. The letters in parentheses show you the file extension of each format.

- **Adobe Flash (.swf).** A video/animation format often used on websites.

- **AVI Movie (.avi).** A video format Microsoft Windows uses for digital video.

- **AVCHD (.m2ts, .mts, .m2t).** Used by hard disk, DVD, and memory-card camcorders to store high-definition video.

- **DV Stream (.dv).** Used to record video to MiniDV, Digital8, and other types of video tape.

- **Filmstrip (.flm).** Used by Premiere to output video as a sequence of individual frames.

- **MPEG Movie (.mpeg, .vob, .mod, .mpe, .mpg, .mpg, .m2v, .mpa, .mp2, .m2a, .mpv, .m2p, .mlv, .mp4, .m4v, .m4a, .aac, .avc, .264).** MPEG stands for *Motion Picture Experts Group*—an organization that defines video standards. There are several MPEG video file formats, as you can tell by the list above. Some represent standard video and others are high-definition formats.

- **QuickTime Movie (.mov, .3gp, .3g2, .mp4, .m4a, .m4v).** Developed by Apple for playing video on the Mac, but you can also get a QuickTime player for Windows.

- **TOD (.tod).** A high-definition video format used by JVC camcorders.

- **Windows Media (.wmv, .asf).** Formats used by Windows, often to send video over the Internet.

Table 2-1. *Popular device resolution dimensions*

Device/standard	Resolution (in pixels)
Apple iPhone	640 × 480
DVD video	720 × 480
DV NTSC (Standard DV)	720 × 480
HDV 720p	1280 × 720
Pure Digital Flip MinoHD	1280 × 720

Table 2-1. *Popular device resolution dimensions (continued)*

Device/standard	Resolution (in pixels)
HDV 1080i	1440 × 1080
Canon VIXIA HV30	1440 × 1080
HDTV 1080p	1920 × 1080

Add Raw Footage

Getting video from your camera into you computer used to be quite a hassle, but with Premiere it's just a matter of a few clicks and a bit of a wait. As shown in Figure 2-2, go to Premiere's Organize tab and click the Get Media button. The Organize panel displays icons for different types of video devices. Click the icon for your gadget, and Premiere uses one of two tools to import video clips to your computer: the Capture panel (Figure 2-3) or the media downloader (Figure 2-4). In general, tape-based camcorders and webcams use the Capture panel. Hard disk camcorders, DVD camcorders, and memory-based devices use the media downloader. Table 2-2 shows which gadgets use which tool.

Tip: You can also add footage by choosing File → Get Media From and then choosing your source. The menu lists all the media options shown in Table 2-2.

Table 2-2. *Premiere Elements can import video from several types of devices*

Device	Media format	Import tool
DV camcorder	Digital video on MiniDV or Digital8 tape.	Capture panel
HDV camcorder	High definition video on MiniDV tape cassette.	Capture panel
DVD (in camcorder or PC disc drive)	DVD or Mini DVD.	Media downloader
AVCHD or other hard disk/ memory camcorder	AVCHD video on hard drive, DVD, or SDHC memory card. Also use this option for camcorders that store video on internal memory chips or removable memory cards.	Media downloader
Digital camera	Video on a digital camera's internal memory chip or removable memory card.	Media downloader
Mobile devices	Video stored on a cellphone, iPod, or other media player.	Media downloader
Webcam or WDM device	Video on a webcam or device connected to your PC.	Capture panel
PC Files or Folders	Video stored on your hard drive (including video from any earlier Premiere projects).	Media downloader

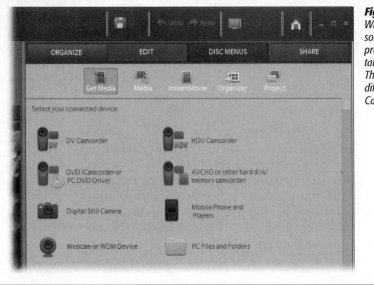

Figure 2-2:
Whenever you want to add video, sound, or other assets to your project, go to Premiere's Organize tab and click the Get Media button. The panel displays links for different media sources, like DV Camcorder or PC Files and Folders.

Figure 2-3:
Premiere's Capture panel is one way to import raw footage. You don't have to import an entire clip; you can use the capture panel's navigation buttons to choose just a portion of it.

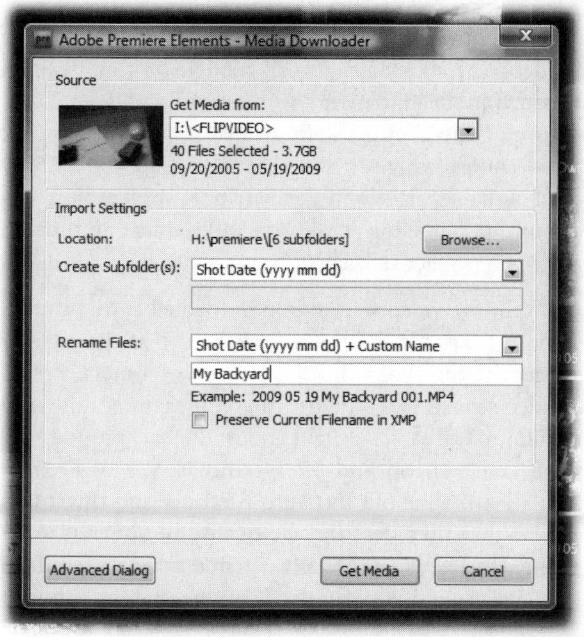

Figure 2-4:
The media downloader doesn't let you import a portion of a clip; it's an all-or-nothing proposition. However, if your hard disk, memory device, or PC folder has several clips, click the Advanced Dialog button to choose the clips you want.

Tour the Capture Panel

When you import video using the Capture panel, you use a process called *device control,* which means that your PC and Premiere take control of your camcorder or other device. The capture panel looks like a TV monitor with DVD-type navigation buttons at the bottom (Figure 2-5). You control the device in Premiere, using the fast forward, rewind, and play buttons to navigate to specific portions of your stored video. When you click the red Capture button, Premiere records that video to files on your PC. When Premiere finishes, you can disconnect your camcorder, and Premiere uses the computer files to edit and create your movies. Here's how to use each of the features in this panel.

Capturing source

At the top of the window, the label "Capturing Source" appears beside a drop-down menu where you select your source device. For a webcam or something similar, you also see an Audio menu where you can select a sound source. When you hook a camcorder up to your PC, the source is usually set to *Microsoft DV and VCR.* In most cases, Premiere can use generic device control settings to communicate with your camcorder. The Capture button starts and stops the capture process. Be patient—device control isn't always an instantaneous process.

Tip: If Premiere and your camcorder aren't talking to each other, try manually setting up your capture source as described on page 49.

Capture settings

A sidebar with capture settings appears on the right side of the window. You can collapse and expand this sidebar by clicking the small triangle button. Collapsing the sidebar lets you see the video in the entire window, as shown in Figure 2-3. You may not need to change any of the capture settings, but if you want, you can rename your video clips and choose where to store the files. Checkboxes let you choose to capture video and audio separately. If you assemble your project as you go along, turn on the "Capture to Timeline" checkbox so Premiere automatically adds imported clips to your open project's timeline.

Premiere offers two ways to split the video stream into individual clips: by content or by timecode. If you choose timecode, Premiere makes note of the times you stopped and started the camera as you shot video. If you choose content, Premiere guesses where to split the video stream based on the image; it examines the objects or faces in the image and notes major shifts in light and in the background. At the bottom of the settings, you can turn on and off specific aspects of Premiere's smart-tagging feature. (You'll learn all about the Auto-Analyzer and smart tags in Chapter 4, but for now know that they describe the quality of your video clips, using labels like Low Volume, In Focus, and Shaky. Premiere uses this information when it creates InstantMovies, and you can use it when you select clips for a project.)

Navigation buttons

The capture panel's navigation buttons look much like the ones on a DVD player. In addition to the usual play/pause, fast-forward, and rewind buttons, there are also buttons that let you move through your video a frame at a time (Figures 2-5 and 2-6). The Shuttle tool lets you move through the video at variable speeds—the further you push the shuttle to the left, the faster the video plays. Don't forget the two buttons on the far left, which jump to the previous and next scenes or clips. Click the red Capture button to start copying video to your PC, and then click the same button to pause the capture process.

Import Digital Video Tape Files (DV or HDV)

Importing raw video from a tape-based camcorder (MiniDV or Digital8) takes a few steps. You connect your camcorder to your PC using a FireWire or USB cable. Then use your PC and Premiere to control the camcorder. You can fast-forward and rewind the tape to find a specific clip you want to import, or you can import lots of clips at once. Either way, Premiere saves the clips on your computer and then runs the Auto-Analyzer to apply smart tags (page 120) based on the quality of the video. The entire process is pretty much the same whether you import standard DV or HDV video clips.

Capturing Source   Clip Name   Save To

Figure 2-5:
There's a lot going on in the capture panel, but Premiere is pretty good at setting things up automatically. Usually all you have to worry about is using the navigation controls to find and capture the video you want.

Navigation Controls   Capture/Pause   Capture Settings

Here are the steps:

1. **Plug your camcorder into an outlet and turn it on. Set it to Play, VTR, or VCR mode, which lets your PC recognize your camcorder.**

   You can run your camcorder off of its battery when you import video, but why risk the battery going dead before you finish?

2. **Connect your camcorder to your PC.**

   Your camcorder connects to your computer using either a FireWire or a USB 2.0 cable. For details about the type of cable and connections, see page 51. If your camcorder is properly powered up and plugged in, you'll probably hear a lovely tone when your PC recognizes the newly connected device.

3. **Start Premiere.**

   Choose either New Project or Open Project as described on page 16.

4. **In the Tasks panel, click the Organize tab.**

   It displays any media already in your Organizer catalog (see page 101). You see several buttons at the top of the panel, including Get Media.

5. **Click Get Media.**

The Tasks panel displays several icons showing devices that hold raw video files, like "DV Camcorder" and "DVD (Camcorder or PC DVD Drive)".

6. **Click DV Camcorder (or HDV Camcorder, if that's what you have).**

The capture panel appears, as shown in Figure 2-5. You're in device control mode, which means that Premiere and your PC are controlling your camcorder's playback. At the top of the Capture panel, the Capturing Source drop-down menu probably displays "Microsoft DV Camera and VCR". Below, a message reports the device's status—Stopped, for example, when you're not rewinding or playing your camcorder's video. If it doesn't seem like your computer and camcorder are communicating, go on to the next step. Otherwise, skip to step 8.

7. **If necessary, click the Capturing Source drop-down menu and select your camcorder or device.**

These days, camcorders and Premiere are pretty good at talking to each other, so this step is becoming less and less necessary. Under the Capturing Source menu, Premiere displays a message about the current status of the connected device. A message like Stopped, Paused, Capturing, or Playing means your camcorder is connected and all is well. If the camcorder and computer aren't talking to each other, you're likely to see something like "Capture Device Offline" or "No DV camera detected." If you're having trouble, consult the steps in the box on page 49.

8. **In the Clip Name box, type in a name, like *Amy's 16th Birthday Cake.***

You can use any name, but make it descriptive enough so that you'll recognize it two years from now when you're rummaging through your clips.

Tip: If the capture window's sidebar is closed, you won't see the Clip Name box or the other sidebar settings. Click the tiny triangle to expand and collapse the sidebar (Figure 2-6).

---

9. **(Optional) Click the "Browse for Folder" button and choose a location.**

Premiere automatically stores your imported clips in the location specified in Edit → Preferences → Scratch Disks → Captured Video. You can choose a different location using "Browse for Folder".

10. **(Optional) Choose "Capture to Timeline".**

Turn this option on and Premiere automatically adds imported clips to the next open spot in your project's timeline (see page 156).

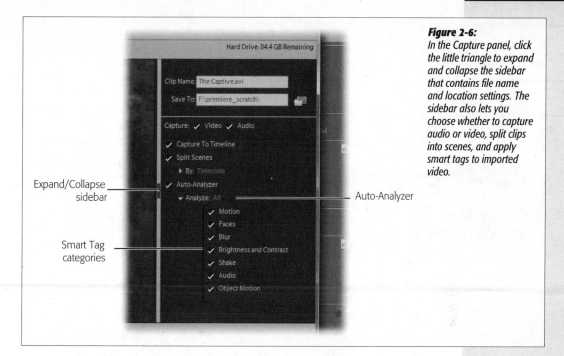

Figure 2-6:
In the Capture panel, click the little triangle to expand and collapse the sidebar that contains file name and location settings. The sidebar also lets you choose whether to capture audio or video, split clips into scenes, and apply smart tags to imported video.

11. **(Optional) Turn on Split Scenes and then choose Timecode or Content.**

When you import digital video from a tape-based camcorder, Premiere automatically checks the time stamp on the video stream. It breaks up your video where it detects that you started and stopped the camera. If you prefer, you can choose Content, to make Premiere look for changes in the image and create scenes based on what's in the image. For an explanation of timecode, see page 50.

12. **Select Auto-Analyzer and Analyze All.**

The Auto-Analyzer checkbox appears in the sidebar. When you turn it on, Premiere applies smart tags to clips after it imports them. Click the Analyze button, and you can choose which smart tags to apply. Here are the options: Motion, Faces, Blur, Brightness and Contrast, Shake, Audio, and Object Motion. (For more on the Auto-Analyzer, see page 120.)

13. **Use the navigation buttons at the bottom of the capture panel to find the beginning of the clip you want to import.**

The navigation buttons (Figure 2-7) work as they do on most DVD or media players. The two buttons at the far left let you jump from one scene (video clip) to another. If you want to jump to an exact location and you know the time and frame, you can click the timecode numbers and type in a new time (see page 50 to learn how to interpret timecodes).

Tip: There's a quick and easy way to jump to a new time in the Capture window. It's called *scrubbing,* and you can use it throughout Premiere to change numerical settings. When you hold your cursor over the timecode, the cursor changes to display two arrows. Drag to the right to increase the number; drag left to decrease it.

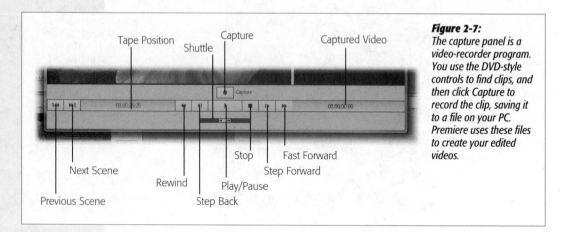

Tape Position Shuttle Capture Captured Video

Next Scene
Previous Scene Rewind Step Back Play/Pause Step Forward Stop Fast Forward

Figure 2-7:
The capture panel is a video-recorder program. You use the DVD-style controls to find clips, and then click Capture to record the clip, saving it to a file on your PC. Premiere uses these files to create your edited videos.

14. **Click the red Capture button.**

    The video starts playing in the capture panel. A red line around the video indicates that Premiere's capturing video and recording it to your PC. If your camcorder has an LCD viewing screen, you probably see the video displayed there, too.

15. **When you reach the end of the clip you want to capture, click Stop.**

    As Premiere imports your video, the capture button turns into a stop button. Click it and Premiere stops recording (and playing back) the video.

    Premiere analyzes the captured video and applies smart tags to it. Later, as you edit your project, the smart tags describe the quality of your clips (for more detail on smart tags, see page 120).

Tape-based camcorders have a lot of advantages. For example, MiniDV tapes are affordable, reliable, and easy to store as backups. During a long video-recording session, you can always pop in a new tape and keep working. Furthermore, for technical, video-compression reasons, the image on DV tape is often better than video stored other ways. The biggest negative about DV tape camcorders is that you have to fast-forward or fast-reverse to find individual clips on the tape, while hard disks, memory chips, and DVD camcorders can jump directly to any bit of stored video.

Import multiple scenes from tape

One MiniDV tape holds about an hour of standard video. If you've got room on your hard drive, you may want to import most or even all the scenes on the tape.

Troubleshoot Your Camcorder Connection

If your computer and camcorder aren't playing well together, you can try a few simple steps to bring about peace and cooperation.

1. Turn off your camcorder.

2. Double-check the cable connection. It may help to unplug and then re-plug the connectors on both ends. You may also want to use a new cable, in case you've got a bad one.

3. Turn your camcorder back on.

4. Make sure the camera is in Play, VTR, or VCR mode.

As simple as it sounds, those steps may be enough to reestablish rapport between the two machines. If that fails, you can try a more elaborate version of the on/off fix:

1. Turn your camcorder off.

2. Save your Premiere work and other work you may have in progress.

3. Restart your computer.

4. Start Premiere, but avoid running additional programs. (C'mon, you can live without iTunes for a few minutes.)

5. Double-check your cable connection.

6. Turn your camcorder back on, making sure it's in Play, VTR, or VCR mode.

7. Click the Organize tab and Get Media button and try again.

If these steps don't solve your problem, you can try manually setting up your capture device, as described below.

Set up your PC and computer to capture video as described in the steps beginning on page 44. Rewind your camcorder to the beginning of the tape and then click Capture. Then you can take a walk around the block or do anything else that takes about an hour. Premiere records the video as your camcorder plays it, but rather than create one big video clip, it breaks the clip into scenes. For example, Premiere can tell when you stopped and started the camcorder, and it uses those breaks to start and end scenes.

Manually set up your capture source

Most of the time, Premiere can use generic settings to communicate with video camcorders and other capture sources. If Premiere and your camcorder don't want to talk to each other, first try the fixes described in the box above. If those steps fail, you can try setting up your capture source manually in Premiere's preferences settings:

1. **Choose Edit → Preferences → Device Control.**

   The Preferences window opens with the Device Control settings selected.

2. **Click the Options button.**

   The DV/HDV Device Control Settings window opens (Figure 2-8).

UP TO SPEED

How to Read a Video Timecode

As you work with video clips, you'll notice that Premiere displays clip duration in an odd way, as a series of numbers separated by semicolons. That's called a timecode. Here's how it works. The timecode represents time in the format hours;minutes;seconds;frames. For example, 02;34;16;22 translates to 2 hours, 34 minutes, 16 seconds, and 22 frames. Why such an exacting number? As you edit a project, you often want to cut scenes and add transitions at very precise locations. Timecodes describe those locations down to the smallest increment possible for video editing—

a clip's frame number. Write down a timecode as you review a clip, and you can go back to that exact location to add a cut or transition.

Video captured according to the NTSC standard—the one used in North America and Japan—records video at about 30 frames per second (technically, it's 29.97). The PAL format—used in Europe and a few other places—records 25 frames per second (fps). For more details about the two video systems, see page 25.

Figure 2-8:
As a last resort, if Premiere doesn't recognize your camcorder or video device, you can manually change the Device Control Settings. Here the device is defined as a Sony DCR-TRV-900 camcorder. The Check Status setting shows that the camcorder is online and communicating.

3. **In the Video Standard drop-down menu, choose NTSC or PAL.**

   Choose the video system that matches your camcorder and TV. (For more details on the NTSC and PAL video systems, see page 25.)

4. **Use the Device Brand drop-down menu to select the maker of your camcorder.**

   For example, choose Sony, Canon, or JVC.

5. **In the Device Type drop-down menu, select the model number for your camera.**

   The menu contains a generous number of models for most popular camcorder manufacturers. If you can't find your model, you can experiment by choosing model numbers that are close to yours.

6. **Leave the Timecode Format set to Auto Detect.**

The two choices on the drop-down menu are Non–Drop Frame and Drop Frame, and they relate to the way the PC records video frames in the file. In most cases, Premiere can detect which method your PC uses.

7. **Click the Check Status button.**

You should see the word Online next to the Check Status button if your camcorder or device is connected, turned on, and set to Play, VTR, or VCR mode.

8. **Click OK.**

The Device Control Settings window closes.

9. **Click OK.**

The Preferences window closes, and you're back at the capture panel ready to import video.

UP TO SPEED

How to Connect Your Camcorder and PC

Two kinds of cables connect camcorders to PCs: FireWire and USB. Your computer and camcorder may have one or both of these connections. The only "gotcha" is that your computer and camcorder have to use the same type of connection: FireWire to FireWire, or USB to USB. Generally, Firewire is used with tape-based camcorders while USB is used for memory, disc, or hard drive camcorders.

FireWire is also known as i.Link by Sony or its catchy technical specification IEEE 1394a. FireWire cables may have a small connector on one end and a large one on the other. Typically, you plug the large end into your PC and the small end into your camcorder. The socket on your camcorder may be labeled FireWire, i.Link, or DV IN/OUT.

FireWire 800 (a.k.a IEEE 1394b) is a new, improved version of FireWire that sends data even faster. It's used on new Macintosh computers and has different connectors than the older version. (They always manage to make it difficult, don't they?) At the time this was written, it was hard to find camcorders using FireWire 800. The older FireWire connection is fast enough to transfer video between camcorders and PCs. However, if you find yourself in a bind—

for example, with FireWire 800 on your PC and FireWire 400 on your camcorder—you can find cables and adapters to convert one end to make the connection.

USB 2.0 is the standard USB (Universal Serial Bus) connection you find on most computers made since 2002. As with FireWire, USB connectors can be big or small, so make sure you get a cable with a small connector that matches your camcorder and a larger connector that plugs into your PC. Beware: Some really old computers use USB 1.0, which doesn't operate fast enough for video work. You can upgrade such a computer with a new USB 2.0 card, but chances are the other parts of the PC won't be up to speed for video editing or Premiere Elements 8.

Whether you connect via a FireWire or USB cable, your computer usually makes some sort of sound when it recognizes a newly connected device. The first time you connect the camcorder and your PC, you may see a message explaining that Windows is finding and installing a driver (providing your PC is tapped into the Internet, that is). That means Windows is automatically getting a mini-program that helps your computer and camcorder talk to each other.

Import Webcam Video

Webcams are simple audio/video recorders that you often find built into laptops—but you can attach one to any PC with a USB cable, too. Their lens and mic are basic quality, but what do you expect for $40? Webcams make fine Internet video-phones, which is what folks usually use them for. Still, Premiere is more than happy to use them as a video source.

1. **Make sure the webcam is plugged in and turned on.**

   Webcams that connect via a USB cable are powered on when you connect the cable. If you have a built-in webcam, turn it on using its control panel.

2. **In the Tasks panel, click the Organize tab.**

   The Organize tab displays any media already stored in your project. At the top of the panel, you see several buttons, including Get Media.

3. **Click Get Media.**

   The Tasks panel displays several icons showing devices that hold raw video files, such as "DV Camcorder" or "DVD (Camcorder or PC DVD Drive)".

4. **Click "Webcam or WDM Device".**

   The Capture panel opens (Figure 2-9). Your webcam is probably already selected as the Capture Source and the Audio Source. If everything is working properly, you'll see an image in the Capture panel monitor even though you're not actually capturing the video stream yet.

Note: The term "WDM Device" refers to the Windows Driver Model—a system for connecting gadgets to Windows PCs.

   If your webcam isn't showing as the Capture Source and you don't see an image in the capture panel's monitor, click the drop-down menu and choose your webcam from the list. (If the list doesn't include your webcam, try the troubleshooting options in the box on page 49.)

   Webcams use small programs called *drivers* to communicate with your computer. The first time you connect your webcam to your computer, Windows guides you through the process of installing the drivers.

5. **In the Clip Name box, type in a name, like *Webcam Address to Nation*.**

   You're welcome to use a more creative or meaningful name.

6. **(Optional) Click "Browse for Folder" and choose a location.**

   Premiere automatically stores your imported clips in the location specified in Edit → Preferences → Scratch Disks → Captured Video. You can choose a different location now using "Browse for Folder".

7. (Optional) Select Capture to Timeline.

With this option, Premiere automatically drops imported video in the next open spot in the editing timeline.

8. (Optional) Turn on Split Scenes and choose Timecode or Content.

When you import digital video from a tape-based camcorder, Premiere automatically watches your video stream's time stamp. It breaks up your video where it detects that you started and stopped the camera. If you prefer, choose Content, and Premiere looks for changes in the image and creates scenes based on when the image changes significantly.

9. Select Auto-Analyzer and Analyze All.

The Auto-Analyzer checkbox appears in the sidebar. When you turn this feature on, Premiere applies smart tags to clips after it imports them. Click the Analyze button, and you can choose which smart tags to apply. Your options are Motion, Faces, Blur, Brightness and Contrast, Shake, and Audio. For more on smart tagging, see page 120.

10. Click the red Capture button.

Premiere begins to capture video and displays a red line around the video image as a signal that it's capturing the video.

11. **When you finish capturing video from the webcam, or if you want to pause, click the Pause button beneath the video image.**

When you click Pause, the Capture panel goes into standby mode. Premiere analyzes the video (and applies smart tags if you turned that feature on in Step 9). You still see the video image, but there's no longer a red line around it. To restart the capture, just click Capture again. If you're finished, go on to the next step.

12. Click the X button in the upper-right corner of the Capture panel.

The Capture panel closes. If you chose Split Scenes or Smart Tagging, Premiere takes a few moments to analyze your clips before displaying them in the Organize tab.

Capture Time-Lapse or Stop-Motion Video

Most of the time, you want to create videos that represent real time—2 minutes of video is the same as 2 minutes in the real world. On the other hand, you can create some entertaining, time-bending effects with time-lapse or stop-motion video. Time-lapse video is where 2 minutes of video may cover 12 hours' worth of events in the real world, like movies where clouds zip rapidly across the sky or flowers open to full bloom in a matter of seconds. Stop-motion video makes seemingly inanimate objects, like rocks, scoot around or jump from one spot to another (think Wallace and Gromit or Mr. Bill). Some video cameras let you create time-lapse or stop-motion video, but if yours doesn't, you can create these effects when you capture camcorder or webcam video in Premiere.

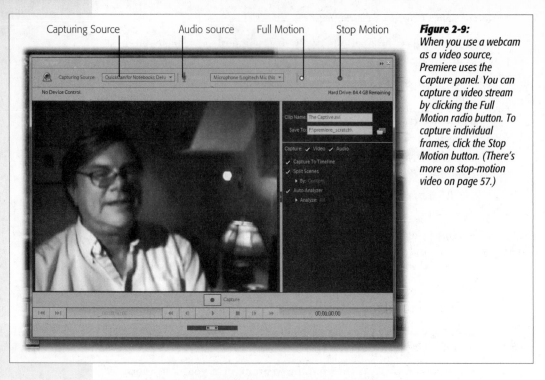

Capturing Source   Audio source   Full Motion   Stop Motion

Figure 2-9:
When you use a webcam as a video source, Premiere uses the Capture panel. You can capture a video stream by clicking the Full Motion radio button. To capture individual frames, click the Stop Motion button. (There's more on stop-motion video on page 57.)

Capture previously recorded video as time-lapse video

In time-lapse video, you record a few frames at regular intervals and put them in a video clip. When you play back the clip, you see a compressed version of time. There are two critical settings that control the action—frequency and duration. For example, if you want to capture clouds moving in the sky, snagging 1 second of video every 5 minutes shows smooth, steady motion. If you want to monitor the activity at your bird feeder, 5 or 10 seconds every 10 minutes captures individual birds' motion better. Usually, it takes some test-runs to find the right formula for a particular event. Follow these steps to create a time-lapse video from a video you took with your camcorder:

1. **Connect your camcorder to your PC and turn it on in Play, VTR, or VCR mode.**

   For more details on connecting your camcorder for use with the Capture window, see page 44.

2. **In the Tasks panel, click the Organize tab and then choose Get Media.**

   The Organize tab shows the different devices you can choose to import video.

3. **Click DV Camcorder.**

   The capture panel opens. Make sure Capturing Source is set to "Microsoft DV Camera and VCR".

4. **To the right of Capturing Source, select Stop Motion.**

Radio buttons let you choose either Full Motion (the standard video-capture mode) or Stop Motion. As shown in Figure 2-10, when you choose Stop Motion, you see a button that says Create New Stop Motion and the instruction "Drag existing clip here to continue." New settings appear below the video image: Time Lapse, Set Time, and Delete Frame.

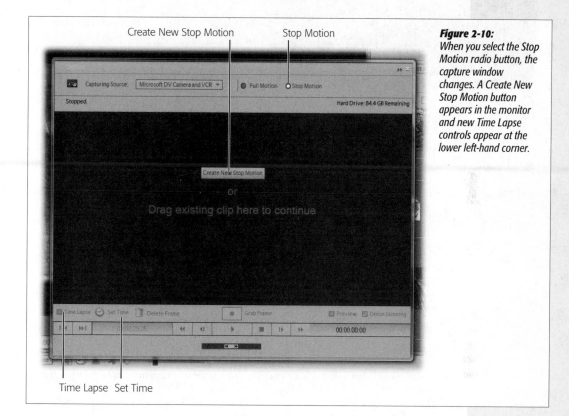

Create New Stop Motion   Stop Motion

Create New Stop Motion
or
Drag existing clip here to continue

Time Lapse   Set Time

Figure 2-10:
When you select the Stop Motion radio button, the capture window changes. A Create New Stop Motion button appears in the monitor and new Time Lapse controls appear at the lower left-hand corner.

5. **In the video image area, click the Create New Stop Motion button.**

After a moment, the Time Lapse checkbox is activated—it's no longer grayed out.

6. **Turn on the Time Lapse checkbox.**

The Time Lapse checkbox controls whether you capture time-lapse video or stop-motion video. When you turn on Time Lapse, Premiere activates the Set Time control (with a clock icon).

7. **Click Set Time.**

The Set Time panel opens, as shown in Figure 2-11.

Figure 2-11:
Use the Set Time panel to set the interval frequency and duration for time-lapse video. If you want to capture smoother motion, keep the duration short, about 1 to 5 seconds.

8. **Set Frequency to 5 minutes and Duration to 1 second.**

   This way, Premiere will capture 1 second of video every 5 minutes. This setting works well for capture events in the sky, like the motion of clouds or the sun setting.

9. **Click OK.**

   The Set Time panel closes.

10. **Click the red Start Time Lapse button.**

    The video begins to play and every 5 minutes, Premiere grabs 1 second of video.

11. **Click the Stop Time Lapse button.**

    It's just the Start Time Lapse button in its alternate identity.

12. **Click the X button at the capture panel's upper-right corner.**

    A panel appears asking "Do you want to save the captured images as a movie file?"

13. **Click Yes.**

    The program creates your time-lapse video from the captured images. The Capture window closes, and you're back on the Organize tab.

Capture live video as time-lapse

You can capture new video as a time-lapse video clip as you record it live with a webcam or a camcorder. The process is nearly identical to the one for previously recorded video. Instead of capturing frames from the video tape, Premiere captures frames from the connected camera. Follow the steps starting on page 54, but in Step 1, instead of putting your camcorder in Play, VTR, or VCR mode, turn it on in Camera or Record mode and start shooting. The rest of the steps are the same, except that Premiere uses the live image as a source rather than previously recorded video.

Capture stop-motion video

Stop motion works much like a still camera, capturing frames when you click Capture. Here's how you can use it to make a stop-motion video of a tricycle moving itself across a driveway: Put the trike on the driveway. Capture a few frames of video. The camera stops. Move the trike a couple of inches. Capture a few more frames. Continue on until the trike completes its journey. (Of course, you have to have a laptop or some way to get your PC out into the driveway.)

Here are the complete steps needed to capture stop-motion video with Premiere:

1. **Connect your camcorder to your PC and turn it on in Camera or Record mode.**

   For more details on connecting your camcorder for use with the Capture panel, see page 51.

2. **In the Tasks panel, click the Organize tab and then choose Get Media.**

   The Organize tab shows the different devices you can choose to import video.

3. **Click DV Camcorder (or Webcam).**

   The Capture panel opens. The Capturing Source should be set to "Microsoft DV Camera and VCR".

4. **To the right of Capturing Source, select Stop Motion.**

   Radio buttons let you choose either Full Motion (the standard video capture mode) or Stop Motion. As shown in Figure 2-10, a button appears in the video monitor that says Create New Stop Motion and the instruction "Drag existing clip here to continue". New settings appear below the video image: Time Lapse, Set Time, and Delete Frame.

5. **Click Create New Stop Motion.**

   The monitor shows the video from your camcorder.

6. **Arrange the scene the way you want.**

   Now's when you position the trike on the driveway.

7. **Click Grab Frame.**

   Premiere captures video and then stops.

8. **Repeat Steps 6 and 7 until you capture the complete scene.**

   Keep changing the scene and capturing frames until you're happy with your video.

9. **Click Preview.**

   Premiere Elements goes into preview mode, and you see the captured frames playing in the monitor. It goes by pretty quickly if you only have a few frames of video. If you want to see it again, click Play.

10. **Turn off Preview.**

Remove the checkmark from the Preview box, and you're back in Capture mode.

11. **(Optional) Turn on Onion-Skinning.**

Onion-skinning is a preview tool. It shows more than one captured image at a time by making the images semi-transparent and superimposing them over each other. This doesn't change your movie clip, you only see this effect as you preview and capture frames. You use onion-skinning to make sure one frame is aligned with the next. (For details see the box.)

12. **When you're done with your Stop Motion video, click the X in the upper-right corner.**

A dialog box asks "Do you want to save the captured images as a movie file."

13. **Click Yes.**

Premiere saves the clip, and you can find it with the others in the Organize tab. You can use the clip just like any other video clip. If you click No or Cancel, the clip isn't saved.

FREQUENTLY ASKED QUESTION

Onion-Skinning to See Multiple Frames

Do I need onion-skinning? I don't even like onions.

Onion-skinning is a tool used in video and animation programs that superimposes one frame over another as you work. The effect looks like a double-exposed photograph. Onion-skinning is only a preview effect. It doesn't change the look of your finished clip, but it can be helpful when you try to align multiple frames in stop-motion or time-lapse video. For example, you may want to make sure all the objects remain in place as you move one object, say a tricycle. If everything is going according to plan, you should see more than one trike superimposed in the image, while all the other objects stay in place. In Premiere, you turn on onion-skinning with the checkbox in the lower-right corner of the capture panel.

If you find onion-skinning helpful for your project, you may want to tweak the preferences so it works even better. In the upper-right corner of the capture window there's a button that opens the Capture panel menu (See Figure 2-12). Choose Stop Motion Preferences from the menu, and you see three boxes where you can make adjustments. Normally, onion-skinning superimposes three images: the current, the previous, and the next. You can change this number in the Number of Skins box. In the example, where the tricycle moves across the driveway, suppose you want to see more of its path. To see more onion-skinned images, first set the opacity to a lower number—it starts out set to 50 percent. Then increase the number of skins. The Playback box sets the rate for number of frames displayed per second.

Tour the Media Downloader

The media downloader is the tool for you if your camcorder stores video on DVDs, hard disks, or memory chips. If you want to capture all the video on your camcorder, you can use the media downloader as it appears in Figure 2-4. If you want to pick and choose the clips you import, click the Advanced Dialog button in

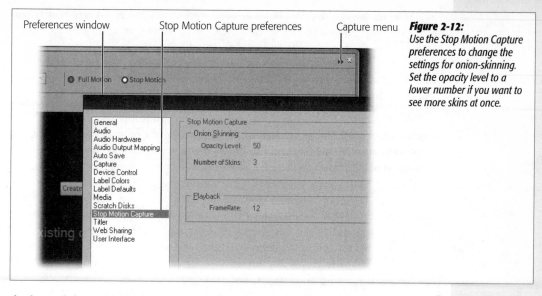

Preferences window   Stop Motion Capture preferences   Capture menu

Figure 2-12:
Use the Stop Motion Capture preferences to change the settings for onion-skinning. Set the opacity level to a lower number if you want to see more skins at once.

the lower-left corner, and the media downloader expands to look like the one in Figure 2-13. Just turn on the boxes for the clips you want to download. Unlike the Capture panel described on page 43, the media downloader captures entire video clips; it doesn't let you select portions of clips. But it *does* let you import video files that live on your PC into Premiere.

The expanded media downloader is divided into two general territories: Source and Save Options.

Source

Use the drop-down menu to choose the camcorder, device, or computer folder that holds the video you want to bring into Premiere. The list automatically shows the camcorders, still cameras, and scanners attached to your PC. Below the drop-down menu, you see a message that lists the number of files you've selected. Another helpful bit of info is the amount of space required to store the selected files. Under Source, you see three buttons that show and hide video, still images, and audio files in the list. If you're only interested in using video, deselect the other two options. The largest area of the display is devoted to thumbnails of your media. You can view video clips by clicking their triangle buttons. Turn on the checkboxes to select the media you want to download—in other words, copy—from your gadget to your PC.

Save Options

The Save Options settings let you organize and name the files as Premiere copies them from your camcorder to your PC. Click the Browse button to choose where you want to store the files. To organize your clips into subfolders, click the Create Subfolders drop-down menu and choose whether to organize your files by date or name. If you plan to do most of your video work in Premiere, using dates to organize video clip folders and files works well, because you can combine date ranges with Premiere's other organizing tools (albums and tags) to help you find clips. Use the Rename Files drop-down menu to determine how Premiere names the clips when it stows them on your PC. You can choose not to rename the files, give them a name of your own choosing, or use the date in combination with a custom name. That last option is cool because it gives you two ways to identify a file in the future.

Video and photo files can store addition text information, called *metadata*, along with the images. Metadata comes in handy if you someday have to credit the file's creator, provide copyright details, and so on. If you turn on "Preserve Current Filename in XMP", Premiere stores the original filename in the metadata. Click the triangle next to Apply Metadata, and you see a few other ways you can add text to your video and photo files. Under "Template to use", choose None if the whole topic bores you and you're not interested in adding metadata. If you choose Basic Metadata, you can add your name as creator and whatever copyright details you want. Also, Premiere stores any metadata your camcorder or camera attaches—like the frame rate and other technical details.

Note: Premiere stores metadata in the folder you specify in Location, along with your video clips. The files with .xmp extensions are text files that hold the metadata Premiere and your camcorder add to the video clips.

Figure 2-13:
The media downloader looks like this in Advanced Dialog mode. You see thumbnails of your photos and video, and you can even preview video clips by clicking the triangular Play buttons. Use the three buttons above the thumbnails to show and hide video clips, audio clips, and still photos.

Import from Hard Disk or Memory Camcorder

The steps for importing video from hard-disk-based and memory-card camcorders are nearly identical. For the most part, Premiere doesn't care whether the video is stored on a hard drive or memory chip. It just needs to know which files to import and how you'd like to name the clips.

1. **Connect your camcorder to your PC.**

   Some camcorders use a USB cable. Others, such as the new minicamcorders, have a USB connector built in to the camera. (For details about USB and FireWire cables, see the box on page 51.)

2. **Start Premiere.**

   Choose either New Project or Open Project, as described on page 16.

3. **In the Tasks panel, click the Organize tab.**

   The Organize tab displays any media that's already stored in your project. At the top of panel you see four buttons: Get Media, Media, InstantMovie, and Organizer.

4. **Click Get Media.**

   The Tasks panel displays several icons showing devices that hold raw video files, like "DV Camcorder" or "DVD (Camcorder or PC DVD Drive)".

5. **Click "AVCHD or other hard disk/memory camcorder".**

   The media downloader window appears, where you can choose the camcorder or device that holds your video clips. As explained on page 58, you can view the media downloader in either of two modes: Standard Dialog (as shown back in Figure 2-4) or Advanced Dialog (Figure 2-13). The button that lets you choose is in the lower-left corner.

6. **If necessary, click the Advanced Dialog button.**

   The media downloader expands to the larger view shown in Figure 2-13. On the left side, you see the Source settings. On the right side, you see the Save Options. The Advanced Dialog also shows you thumbnails of the downloadable video clips and other media.

7. **Turn on the checkboxes under the thumbnails that you want to import.**

   If you want to preview a video clip, click the triangle Play button below the thumbnail. At the bottom of the window, you see buttons to Check All or Uncheck All of the thumbnails.

8. **Click Get Media.**

   Premiere copies the files from the camcorder or other device to your hard disk. You see a progress bar as the files transfer. When the process is over, the media downloader closes, and you see the video clips in the Organize tab ready for editing.

Import DVD Camcorder Video

DVD camcorders record video onto mini-DVDs that are 3 inches in diameter. Single-layer, single-sided discs hold 1.4 gigabytes of video, which is about half an hour of standard digital video. You can also get double-sided discs—you flip them over to record on the second side. Since 2006, you can get single-sided dual-layer discs that record twice as much, but your camcorder, PC, and DVD player must all support dual-layer discs. As with their bigger 5-inch brothers, these mini-DVDs may record once (DVD-R or DVD+R) or they can record, be erased, and recorded on again (DVD-RW or DVD+RW). The key here is to learn (and remember) which discs your equipment supports. The one format that you can use on almost any equipment is the DVD-R (record-once) format.

DVD camcorders compress video and can store it in a couple of different formats, including one of the many MPEG formats or AVCHD. Depending on your camcorder, you may be able to import video using the steps described below, "Import from Hard Disk or Memory Camcorder", or you can import from the recorded DVDs using the steps described in "Import Video from DVD" on page 63.

Import Video from PC Hard Disk

There are a lot of reasons why you might have video clips on your PC that you haven't imported into Premiere. For example, someone may give or email you some videos, or maybe they're from earlier video projects. If you want to follow the exercises in this book using the same video clips shown in the examples, see the box on page 63. You can download the clips and then use these steps to import the clips into Premiere. In any case, you're free to import files on your PC into Premiere so you can use them your projects. Follow these steps to use the media downloader to import video from your PC's hard disk.

1. **In Premiere's Tasks panel, click the Organize tab and then choose Get Media.**

   The Organize tab shows the different devices you can choose to import video.

2. **Choose "PC Files and Folders".**

   The Add Media window opens.

3. **Navigate to a specific file or folder you want to import.**

   Premiere Elements can import selected files, or it can import all the video clips in a particular folder.

4. **Select the files or folder you want to import.**

   You can select a single file or multiple files using Ctrl-click. If you want to import all the video files in a folder, just select the folder.

5. **Click Open to import files or click Add Folder to import all the video files in a folder.**

   Premiere Elements displays a progress bar as it imports the files. When it's done, the Add Media window closes and you see the video files in the Organize tab.

Download Clips for Book Exercises

Here's another chance to practice your "import video from hard disk" skills. The remaining chapters of this book include several exercises that cover assembling and editing a movie, adding transitions and effects, and sharing a movie to discs or websites. You can follow along using your own video project, or if you want to follow the examples exactly as they appear in the book, you can use the clips referred to in this book. First you need to download these 13 media clips from *http://missingmanuals.com/cds*. There are 12 video clips and one audio clip:

- 01-House.mp4
- 02-Street.mp4
- 03-Birds.mp4
- 04-Cars_Street.mp4
- 05-House_Fence.mp4
- 06-Pickets.mp4
- 07-Trail.mp4
- 08-Stream.mp4
- 09-Splash.mp4
- 10-Bridge.mp4
- 11-Corner.mp4
- 12-Stop.mp4
- 01-Nobody Knows.mp3

You can preview each clip before you download it, and if you want a sneak peek at the final project go to *http://missingmanuals.com/cds/premelements8tmm/*. Be forewarned, these raw video clips are big (about 30 megabytes each) and will take a while to download.

Once you download them, follow these steps to get started:

1. Choose File → New → Project to open the New Project window.

2. In the Name box type *Lola's Big Splash*.

3. (Optional) Choose a folder where you want to save the project, or you can use the location Premiere suggests.

4. Click Change Settings and choose *NTSC → HDV → HDV 720p 30*.

5. Click OK.

Premiere creates a new project, called "Lola's Big Splash," which you can use for the rest of the exercises. The first exercise is to add the files you downloaded to the project file. So, follow the steps on page 62 to Import Video from PC Hard Disk to add the 13 media clips to your new project.

Import Video from DVD

Besides the DVDs that your camcorder records, you may have DVDs your friends or family made that you want to work with in Premiere. All DVDs store video in container files that have a *.vob* extension. Some DVDs—such as those containing the latest blockbuster movies—are copy-protected. You can't import protected DVDs with Premiere, but you can import DVD video from camcorders. Premiere brings in the entire VOB file, and you can edit it as you would any other video clip. Here's how to move VOBs from DVD to your PC:

1. **In the Tasks panel, click the Organize tab and then choose Get Media.**

   The Organize tab shows the different devices you can choose to import video.

2. Choose "DVD (Camcorder or PC DVD Drive)".

The media downloader window opens. As explained on page 58, you can view the media downloader in either of two modes: Standard Dialog or Advanced Dialog.

3. Under Source, use the "Get Media from" drop-down menu to select your DVD drive (Figure 2-2).

Thumbnails of the VOB files appear in the media downloader. If you don't see the thumbnails, make sure that the Video button is selected.

4. If necessary, click the Advanced Dialog button.

The media downloader expands to the larger view as shown in Figure 2-13. On the left side of the window you see the Source settings. On the right side of the window you see the Save Options.

5. Turn on the checkboxes under the thumbnails you want to import.

It takes a while for Premiere to load all the files on a DVD, but be patient. Once they're loaded you can preview the individual VOB files as you would any clip. Just click the Play button. Under each thumbnail you see its file name. Some are marked "(Menu)", and they're probably not the ones you want. Other VOB files have sequential names such as VTS_01_1.VOB, VTS_01_2.VOB, VTS_01_3.VOB, and so on. These sequential files may divide larger content into equal parts, so it's organized by size rather than subject matter.

6. Click Get Media.

Premiere copies the files from the DVD to your hard disk. Be patient; these files are sometimes very big, and DVDs aren't all that fast at sending data. You'll see a progress bar as the files transfer. When the process is complete, the media downloader closes and you're ready to edit.

Import from VHS Videotape or Other Analog Source

As time marches on, there'll be fewer analog sources of video that you want to pull into your Premiere projects. But if you're like most people, you still have a collection of old family VHS vids. Or you may come across a training video at work that's on Hi8, but it's otherwise still good. The image quality isn't likely to be great, but it's worth saving the movies for posterity. Premiere only works with digital video, so you must convert these ancient gems into digital video before Premiere can slurp them up. You can do the job in a couple of ways:

• **Use a camcorder as a pass-through.** Some camcorders can act as an analog-to-digital go-between. You plug the output from an old VHS VCR into the inputs on your camcorder, and then plug your camcorder into your PC. As you play the videotape in the VCR, the camcorder converts the analog image to digital, and Premiere saves the digital video to your PC.

Note: Unfortunately, video input connections are most common on older MiniDV tape-based camcorders. Most of the newer, smaller, and less expensive camcorders don't provide this feature.

- **Use a camcorder as a recorder.** Even if your camcorder doesn't do pass-through, you may still be able to record the analog video on your camcorder. Then you can import it in the usual fashion. To do so, your camcorder must have video inputs so you can connect it to your old VCR.

- **Use an AV/DV converter box or card.** If your camcorder refuses to help, you can beg, borrow, or buy an analog-to-digital video converter from a company like Blackmagic Design, Creative Labs, Grass Valley (Canopus), or Pinnacle. These units have multiple audio/video input connectors. The output is usually the same kind of FireWire or USB connector you find on camcorders. Plug your VCR into the box and then connect the box to your PC. Converters give you excellent analog-to-digital quality. The downside is that the boxes ($100 to $500) can cost as much as an inexpensive or used camcorder.

- **Use a video service company to convert for you.** There are a number of companies that convert analog video to digital for you. You might be able to find some in your home town. If not, you can find them on the Web. For example, iMemories (*www.imemories.com*) converts video, audio, still photos, and home movies to DVDs. They'll even send you a FedEx box so you can track your original stuff when you ship it back and forth.

Import Sound, Still Pictures, and Animation

Say you've been charged with producing the official video for your upcoming family reunion. Depending on how "Hollywood" you want to go, your movie may include background music, a few sound effects, cutaways to old family photos, and baby pictures of everyone who's coming. And you might want to jazz up the closing credits with a narrated animation of a harried you pulling all this together. None of these elements are video clips, of course, but so long as you can get them into your computer, you can use them in your Premiere project.

In this chapter, you'll learn how to add music and other sound files to your video and how to create and record sound effects and narration. You'll also learn how to add still images and animation and how to avoid some of the common pitfalls of mixing and matching media.

Add Sound Clips

When you hit the Record button on your camcorder, you capture both images and sound. The camera picks up conversations, rumbling trucks, and the wind as it rushes by the mic. But let's face it, camcorder audio doesn't always make the perfect soundtrack. So borrow a trick from Tinseltown and make your movie sound as good as it looks: Use the audio from your camcorder where appropriate, but don't stop there. Add background music to convey the mood of your video (and to mask unwanted background noise the camcorder picks up). And what about sound events you didn't capture, such as closing doors, thunderclaps, laughter, or screeching tires? In cases like these, you need to add sound effects, also known as SFX.

You can record your own or snag them from an SFX library. (See page 70 for more details about Foley artists, sound effects, and sound libraries.) Finally, you can have your main character narrate a backstory as your movie's plot unfolds.

Sound Formats

As you start working with sound files, you soon discover that they come in as many formats as radio stations. The good news is that they break down into two major groups: compressed files and uncompressed files. As you might expect, there are pluses and minuses with each.

Compressed files record sound with an eye toward your hard drive's limited storage capacity; stripping out notes and tones you're less likely to hear in the cause of saving space.

Uncompressed files, on the other hand, convert every note and tuba blast into the ones and zeroes of a high-fidelity digital recording, resulting in a file that, while faithful to the original source, is huge—sometimes 10 times as large as a compressed file.

Premiere works with almost all types of sound files, compressed and uncompressed, including the two major Windows formats, MP3 (compressed) and WAV files (uncompressed). See Table 3-1 for the complete list.

Table 3-1. Sound file formats

Format name	File extension	Description
Advanced Audio Coding	.aac	Similar to MP3, the AAC format compresses audio files to make them smaller. Apple's iPods and the iTunes store use AAC compression, even though the filenames have a different extension, like M4A (unprotected) or M4P (copy-protected). You can use M4A files with Premiere but not M4P.
Dolby AC-3	.ac3	Dolby Digital audio is stored in AC3 files which can store the six channels of sound used by today's home theaters. Usually known as 5.1, the six channels are one center, two front, and two rear—the subwoofer is the .1 in the nomenclature. When you want to impress your audience with spatial sound effects, this is the way to go.
Macintosh Audio	.aif, .aiff	The Mac's equivalent of uncompressed WAV files is the AIFF (Audio Interchange File Format). This format is useful when you share music or sound effects on a Mac.

Table 3-1. *Sound file formats (continued)*

Format name	File extension	Description
MP3 Audio	.mp3	Technically known as MPEG-1 Audio Layer 3, the MP3 format is a byproduct of a movie encoding standard that took on a life of its own when it came to creating music files. You'll find lots of opportunities to use MP3s in your movies, but it's not your best choice because MP3s lose audio quality when they're compressed. If you're creating the MP3s, you can control this by using a high bit rate in the encoding. For example choose 320 bits per second instead of 128 bits per second. However, the best option is to use WAV files, which are bigger, but of higher quality.
QuickTime	.mov, .m4a	Apple developed QuickTime as the multimedia centerpiece for Macintosh computers. The Quick-Time player, available for both Mac and Windows PCs, plays several video and audio formats, including MOV and M4A. You can think of M4A files as a new, improved MP3 format. Both are based in the MPEG (Motion Picture Experts Group) standards. Keep in mind that files in the M4P format (often purchased from the iTunes store) are copy-protected so you can't use them in Premiere Elements.
Windows Media	.wma	Created by Microsoft as a competitor to the MP3 format, WMA files are compressed creating a loss in fidelity. There are a few different flavors of WMA, some of which may be copy-protected.
Windows WAVE	.wav	The name stands for Waveform, and it's a standard created jointly by Microsoft and IBM for storing uncompressed audio. WAV files are higher quality but bigger than MP3s. Usually, they're you're best option if you want a top-quality audio track.

So, which type of file should you use in your project? Wherever possible, use uncompressed files, such as WAV (pronounced "wave") or AIFF files. That's because Premiere takes advantage of all the uncompressed fidelity you can send it. Sure, when you export your project to turn it into a movie file, Premiere compresses the audio (and the video) to match the intended media (if your movie's headed to YouTube, for example, everything's compressed more than if it's destined for a DVD). But audio files always sound better if you compress them just once, so start off with uncompressed audio if you can.

On the other hand, if the only source files you have are in compressed format, such as MP3 or AAC files, that's okay. Just try to use the best-sounding files you can.

After you import a sound file, it appears in the Organize tab along with all your other assets (Figure 3-1).

Audio

Video · Stills · Set Date Range

Audio clip

Figure 3-1:
The Organize tab shows all the assets for your project. Use the Video, Audio, and Stills buttons to show and hide different types of assets. Use the Set Date Range to display assets imported during a specific time period.

Sound Effects and Jack Foley

Hollywood pros who create sound effects are known as Foley artists. The name is a tribute to Jack Foley, who worked in film during its transition from silent movies to talkies. Foley pioneered many techniques for capturing sound. You can follow in his audible footsteps (clack, click, clack) by recording your own sound effects.

Keep in mind that sounds aren't always what they seem. Sometimes thunder is just a piece of sheet metal snapped back and forth. If you're creative, you'll see ways to make interesting sounds everywhere you look. Crumple a piece of paper to reflect frustration. Maybe your garage door opener sounds like an airplane engine starting up.

If you need inspiration, start off in your kitchen and check out the utensils, pots, and pans (and don't forget the food processor). If you're serious about recording sound effects, you may want to check out the following websites. Audio-Cookbook has an interesting blog, *One Sound Every Day*, where Foley artists explain how they capture certain sounds.

http://FilmSound.org

http://AudioCookBook.org

As an alternative to recording your own effects, you can visit online libraries that let you download free sounds. Googling something like *free sound effects library* should do the trick. You're not limited to film-related sites, either. If you're going for something specific, like a bird call or the croak of a toad, it's worth checking out fan sites that are bird- or toad-specific. Here are some sites to get you started:

www.acoustica.com/sounds.htm

www.ljudo.com/

www.pacdv.com/sounds/

SmartSound and Other Sources for Music

So where do you start your search for music and sound effects? Sure, you can search online, but why not start with your own computer? You might be surprised at the number of sound files stored there. The first place that comes to mind is your iTunes or Music folder. If you're like most people, your folders have a combination of copy-protected files and non-protected files from iTunes or another music service, or copied from CDs you own. (For tips on using commercial music in your videos see "Staying out of Copyright Trouble" on page 72.)

In addition to music, your computer probably has lots of other sound files installed as part of programs or games. You can find them by pressing Windows+F and then typing *.wav* or *.mp3* into the search box. For the biggest list of sound files, make sure your search includes program and system files.

Want to add some professional-quality music to your project, but don't know your bass from your treble clef? Premiere comes with a SmartSound plug-in that amounts to an online store for music. To start the plug-in, click the Audio Tools button in the upper-right corner of the timeline (Figure 3-2). Choose the Smart-Sound option, and the SmartSound Quicktracks window opens.

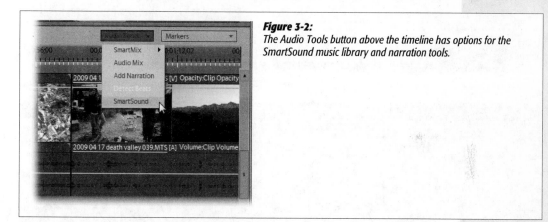

Figure 3-2:
The Audio Tools button above the timeline has options for the SmartSound music library and narration tools.

Click the text next to "Name", and a second panel named SmartSound Maestro opens, filled with clips, as shown in Figure 3-3. Each clip has a descriptive title. Double-click it to preview the clip before you use it.

To add a clip to your project, click the Select button. Your selection appears in the Quicktracks window, which also shows you the clip's length and variation. Click OK, and Premiere downloads the music to your computer. It then appears in your project panel.

The SmartSound music you download is "royalty-free." That means the artist still holds the copyright to it, but you can use it for most non-commercial purposes. If your movie is a feature film or it's going to be broadcast on television, however, you're going to have fork over some money to the artist.

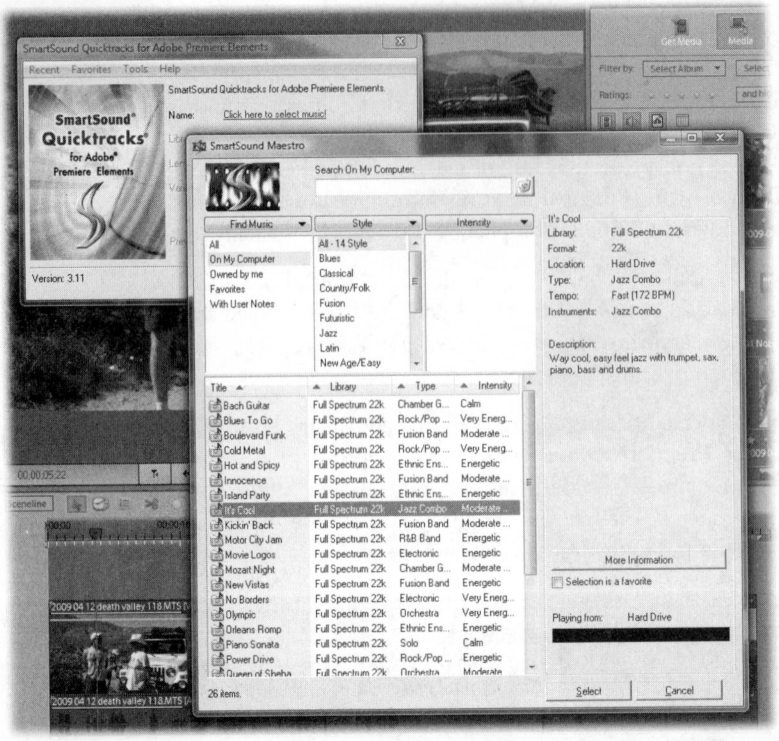

Figure 3-3:
The SmartSound Maestro window sorts music by style, such as Blues, Classical, Jazz, and Rock, and by Intensity, such as Calm, Moderate, and Very Energetic.

SOUND ADVICE

Staying out of Copyright Trouble

Movies and TV shows shell out big money to use famous hits from the best musicians. You know your latest video would be oh-so-much-better if only you could put your favorite tune on the soundtrack, but you'd rather not end up in court. Well, there are some cases where you probably won't get targeted by lawyers from the Recording Industry Association of America. Here are some tips that should keep you out of the defendant's chair:

- Don't use commercial music for any video you sell or profit from. It's not fair to the musician if they don't get a share.

- Don't use commercial music for a project that's going to be viewed publicly. That means don't use music you don't own for submissions to an independent film festival or for uploads to a public website.

That said, you probably won't get in trouble for adding commercial music to the soundtrack of your family reunion that you distribute by disc, email, or on an invitation-only website.

For the other cases, make your own music, hire a local band, or hunt down music that's free to use. It's worth noting that "free to use" and "royalty free" are two different things. "Free to use" means you don't have to pay anything. "Royalty free" often means you pay once for the rights to use the music on different projects—you just don't have to pay a royalty every time it is viewed or broadcast.

Tip: Looking for other sources of music for your movie? Try this site *http://freemusicarchive.org*. Music is organized by genre. Much of the music comes under the Creative Commons usage license. For each track, check the column on the right for copyright details. For classical music, try *www.musopen.com*.

Preview Audio Clips

You probably want to audition sound clips before you go to the trouble of importing them into your project. If you find downloadable clips online, you'll usually see a player embedded in the web page so you can preview the clip.

For sound clips on your PC, all you have to do is double-click the file to open and play it in Windows Media Player, iTunes, QuickTime, or another pre-installed media player. This works for most of the sound file formats listed on page 68.

Which media player pops up depends on what you have installed on your system and how it's configured. To choose a specific media player, right-click the sound file and choose Open With, as shown in Figure 3-4.

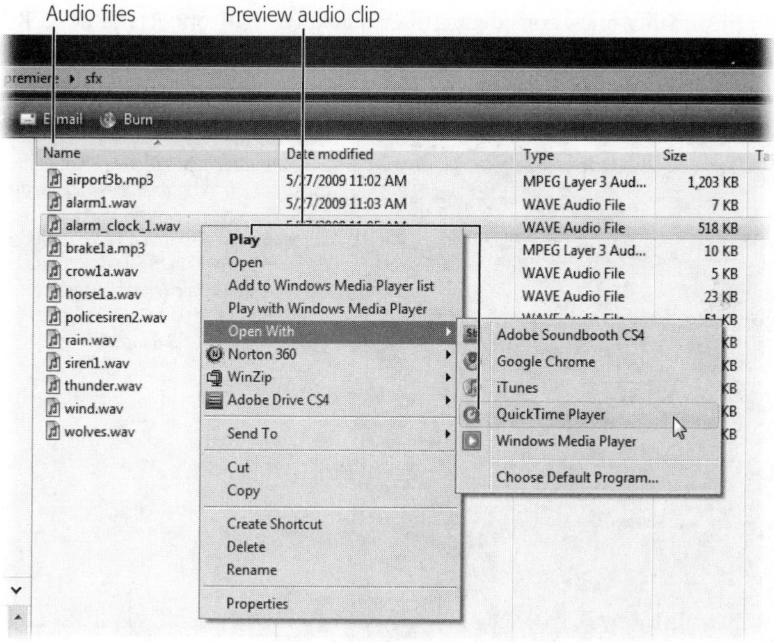

Figure 3-4:
You can play most audio or video clips by double-clicking them in Windows Explorer. If you want to choose a specific media player, right-click the clip, then choose Open With and choose a player from the list.

Record Your Own Sound Effects

Sprinkle some key sound effects throughout your movie and the soundtrack goes from blah to BAM! Your camcorder captures sounds, but often the camera is too far away from the sound source to get a really good recording. You can improve your soundtrack and add dramatic impact by recording sound effects and placing them at key moments in your movie.

Connect a Mic to Your Computer

To record your own sound effects, you need a mic. Many laptops have built-in mics, as do most webcams, though the sound quality is probably only so-so in both cases.

To get better sound, you need a better mic. Let your wallet be your guide—mic prices range from cheap to ridiculous. For recording sound effects and instruments, dynamic microphones work best, and they're rugged if you need to take them into the field. For voice recordings like narration (covered in the next section), consider a condenser microphone. The large-diaphragm models cost more, but they capture the nuances of your voice better, just as audio speakers with larger surfaces produce better sound detail. (For more tips on mics, see the box on page 75.)

Tip: If a dedicated mic is out of your reach and you don't have a laptop or webcam with a built-in mic, connect your camcorder to your PC and record live audio through it.

If you use your mic primarily with your computer, it makes sense to get one of the newer models that plugs into a USB port (Figure 3-5). If you've already got a stable of great pro-quality mics, consider getting an adapter that connects these XLR pro mics to USB ports.

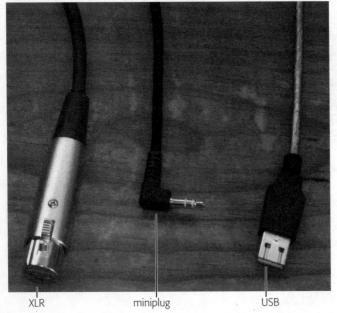

Figure 3-5:
Here are three types of plugs that mics use, from left to right: XLR, miniplug, and USB. Windows recognizes and automatically sets up mics that use USB plugs, making them the easiest to use. Use a miniplug mic (center), and the setup chores are up to you. XLR mics need an XLR-to-USB adapter.

XLR   miniplug   USB

SOUND ADVICE

Choose a Mic

Buying a mic is like buying a camera or a camcorder. There are lots of options and a ton of technical jargon—and everyone has an opinion (especially the salesperson). Of course, your needs and budget determine the type of mic you get, from cheap, under-$50 models to super-expensive over-$1,000 gems. In the midst of this, there are mics that'll do the job you want and some of them may even be close to your budget.

To Record Live Sound, you may need a couple of different types of mics. The mic on your camcorder tries to do everything, often from a distance. If you're recording a voice and it's not close to the camera, you may want to get a lavalier mic (often just called a "lav"). These are the little mics you see clipped to newscasters' lapels. You want your lav as close to the person's mouth as possible. It's okay for the news "talking heads" to have a mic show, but if you're shooting a dramatic scene set in 1776, you have to hide the lav under some clothing, which may affect the sound quality.

Another staple of sound engineers is the shotgun mic. They're bigger and often kind of long. Designed to pick up sound from a distance, shotguns are directional. That means you point the tip of the mic at the sound you want, and it doesn't pick up much sound from the sides or the rear. Some shotguns mount on your video camera, and others use a separate boom—a long pole that requires a person to point it in the right direction.

The tone and quality of sound you get from a lav or a shotgun mic is likely to differ. If you can, experiment with both. In some cases, you may want to record with both. Then, when you edit, you can choose the best recording or maybe mix the two.

To Record Musical Events, try to use multiple microphones with at least one mic for every instrument, including voices. Unfortunately, circumstances and finances don't always permit that kind of production. Short of that, follow the rule about getting your mic as close to the sound source as possible. Perhaps you can place a couple of mics on or near the stage. Or maybe you can use two camcorders for the shoot and keep one close to the performers, recording closeups and good-quality sound. A second camera could be further from the stage recording group shots and audience reactions.

To Record Narration, you want a mic that can sit on your desktop and capture your voice at close range. A lot of different mics can do that. On the low end, you can use the mic built in to your computer (common on laptops) or an inexpensive mic that plugs into your USB port (cheaper USB mics cost $10 to $40). The sound quality isn't great, but they might do for your needs.

A step up from USB teleconferencing mics are a newer breed of USB mics like the Snowball from a company called Blue or Audio Technica's Condenser Mic (model AT2020USB). These mics range in price from $100 to $200.

If you already have some good-quality mics, like those used for home studio recording or live performances, you may want to get an adapter that converts mics with XLR connectors to USB. Shure, one of the big dogs in the mic biz, offers X2u adapters for about $130, or you can get the adapter and a good mic for a couple of hundred dollars.

Some mics have miniplug conectors, similar to the plugs for iPod or other MP3-player headphones. See Figure 3-5 for the different types of mic connectors. You can plug these directly into your computer, but setting them up is more work than setting up a USB mic. When you plug in a USB mic, your computer automatically installs the needed drivers and lets you know it's ready to go by sounding a tone.

SOUND ADVICE

Make Your Miniplug Mic Work

As explained on page 74, USB mics are easy to connect to your computer because Windows recognizes them when you plug them in and installs any drivers they might need. When you plug a miniplug mic into your computer or soundcard, Windows doesn't know it's there and it's up to you to make sure it works. (Miniplugs look like the little plug on the end of your headphone cord.)

1. **Plug your miniplug mic into your computer.**

   If you're lucky, your desktop computer has a socket for a mic plug in the front. It may be hidden under a panel. If not, you'll have to get around to the back of the computer and plug it into the sound card. It may be hard to see, but most sockets have little icons to indicate whether the socket is for headphones or a mic. The mic sockets for notebook computers are usually on the side.

2. **Choose Windows → Control Panel › Hardware and Sound › Sound → Manage audio devices.**

   Initially, the Sound panel opens to the Playback tab, where you see headphones and other playback gadgets.

   If the Control Panel is set to the Classic view, you won't see "Hardware and Sound" you just see Sound among the many Control Panel options. In that case, click Sound to open the Sound panel.

3. **Click the Recording tab.**

   The Sound panel displays Audio input devices, but this is where it can be a little confusing. Your computer knows about the capabilities of your sound card, but it doesn't necessarily know what's plugged in. You may see devices that you don't have. For example, the Sound panel in Figure 3-6 shows Line In even though the option isn't enabled.

4. **If necessary, right-click Microphone and choose Enable from the shortcut menu.**

5. **If you don't see a checkmark on Microphone, you need to enable it. The shortcut menu shows several options for Microphone, including a link to the Microphone Properties panel.**

6. **Talk directly into your mic.**

   As you speak, the green bars to the right of Microphone show the level (volume) for the mic. It should be moving well past the midpoint as you talk, but not pinned to the top of the level indicator. If you're happy with the results, your Mic setup is done and you can click OK to close the Sound and Control Panel. If you're not getting the level you'd like, keep on reading.

   If there's no signal in the level meter, double-check a few things. Some mics have on/off switches and volume controls. Make sure yours is on and the volume is cranked up. Some mics use batteries (and it's not always obvious). Make sure your mic has a good battery. Last, but not least, double-check that you're mic is plugged into a mic socket. The input and output sockets on sound cards are small and look the same. It's easy to plug into the wrong spot.

7. **If you need to adjust the level of your mic, click Properties and then choose the Levels tab.**

   The Microphone Properties panel opens with tabs along the top. When you choose the Levels tabs, you see two sliders that help you control the mic level.

8. **First, adjust the Microphone slider.**

   Use the Level slider like any volume control—drag to the right to increase the mic level.

9. **If necessary, adjust the Microphone Boost.**

   The Microphone Boost slider changes the power of the signal coming from the mic, showing the gain in decibels. Again, drag to the right to increase the level.

When you plug in a miniplug mic, the computer doesn't necessarily know it's there, and it's up to you to make sure that your sound card recognizes the mic and works with it. See the box on page 77 for some help. (There are more details on mics and recorders in Chapter 10, page 291.)

If you plan to record a lot of sound effects, consider investing in a portable digital recorder. Lots of good sounds aren't within range of your computer. Just like camcorders, you can get portable recorders that save sound to memory card, disc, or hard drive. It's best to get the type used to record music rather than the ones used for office dictation. They cost more (upwards of $100), but you get much better sound and they're more computer-friendly. Some of the handier ones record to both the MP3 format and the higher-quality WAV format.

To copy files to your computer, connect the recorder using a USB cable or pop the recorder's memory card into your PC.

Tip: In a pinch, you can always use your camcorder or cellphone as a field recorder. Just keep in mind that the sound quality won't be as good as that from a dedicated, digital recorder.

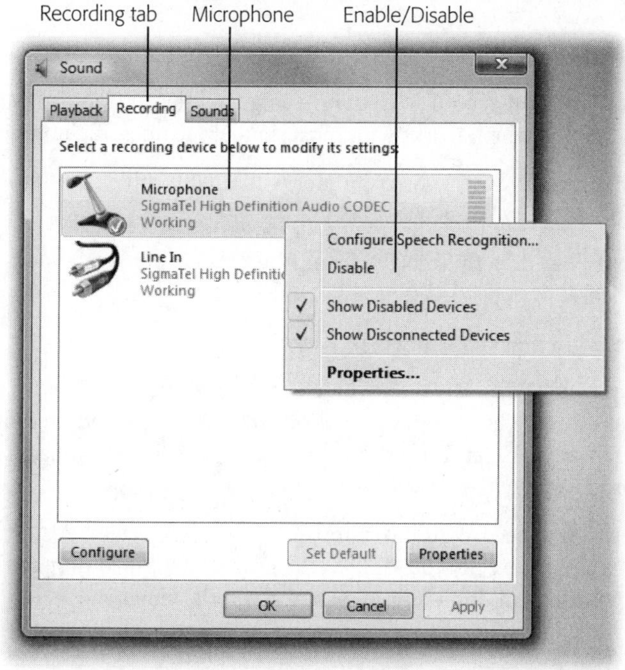

Figure 3-6:
Use the Sound control panel to set up your miniplug mic or other audio devices that you plug directly into your computer. The checkmark next to Microphone indicates that the device is enabled. The Line In option is disabled.

Test Your Computer Mic

If you want to test your mic, you can use Windows' built-in Sound Recorder program. Click the Windows button and type *Sound Recorder* or go to Windows → Programs → Accessories → Sound Recorder. Click the Start Recording button and jabber away or make some other sound. Click Stop Recording when you're done. A Save As window opens, giving you the option to name and save your sound. If it's just a test, you may want to save it to your desktop to make it easy to find and play.

Windows stores sound clips recorded with the Sound Recorder in WMA format, which Premiere understands. You can add WMA files to your project using the steps described on page 85. There's one main drawback to using Sound Recorder if your computer uses Windows XP or an earlier operating system—it limits the clips to 60 seconds. That's not so bad for short sound effects, but it's easy to bump against the limit for voice, music, or other recordings.

Famous Movie Moment: The term MOS is Hollywood jargon for shooting film without sound. Some folks like to say the term comes from some of the early German directors like Ernst Lubitsch or Fritz Lang, who might have said "Mit out Sprechen" or "Mit out Sound." More likely, the term has technical origins and comes from the phrase "motor only shot," meaning the camera motor is running but not the sound.

Capture Live Sound

Once you have a mic, you can record live sound using Premiere's Capture panel (see the instructions below), which works with most standalone mics, including:

- USB mics that plug directly into your computer with a USB cable or mics that connect with a USB adapter.
- Miniplug mics that plug directly into the front of your computer or into your computer's soundcard.
- Webcams that include a mic and connect to your computer via USB.

You can also connect your DV or HDV tape-based camcorder to your PC and use its mic as your sound source. This setup won't work with hard-drive and memory-based camcorders, however, because they use Premiere's Media Downloader to move media clips into Premiere.

In each of these cases, you record sound directly to Premiere (via the Capture panel). The process is almost exactly the same as the process described on page 44. The major difference is that you don't have to worry about the video.

As an example, here are the steps to capture only sound from a webcam:

1. **In Premiere Elements, click the Organize tab and then choose Get Media.**

   You see the icons that represent the sources for media, including Webcam or WDM Device.

2. **Click Webcam or WDM Device.**

The Capture panel opens, displaying the Capturing Source drop-down menus at the top.

3. **Click the menu next to Audio and select the mic for your webcam.**

There may be a couple of audio sources listed in the menu. You don't need to worry about setting the video source, because you deselect video in the next step.

4. **On the right side of the Capture panel, next to "Capture", deselect Video and select Audio.**

As shown in Figure 3-7, you can choose to capture audio and video or just one media stream. Even if you choose to capture sound only, you probably still see video previewed in the Capture panel's monitor.

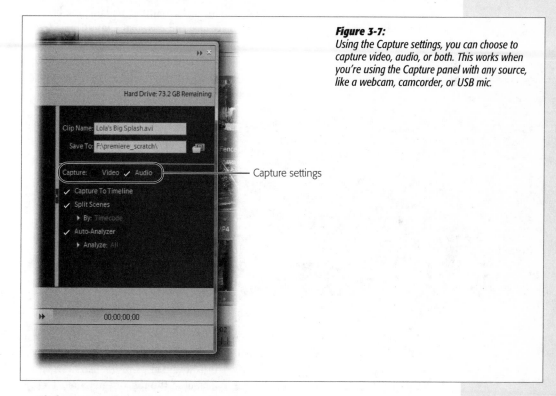

Figure 3-7:
Using the Capture settings, you can choose to capture video, audio, or both. This works when you're using the Capture panel with any source, like a webcam, camcorder, or USB mic.

Capture settings

5. **Click Capture and make some noise.**

You can record voice or sound effects as long as you get the sound source close to your mic.

6. **Click Pause when you're through recording.**

Premiere saves the sound clip and adds it to the Organize tab. You can continue to capture clips by clicking the Capture button again, or you can close the capture panel as described in the next step.

7. **Click the X in the upper-right corner of the Capture panel.**

The Capture window closes, and you see your audio clip in the Organize tab.

Once you capture a sound clip in Premiere, you can preview it a couple of ways:

- Double-click an audio clip, and it opens in the Preview window. Instead of a video image, you see an audio waveform in the window. Press the Play button to hear the clip.

- Drag a clip to one of the Audio tracks in your timeline, and then use the monitor controls to play the clip (see Figure 3-8). If the Capture to Timeline box was checked in the Capture panel, a copy of your sound clip is already there.

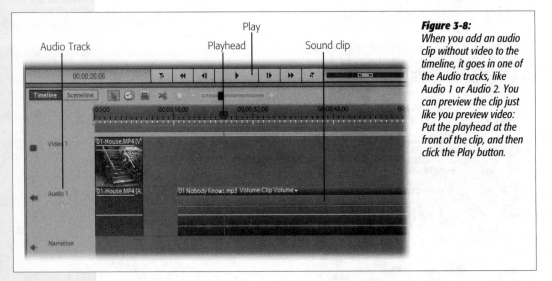

Figure 3-8:
When you add an audio clip without video to the timeline, it goes in one of the Audio tracks, like Audio 1 or Audio 2. You can preview the clip just like you preview video: Put the playhead at the front of the clip, and then click the Play button.

Another option is to choose Window → Available Media in Premiere. The Organize tab changes to show your media clips in list form, displaying details such as duration and media type. If you want to see only audio clips in the list, deselect the Video and Still options beside the "Filter by" label at the top of the panel. To preview your recently recorded clip, double-click it. A preview window opens, showing your sound clip as a waveform. You can use the control buttons at the bottom of the window to play the clip.

Tip: If you can't get Premiere's Capture panel to recognize your USB microphone using the Webcam or WDM device setting, it may have to do with the mic's drivers. If that's the case, you might still be able to record sound clips using Windows Sound Recorder, as described on page 78. Then you can add the sound files to your project using the steps described on page 85.

Add Narration

When you sit down to edit your movie, most of the soundtrack is in place. But there's one audio element you add while you're in your editing room: the narration. Premiere makes it easy to add "voiceover" as you watch your video play back in the monitor. You probably want to record your narration *after* you finish editing. That way, you won't be narrating scenes that get cut.

Exactly how much narration there is in a movie varies a lot. Sometimes, movies use it only at the beginning or the end. But if you've got a Sam Spade character in your movie, perhaps he's wisecracking all the way through.

You need to decide whether you want to script your narration beforehand or if you want a more off-the-cuff feeling. Usually, the audience can tell when someone narrates from a script, and the results often sound a little stiff. To avoid that, try creating bullet points with just a few words to remind you of each topic you want to cover. Of course, you've also got the images to help you out. Like any public speaker, try to keep the "ums" to a minimum.

It's best to try and record all your narration in the same sitting, because your voice, and even the sound of your room, change over time. On the other hand, during that session, don't be afraid to stop and rerecord parts if you make a mistake. You can also use the sound-editing techniques described in Chapter 10 (page 291) to clean up and edit your narration.

Set Up Your Mic for Narration

When you're ready to roll, plug your mic into your computer. Before you start recording in Premiere, it makes sense to check your mic in Windows to ensure it's working and the volume (sometimes called gain) is adjusted properly. To do that, go to Windows → Control Panel. The control panel looks different depending on which version of Windows you have (and on a few other settings, too). What you want is Windows' tool for setting the recording levels of attached mics. You may see a category in the Control Panel called "Hardware and Sound", or "Sounds, Speech, and Audio Devices", or you may see an item named "Sound".

Whichever you have, open the sound panel to the Recording tab, as shown in Figure 3-9. When you talk into your mic, you should see one of the green level meters go up and down. Nothing happening? Double-check your cable connection, and see if your mic has an on/off switch set to Off. Some mics use batteries, so pop in a spare if you have one. Once you get a level reading, check to see if it's too low or too high. If it is, click Properties and then, in the Microphone Properties panel, click Levels. Adjust the Microphone slider as you speak until you get the level right.

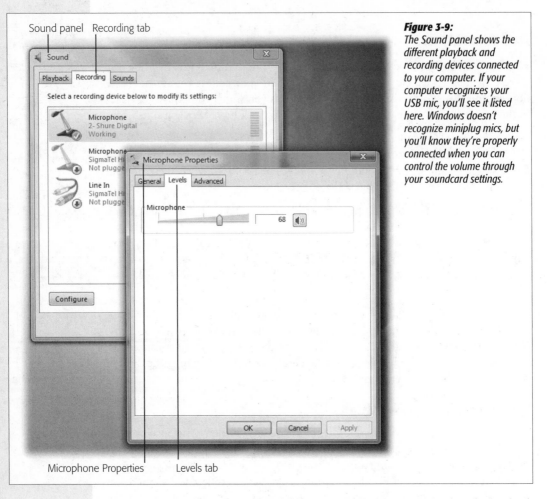

Sound panel   Recording tab

Figure 3-9:
The Sound panel shows the different playback and recording devices connected to your computer. If your computer recognizes your USB mic, you'll see it listed here. Windows doesn't recognize miniplug mics, but you'll know they're properly connected when you can control the volume through your soundcard settings.

Microphone Properties   Levels tab

You need to tell Premiere what hardware you're using to record and play back sound. To do that, go to Edit → Preferences → Audio Hardware. Then, click the ASIO Settings button. The Audio Hardware Settings panel opens. It has two tabs: Input for your microphone and Output for speakers or headphones. Click the Input setting and make sure that your mic is selected, as shown in Figure 3-10.

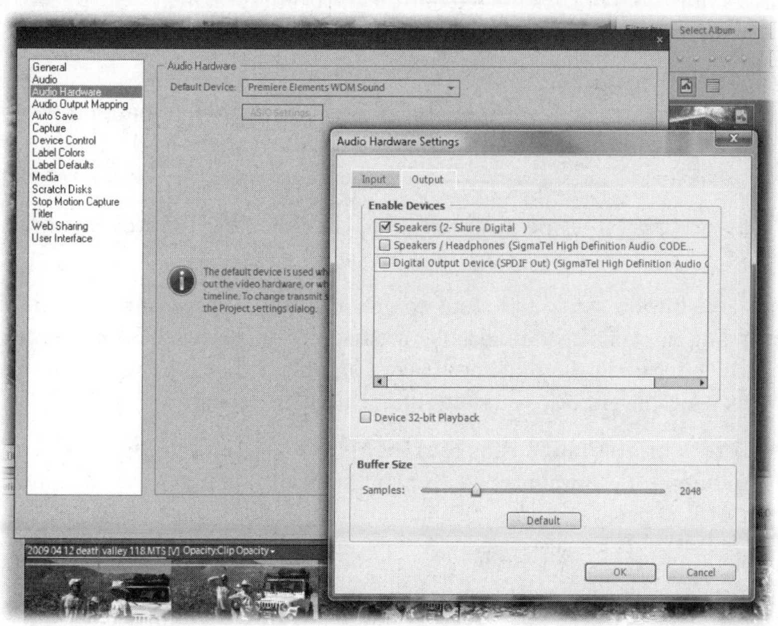

Figure 3-10:
Two preferences panels are shown here. The first, Preferences, is set to Audio Hardware. The second, Audio Hardware Settings, lets you select which mics, speakers, or headphones you want to use with Premiere.

Record Narration

The moment has arrived when you put voice to mic and add narration to your project:

1. **Position the playhead where you want to start narrating.**

   Premiere gives you a handy 3-second countdown before it starts recording, but if that isn't enough, move the playhead forward a couple seconds.

2. **Click Audio Tools and choose Add Narration.**

   The Record Voice Narration window opens, as shown in Figure 3-11, with just a few controls for chores like starting and stopping the recording and playback.

3. **Turn on the "Mute audio while recording" checkbox.**

   You don't want your voice and the other audio coming back at you as you record. At best, it's a little confusing. At worst, it creates feedback as your mic picks up sounds from the speakers.

4. **Take a deep breath, relax, and sit up straight.**

   These are tips from the voice coach.

5. **Press G (for "go") or click the red button and begin speaking.**

The video plays in the monitor as Premiere records your narration. The level meter in the Record Voice Narration panel bounces up and down as you speak. You want the meter to hit the yellow point every so often, but you want to avoid the red peaks as much as possible. You can adjust the level with the slider next to the meter.

6. **When you finish a segment of narration, click the Stop Recording Narration button.**

The same button starts and stops the recording—it just changes appearance depending on what it's doing at the moment. After you click Stop, the narration clip appears in the timeline. There's another copy of the narration in the Project panel, just in case you muck up the timeline version.

Premiere names narration clips Narration_1.wav, Narration_2.wav, and so on. If you think you can improve on that, right-click the clip in either the timeline or the Project panel and choose Rename from the shortcut menu.

Premiere automatically positions the playhead at the beginning of the segment you just recorded, making it easy to listen to the results.

7. **Press the space bar or click the Play button.**

As you listen to the narration, check to make sure it matches the video. If it doesn't match perfectly, is it something you can fix with a little audio editing? Are there any "ums" you need to delete? Any phrases or sentences that could stand some rerecording?

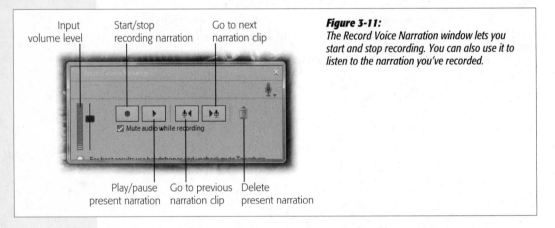

Input volume level | Start/stop recording narration | Go to next narration clip

Play/pause present narration | Go to previous narration clip | Delete present narration

Figure 3-11:
The Record Voice Narration window lets you start and stop recording. You can also use it to listen to the narration you've recorded.

It's easier to make corrections and additions if you record your narration in short chunks. Give yourself some pauses between statements—they make great places to split a clip in case you need to swap in a new, improved version. And don't be afraid to hit the Delete Present Narration trashcan button and give it another try.

Import Sound Files to Your Project

Whether you import sound from a CD, download it from an online source, or record it live, all you have to do to use it in your project is add it to Premiere. Here are the steps:

1. **In Premiere, click the Organize tab and then click Get Media.**

   The Organize tab displays the different sources for media.

2. **Choose PC Files and Folders.**

   The Add Media window opens, providing standard Windows tools for browsing through files and folders.

Tip: As an alternative to the Organize tab, you can choose File → Get Media from → PC Files and Folders.

---

3. **Navigate to the folder that has your sound clips.**

   Use the "Look in" drop-down menu, which displays folders and other computer locations, or use the shortcut buttons on the right for Recent Places, Desktop, Your User Folder, Computer, and Network. If you need a bigger window to see your folders and files, drag any of the edges of the Add Media window to expand the view.

4. **Select one or more files to add.**

   Use any of the standard selection techniques:

   - Click to select a file. Shift-click to select adjacent files.

   - Ctrl-click to select/deselect more than one file.

   - Click and drag to get a bunch of files at once.

   You can include video clips or stills in this selection—Premiere is perfectly happy to add different types of media all at once.

Tip: If you want all the files in a folder, don't open the folder, just select it and then click the Add Folder button.

---

5. **Click Open.**

   Premiere imports the files into your project, displays them in the Organize tab, and closes the Add Audio window.

   Not only does the imported file appear in Premiere, it also appears in a related program called Elements Organizer, a separate program from Premiere Elements you'll learn about in detail in Chapter 4. Both Premiere Elements and Photoshop Elements use it to organize and tag media. When you add or import a file in Premiere, it automatically adds the file to Elements Organizer, too, as

---

shown in Figure 3-12. As with video clips, Premiere and the Organizer create links to the audio clips stored on your computer. When the files are added, Premiere "conforms" the clips to match the audio settings for your project. For larger files, you may see a progress bar during the process. Premiere stores the new conformed audio file with your project file.

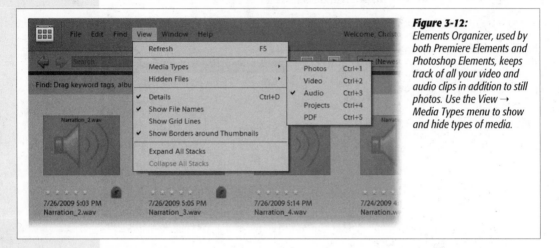

Figure 3-12:
Elements Organizer, used by both Premiere Elements and Photoshop Elements, keeps track of all your video and audio clips in addition to still photos. Use the View → Media Types menu to show and hide types of media.

If you want to add a sound file to Premiere that's on a device other than your PC, like a camcorder, cellphone, memory card, or sound recorder, follow the steps above but in Step 3, navigate to the device that holds the sound clip.

Once you import clips to Premiere, you can use them immediately. Just drag them to the audio track in your project's sceneline or timeline.

Import Still Pictures

There are plenty of reasons you might want to import still pictures into your video. You might have an old family picture or some subject that exists as a photo only (it's not like you've never seen a Ken Burns documentary!). Aside from availability, you may like the impact of pausing on a still image. And, of course, just because an image is still doesn't mean you can't pan and zoom on it within your video frame. There are a few things to keep in mind as you import still pics: frame sizes, aspect ratios, and file formats. Frame sizes and file formats are the most important issues to understand. Aspect Ratio is the most complicated, geeky issue. Fortunately, it's the least likely to cause you a problem because Premiere Elements is pretty good at managing aspect ratio.

About Frame Size

Your video has a "frame size," measured in pixels. Frame size is the size of your playback window. The frame size for standard digital video, for example, is similar to that for DVDs: 720×480 pixels. If you need to double-check the frame size for your project, go to Edit → Project Settings → General and then under Video find the Frame Size boxes. You can add still images with frame sizes up to 4096×4096. Unless you give Premiere specific instructions, it scales your imported stills to match your project settings. It's always better to scale down (shrink an image) than it is to scale up. When Premiere scales up an image, you're likely to notice blockiness in the picture, called *pixelation*.

Sometimes, you might want a very large still imported into your project. Perhaps you're planning on panning and zooming over the image. To stop Premiere from automatically scaling your stills when you import them, go to Edit → Preferences → General and turn off the checkbox next to "Default scale to frame size".

About Aspect Ratio

If you've ever watched video on your computer or TV and seen football-shaped heads (Stewie Griffin aside) or squares that have become rectangles, you've observed a problem with aspect ratio. *Aspect ratio* is the relationship between the vertical and horizontal measurements of an object. Standard TVs have an aspect ratio of 4:3, for example, and movie-theater screens have an aspect ratio of 16:9.

When the horizontal and vertical measurements remain proportional from the time you shoot a picture to when you play it back, everything looks fine. But if you shoot an image or video in one format (say, with a ratio of 4:3), and then play it back in widescreen format (16:9), you've got the video equivalent of a Silly Putty impression. Or if you crop a still photo (that is, trim its edges) it can have almost any aspect ratio.

Not only is a consistent width-to-height aspect ratio in an image or video clip important for proper-looking playback in a movie, so is a consistent *pixel* aspect ratio. Pixel stands for "picture element," and most people think of a pixel as a little dot of light on a screen. Cram enough dots onto a screen, and you create an image. But it turns out that pixels aren't actually dots, they're either squares or rectangles; monitors use square pixels, TVs often use rectangular ones. So, adding a photo to a movie that's destined for TV playback could be a problem.

The good news is that most of the time, you don't have to worry about the intricacies of pixel aspect ratios because Premiere does a good job of identifying and correcting aspect ratio problems in still photos and video clips as you add them to your project. Occasionally, you may notice a problem if, for example, your project mixes NTSC video (American) with PAL video (European), but you'll probably rarely, if ever, do that.

Here's how it works: When you choose a project preset (see page 25), you tell Premiere which pixel aspect ratio to use. When you import stills (or video) Premiere makes changes as needed so your imported footage conforms to the project. Later, when you choose to export your movie to YouTube or DVD, Premiere again makes the necessary adjustments.

Tip: If you want to check the aspect ratio for a particular project, go to Edit → Project Settings → General and find the Frame Size and the Pixel Aspect Ratio settings. You won't be able to make changes, but you can see the pixel aspect ratio used by the preset.

You can review the aspect ratio Premiere uses for individual clips by following these steps:

1. **Choose Window → Available Media.**

   You see your imported and added media in list form.

2. **Right-click on a clip and then choose Interpret Footage.**

   The Interpret Footage dialog box displays several details about the media, depending on its type and content. The box is divided into three sections: Frame Rate, Pixel Aspect Ratio, and Alpha Channel. Under Pixel Aspect Ratio are two radio buttons. The top button is labeled "Use Pixel Aspect Ratio from File:" followed by a description such as "Square Pixels" or "D1/DV NTSC". The second button is "Labeled Conform to". To change the pixel aspect ratio for a clip, click this button and choose one of the options on the menu, as shown in Figure 3-13.

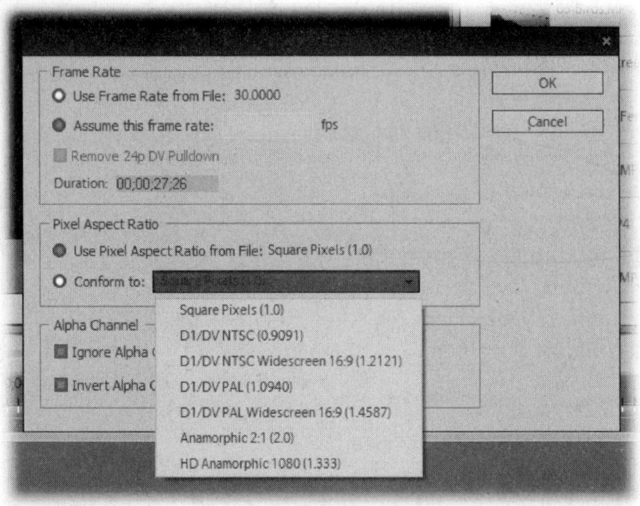

Figure 3-13:
Use the Interpret Footage dialog box to review and change the pixel aspect ratio for a media clip.

Still Image File Formats

Like sound files, still images come in a host of file formats (see Table 3-2 for the list). Some formats excel at displaying photographs, while others are better for drawings or line art. Each format was developed to solve specific computer issues, even if that was only to get an edge on the competition.

No matter. The only thing you need to worry about is image quality and resolution. For quality, the rule of thumb is the same as for video: Use the best quality image you can get, and let Premiere massage and compress the file when you share it. In short, wherever possible, avoid formats that compress images.

As for resolution, you want your still images to be equal to or larger than the size, in pixels, of your video frame. That's 720×480 pixels for most movies (for more detail, see page 25).

Table 3-2. Formats for image files

Format Name	File Extension	Description
Adobe Illustrator	.ai	The file format used by Adobe's vector graphic editing program. The Illustrator program is so widely used that the AI format is a standard in the graphic arts community.
Adobe Photoshop	.psd	The file format used by Adobe's photo editing program. Photoshop is also an industry standard. PSD files have an advantage over JPEG images because it is an uncompressed format.
Adobe Premiere Elements title	.prtl	A file format used by Premiere to store movie titles.
Bitmap	.bmp, .dib, .rle	One of the earliest image formats used by IBM-PC–compatible computers. You don't see this format used in the pro graphics community very much, but it's one of the formats used by Windows Paint. It's the format used by Premiere Elements when you use the Freeze Frame command (page 222).
Compuserve GIF	.gif	A lossless format originally developed by CompuServe, an online information service popular before the Internet became everyone's favorite. The GIF format is great for making small files from non-photographic images. You can make some parts of the image transparent. At one point, there was concern that GIF would not be available for Internet use due to patent issues. One of the results was the development of the PNG format.
Encapsulated PostScript	.eps	Often used in page layout, EPS files use the PostScript language to define images.
Fireworks	.wbm	The WBM or WBMF format stands for wireless bitmap and was designed specifically to transmit over wireless networks. It's one of the many formats available in Adobe Fireworks.
Icon	.ico	The format that is used to show icons, such as those on your desktop.
JPEG	.jpg, .jpe, .jpeg, .jfif	The most popular format for displaying photographs on the Internet, JPEG images can be compressed to various degrees, but the compression results in a loss of image quality.

Table 3-2. *Formats for image files (continued)*

Macintosh PICT	.pct, .pic, .pict	A graphics file format developed for Macintosh computers. PICT files may include both bitmapped and vector images.
PCX	.pcx	Another file format that was popular on IBM-PC–compatible computers in the days before Windows. PCX was developed for use with a program called PC Paintbrush and became relatively popular for a while.
Pixar Picture	.pxr	A file format developed by Pixar, the animation production company, originally a division of LucasFilm and subsequently bought by Steve Jobs and then the Walt Disney Company.
Portable Network Graphic	.png	A lossless image file format standard that works well for both photographic and non-photographic images.
RAW	.raw, .raf, .crw, .cr2, .mrw, .nef, .orf, .dng	Cameras use the RAW file format to record photos. Different camera companies use different RAW formats, and the RAW files are larger than the same image saved as a JPEG or TIFF.
TIFF	.tif, .tiff	The acronym stands for Tagged Image File Format. TIFFs are used to store all types of images including photos. A favorite for print layout artists because, unlike JPEGs, the TIFF format is lossless.
Truevision Targa	.tga, .icb, .vst, .vda	An early graphic file format developed for IBM PCs in the days before Windows.

Import Still Images

You import still photos from your camera, cellphone, or other device using Premiere's media downloader. As you learned in Chapter 2, the media downloader copies files from a source device to your computer. During the process, you can rename the file and choose a destination folder. The downloader works the same for all kinds of media—still photos, audio clips, and video clips. As far as Premiere is concerned, a media file is a media file. Here are the steps for importing stills from a digital camera:

1. **In Premiere Elements, click the Organize tab and then click Get Media.**

   The Organize tab displays the devices that can hold media.

2. **Choose Digital Still Camera.**

   The media downloader window opens with the Source settings on the left and the Save options on the right.

   If your media is stored on a different type of device, like a memory card or DVD camcorder, choose that option. The options that open the media downloader are: DVD (Camcorder or PC DVD Drive), AVCHD or other hard disk/ memory camcorder, and Mobile Phone and Players.

3. **In the lower-left corner, click the Advanced Dialog button.**

   The media downloader has two modes: Standard Dialog and Advanced Dialog. Use Standard Dialog when you want to import the entire contents of a device. Use the Advanced Dialog when you want to pick and choose the media to import.

4. **Under Source, use the "Get Media from" drop-down menu to select your camera.**

   Keep in mind that cameras and other devices connected to your computer may look like a computer drive, complete with a drive letter, like the one shown in Figure 3-14.

   After you select the camera, a dialog box displays the media files stored on the camera.

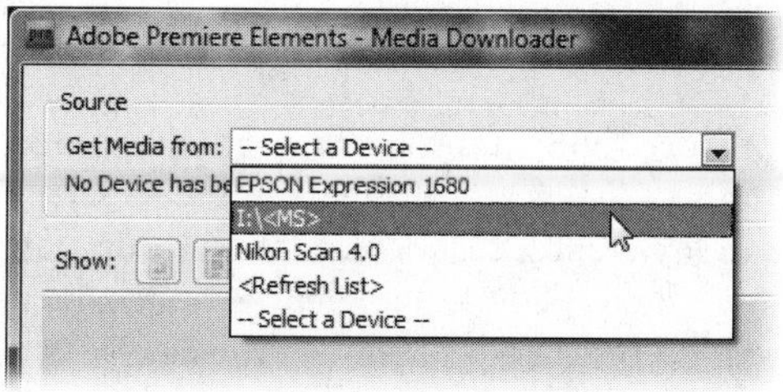

Figure 3-14:
When devices like camcorders and still cameras are connected to your computer via USB, they look like hard drives or DVD discs. Here, a Sony still camera is named I:\<MS>.

5. **On the right side, under Save Options, use the Browse button to select a folder for the imported pics.**

   If you don't change the location, Premiere uses your Pictures folder.

6. **Use the Create Subfolders drop-down menu to create a naming convention for the folders that hold imported images.**

   Choose *None* if you don't want to store the imported media in a subfolder. If you want to provide your own folder name, choose *Custom Name* and type a name in the box below the menu. Choose one of the date options to name the subfolders by the date the media was shot or the date the media was imported.

7. **Use the Rename Files options to create a naming convention for the imported still photos.**

   The options are similar to those for naming folders. Choose *Do not rename files* if you want to keep the names that were used on the still camera. You can choose *Today's Date* to name the files for the import date, or you can name the files according to the date the images were shot. And again, you can mix and match dates with a custom name, such as *Malibu Beach 2009*.

8. (Optional) Use the Apply Metadata settings.

Metadata is a method for attaching text information, such as the Creator's name and copyright details, to visual files. Under "Template to use", choose *None* if you don't want to include metadata. Otherwise, set the menu to Basic Metadata and type in your name and copyright details.

9. Turn on the checkboxes under the stills (or other media) you want to import.

You can import still photos at the same time as you import audio or video clips.

10. Click Get Media.

A progress bar appears as Photoshop copies the still photos and other media to your computer. When the process is done, you see the media in the Organize tab. The imported media is also available in Elements Organizer.

Change the Duration for Stills

A still image is like a single frame of video, but you probably want your image to stay on screen longer than a single frame. The length of time a still is on screen is called its *duration*. There's a setting in Preferences that determines the duration of all still images when they're imported. Choose Edit → Preferences → General and look for the Still Image Default Duration box. It's probably set to something like 150 frames (about 5 seconds). You can change this setting if you want. More important, you can change the timing for any individual still image after you drop it into your movie. In the timeline, click and drag one edge of the still clip. When you do this, the clip stretches or shrinks along the timeline, changing its duration. For more on editing with the timeline, see page 162.

Create New Photoshop Still Images

If you have both Premiere Elements and Photoshop Elements, there's another way to cope with the frame size and aspect ratio issues discussed on page 87. You can create a new Photoshop image using a command in Premiere Elements. Photoshop automatically sizes the image, which begins as an empty frame (Figure 3-15), to match your Premiere project. At that point, while you're in Photoshop Elements, all you have to do is *place* an image in the frame. As a bonus, while you're in Photoshop, you can take advantage of all of Photoshop Elements' tools, text features, and effects. Here's a step-by-step description of the process:

1. In Premiere, choose File → New → Photoshop File.

The Save Photoshop File As window opens.

2. Name your file, choose a folder to save it in, and click Save.

Premiere creates an empty file, and then automatically opens Photoshop. Why do you have to name the file at this point? Premiere needs to keep track of the file, so it can automatically add it to your project.

3. **In Photoshop, choose File → Place.**

The Place window opens.

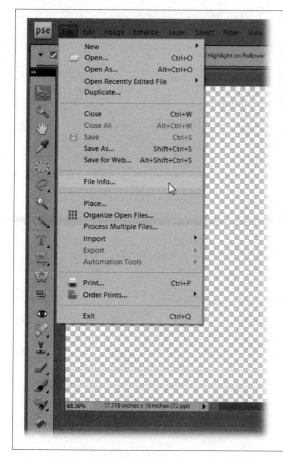

Figure 3-15:
One of the easiest ways to make a still image with a frame size that matches your project is to use Premiere's File → New → Photoshop File command. Photoshop Elements starts automatically and creates an empty image with just the right proportions. All you have to do is place or create a real image in the frame.

4. **Navigate to the folder with the image you need.**

The Place window looks like your standard file and folder browser. Use the "Look in" drop-down menu at the top or the shortcut buttons to the left to navigate.

5. **Click the image you want to import and then click Place.**

The selected image is sized to match the frame and placed in the Photoshop document. There are guidelines displayed over the placed image, as shown in Figure 3-16. The area within the outermost lines is called "video safe." TVs have a tendency to crop off parts of an image, and the video safe area indicates what will be visible on most TVs. (The area within the innermost guides is known as the "title safe" area. You certainly don't want to crowd any titles in your image, so keep your text within the title safe area and you're in good shape.)

6. **Edit the image.**

   You can use all Photoshop's tools and all your skills to create an image for your video. Keep in mind that most of the time, simpler works better in video. If you're using type, make sure it's large with a color that contrasts well with the background.

7. **When you're finished editing the image, click File → Exit.**

   A dialog box opens, asking if you want to save your changes.

Tip: If you want to keep Photoshop Elements running, you can choose File → Close. Just keep in mind that running both Photoshop and Premiere Elements at the same time may make your computer run a little slowly.

---

8. **Click Yes.**

   The Save As window opens, displaying the filename and folder you specified in Step 2.

   If you don't want to save your changes, you can click No. In that case, Photoshop closes, and you're back where you were in Step 1. If you decide the image needs editing, click Cancel and you're back in Photoshop.

9. **Click Save and then, in the alert box click OK.**

   When you click Save, yet another alert box appears, double-checking to make sure it's okay to replace the existing, empty Photoshop file you created in Step 2. When you click OK this last time, Photoshop actually saves your still image and returns you to Premiere.

Edit Pictures with Photoshop Elements

As mentioned above, Premiere Elements and Photoshop Elements share a common helper program called Elements Organizer, which displays your media as thumbnails. The menus and tools in the Organizer are similar to those in Premiere and Photoshop, so this threesome makes a great team. You'll learn more about the Organizer in the next chapter, which is all about tags, albums, and, well, organizing. For this section on still images, it's helpful to know that you can use the Organizer to open and edit still images.

To open Elements Organizer from Premiere, click Premiere's Organize tab, and then click the Organizer button. It may take a few seconds to launch. When that's done, you see video clips, stills, and other media displayed as thumbnail images. Click on an image to select it, and you can apply any of the quick fixes under the Fix tab. If your image needs more than the quick fixes available in the Organizer, right-click the image and choose Full Edit from the pop-up menu. That opens Photoshop Elements, where you can make more extensive changes. If you want to add an image that's in the Organizer to your Premiere project, just drag the thumbnail from the

Video safe line   Title safe line   Info window

Figure 3-16:
When you use Photoshop's Place command, the image you select is automatically sized to fit the frame size. You don't have to worry about all those numerical details. As icing on the cake, the image shows guides for the "video safe" and "title safe" areas, as described in Step 5.

Organizer onto the Media panel (Organize tab → Media) or the Project panel (Organize tab → Project.

This sharing between Premiere Elements and Photoshop Elements is very handy and works both ways. Using Photoshop, you can create fancy images, titles, and menus for your movies. Using Premiere, you can snag individual frames from your video and then make them even better-looking using Photoshop and its bundle of photo fixes. Using Photoshop Elements, you can create a slide show, complete with captions and transitions. Then you can send the project over to Premiere for more editing, video effects, and burning to a DVD. Elements Organizer is your central station for organizing and opening media files in either program.

Note: For a complete guide to Photoshop Elements, get hold of Barbara Brundage's *Photoshop Elements 8: The Missing Manual.*

Import Animation

Unlike videos, which feature live action, animations are drawings played back-to-back. Think *Toy Story, WALL-E,* and *Up.*

Premiere isn't the only kid on the block when it comes to creating moving pictures. Other programs animate images, too. Adobe Flash, for example, outputs a series of images for animation. Even the lowly GIF file, described on page 89, was designed to hold multiple images so it could display simple animations (like the ones that annoy you on web pages).

Animations are made up of many files displayed one after the other, and their individual file names reflect their serial nature. For example, an animation might include files with names like Horse_Running_001.PNG, Horse_Running_002.PNG, Horse_Running_003.PNG, and so on. Because animations play back at the standard rate of 30 frames for each second of video, you're talking about a lot of Horse_Running images.

Note: You can download a short animation for use with this example. The file *car_go.zip* is included in the Missing CD for this book (*http://missingmanuals.com/cds*).

Here are the steps to import an animation that consists of sequenced images:

1. **In Premiere, click the Organize tab, and then click Get Media.**

   You see the familiar grouping of icons that represent camcorders, still cameras, and PC files and folders.

2. **Click PC Files and Folders.**

   The Add Media window opens.

3. **Navigate to the folder that holds the sequence of images that make up the animation.**

   The filenames must be identical except for the number on the end. For example, here are a group of PNG files that are part of an animation: Horse_Running_001.PNG, Horse_Running_002.PNG, Horse_Running_003.PNG.

4. **Select the first image in the animation sequence, and then turn on the Numbered Stills checkbox.**

   When you select a numbered image, the Numbered Stills checkbox at the bottom of the Add Media window is activated—meaning it's not grayed out and you can click it (Figure 3-17).

5. **Click Open.**

   Premiere finds all the images in the sequence and converts them into a single sequence that you can use in your project. In the Media panel (Organize tab → Media) you see a single still image, but in the Project panel (Organize tab → Project) you see that Premiere turned all the numbered stills into an movie clip.

First image in animation

Numbered Stills checkbox

Tips for Creating Animations in Other Programs

You can create sequences of animated images from many graphics programs, including nearly the entire stable of Adobe professional graphics programs: After Effects, Fireworks, Flash, and Photoshop. There are a few things to keep in mind when you create these images. Still images used in an animation sequence can't include layers. So, if you're using a program like Photoshop CS4, you need to "flatten" any images you want to use in a sequence. Also, you want the frame size and aspect ratio of your animation to match your video project. Programs such as Photoshop CS4 have presets that will help you create graphics that match video standards.

Organize Your Clips

As you edit more and more projects in Premiere, it won't be long before you're overwhelmed with video and other media clips. In fact, all it takes to get there are a couple of vacations, some family celebrations, and maybe a school project or two. Suffering from media overload, you click Premiere's Organize tab and scroll through tons of clips but can't find the one you want. What you need is a way to organize your media files.

You've come to the right place. This chapter introduces you to a tool that helps you tame your growing media collection: Adobe's Elements Organizer, a high-powered, standalone program that comes with Premiere Elements. (Don't confuse Elements Organizer with the simpler Organize tab in Premiere; to understand the differences, see page 100.)

In this chapter, you'll learn how to rate your clips, apply searchable tags to them, and organize them into albums. All these techniques make it easy to find the clip you need when you're in the midst of editing.

Of course, when you're eager to start splicing clips together to create a movie, organizing clips may seem like a tedious waste of time. It's actually the opposite. Spend a few minutes tagging clips and arranging your videos in albums, and your projects will go much faster. Not only that, three years from now, when you want to see that clip of your basset hound Clementine next to a Sequoia in Yosemite National Park, you'll actually be able to find it.

The Organizer Application

From the outset, you should understand that the standalone program called Elements Organizer and the tab in Premiere Elements called "Organize" are two different beasts. Yes, they perform similar functions, and yes, their names are confusingly similar, but of the two, Elements Organizer is much more powerful. Why the duplication? Well, previous versions of Premiere Elements didn't use Elements Organizer; it was a part of Photoshop Elements, Adobe's photo-editing program. Adobe decided that, with Version 8 of both programs, they could share the same media library. So if you install either Premiere Elements or Photoshop Elements on your computer, you also install Elements Organizer.

Now, if that isn't confusing enough, Elements Organizer also has a tab called "Organize." This chapter focuses mostly on Elements Organizer as a standalone application. Just keep in mind that, in this chapter and in the rest of the book, the term *Organizer* (with an "r" at the end) means Elements Organizer, the standalone tool. When the book refers to the Organize tab, the text will make it clear whether it's referring to Premiere Elements or Elements Organizer.

On to the Organizer

You launch the Organizer in one of two ways. From Premiere's splash screen, click the Organize button (yes, incredibly enough, Adobe refers to the Organizer as "Organize" on this screen—go figure). If you're working within Premiere, go to its Organize tab and then click the Organizer button near the top-right corner.

Note: It doesn't help the Organizer/Organize confusion that the Organize button in the splash screen leads to the Elements Organizer program. When you use it, just focus on the Organizer icon and don't think about the missing "r."

No matter how you launch the Organizer, it provides a slightly different view of your media clips and slightly different tools than Premiere's Organize tab does—see Figure 4-1. And when you look closely, you see that there are major differences between the two. For example, you can create and apply keyword tags using the Organizer, but not in Premiere's Organize tab. And you can create Albums in the Organizer, but not from Premiere. Use the Organizer application to sort, group, and manage your ever-growing collection of media. Use Premiere's Organize tab to view your media as you edit video.

Tour the Organizer

The Organizer displays miniature versions of all the media files you import—videos, photos, and songs—neatly arranged in rows and columns. The screen actually looks like a photographer's lightbox, which makes sense given the Organizer's

Figure 4-1:
*The Organizer
application, with its
tabbed Tasks panel on
the right and large work
space, looks a lot like
Premiere. But the
Organizer does a
different job: It focuses
on organizing your
media. You use it to
apply descriptive tags to
media files and to group
files into albums.*

roots as an image-organizing tool for Photoshop Elements (in fact, this book will refer to the Organizer's main screen as "the lightbox"). Adobe refers to this collection of media as your *catalog*.

At the top of the Organizer screen, a menu bar provides commands for importing and viewing your clips. Choose File → Get Photos and Video, for example, to import media from your camcorder or computer. Under the Organizer's Find menu, you see unique ways to view your clips (for example, by file type or by date). Need to hunt down that video of a hummingbird you snapped 7 months ago? No problem.

A search box sits below the menu bar, along with a slider that enlarges or reduces your thumbnail images.

On the right side of the lightbox, you see a Tasks panel with four tabs (Figure 4-2):

- **Organize.** Because a primary function of the Organizer is to classify your clips, you'll spend most of your time here. You can rate your clips (from zero to five stars), attach key words to them so you can search them later, and group them into albums. All these techniques help you quickly find the media you need as you edit a project.

- **Fix.** Use the Fix tab to touch up still images. It includes options like Auto Color to correct a picture's color balance and contrast, Auto Contrast to improve an image's contrast without affecting its color, and Auto Red Eye Fix.

- **Create.** Look at the Create tab, and you can see the Organizer's still-photo roots. Most of the options handle projects like photo books, calendars, and greeting cards. As a videographer, the buttons you're likely to use are Slide Show, InstantMovie, and DVD with Menus. When you click on the latter two, the Organizer sends you to Premiere. For example, if you click InstantMovie, the Organizer launches Premiere and opens its InstantMovie panel.

- **Share.** The Share tab includes options to burn DVDs and BluRay discs and upload videos online. Again, either option sends you to Premiere.

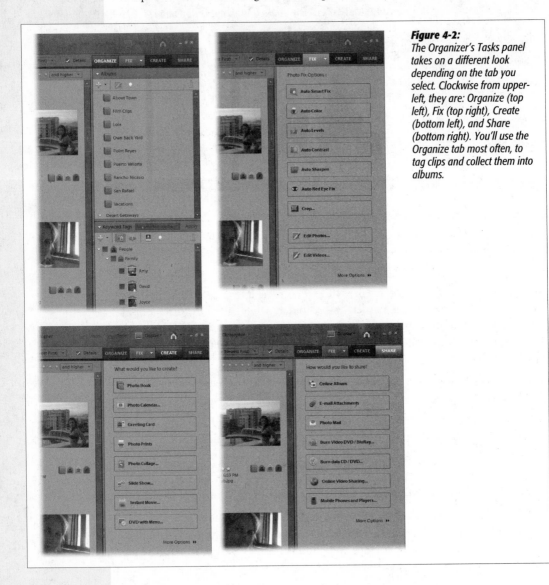

Figure 4-2:
The Organizer's Tasks panel takes on a different look depending on the tab you select. Clockwise from upper-left, they are: Organize (top left), Fix (top right), Create (bottom left), and Share (bottom right). You'll use the Organize tab most often, to tag clips and collect them into albums.

Import Media to the Organizer

Although any media you import through Premiere automatically appears in the Organizer, being able to import video, sound files, and still photos directly into the Organizer itself is handy, because it's the same program you use to categorize that media—to rate and tag it and assign it to albums. You can import media from many sources, like camcorders and still cameras, or you can import media that's already on your computer. (The one thing the Organizer *doesn't* provide is "Device Control," so, if you want to import video from a tape-based DV or HDV camcorder, you must use Premiere Elements and the steps described on page 44.)

Import Media from a Camera

Here are the steps to import media from a tapeless camcorder directly into the Organizer:

1. **Connect your camcorder to your PC.**

   Some camcorders use a USB cable. Others, such as the new mini-camcorders like the Flip line of cameras, have a USB connector built right into the camera.

2. **In the Organizer, choose File → Get Photo and Videos → From Camera or Card Reader.**

   The Organizer's Photo Downloader window opens. This window works just like Premiere's media downloader described on page 58.

3. **Click the Select a Device menu and choose your camcorder.**

   Your camcorder looks like a removable storage device to Windows and the Organizer. It even has a drive letter, like E: or F:.

4. **(Optional) Click the Advanced Dialog button to select individual clips.**

   To import all the media on your camcorder, skip this step. If you want to pick and choose individual files, click the Advanced Dialog button to see them listed, as shown in Figure 4-3. Check the boxes under the clips you want to import.

5. **Click Get Media.**

   The Organizer copies clips from your camcorder to your computer. The imported media appears in the Organizer and in Premiere's Organize tab, too.

Note: For more tips on using the Photo Downloader's file renaming and metadata features, see the description of the Media Downloader on page 58.

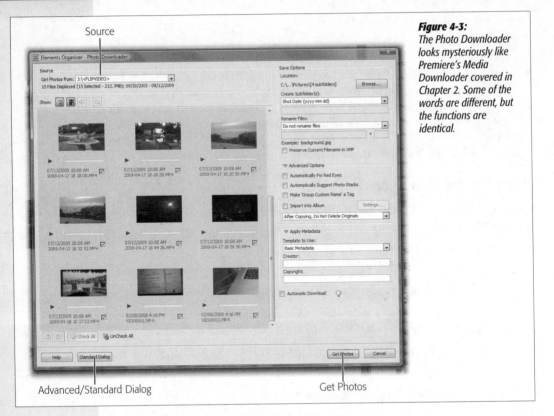

Source

Figure 4-3:
The Photo Downloader looks mysteriously like Premiere's Media Downloader covered in Chapter 2. Some of the words are different, but the functions are identical.

Advanced/Standard Dialog

Get Photos

Import Media from PC Files and Folders

To grab media on your computer in a file or folder, follow these steps:

1. **In the Organizer, choose File → Get Photo and Videos → From Files and Folders (Figure 4-4).**

   The Get Photos and Videos Files and Folders window opens as shown in Figure 4-5. As an alternative, Ctrl+Shift+G also opens this window.

2. **Select the files or folders you want to import.**

   Select a folder to import all the media inside of it or double-click the folder to choose individual files within it. The usual selection tricks work to select multiple files:

   • Click to select. Shift-click to select adjacent files.

   • Ctrl-click to select/deselect more than one file.

   • Click and drag to box in and import a bunch of files at once.

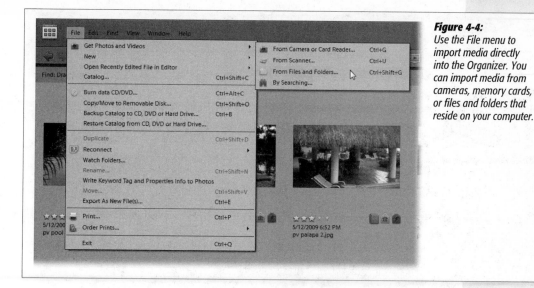

Figure 4-4:
Use the File menu to import media directly into the Organizer. You can import media from cameras, memory cards, or files and folders that reside on your computer.

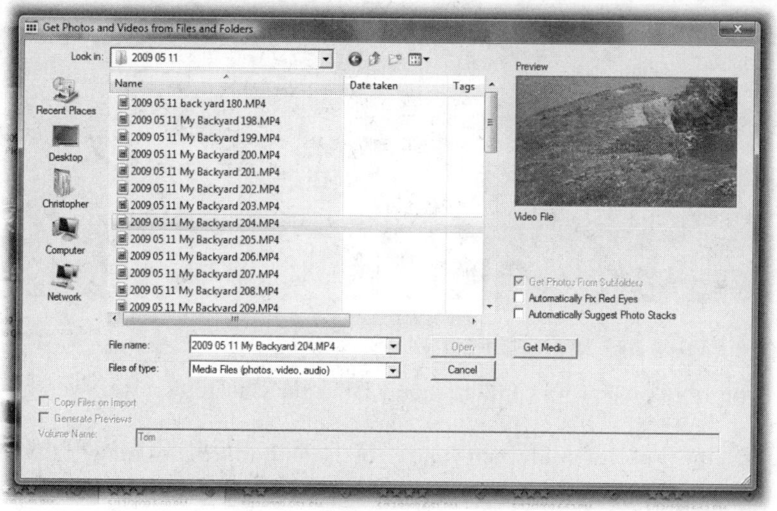

Figure 4-5:
The window you use to import media from files and folders lists the media clips and previews the first frame of each clip. Select a folder if you want to import all the media inside. Otherwise, you can pick and choose individual files.

3. **Click Get Media.**

The Organizer imports the clips into your catalog. The same clips appear in Premiere's Organize tab, too.

Once you import your clips in the Organizer, you can see them in the lightbox and they're available in Premiere's Organize tab; it's all part of the Organizer Philosophy described on page 106.

The Elements Organizer Philosophy

As you work in either Premiere Elements or Photoshop Elements, it helps to understand why Adobe made a third program, Elements Organizer, common to both programs. You might call the company's rationale the Elements Organizer Philosophy. It goes something like this: Since media files are big, you don't want to have multiple copies of the same file stashed in folders all over your computer or network hard drives. That's a huge waste of space, and it can lead to trouble if you update one copy of the file but not another; you might inadvertently use the unimproved copy in a project.

So Adobe decided you should keep just a single copy of your media. So far, so good. But if you do that, you need a way for Premiere and Photoshop to know where those files are. Enter Elements Organizer, the central registry for your media file locations.

The Organizer keeps track of your media no matter where you store it. It could be in folders on your computer or on some other computer on your network. In fact, you can keep your media on removable hard drives, CDs, or DVDs. As long as you add your media via the Organizer (and thus "register" it), Premiere or Photoshop can always find it because they consult the Organizer for the location.

The Organizer also tracks all sorts of other details about your clips, including keyword tags, smart tags, assigned albums, projects, dates, and file sizes. Using this info, the Organizer can locate and display the clips you want for a project and hide the ones you don't—a process called filtering. The Organizer offers a lot of ways to filter your clips, as you'll see in this chapter.

The Organizer Philosophy works pretty well, but you do have to follow some of the standard practices to make it work. First of all, if you keep all your media in one giant pool, use tags and albums as organizational tools so you can easily find the clips you need. It's also important that you use the tools in the Organizer to move media from one folder location to another. For example, suppose you get a new humongous hard drive for all your video clips. If you use Windows Explorer to move your clips to the new drive, the Organizer won't know where they are. Instead, you should move your media using the tools in the Organizer, as explained on page 107.

Change Views in the Organizer

When you work on a project and have only 20 media clips to deal with, you might not need the Organizer's help. When you've got 200 clips, you're beginning to appreciate the problem. And when you've got 2,000 or more clips in several different projects, you're desperate for a way to order your clips. Organizer to the rescue! Here's how it works:

1. From Premiere's splash screen, click the **Organize** button to launch the Organizer. Alternatively, within Premiere itself, click the **Organize** tab and then click the **Organizer** button to launch the Organizer.

   The Organizer displays your catalog, all the media you've imported, in other words. If you added photos to the Organizer from Photoshop Elements, you'll see those here, too.

2. **If displayed, click the Show All button.**

The Show All button appears only if you filtered the lightbox view earlier in the same work session. So if you were working in the lightbox in a filtered view (like View → Photos), switched windows to complete another task, and then came back to the lightbox, the filter remains in place. In such a case, you have to click Show All to see all your files. But every time you quit the Organizer program, the lightbox resets to Show All. The only thing is, you won't see the Show All button because the Organizer displays all your files by default.

3. **Use the Display menu to sort and view your clips in different ways.**

Click the Display button in the upper-right corner of the Organizer. Here's a rundown of the views available from the drop-down menu:

Thumbnail View (Ctrl+Alt+1) is the standard view. It displays miniature versions of all your media—video clips, images, and songs. Everything is in one big pool, which is great for tagging clips and creating albums.

Import Batch (Ctrl+Alt+2) Organizes your clips according to the dates you imported them to the Organizer.

Folder Location (Ctrl+Alt+3) opens a Windows Explorer-like sidebar to the left of the lightbox that displays the folders on your computer. You're probably used to clicking a folder to see the files inside. The Organizer doesn't work that way—in fact, it's just the opposite. When you're in this view, click a file in the lightbox and the sidebar on the left displays the folder it's in.

Think of this view as a tool to tell you where your clips are on your computer. It's part of the all-in-one-big-pool Elements Organizer philosophy. If you want to move a clip, you can drag it from the lightbox to a different folder. As mentioned earlier, you don't want to use Windows to move media you import. If you do, the Organizer loses track of the file. Instead, use this view to move clips from one folder to another.

Date View (Ctrl+Alt+D) displays a calendar that highlights the dates on which you imported files. You can change the display to view the calendar by year, month, or day. Click on a highlighted date to preview that day's imported media.

View, Edit, Organize in Full Screen (F11). In this view, most of the Organizer tools disappear to give you a great full-screen view of your media. You get a limited number of tools in collapsible menus on the left side of the screen for editing (Smart Fix and Auto Color, for example) and organizing (Add to Album and Add Keyword) your media. To return to the standard view, hit Esc.

Compare Photos Side by Side (F12). You see the same full-screen view described above, except that the Organizer displays two photos or video thumbnails side by side. You can preselect the images you want to compare (use Ctrl-click), or you can change the images once you're inside the view. Click the image and use the arrow buttons that pop up along the bottom of the screen to navigate through your media collection.

4. **You can show and hide specific types of media in the Organizer's lightbox (just as you can in the Organize tab of Premiere).**

   For example, to see only video and audio files, choose View → Media Types and deselect Photos, Projects, and PDF, making sure that just Video and Audio are selected.

   As you can see in Figure 4-6, each filter has a shortcut key, which is faster than using the menu:

   Photos: Ctrl+1
   Videos: Ctrl+2
   Audio: Ctrl+3
   Projects: Ctrl+4
   PDF: Ctrl+5

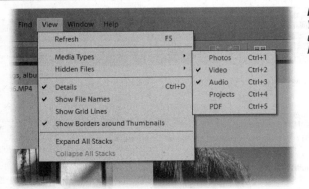

Figure 4-6:
You can show and hide different types of media using either a menu command or the shortcut keys shown here.

5. **Near the top-center of the window, click and drag the slider to resize your thumbnail images.**

   Drag the slider to the right to display larger but fewer thumbnails, and to the left to display smaller but more thumbnails.

6. **Click the Date menu next to the slider to sort thumbnails by date.**

   The Date menu has two options: Date (Newest First) and Date (Oldest First). Newest First zeroes in on the most recent batch of clips you imported. Oldest first is helpful when you view clips that follow a logical timeline, such as a wedding or birthday party—you can review the clips in the order you captured them.

7. **Next to the Date menu, turn on the Details checkbox.**

When you select Details, additional information shows up beneath each clip (providing your thumbnails are large enough). This information includes the clip's star rating (page 109), keyword tags (page 113), smart tags (page 120), album icons (page 126), capture date, and file name.

You won't see tag and album icons until you apply them to your clips, of course, which you'll learn to do a little later in this chapter. If you can't see the file names, make sure the thumbnail slider is set large enough to display them, and check to see that the filenames display is turned on by choosing View → Show Filenames. (While you're in the View menu, it's worth noting that you can show and hide file details by choosing View → Details or using the shortcut Ctrl+D.)

8. **If you see a scroll bar on the right of the lightbox, you can use it (or the scroll wheel on your mouse) to maneuver through your clips.**

Drag the scroll bar up or down to move quickly. Click the arrows at the top and bottom of the bar to move one row at a time.

You can drag the bar that separates the lightbox and the Task panel left and right to change the space available to your thumbnails. The same is true for the horizontal bar between the Albums and Keyword Tags panels. If either of those panels is closed, click the triangle button next to its name.

9. **Use the search box that sits below the menu bar to execute a search.**

For example, type in a few letters from one of your clips' filenames. When you press Enter, the Organizer limits the media it displays to files that match the word or characters you entered.

The Organizer looks at more than file names when it searches; it searches album names, keyword tags, smart tags, and dates. As it searches, it tells you what it's searching for, like "Find: Items matching 10/12/2009."

10. **In the upper-left corner, click the blue Back arrow.**

The view changes to the previous view, filtered by the date. Click the back button again, and you see the view before it was filtered by the date. You can use the Back and Forward arrows to move through your view history.

Now that you have some viewing tips and tricks under your belt, it's a great time to learn how to rate and filter clips, also known as filtering your catalog.

Rank Your Clips with Star Ratings

Suppose you spend a day shooting buffalo—with your camcorder, that is. Back home, you import your clips and you're ready to edit. But it's hard to tell the good buffalo clips from the bad ones when all you see is a thumbnail still of each clip.

As much as you want to jump in and start working on a project right away, take a little time to winnow the good clips from the bad by ranking them. Premiere gives you a quick and easy way to do so: star ratings. In the Organizer lightbox, five little ghosted-out stars appear under each clip (or image or song). As you play each clip, click on one of the stars to rate it.

Here's a proven strategy for figuring out how to rate a clip: On the first pass, separate usable clips from unusable ones by giving the former a single star and the latter no stars. Then filter your view of the clips to hide those you deemed unusable: in the Organizer, click one star in the Ratings filter at the top-right of the lightbox. As you continue to review and compare clips, upgrade the ratings on the usable clips to good and maybe even great by applying two, three, or more stars. (Later, if you feel you were too generous or too stingy, you can come back and change the rating.)

While this may seem like a tedious process at first, it saves tons of time in the long run because you can filter your clips by star rating as you edit your project. That way, you won't be reviewing bad clips. For example, if you only want to see buffalo clips with a rating of three stars or better, click the appropriate star in the Ratings filter (Figure 4-7).

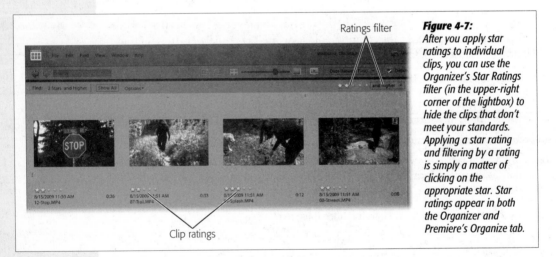

Ratings filter

Clip ratings

Figure 4-7:
After you apply star ratings to individual clips, you can use the Organizer's Star Ratings filter (in the upper-right corner of the lightbox) to hide the clips that don't meet your standards. Applying a star rating and filtering by a rating is simply a matter of clicking on the appropriate star. Star ratings appear in both the Organizer and Premiere's Organize tab.

In practice, of course, you'll probably work on all types of video projects—some serious, some frivolous. So let the nature of your project determine how much time you spend reviewing and rating clips. If it's a serious project, you may want to take several passes through each clip. On the other hand, if your project is a quick-and-dirty YouTube video, forgo the multiple-pass rating and upgrade and downgrade clips as you work with them.

Apply Star Ratings

Rating your clips couldn't be easier. Just click one of the five stars under the clip. Star-rating a clip works the same way whether you're in the Organizer or Premiere's Organize tab. (The steps below describe the process within the Organizer.)

Before you preview clips and apply star ratings, you may want to filter the catalog so that it displays only clips from, say, the great buffalo shoot or your most recent project. You can sort files using the Organizer's menu bar or drop-down menus at the top of the screen. So you can, for example, sort files by selecting "Date (Newest First)" in the drop-down menu, or you can choose Find → By History → Imported on to display clips added on a specific date. (Fortunately, you don't have to rely on your memory for the date. As shown in Figure 4-8, the Organizer presents a handy window that lists the dates you imported media, along with some other details.)

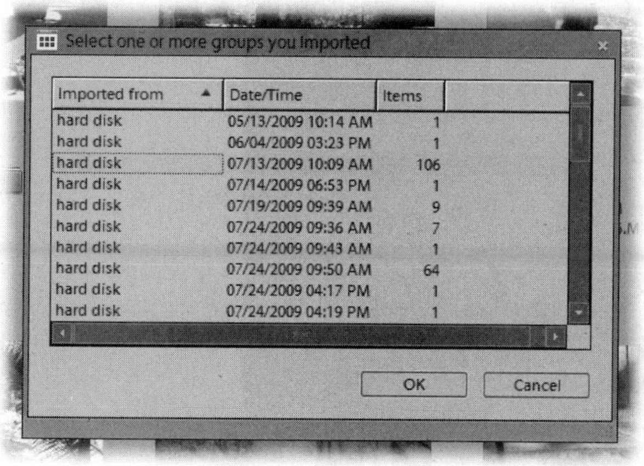

Figure 4-8:
This handy window shows you the source of the media clips, the date and time you imported them, and how many clips you added to the catalog. Choose one of the dates, and the lightbox shows you the clips.

Once you've got the right clips in the lightbox, follow these steps to preview your videos and apply star ratings:

1. **Right-click the first clip, and then choose View Photos and Video in Full Screen.**

   The Organizer window displays the clip in Full Screen mode, as shown in (Figure 4-9). Along the right side of the monitor, a film strip displays your media. At the bottom, a toolbox has controls for playing clips and for showing and hiding the other panels. Move your mouse to the left side of the screen, and a Quick Edit panel pops out, displaying different tools and, in the top-left corner, the star rating.

2. **Click the Play button.**

   You may want to play a clip a couple of times before you decide what rating to give it—and whether you even want to use it. But keep in mind that you don't have to use an entire clip. You may want to use just a portion of it, so don't throw out a clip with good sections in it. As you'll see later in this chapter, Premiere offers some help in assessing your clips with its Auto-Analyzer feature, but for now, you're the one who knows what you want from your video. Review the clip as many times as needed to star-rate it.

Quick Edit palette

Previous media | Next media

Play

Film strip

Figure 4-9:
*The Full Screen view
gives you the big picture.
Use the film strip on the
left or the buttons at the
bottom to choose a clip
to preview. The Quick
Edit palette hides until
you move your mouse to
the edge of the screen.*

3. **If the clip is acceptable, move your mouse over the Quick Edit palette and click the one-star rating.**

   The rating displays as one big gold star and four ghosted-out stars. It appears in the Organizer and Premiere's Organize tab. You can use the star rating to filter your clip catalog in both programs.

   It's hard to judge one video clip compared to another, especially if you haven't seen all the clips yet. That's why it makes sense to set the bar low on your first pass. Don't give any stars to the really bad clips. Give acceptable clips a one- or two-star rating. As you pare down the clips and re-review the rated ones, you can elevate the better clips to a higher rating.

4. **Repeat the process for all the media clips.**

   Depending on how much video you shot, it can be a little tedious to view each and every clip more than once. Just keep in mind that the time you spend now will save you lots of time later on. At this stage, your primary mission is to eliminate all the truly bad clips. You won't ever have to watch that bad video again.

Get a Good View

There's more than one way to preview video clips in the Organizer and in Premiere, and you may find that one tool works better than another for your video format. So, if the Organizer's Full Screen view gives you fuzzy clips or the playback stutters, try one of these options for previewing and rating clips:

1. In the Organizer's lightbox, right-click the clip and choose Play Video or Audio to open the media player.

2. Click Play to preview the clip.

3. Close the media player by clicking the X button in the upper-right corner.

4. In the lightbox, set a star rating for the clip. If you don't see stars under the thumbnails in the lightbox, press Ctrl+D to show details.

5. Choose the next clip and repeat the process.

Preview and Rate in Premiere

If neither of the Organizer methods works for you, try previewing and rating your clips using Premiere. Follow these steps:

1. In Premiere, click the Organize tab and then click the Media button to display your clips.

2. Set the Media Arrangement menu to show Newest First.

3. Turn on the Details check box to display the star rating for clips (Figure 4-10).

4. Double-click a clip to open it in the Preview window.

5. If necessary, drag one of the edges of the Preview window to resize it.

6. Click play to Preview the clip.

7. Close the media player by clicking the X button in the upper-right corner.

8. Click a star under the clip to set the star rating.

9. Choose the next clip and repeat the process.

Apply Keyword Tags to Clips

The star rating system doesn't specify much detail about the contents of a clip; it simply lets you broadly label a clip as relatively good or bad. Keyword tags, described in this section, and smart tags, up next, give you the opportunity to be more specific.

When you look at media files in the Organizer or in Premiere's Organize tab, all you see is a still frame of a clip. You may wonder who's in the clip, where was it shot, when was it shot, and probably half a dozen other questions.

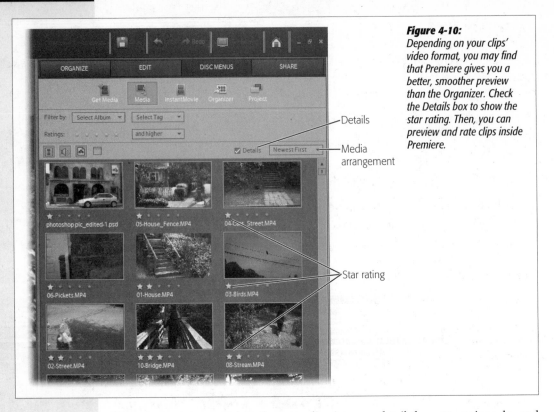

Figure 4-10:
*Depending on your clips'
video format, you may find
that Premiere gives you a
better, smoother preview
than the Organizer. Check
the Details box to show the
star rating. Then, you can
preview and rate clips inside
Premiere.*

Tags give you a way to describe your clips in more detail than star ratings do, and
they can answer important questions like those above. Once you tag your clips,
you've got a powerful way to zero in on just the clip you need. Get used to working with keyword tags, and you can really cut through the media clutter.

Here's an example: Suppose you travel the country with your faithful basset hound
Clementine and fussy Siamese cat Jasmine. Naturally, you shoot video every step of
the way. As you import the video into the Organizer, you tag all the Clementine
clips with her name and do the same for Jasmine. You also tag clips by location,
like Yosemite National Park, the Grand Canyon, and Mississippi. You can apply
multiple tags to clips, so some clips might end up with three tags: Clementine, Jasmine, and Grand Canyon. Then, as you edit your project, it's easy to apply filters
so you see, for example, only those clips with both Clementine and Jasmine at the
Grand Canyon.

You can filter your view in either the Organizer or Premiere's Organize tab using
keyword tags. However, to *create* and *apply* tags to clips, you have to be in the
Organizer. Here's how you do that:

1. If you're in Premiere Elements, click the Organize tab and then click the Organizer button. Alternatively, click the Organize button from Premiere's splash screen.

   The Organizer application opens, showing your media in the lightbox, with the tabbed Tasks panel on the right and the Organize tab selected. It displays Albums at the top and Keyword Tags below, as shown in Figure 4-11. You'll learn about albums in more detail beginning on page 126, but for the time being, it's helpful to know that they're simply another way to group clips.

   Initially, the Organizer displays all your media files. Before you apply keyword tags, you can use filters to bring the number of clips down to a more manageable quantity. The next steps describe your options.

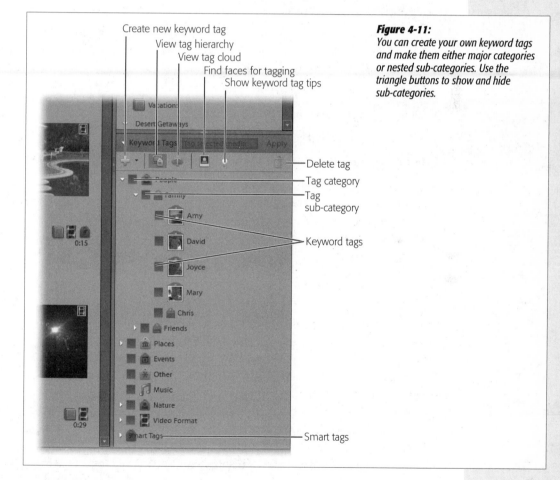

Create new keyword tag
View tag hierarchy
View tag cloud
Find faces for tagging
Show keyword tag tips

Delete tag
Tag category
Tag sub-category
Keyword tags

Smart tags

Figure 4-11:
You can create your own keyword tags and make them either major categories or nested sub-categories. Use the triangle buttons to show and hide sub-categories.

2. Click the Show All button, if available.

   When you do so, the Show All button disappears and the Organizer displays all the media in your catalog. As you learned above, the Show All button appears only if you filtered the lightbox view earlier in the same work session.

3. In the Albums panel, choose the project or album that has the files you wish to tag.

   You can choose only one project or album at a time. When you click on a name, the Organizer displays only the media for that project or album.

   Projects are described on page 13. Albums are covered in more detail on page 126.

4. (Optional) **To sort your media by star rating, click a star in the upper-right corner of the lightbox and then choose an option from the menu.**

   After you click one of the stars, you can choose "and higher", "and lower", or "only" from the drop-down menu. For example, to see all the clips with a three-star or better rating, click on the third ghosted star to highlight it, and make sure "and higher" is selected in the menu.

5. **Select the clips you want to tag.**

   If you're tagging a single clip, you don't need to make a selection first—just drag the tag to the clip. If you want to tag several clips at once, you can use any of the usual multiple-selection techniques:

   • Ctrl-click to select multiple clips.

   • Shift-click to select a range of adjacent clips.

   • Click and drag a selection box to select a group of clips.

6. **Select one or more tags.**

   Premiere provides several categories and sub-categories of tags. For example, you can select the People category and tag clips with subcategories that include Family and Friends.

   If you want to apply multiple tags to the selected clips, Ctrl-click or Shift-click to highlight the tags.

7. **Drag one of the selected tags to one of the selected clips, as shown in Figure 4-12.**

   The Organizer applies the selected tags to all the selected clips.

By selecting multiple clips and applying multiple tags, you can speed up your tagging chores.

Create a New Keyword Tag

You're not limited to the Organizer's tags, however. You can create your own. For example, within the Family sub-category, you might want to create a tag for individual family members. Then, you can not only find all the clips with Amy in them, but you can also find all the clips that have Amy, Mary, and Joyce together.

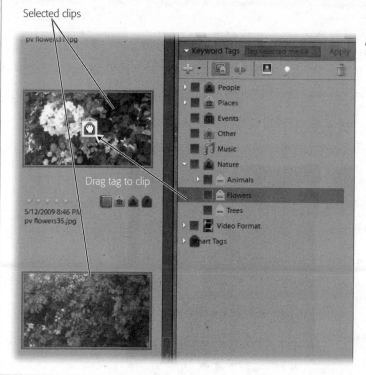

Figure 4-12:
To apply tags to more than one clip, preselect the clips and then drag the tag onto one of the selected clips.

You can only create new tags from within the Organizer. Choose the Organize tab in the Task panel. If the Keyword Tags panel is closed, click the triangle button to open it. You can display tags two ways: Tag Hierarchy (click the button that looks like a TV screen with a tag beside it) or Tag Cloud (click the cloud with the big "T" on it). The Tag Hierarchy displays tags you can checkmark to narrow your view to clips that have that tag. The Cloud view displays tags as a word list; click a word to sort by that tag.

When you create a new tag, it's easier to use Tag Hierarchy because you can see the main categories (People, Places, and so on) and their sub-categories (Family and Friends under People, for example).

To create a new tag, click the big green + button to open a menu with several options:

- **New Keyword Tag.** This opens the Create Keyword Tag panel (Figure 4-13) where you have a few options. Click the Edit Icon button to choose a label, color, and icon for the new tag. Premiere displays this icon on the clip's still frame, so it provides a quick reference as you edit. For example, if you create a tag for your basset hound Clementine, you might use her picture as the icon image.

Next, you have to tell Premiere where, in the list of all the tags, to put this new tag. Use the Category drop-down menu to position it as a sub-category of an existing tag. For example, to add a tag for Clementine under "Pets", choose the Pets category. Then, when you create the tag by clicking the OK button, "Clementine" shows up under "Pets", replete with a little picture of your hound dog in the tag.

You may also choose to place your tag on a map and provide additional notes about the tag.

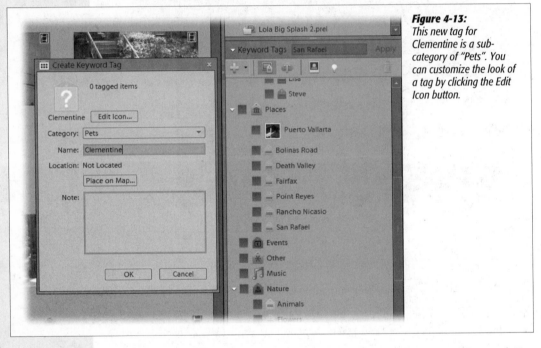

Figure 4-13:
This new tag for Clementine is a sub-category of "Pets". You can customize the look of a tag by clicking the Edit Icon button.

- **New Sub-Category.** This option is really a subset of the New Keyword Tag option; it also lets you create and position a new tag. The difference is that here you can't specify a tag color or image. Your new sub-category adopts the tag characteristics of the parent category. So if you add a sub-category to Events, it shows up as a red tag with a couple of ersatz lines of text in it.

You might wonder, if New Sub-Category does the same thing as the option above, why is it here at all? That's because New Sub-Category lets you set up a tag without specifying a tag color or icon image. If you know you're going to shoot footage of a vacation on Martha's Vineyard, for example, you can set up a tag in the Event sub-category called "Martha's Vineyard Vacation" so it's all ready for you when you return.

If you choose this option, the Create Sub-Category panel opens as shown in Figure 4-14. At the top, type in the tag name in the Sub-Category Name box. Then, in the Category drop-down menu, choose a parent category or existing sub-category from the list.

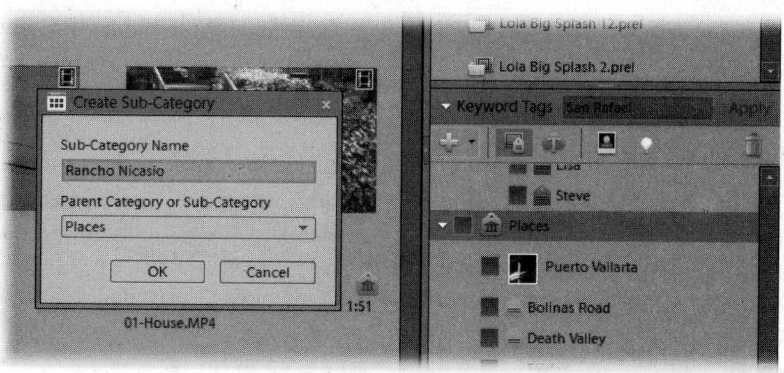

Figure 4-14:
The Organizer orders tags in a hierarchy, and you can create sub-categories that branch down several levels. Though you can create a complex tagging structure, it's probably best to keep it simple when you start.

- **New Category.** In Elements lingo, a "category" is the top level of keyword tags. People, Places, and Events all represent categories, for example. Everything else belongs to a sub-category.

  To create a new top-level tag, choose this option, name the category, and then choose a tag color and icon.

Tip: After you create a keyword tag, you may decide that you put it in the wrong category. If so, in the Organizer's Keyword Tags panel, simply drag the tag to a new category.

Remove Keyword Tags

As you work on projects, you may change your mind about a keyword tag. No problem, you can remove a tag with a couple of clicks. Right-click the blue keyword tag under a clip and a menu pops up with options like "Remove Clementine Keyword Tag." Click on the tag you want to remove, and Premiere deletes it instantly—you won't see an alert box to double-check your intentions, so be forewarned. As an alternative, you can right-click on a thumbnail and then choose Remove Keyword Tag. This method displays a submenu with both the keyword tags and the smart tags described later.

Tip: You can use the Remove Tag feature to see just what tags Premiere applied to a clip. Follow the steps above, but don't click on a tag (otherwise, you'll remove it). Just click away from the menu by placing your cursor elsewhere on the screen and left-clicking.

Apply Smart Tags to Clips

In addition to keyword tags, Premiere offers another type of tag, called a smart tag. Smart tags don't know anything about you, your basset hound, or, unfortunately, upcoming Lotto numbers. They simply reflect Premiere's assessment of the quality of a video clip. Ask Premiere to analyze a clip, and it identifies problems like shaky camera work, low light, and inaudible audio. It lets you know about the good things in your clips, too, with tags such as High Quality and In Focus. It then labels the clip with these assessments, and those labels become purple smart tags under your media clips. So, how do smart tags help you when you edit video? It's like having an assistant who pre-screens your clips and flags the good and bad parts.

Premiere smart-tags your clips using a tool called Auto-Analyzer. Auto-Analyzer doesn't simply look at each clip as a single object—it actually analyzes your footage frame by frame, looking for specific deficiencies and attributes (see Figure 4-16 for the complete list). You can't create or add your own smart tag definitions, however.

Premiere uses smart tags in a number of ways. For example, if you attempt to use footage tagged as dark or low-contrast, Premiere asks if you want to apply Auto Contrast to improve the clip. And if you choose Premiere's InstantMovie option, it uses the smart tags to select footage, create transitions, and apply effects.

As part of the smart-tagging process, Auto-Analyzer detects dramatic image changes in the video and, based on that, divides each clip into multiple scenes. For details on these newly created scenes, go to page 124.

Smart-Tag with Auto-Analyzer

You can run Auto-Analyzer from the Organizer or from inside Premiere, and you can analyze either a single or multiple clips at once (to analyze multiple clips, use the multiple-clip selection process described on page 116).

To start Auto-Analyzer in either the Organizer or Premiere, right-click the selected clip or clips and choose Run Auto-Analyzer from the shortcut menu. A small window displays a progress bar like the one in Figure 4-15, along with status messages such as "Detecting scenes" and "Analyzing media." If it's taking too long or you change your mind, click Cancel to stop the analysis.

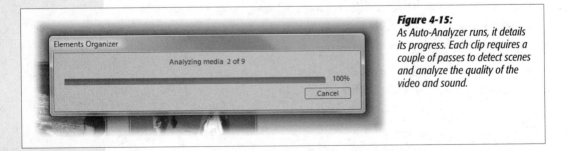

Figure 4-15:
As Auto-Analyzer runs, it details its progress. Each clip requires a couple of passes to detect scenes and analyze the quality of the video and sound.

You might expect Premiere to display a report once it finishes analyzing your clip, but it doesn't. Instead, it adds a purple smart tag to the lower-right corner of your clip. To see the results of the analysis, hold your cursor over the smart tag, and a tooltip lists the tags Auto-Analyzer applied. You can see the full list of smart tags in Figure 4-16.

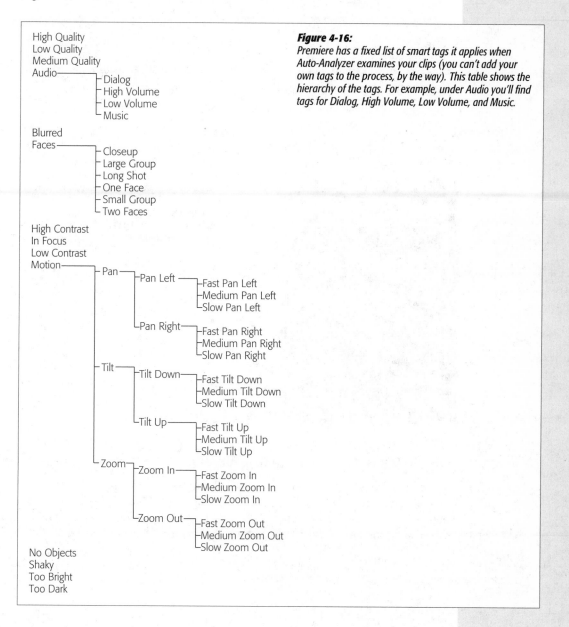

Figure 4-16:
Premiere has a fixed list of smart tags it applies when Auto-Analyzer examines your clips (you can't add your own tags to the process, by the way). This table shows the hierarchy of the tags. For example, under Audio you'll find tags for Dialog, High Volume, Low Volume, and Music.

Apply Smart Tags During Capture

You can analyze and smart-tag your clips as you capture video, too, but only through Premiere and only with footage from a DV camcorder or an HDV camcorder (see page 44) or a webcam (you can't auto-analyze video from an AVCHD camcorder, a mobile phone, or a PC file; to analyze those files, see the section below).

Under Premiere's Organize tab, click Get Media and select either DV or HDV camcorder or webcam as your video source. A window of capture and smart-tagging options appears, as shown in Figure 4-17. Click the Auto-Analyzer option. If you want to pick and choose which characteristics Premiere analyzes, click the triangle beside the Analyze label and select from Motion, Faces, Blur, Brightness and Contrast, Shake, Audio, and Object Motion.

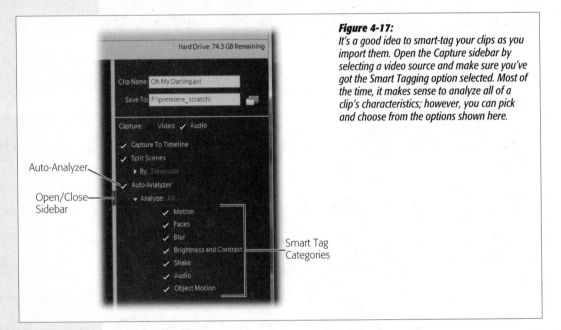

Figure 4-17:
It's a good idea to smart-tag your clips as you import them. Open the Capture sidebar by selecting a video source and make sure you've got the Smart Tagging option selected. Most of the time, it makes sense to analyze all of a clip's characteristics; however, you can pick and choose from the options shown here.

Apply Smart Tags From the Organizer

If you import video from a DVD or AVCHD camcorder, a digital still camera, or a mobile phone, or if you add clips using PC Folders and Files as a source, you can only analyze clips *after* you import them. Select the clips you want to tag, then right-click one of the clips and choose Run Auto-Analyzer from the shortcut menu.

Change Smart Tag Options in the Organizer

In most cases, it makes sense to let Auto-Analyzer analyze all the characteristics of a clip, and when you start out, that's the way Auto-Analyzer's set up. Later on, you may want to look for certain clip qualities. To do that, choose Edit → Preferences → Auto-Analyzer Options in the Organizer. The Preferences window opens, as shown in Figure 4-18. You can choose from major categories such as Audio, Face, and Object Motion, but you can't specify the sub-categories, such as Pan and Fast Zoom In.

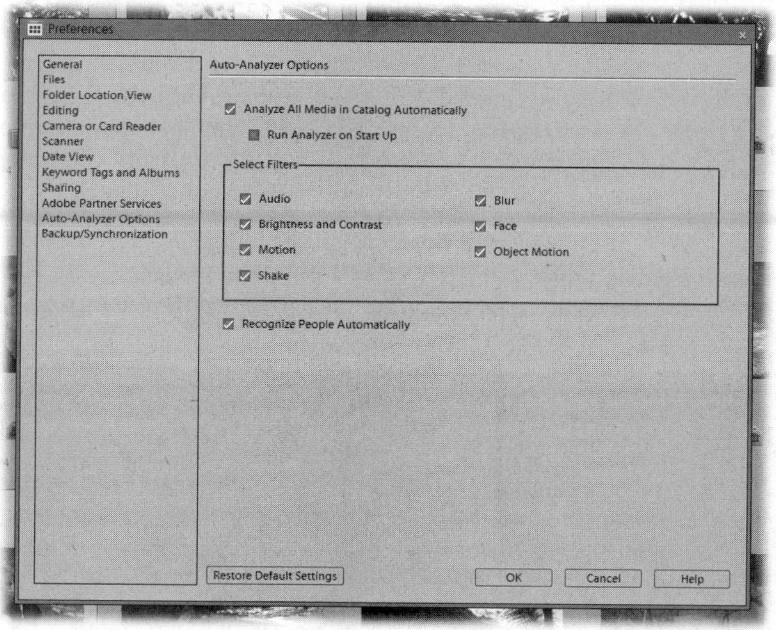

Figure 4-18:
When you import clips through the Organizer, you can choose which characteristics Auto-Analyzer considers during the smart-tagging process. Initially, Auto-Analyzer is set to look at all of a clip's characteristics.

Apply Smart Tags Automatically

If you wait impatiently while Auto-Analyzer does its work, you may wonder if there's a faster way to do the job. In fact, you can automatically start Auto-Analyzer in a couple of ways.

When you first install Premiere, the program sets Auto-Analyzer to run automatically whenever you have the Organizer open. Left this way, all the clips in your catalog will eventually sport that snazzy purple tag. That's a great system so long as it doesn't take a toll on Premiere's performance, such as when you're trying to play back a scene or render a clip. If Auto-Analyzer turns out to be a problem, turn it off. Go to Edit → Preferences → Auto-Analyzer Options (Figure 4-18). Click the check mark beside the option "Analyze All Media in Catalog Automatically" to remove it. If you want to stop the Auto-Analyzer for just a few moments, click the purple tag in the status bar below the catalog; it acts as a pause button.

But there's another option that may work even better: You can run Auto-Analyzer even when you're not using the Organizer or Premiere. You can set a preference so that the program automatically runs when you start up your computer. The idea is that when your PC isn't busy doing other things, it spends its spare brainpower analyzing your videos.

The Organizer normally has this option turned on. To toggle it on or off, go to Edit → Preferences → Auto-Analyzer Options and check the box "Run Analyzer on Start Up".

Smart-Tagged Video Groups

As you learned earlier, when Auto-Analyzer detects dramatic changes in a video clip, it breaks the clip into scenes. It assumes that, because the image changed so abruptly, the subject has also changed. This gives you the opportunity to treat each auto-analyzed scene as a separate entity. You may want to apply transitions between the scenes, for example. (Remember, as always, the original clip remains unchanged. Premiere still stores it as a single video file on your computer.)

You can tell when Auto-Analyzer divided a clip into multiple scenes—the thumbnail of the clip sports a thick, light-gray border, and it has an Open Group button on the right side (see Figure 4-19, top). Click the button and the clip expands into its multiple scenes (see Figure 4-19, bottom).

GEM IN THE ROUGH

Stack Still Images

If you use a lot of still photos in your projects, at some point they're going to clutter up your workspace. One solution is to group the photos into "stacks." You can stack multiple still images under a single picture similar to the way that Auto-Analyzer tucks several scenes under a single clip image. Stacking stills is a good way to organize images that have a common theme, and it reduces the clutter.

To stack stills, select the pictures (make sure there aren't any video or audio clips in the selection or it won't work) and then right-click one of the stills. Choose Stack → Stack Selected Photos. Once you do, the stacked photos carry the same visual cues as stacked clips: a hefty light-gray border and an Open Group button on the right (see Figure 4-20).

You probably want to pick a representative image for the top of the stack. Expand the stack, right-click any of the stills, and choose Stack (Image Only) → Set As Top Item. When

you close the stack, the chosen image sits at the top of the pile; it will also occupy the number-one spot when you next expand the stack.

If you get to the point where you want to unstack the images, right-click on the stack and choose Stack → Unstack Photos. You can remove individual items from a stack, too. Expand the stack by clicking on the Expand icon or by right-clicking a stack and choosing Stack → Expand Photos in Stack. Then select one or more stills you want to remove. Right-click one of the selected images and choose Stack → Remove Photo from Stack.

Drag a tag to a closed stack of photos, and Premiere applies that tag to every photo. On the other hand, if you open the stack, you can add tags to or remove them from individual photos.

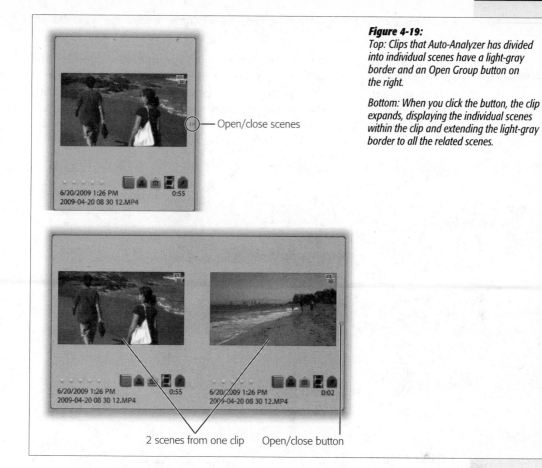

Figure 4-19:
Top: Clips that Auto-Analyzer has divided
into individual scenes have a light-gray
border and an Open Group button on
the right.

Bottom: When you click the button, the clip
expands, displaying the individual scenes
within the clip and extending the light-gray
border to all the related scenes.

Open/close scenes

2 scenes from one clip   Open/close button

Stacked Photos icon

Expand
stack

Figure 4-20:
Stacked still images look similar to grouped video
scenes. Stacked photos display an icon in the upper-
right corner. Click the Open Group button on the
image frame to see all the photos.

If you apply a tag to an Auto-Analyzed clip, Premiere applies the tag to all the scenes in the clip; you can't apply a tag to an individual scene.

In the next chapter, you'll learn all about adding clips to Premiere's timeline and sceneline. For now, know that if you want to add all the scenes in a group, make sure the group is closed and then drag it to the timeline or sceneline. To add just a single scene from within a group, expand the group and drag the scene. If you happen to smart tag a clip *after* you add it to the timeline, it gets divided into separate scenes in the timeline (Figure 4-21). In the sceneline, the clip is separated into separate boxes, each holding a scene.

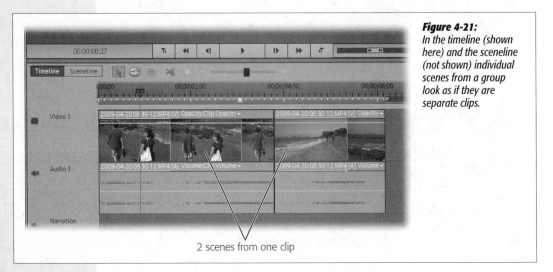

Figure 4-21:
In the timeline (shown here) and the sceneline (not shown) individual scenes from a group look as if they are separate clips.

2 scenes from one clip

Remove Smart Tags

As you review a clip's smart tags, you may feel that Auto-Analyzer improperly tagged a clip. Just as with keyword tags, you can remove a smart tag. Right-click the clip and, in the menu that pops up, move your cursor over the Remove Tag option. The clip's smart tags appear at the bottom of the menu—they have the typical purple smart tag icon, as shown in (Figure 4-22). Click the tag you want to remove, and Premiere deletes it immediately—you don't get a chance to confirm the cut.

Organize Clips into Albums

Premiere Albums are another great tool for organizing your media. They work according to the Organizer Philosophy explained on page 106, and they work exceptionally well.

There's one important thing to keep in mind when you create an album and add clips to it. You're never copying or moving clips from one place to another—from the Organizer, say, to an album called "Beach Vacation". You're just creating links

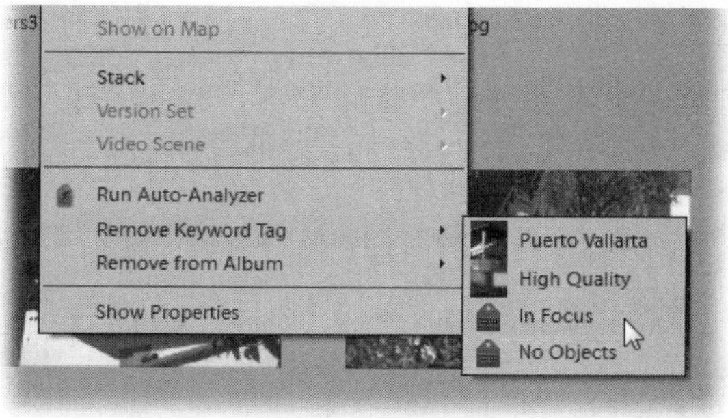

Figure 4-22:
Use the pop-up menu to remove a tag from a clip. The clip shown here is about to lose its High Quality smart tag.

so that Premiere can display the clips in that album. That way, a single clip of Clementine can appear in several different albums, such as Clementine's Favorite Moments, The Grand Canyon, and Dogs with Long Ears. No matter how many albums you add Clementine to, there's still only one Clementine clip.

Create a New Album

You create albums inside the Organizer application. These steps create an album called "Gone Gobi."

1. **Click the Organize tab.**

   The Albums panel sits at the top of the Tasks pane. If necessary, click the triangle button to expand the panel.

2. **Click the big green + button and choose New Album.**

   The panel changes to display Album Details (Figure 4-23).

3. **In Album Name, type "Gone Gobi".**

   The album name should be descriptive because it's the only thing you'll see in Premiere's Filter by menu, shown in Figure 4-24.

4. **Choose an Album Category from the drop-down menu.**

   You can collect albums in album groups, described in the next section.

5. **Click the Content tab, and then drag clips from the lightbox into the Gone Gobi album.**

   You can add clips one at a time or select groups and drag them to the album. Later, you can add new clips by dragging them on to the album in the Albums panel.

6. **Click Done.**

   The Album closes and it appears in the Albums panel.

If you want to make changes to your Gone Gobi album later, right-click the album in the Albums panel and choose *Edit Gone Gobi Album*. The Album Details panel described above opens, and you can make your changes.

Figure 4-23:
When you create a new album, you see this panel, where you can name the album, choose a group for the album, and add clips.

Figure 4-24:
In Premiere, the Filter by Albums menus displays albums, album categories, and projects. Album categories hold more than one album, and you can nest one album category inside another album category.

Create a New Album Category

As your collection of media clips grows, you may want to create *groups* of albums. If you shoot a lot of family events, for example, you may create albums for birthdays, weddings, and graduations. Then, within these albums, you may have sub-albums for specific events, like Mary Frances's Wedding and Steve's Wedding.

Creating album groups is similar to creating a new album. In the albums panel, click the green + button and choose Create Album Category. Then you see the Create Album Category dialog box (Figure 4-25), where you name the Album Category and, if you like, nest it inside another album category.

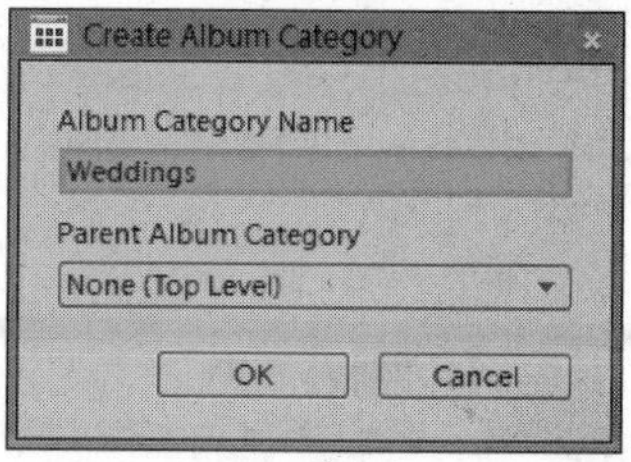

Figure 4-25:
To create a new album category, give it a name and choose whether it's at the top level or within another album category.

Projects vs. Albums

Your video projects show up at the bottom of the album panel, as shown in Figure 4-24. Technically, these projects aren't albums, so they have their own category and different icons than albums. In Premiere, whenever you drag a clip onto the sceneline or timeline, that clip gets added to your project file. If you have a project open in Premiere and you import clips, Premiere adds those clips to that project.

In Premiere, you view the clips in a project by opening the project when you launch Premiere, clicking the Organize tab, and then clicking the Project button. In the Organizer, you view the clips in a project by selecting the project in the Album panel.

Create Smart Albums Automatically

Smart Albums are nifty containers for your clips. You never have to drag clips to smart albums; all you have to do is tell the Organizer what type of clips to include in them. You provide a set of rules, which Premiere calls "criteria," and Smart Album uses those rules to decide which files to include in which albums. Other than that, a Smart Album is like any other album. For example, you find your Smart Albums listed in Premiere in the Select Album menu on the Organize tab.

You create a smart album from the Albums panel. Click the green + button and then choose New Smart Album. The New Smart Album panel opens as shown in Figure 4-26. Name the album and then use the drop-down menu to build your set of inclusion rules. Each rule comprises three parts. First you choose a characteristic of the clips you want to include, which can be as diverse as a keyword tag, a capture date, or an author.

Next you choose a modifier, such as "Starts With" and "Includes". The modifier changes depending on the object; for example, if you choose to include clips based on their keyword tags, the only available modifier is "Includes".

Finally, in the third menu, you choose the boundaries for the modifier. In the above example, you'd choose from a list of existing keyword tags. On the other hand, if you elect to include clips based on their capture date, the modifiers include: "Is", "Is before", "Is after", and "Is within the last". After you make your choice, you then choose a date ("is before 9/25/09") or time period ("is within the last 8 days").

Premiere applies the criteria you establish two ways. You can choose to match "Any one of the following search criteria" or "All of the following search criteria".

Once you finish setting up the rules, the Organizer automatically searches your media and adds it to the album. And if you import or add new media that matches the criteria, the Organizer automatically adds that, too.

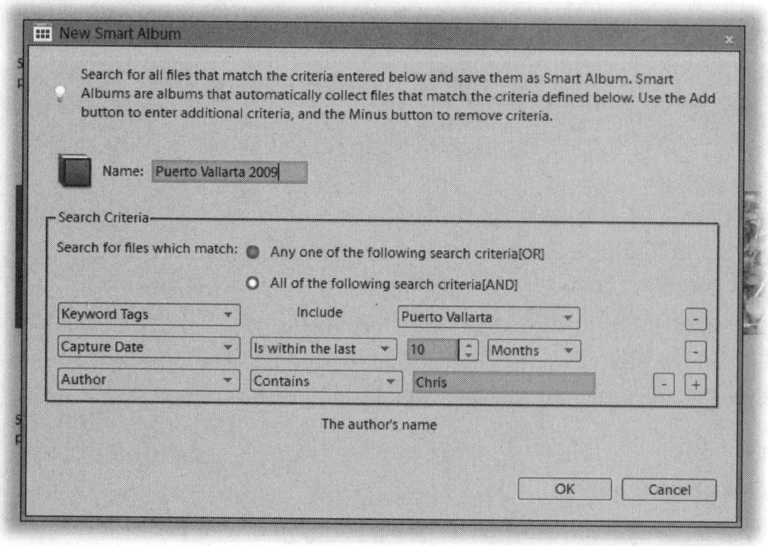

Figure 4-26:
You set the rules for clips that should appear in a smart album. Here, you're creating the rules for a smart album named Puerto Vallarta 2009. The rules state that, for the Smart Album feature to include them, clips must have the keyword tag "Puerto Vallarta", a capture date within the past 10 months, and an author name that contains "Chris".

Delete a Smart Album

If the time comes when you no longer need your Puerto Vallarta 2009 Smart Album, right-click on the album name in the Albums panel and choose *Delete Puerto Vallarta 2009 album* from the shortcut menu. An alert box appears, asking "Are you sure you want to delete this smart album?" Click OK to go through with it or click Cancel to back out. Naturally, deleting the album doesn't delete the clips. They're still there in your main catalog.

Back Up and Synchronize Albums

Adobe's optional Photoshop.com service can back up your albums (see page 16 for a detailed description of the Photoshop.com service). The best thing about the service is that it's easy, and you don't have to worry about it too much once you set it up. The bad thing about it is that video files are big, and, after you fill up 2 GB of space, Adobe charges you for online storage based on the amount of space you use. You have to decide whether the convenience outweighs the cost (see page 16 for some help). Here's how it works:

• Store the media clips you want to back up in an album.

• In the Albums panel, open Album Details by right-clicking on the album and choosing Edit.

• Under the Album name, check the Backup/Synchronize box.

Once you enable the Backup/Synchronize option, Premiere automatically copies the contents of the album to a synonymously named album on Photoshop.com. If you make a change, like adding or removing clips from the album, Premiere duplicates those changes to the online backup.

Tip: If backing up your video on Photoshop.com sounds too expensive, consider backing up your clips to an external hard drive, as described on page 136.

Filter Your View Using Star Ratings, Keyword Tags, Smart Tags, and Albums

Once you star-rate your clips, tag them with one or more keyword or smart tags, and arrange them in albums, you can use those attributes to filter clips in the Organizer and, more importantly, in Premiere.

In the Organizer, you see all your clips in the lightbox. In Premiere, you see all your clips by clicking the Organize tab and then clicking the Media button. In either view, you can filter the displayed clips by their star rating. For example in Premiere, use the Rating option and the menu next to it (Figure 4-27) to specify which clips get displayed.

Suppose you're looking for video clips of a place called Rancho Nicasio. Of course, you've dutifully applied a keyword tag for Rancho Nicasio after you imported the video. To see the Rancho Nicasio clips, in the Keyword Tags panel of the Organizer, click Places to display the tag sub-categories, which include Rancho Nicasio. When you turn on the checkbox next to Rancho Nicasio, the box displays a pair of binoculars to indicate you've selected that view, and the Organizer shows only the clips with the Rancho Nicasio tag (Figure 4-28).

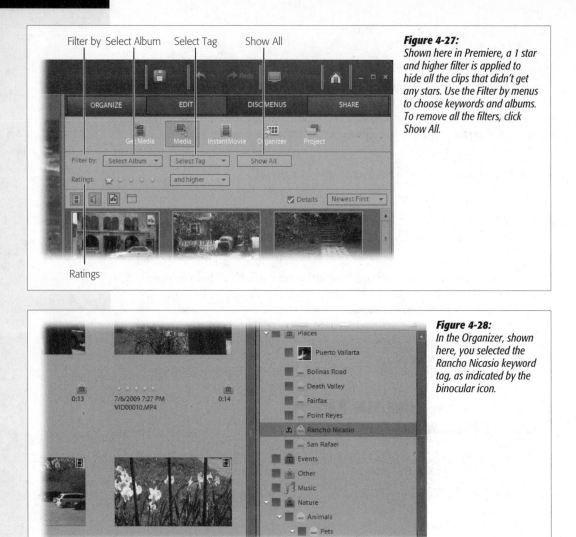

Figure 4-27:
Shown here in Premiere, a 1 star and higher filter is applied to hide all the clips that didn't get any stars. Use the Filter by menus to choose keywords and albums. To remove all the filters, click Show All.

Figure 4-28:
In the Organizer, shown here, you selected the Rancho Nicasio keyword tag, as indicated by the binocular icon.

You can also use tags to *exclude* images from a view. For example, suppose you want to view all the people shots in your catalog *except* for those tagged Rancho Nicasio and, say, Puerto Vallarta. Click the People category, and you see that all the People sub-category tags sport binoculars to show their images are included. Right-click the Rancho Nicasio tag and near the bottom of the shortcut menu choose *Exclude photos with Rancho Nicasio sub-category from search results.* Your keyword tags look like Figure 4-29. Hey, it's a little wordy for a menu option, but it gets the job done. Repeat the operation for Puerto Vallarta, and you're all set.

You can include or exclude any combination of filters, and you can use keyword tag filters along with smart tag, star rating, and album filters.

Figure 4-29:
Here, you've selected all of the sub-categories under People by simply selecting the People tag itself. In addition, you've excluded clips tagged Rancho Nicasio by right-clicking the check box and selecting "Exclude media with Rancho Nicasio sub-category from search results".

To filter your view by smart tag, follow the same procedure but select and deselect tags in the Smart Tags panel of the Organizer, where you'll find the labels that Auto-Analyzer applied to your clips.

You have to sort clips by album or by project. In the Organizer, click on the album or project in the Albums panel. In Premiere, use the Filter by drop-down menu shown in Figure 4-27.

It's great to be able to fine-tune what appears in the Organizer lightbox using filters, but you really need the filters as you're editing in Premiere. Fortunately, you filter your clips in pretty much the same way there. Go to Premiere's Organize tab and click the Select Tag menu. Choose the tags you want to include, and Premiere displays only media with tags that match (Figure 4-30). The only difference within Premiere is that you can't use filters to exclude files.

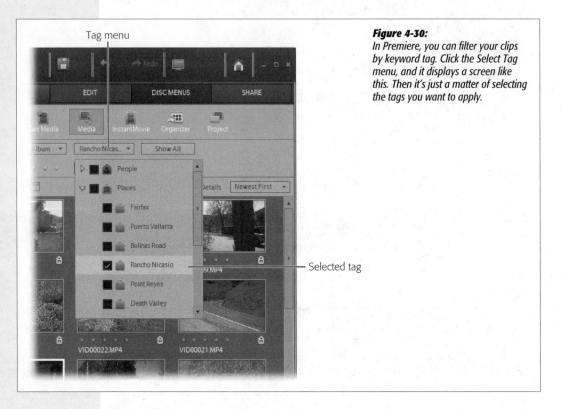

Tag menu

Figure 4-30:
In Premiere, you can filter your clips by keyword tag. Click the Select Tag menu, and it displays a screen like this. Then it's just a matter of selecting the tags you want to apply.

Selected tag

Manage Your Catalogs

Premiere calls your collection of media—that big giant pool of video clips, sound clips, and still photos—a "catalog." If you're like most people, you probably want only one catalog. That way, you only have to search one collection for all your media. Select albums, apply star and tag filters, and you'll find what you need. On the other hand, if you'd like to keep your work files in one big pool and all your family media in another pool, you can create and use two different catalogs.

When you first install Premiere (described on page 385) the Organizer is installed at the same time, and it creates a catalog called My Catalog. If you do nothing, that's the catalog where Premiere stores all your media.

But if you want to create a new catalog, say one called My Business Catalog, follow these steps:

1. **In the Organizer, choose File → Catalog (Ctrl+Shift+C).**

   The Catalog Manager panel opens, listing your existing catalogs in the box at the bottom. If you only have one catalog, it's probably the original one named My Catalog.

2. **In the upper-right corner, click New.**

   A text box appears where you name the new catalog. If you want the catalog to include the free music clips that come with Premiere, check the box labeled "Import free music into this catalog".

   If you have Premiere open, a message box explains that you must close Premiere before you create a new catalog.

3. **Type "My Business Catalog" in the text box and leave the checkbox turned on. Then click OK.**

   The Organizer creates and opens your new catalog. You can only work in one catalog at a time, so Premiere closes My Catalog. That means you're looking at a catalog with no content or maybe just some free music. Its keywords and albums are the barebones ones that Premiere creates when you first start out. It's up to you to fill My Business Catalog with new clips, tags, and albums.

Remove a Catalog

When you no longer need a catalog, remove it from the Organizer. Go to File → Catalog to open the catalog manager. Select the catalog you want to remove and then click the Remove button.

Here are a couple of things to keep in mind:

- You can't remove a catalog if it's currently open, which also means you can't remove the last catalog in the Organizer.

- You always have to have at least one catalog.

- Removing a catalog doesn't delete the clips; it just removes the catalog container.

Repair Your Catalog

A catalog is really just a collection of information that keeps track of where your media clips are. Catalogs track lots of complicated connections, and they have the unfortunate habit of getting fouled up. If that happens, use the catalog repair command to see if the Organizer can make things better. Go to File → Catalog to open the catalog manager. Select your catalog from the list at the bottom. Then, on the right, click the Repair button. A box with a progress bar appears and displays a message "Repairing Catalog." When the process is complete, you may see another box that either says no errors were found or that repairs were made.

Optimize Your Catalog

If the Organizer seems to be running sluggishly, run the Optimize tool to see if it helps. The steps are similar to the Repair process described above. Go to File → Catalog to open the Catalog Manager. Select your catalog from the list at the bottom. Then, on the right, click the Optimize button. A box with a progress bar appears while the Organizer tries to do a better job of organizing. When the Organizer finishes, it returns you to the catalog manager.

Back Up Your Entire Catalog

In general, you don't have to worry about catalogs too much, especially if you plan to have a single catalog. There is one important chore that catalogs can help with, however: backing up your files. It's probably everyone's least favorite chore, and video files are big. So if you're going to back up, make it easy on yourself and buy an external hard drive. They're inexpensive and provide tons of storage.

Plan on spending under $100 for a 500 gigabyte or 1 terabyte external drive. Get a drive that connects to your computer via a USB cable. Almost all computers have USB ports, so if disaster strikes, you can easily move all your clips to a new PC. Then follow these steps to back up everything in your catalog to the hard drive:

1. **Connect your external hard drive to your computer through the USB cable.**

   The first time you connect the drive, Windows may have to install a small helper program, called a driver. Usually, you hear a tone when your computer recognizes the hard drive.

2. **In the Organizer, choose File → Backup Catalog to CD, DVD, or Hard Drive.**

   As you can see from the steps above, you can back up your catalog to CDs, DVDs, or a hard drive. So why is a hard drive recommended? Three reasons:

   • If you back up to CDs or DVDs, you have to sit there and feed discs into your computer.

   • Optical drives (CD and DVD) work much more slowly than hard drives.

   • You'll spend more money backing up your catalog on discs as opposed to doing so on a hard drive.

   That said, go ahead and use discs in a pinch. They're better than no backups at all.

3. **Choose Full Backup and click Next.**

   If this is your first backup, choose Full Backup to back up all the clips in your catalog. Choose Incremental Backup if you want to back up only clips that have changed since the last backup.

   When you click Next, you see the second panel in the backup window.

4. **In the Select Destination Drive box, choose where you want to store the backups.**

The list shows all the drives connected to your computer—CD, DVD, or external hard drive. It even lists any network drives available to you. If you want to select a specific folder within a drive, click the Browse button to locate the folder.

5. **Click Done.**

The Organizer displays a progress bar while it backs up the files. If there isn't enough room on the destination drive, you see an alert box that says "Your system is low on disk space and Elements cannot perform this operation. Try removing some files to free up disk space."

Part Two:
Create Your Movie

2

Edit Your Movie

Now that you've imported, organized, and tagged your clips, it's time to roll up your sleeves and make something out of the bits and pieces of your project. Video editing is similar to other creative activities, like painting or playwriting. Every editor has his own technique. Along the way, you learn a craftsman's tricks of the trade, and, more important, you learn what techniques work for you. At this point, the basic steps include reviewing and selecting clips, trimming them down to just the right frames, and arranging them to tell a story.

In this chapter, you'll start to develop your editing style. For some projects, you may lean more toward an automated, quick-and-easy approach. You'll be interested in Premiere's InstantMovie and Smart Trim features and how you can take advantage of the information Premiere stores in smart tags. For other projects, you may choose a more meticulous, handcrafted approach, where you edit each audio and sound clip with a keen eye.

In either case, you need to know editing tools like the sceneline, timeline, the Monitor window, the Project View, and the Preview window.

Choose Your Editing Style

Premiere is a versatile tool. You can use its automated editing features, letting Premiere make a lot of decisions for you, or you can assemble your movie and fine-tune each clip and transition just as a Hollywood film editor would. The approach you choose depends on the project, your sensibilities, your patience, and the amount of time you can spend on a given project. When you want to piece together a quick video of yesterday's birthday party, you may choose the automated approach. If you're producing a documentary of your bike club's annual race, you might go for the handcrafted approach.

The next two sections describe the tools and techniques for these different approaches, but they're not entirely an "either/or" proposition. You may find yourself mixing and matching approaches depending on the project, so you'll learn both styles. For example, you can use some of the quick-and-easy tools, like Smart Trim, to help you in a handcrafted project. The short lists below identify the tools and techniques available for each method.

The Automated Quick-and-Easy Approach

Premiere Elements 8 has more "smart" features than any of its predecessors. You've already heard about InstantMovie and the Auto-Analyzer. Actually, the Auto-Analyzer does quite a bit of work behind the scenes as it studies your video and audio clips, and it uses the results of that analysis in some of Premiere's other "smart" features to make decisions. Here are some of the things that those smart features can handle for you:

- Split video clips into scenes. See page 124.

- Identify high-, medium-, and low-quality scenes. See page 120.

- Identify image problems and apply fixes. See page 121.

- Trim clips for content and quality. See page 121.

- Adjust soundtrack (music) and live audio volume. See page 310.

- Find and track moving objects within a video.

- Identify clips that have faces in them. See page 122.

- Automatically assemble clips into a movie, complete with transitions and special effects. See page 28.

The quick-and-easy upside: Every decision Premiere makes saves you time. The downside: You and Premiere may, as they say in the film industry, have creative differences.

The Handcrafted Approach

When you edit video using the "handcrafted" approach, you analyze your video and other media and make all the decisions about the clips, including the order in which you want them to play back, how to trim them, and which transitions and special effects best suit your project. You also choose the soundtrack, music, sound effects, and live audio.

For serious projects, you should know your footage backward and forward to make the best editing decisions. In fact, by the time you burn your project to DVD, you may be tired of watching it.

The steps for handcrafting a video look like this, though the order can vary a bit:

- Review and trim clips. See Rough Trim Clips (page 152) and Final Trim Clips (page 166).

- Assemble clips in sequence. See "Assemble Your Movie in the Sceneline" (page 160) or "Assemble Your Movie in the Timeline" (page 162).

- Add transitions. See page 175.

- Add special effects. See page 195.

- Add a soundtrack. See page 291.

- Mix the audio. See page 309.

- Encode the video. See page 315.

- Publish your movie to DVD, website, or computer file. For DVD publishing, see page 337. For web publishing, see page 323. For exporting your movie to computer files, see page 380.

The handcrafted upside: Your video has the look and feel you want. The downside: You spend a lot more time sitting at your computer using Premiere's manual tools.

Gather Clips, Pictures, and Animation

Earlier chapters explained how to start a project, import clips, and organize your media in a general way. This section explains how to gather and review your media while working on a specific project. This is where those earlier organizational chores, like tagging clips and creating albums, pays off. When you assemble your video, you'll be able to quickly put your hand on that great shot of the SUVs making their way through Death Valley. You can spend more time assembling your movie and less time hunting down clips.

The tools you use to control which clips appear in the Media View are near the top of the panel shown in Figure 5-1. You use the "Filter by" menus, the star ratings, and the media buttons. Try to follow this order because the filters have a cumulative effect:

- Next to "Filter by", use the Select Album menu to choose a project or album.

- Use the Select Tag menu to select the tags for the clips you want to see.

- Use the Star Rating option and its adjacent menu to limit the clips displayed.

- Use the Media buttons to show and hide video clips, audio clips, and still images.

- Use the Set Date Range button to limit the displayed clips to a specific time period.

- Use the Sort menu to determine the order the clips are displayed.

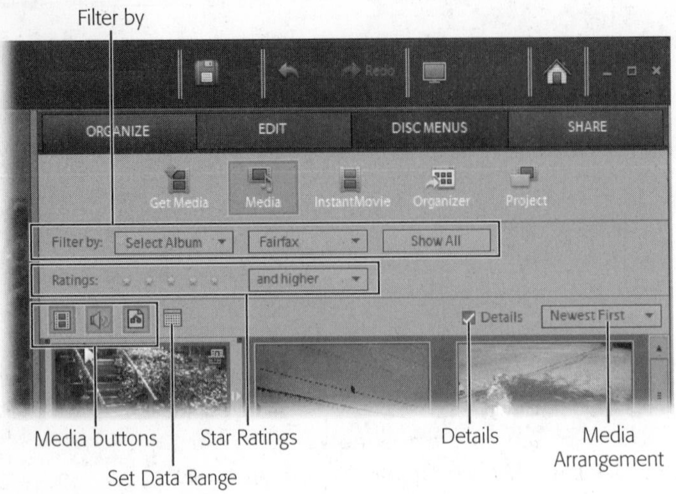

Filter by

Figure 5-1:
*Premiere offers all the tools you need
to select clips at the top of the Media
View on the Organize tab. If you
apply them in order from top to
bottom, left to right, you gradually
winnow down to the few the specific
clips you need for a project.*

Media buttons   Star Ratings   Details   Media
                                                       Arrangement
            Set Data Range

Choose Clips by Project

When you start Premiere, you must choose to work on an existing project or create a new one. Either way, as you import or add media using the Get Media tool,
Premiere considers those clips part of that project. The same holds true for any
clips you add to the timeline or sceneline in a project.

To see your project's clips in the Media View, use Premiere's "Filter by" menu.
There, the Select Album menu (Figure 5-2) lists albums at the top and projects at
the bottom. So if your project's name is "Death Valley Days," you see *Death Valley
Days.prel* toward the bottom of the Select Album menu. (Adobe uses the filename
extension *.prel* to denote Premiere Elements project files.) When you select a
project or album in the list, you see a pair of binoculars next to the project or
album name. Choosing a project from the menu is a handy way to exclude the
clips in your catalog that aren't part of your project. If you don't have either a
project or an album selected, Premiere displays all the media clips in your catalog.

Choose Clips by Album

As explained on page 126, you use albums to collect lots of clips into a single
group. You create albums in Elements Organizer and select them using filters in
Premiere. You can include an individual clip in more than one album. You can
also create album categories to collect albums into groups, and you can nest one
album category inside of another. In fact, it's possible to import clips into the
Organizer and place them in albums without ever bringing them into a Premiere
project. You display the contents of an album using the "Filter by" menu shown in
Figure 5-2.

You can only choose one album or one project at a time. If you choose neither,
Premiere displays all the clips in your catalog.

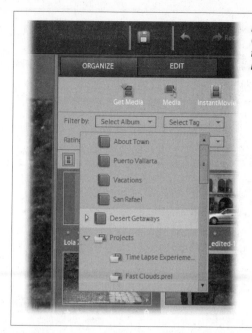

Figure 5-2:
Click the Select Album menu, and you see media albums listed at the top and projects (shown here) listed at the bottom. Project names include the .prel extension.

Deselect a Project or Album Filter

Since you can apply only one project or album filter at a time, selecting a new filter automatically deselects the previous one. But what if you don't want *any* project or album filter? Click the Show All button to remove all filters, including the tag, album, star, and media filters. Choose that option if you want to see absolutely everything in your catalog. However, if you only want to remove a project or album filter, just click the selected filter, which is indicated by the binoculars icon. The icon disappears and the filter is toggled off.

Choose Clips by Tags

You can cumulatively limit the clips the Organizer displays by selecting tags within a project, as shown in Figure 5-3. Next to the "Filter by" label, click Select Tag and choose the tags you want from the drop-down menu. So for example, if you're working on the Death Valley Days project, and you select the "Steve" tag, you only see clips of Steve at Death Valley. You can select several tags at once, so you could choose both the Steve tag and the Karen tag to display clips tagged with both "Steve" and "Karen". You can select both keyword tags *and* smart tags (which appear at the bottom of the Select Tag menu). That way, you can find all the "High Quality" clips with Steve and Karen in them.

Note: In the Elements Organizer application, you can select tags in a way that either includes or excludes clips. In Premiere's Organize *tab,* you can only *include* clips.

Figure 5-3:
In Media View, click to select one or more tags from one or more categories, such as Places, Family, or Friends. Premiere then displays the clips bearing these tags.

Choose Clips by Star Rating

As you learned earlier (see page 110), Premiere's star ratings let you rank clips using a five-star system. You can use any criteria you want for the ratings, but most filmmakers and photographers use the star rating as a general gauge of a clip's quality. To filter your clips using the star rating, click on a star in the Organizer or the Media panel of Premiere's Organize tab. Then, next to the rating, use the menu shown in Figure 5-4 to choose one of the three options: "and higher", "and lower", or "only". When you set a star rating filter, Premiere never displays clips that have no star rating.

Tip: You can add or change a star rating as you work with clips in Media View. Make sure you check the Details box so you can see the star ratings, then simply click the appropriate star under a clip to set the rating.

Filter Clips by Media Type

Under the star rating buttons, you show and hide different types of media using three toggle buttons: Video, Audio, and Still Image. Once you select a button, it has a thin frame around it. Use the fourth button of the group to set a date range for the displayed clips (Figure 5-5).

Sort Clips by Date

Use the Sort menu on the right side of the Organize tab (Figure 5-1) to show clips in chronological or reverse chronological order, the only two options available. Newest First is handy when you just imported or added clips to your project. Oldest First is helpful when you want to arrange clips in the order you shot them.

Figure 5-4:
*You can filter displayed clips by star rating. Click a star and
then choose one of the menu options. Premiere applies the
rating filter in addition to any other tag or album filters
it applies.*

Show/Hide Video
Show/Hide Audio
Show/Hide Still Image
Set Date Range

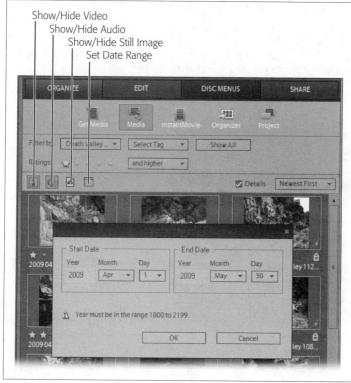

Figure 5-5:
*Click the Set Date Range button and you
see this panel, where you can enter a
start date and an end date for the clips
you want to see.*

Display Clip Details

Sometimes, a thumbnail doesn't provide enough detail about your clips. To learn more, click the Details checkbox (Figure 5-1) to see the clip's file name, star rating, and icons that indicate whether or not you tagged a clip; a purple tag indicates a smart-tagged clip. The other colored tags match the colors assigned to keyword tags. If you hold your cursor over a clip, you see the filename and folder path for it. If you want more details on the clip, use the Available Media panel described in the next section.

Show the Project View

You see thumbnails of your video clips in three places: in the Organizer and under the Premiere Organize tab's Media View and Project View (see Figure 5-6). As explained on page 100, the Organizer is a standalone program that Premiere Elements and Photoshop Elements share. You first learned about Premiere's Media View in Chapter 1 (page 15). The Project View deserves a little more of an introduction. One major difference between the two is that Media View lets you view *all* the media in your catalog, while Project View shows you only clips that are part of your open project. In other words, Project View shows you the clips you added to your project using the Get Media command while you had the project open. If you drag clips from the Media View onto a project's sceneline or timeline, Premiere also adds them to your project and the Project View.

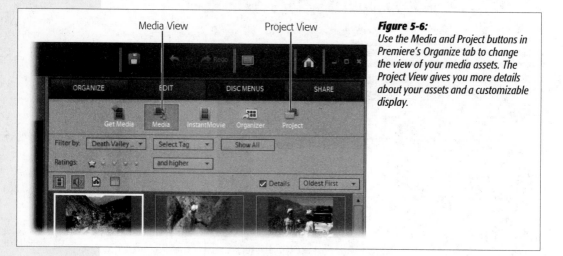

Figure 5-6:
Use the Media and Project buttons in Premiere's Organize tab to change the view of your media assets. The Project View gives you more details about your assets and a customizable display.

If you're a fan of the "handcrafted" video-editing approach, you want to learn all about Project View. It offers several features you don't find in either the Organizer or Media View. Project View is customizable, so you can display details like how many times you used a clip, the timing of the In and Out points, and the duration of the clip. Want to add custom comments, like a client's name, a scene name, or a log note? The Project View gives you the tools.

Open Project View by clicking the Project button or choosing Window → Available Media (if you plan to use the latter option often, you may want to memorize the keyboard shortcut: Alt+W, A). Double-click a clip in the Project View, and it opens in the Preview window, where you trim a clip before placing it in the timeline.

Tip: You can use keyboard shortcuts for nearly every Premiere menu command, even the ones that don't list a shortcut next to the menu option. Press the Alt key and you see underlined letters in the menu names. For example, press Alt and you see the *W* in Window become underlined, so you can press Alt+W to open the Window menu. Then, when Premiere opens the Window menu, each menu option within it has an underlined letter. At this point, you can press *A* to open the Available Media panel, *Z* to see the Organize tab, or *R* to see the Properties window.

The by-now-familiar "Filter by" buttons at the top of Project View let you choose whether you want to display video clips, audio clips, still pictures, or some combination of the three.

Project View gives you the choice of two modes, List View or Icon View. You toggle between them using the buttons in the lower-left corner of the Project panel or by using Ctrl+PgUp for List View and Ctrl+PgDn for Icon View. Of the two modes, List is the most helpful because it offers more details about your clips, including media type (audio, video, or still image), frame rate, duration, and the number of times you used a media file in the current project. Icon mode is similar to the Organize tab view, listing just the file name and clip duration.

You use the other buttons in that lower-corner neighborhood to create folders (to organize clips within the Project View), navigate folders, and delete clips (Figure 5-7).

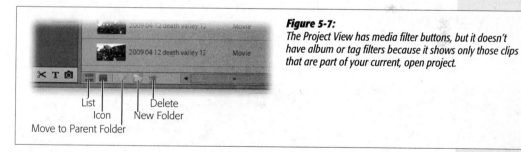

Figure 5-7:
The Project View has media filter buttons, but it doesn't have album or tag filters because it shows only those clips that are part of your current, open project.

List
Icon
Move to Parent Folder
Delete
New Folder

View Clip Properties in Project View

The handiest and most interesting thing about the Project View is the way it displays clip details in table format. Each column in the table presents details about your clip. Here are some examples, not necessarily in the order you first see them:

• **Thumbnail.** This is the same thumbnail image you see in the Organize tab.

• **Name.** Initially, this is the filename for the clip, but you can change the name here by clicking on it and typing in a new, more useful name.

- **Used.** Checkmarks mean the clip is currently in your project's timeline.

- **Media Type.** Lets you know whether the item is a movie, audio, a still or a folder.

- **Frame Rate.** Lists the frame rate in the standard measure, frames per second.

- **Media Duration.** Shows the clip's duration as hrs;mins;seconds;frames.

- **Video Usage.** Displays the number of times you used the video clip in the project.

- **Audio Usage.** Displays the number of times you used the audio clip in a project.

- **Comment.** Here you can add any notes or comments that describe the clip or help you in your work. You can save lots of clip-reviewing time by adding descriptive comments to your clips. For example, a note that says "Great footage of Jeeps in desert, marred by sun flare at 02;18;26" may help you decide whether or not to use a clip without taking the time to review it again.

As helpful as some of these details are, there're even better ones hidden away. For example, if you shot all your video with a single camera, you may not be too concerned about frame rate since all the clips will have the same frame rate. On the other hand, it might be very helpful to see the *In* and *Out* points for your clips.

Customize the Project View

Initially, Project View displays your clips and their properties in a table arrangement as shown in Figure 5-8. You're not limited to this arrangement, though. Click a column heading to sort the clips according to that property. So, by clicking on the Video Usage heading, you can make the clips you use the most jump to the top of the table. A second click reverses the sort order, putting unused and seldom-used clips at the top. You can rearrange the order of the columns themselves by clicking their headings and dragging them to a new location.

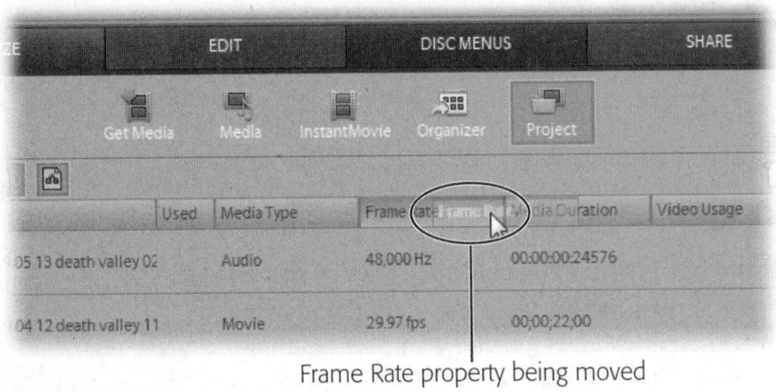

Figure 5-8:
You can customize the Project View in a couple of ways. You can choose which properties Premiere displays and you can click and drag the headings to reorder the properties. Here, the Frame Rate (circled) is being dragged to a less prominent location.

Frame Rate property being moved

The clip properties that Premiere initially displays are only a fraction of those available. To see the whole list and pick and choose among them, follow these steps:

1. **Choose Window → Show Docking Headers.**

   An extra header appears above each of the panels. (When you first install and run Premiere, Adobe keeps the workspace simplified and doesn't display the docking headers. They give you additional ways to customize your workspace.)

2. **Choose the Project View button, if you aren't already in Project View.**

   The docking header for Project View says Tasks on the right side. On the left side, there are two triangle icons that open the Available Media panel menu (Figure 5-9).

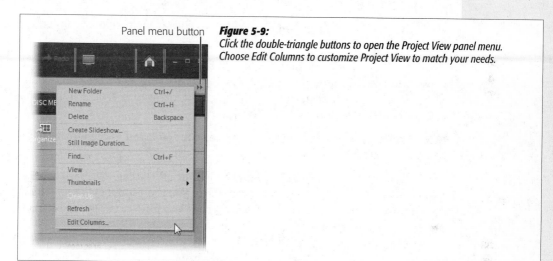

Panel menu button

Figure 5-9:
Click the double-triangle buttons to open the Project View panel menu. Choose Edit Columns to customize Project View to match your needs.

3. **Click the panel menu button and then choose Edit Columns.**

   The Edit Columns panel (Figure 5-10) shows all the properties that Premiere can display in the Available Media panel. Use the scroll bar to see the complete list.

4. **Click to turn on the boxes next to the properties you want to appear in the Available Media panel. You can also deselect properties you *don't* want displayed.**

   Using the buttons on the right side of the Edit Columns window, shown in Figure 5-10, you can rename properties or add new ones. You can change the order of the properties using the Move Up and Move Down buttons, but it's easier to make those changes as described in the following steps.

5. **Click OK.**

   The Edit Columns panel closes and you see just the Project View columns you want.

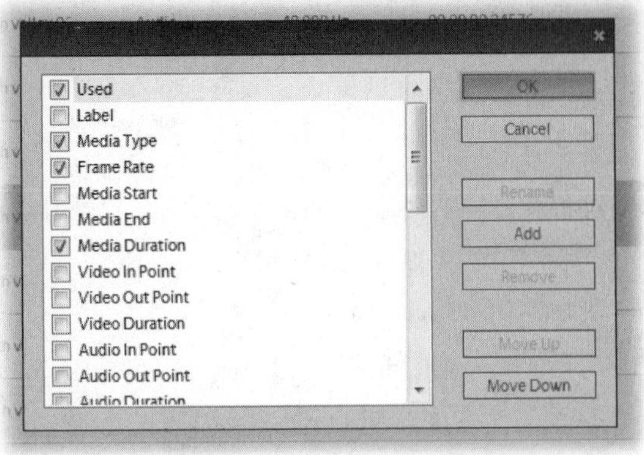

Figure 5-10:
Click an empty box to place checkmarks next to the properties you want displayed. You can even rename properties or add your own, new, properties.

6. (Optional) Click and drag column headers to rearrange the columns' order.

For example, if you want Media Duration right next to the clips' name, drag the header over. You can customize the columns however you want. And if you want to give a column more room, resize it by moving your cursor to the line between column headers and, when the cursor changes to a vertical line with two arrows, drag to a new column width.

Once you have the Project View set up the way you want, you'll see more detail on your clips, including your own comments.

From Project View, you can review and trim your clips using the Preview panel that pops up when you double-click a clip. Then you can drop these rough-edited clips into your timeline. Many editors jump back and forth between Project View and Media View as they work.

Review and Rough-Trim Your Clips

You have to review a clip to decide whether or not it's worthy of your project. In fact, for most handcrafted projects, you'll view your clips over and over as you rate, tag, arrange, and trim them. Fortunately, it's not hard to work with clips. No matter which tools you use to organize and assemble your movie, it's easy to review and trim your clips as you work. When you work in Project View, you use the Preview window. When you work in Media View, you use the tools in the sceneline and timeline.

Review Clips in the Preview Window

If you're in Project View, double-click a clip and the Preview window opens as shown in Figure 5-11. In the Preview window, you can use the standard DVD-like controls to move through your clip. It's also a great place to "rough-trim" your video. A rough trim usually cuts off both ends of a clip, selecting the good bits that

How Premiere Protects Your Original Clips

When you edit a movie in Premiere, you're never working on the raw files you import. If you were and you made a mistake, that raw footage would be lost to the ages—you'll never be able to recreate that charming shot of Junior's first encounter with a dog.

To safeguard against such a calamity, Premiere imports your originals and stores them away (in a location you select). It then creates *copies* of those originals so that when you work in Premiere, you're working on those copies (which Premiere and this book call "previews", not to be confused with the act of previewing an in-progress movie).

Once you finish editing your movie and you're ready to share it with the world, Premiere goes back to those original files, using the "map" you created with the preview clips, and assembles your finished movie using the original files as the source material—that way, you create a finished film using the highest quality video and audio files possible.

Incidentally, the act of assembling and saving a finished video file is also called "exporting" a video.

you're most likely to use. Don't worry about fine-tuning the trim, because you may not be able to make those decisions until you see the clip next to the adjacent clips in the timeline.

Figure 5-11:
The Preview window gives you a great workspace to review and rough-cut your clips. If the view isn't big enough, click and drag an edge of the window to resize it.

In Marker   Playhead (Current Time Indicator)   Good bits   Step Back   Out Marker   Trimmed end   Step Forward

Here's how you review and rough-trim a clip in the Preview window:

1. **Double-click on a clip in Project View.**

   The Preview window opens with the clip loaded.

2. **Click the Play button (or press the space bar) to watch the clip.**

   As you view the clip, identify the portion you want to use. As good a cinematographer as you are, it's unlikely you'll use an entire clip very often. More likely, you'll want just a portion of it. To isolate that portion, you need to tell Premiere where you want the clip to begin (called the clip's *In point*) and where you want it to end (called the *Out point*).

   Use the video control buttons in the Preview window to move through your clip (or use shortcut keys described in the box on page 155). Go through it as many times as you need.

3. **Identify the clip's In point.**

   As you review the clip on a second or third pass, you probably know about where you want to put its In point. You can get to that point a couple of ways:

   • As you review the clip on subsequent passes, press the Pause button to stop playback near the In point.

   • Position the playhead (which Premiere calls the Current Time Indicator or CTI) where you want the *In* mark. You can drag the playhead to any position on the clip.

4. **Fine-tune the In point.**

   Use the transport tools, including the single-frame-forward button (Step Forward) and the single-frame-back button (Step Back), to locate just the right frame.

   When you click the Set In button, the clip's *unselected* segment (the portion from the beginning of the clip to your newly set In point) turns gray. The *selected* segment gets highlighted in purple.

5. **Identify the clip's Out point.**

   Pause playback or position the playhead where you want the *Out* mark, fine-tune it with the frame-by-frame buttons, and then click the Set Out button.

   At this point, you've trimmed off the two ends of the clip and selected the segment you want to use, highlighted in purple.

6. **Click the X button in the upper-right corner of the Preview window.**

   The Preview window closes, but Premiere remembers how you trimmed the clip. Later, when you add the clip to the timeline, Premiere automatically uses only the portion within the In and Out marks. Don't worry, though, you can still use the trimmed portions of a clip if you change your mind later; remember,

Premiere leaves the original clip intact, so if you double-click the clip to bring it into the Preview window, you can reset the In and Out points (or select entirely new points to select a different portion of the clip).

It seems you never stop reviewing clips while you're editing. You can review clips and set In and Out marks while you assemble clips in the sceneline or timeline, as described in the next sections. As you work in the Preview window and the timeline, you can speed things up by using the shortcut keys (page 155).

UP TO SPEED

Shortcut Keys for Viewing Video

When your hand is on the mouse, it's easy to click the Play and Rewind buttons in the preview and monitor windows. But if your hands are on the keyboard, it's faster to use shortcut keys. The shortcut keys are also great for jumping to specific points in your movie. Here's a list of handy shortcuts:

Space bar: Play/Pause
Home: Jump to beginning of movie

End: Jump to end of movie
PgUp: Jump to beginning of clip
PgDn: Jump to end of clip
Right arrow: Move forward 1 frame
Left arrow: Move back 1 frame
Shift-right arrow: Move forward 5 frames
Shift-left arrow: Move Back 5 frames

Review Clips in the Sceneline

Click the Sceneline button, and you see a series of large and small boxes along the bottom of the Premiere window. Drag a clip from the Project or Media window into one of the big boxes, and Premiere adds it to your movie. (The small boxes hold transitions, like dissolves or fades, which you'll learn about on page 175.)

The sceneline is a great tool when you're ready to sequence your video clips. That's because it's actually a storyboard. As you pop your trimmed clips into the boxes, the clips' thumbnails appear there, giving you a sense of what your finished movie will look like.

The sceneline handles some of the same chores as the timeline, but its simplified tools make things like arranging clips a little easier. (For more about the differences between the sceneline and the timeline, see the box on page 159.) The sceneline doesn't display the audio that's synched with a video clip, but there are two tracks at the bottom of it for music and sound effects or narration.

Once you add clips to the sceneline, you can review them in Premiere's monitor. Click a clip, and the monitor displays the scene's first frame, along with a mini-timeline at the bottom of the monitor, complete with In and Out markers as shown in Figure 5-12. To trim a clip here, drag either the In or Out marker. You can change the scale of the mini-timeline to zoom in to see fewer frames or zoom out to see more. Just above the time scale, you see a thin, horizontal bar with arrows on each end; drag an arrow to adjust the scale of the mini-timeline.

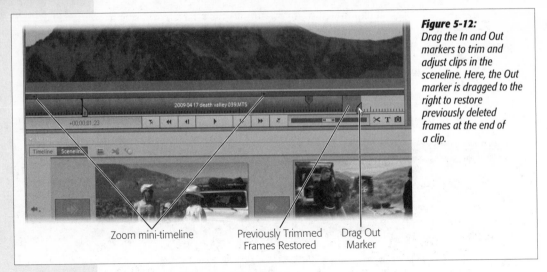

Figure 5-12:
Drag the In and Out markers to trim and adjust clips in the sceneline. Here, the Out marker is dragged to the right to restore previously deleted frames at the end of a clip.

Zoom mini-timeline   Previously Trimmed   Drag Out
                          Frames Restored   Marker

Review Clips in the Timeline

The timeline gives you a different view of the same movie. If you add three clips using the boxes in the sceneline and then click the timeline button, you see those same three clips end-to-end, displayed in the Video 1 and Audio 1 tracks of the timeline (Figure 5-13).

Figure 5-13:
Here are two views of the same movie.

Top: Three video clips appear in the sceneline.

Bottom: The same three clips as they appear in the timeline, where they occupy the Video 1 and Audio 1 tracks.

Timeline
   Sceneline

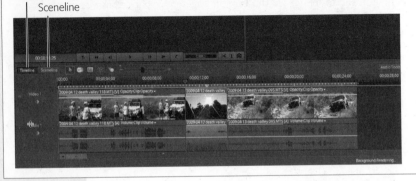

It can be a little hard to tell where one clip ends and another begins in the timeline; click anywhere on a clip, and Premiere highlights it in purple, making the
boundaries of the clip clear. Unlike the sceneline, when you select a clip in the
timeline, it doesn't automatically show up in the monitor. In the timeline, the
image the monitor displays is governed entirely by the position of the playhead, as
shown in Figure 5-14.

Figure 5-14:
*A selected clip appears
highlighted in purple, but
because the playhead
sits over a different
portion of the timeline,
that's the image that
appears in the monitor.*

Playhead   Selected clip

Follow these steps to review and trim video clips while you work in the timeline:

1. **Create and name a new project using the File → New → Project command.**

   Premiere creates a new project with an empty timeline. The Tasks panel displays
   the Organize tab and the contents of your media catalog.

2. **Below the monitor on the left, click the timeline button.**

   If the timeline's already displayed, you can skip this step. In any case, you see
   the timeline view across the bottom of the screen. A time scale appears at the
   top, with labels for the different tracks, such as Video 1 and Audio 1, displayed
   on the left side.

3. **Drag a video clip from the catalog to the beginning of Video 1 track.**

   Place the left edge of the clip all the way to the left end of the track, where the scale reads 00;00;00;00. Sometimes, you need to use the Project window's horizontal and vertical scrollbar to find your spot in the timeline. Use the scrollbar on the right to see the different tracks. For example, above Video 1 you can find the tracks Video 2 and Audio 2.

4. **On your keyboard, press *V*.**

   The keyboard shortcut V changes your cursor to Premiere's Selection tool, which you use to select and trim clips. If you've got your hand full of mouse, you can also click the arrow icon above the timeline (see Figure 5-15).

5. **Move your mouse to the right end of the clip on the timeline.**

   When you have the cursor over the edge of the clip, it changes from an arrow to a trim cursor—a bracket with two arrows. The open end of the bracket always faces the clip you're trimming. This is helpful to know when you put the cursor over a splice where two clips meet—the open bracket always tells you which of the clips you're trimming.

6. **Drag the trim cursor to the right to trim the clip, then release the mouse.**

   As you drag to the right, you make the clip longer by adding frames. You can keep adding frames, as long as they're available in the original clip (at some point, you come to the end of your raw footage). As you adjust the trim, Premiere displays a tooltip showing how much time you're adding or removing from a clip.

   Remember, Premiere never alters your original clips (it creates a copy of it for editing purposes, which it calls a "preview" version), so any frames that were there at the beginning are always available when you edit. Why would you want to extend a clip beyond your initial edit points? You may discover you need a little more footage to accommodate a transition or special effect.

7. **Now, click the edge of the lengthened the clip and drag it to the left.**

   Dragging the edge to the left removes the frames you just added. You can keep tweaking the In and Out points for clips up until you're ready to export your final film.

8. **Click the left edge of the clip and drag it to the right.**

   In this step, you're removing frames from the beginning of the clip. It's the same as setting a new In point for the clip. Notice how the front edge of a clip automatically snaps to the first frame position in the timeline.

As you'll learn later, you assemble a movie by dragging additional clips to the timeline, placing them snug against each other, and fine-tuning their edit points as described above.

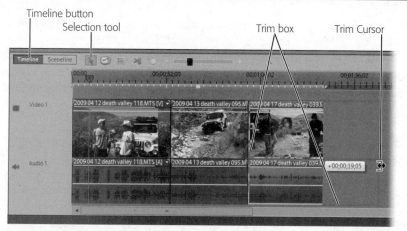

Timeline button
Selection tool
Trim box
Trim Cursor

Figure 5-15:
Use Premiere's Selection tool (V) to trim clips in the timeline. When you hold the cursor at the edge of a clip, it changes to the trim cursor (shown here). Click and drag to trim your clips.

Sceneline vs. Timeline

Should I use the sceneline or the timeline?

The sceneline and the timeline give you two different views of the same territory—your movie (Figure 5-13). There's nothing wrong with choosing the tool that works best for you. In general, the sceneline meshes with the quick-and-easy approach to editing, while the timeline lends itself to the handcrafted approach.

The **sceneline** works like a storyboard. For ages, filmmaker's have used storyboards to plot out their movies. Individual frames (usually hand-drawn) represent a segment of a scene. Piece together a few of these segments, and you have a quick way to communicate the way a story sequence unfolds. You can use the sceneline this way.

A single video frame represents each clip and visually tells part of the story. By glancing at the sceneline boxes, you can understand how one action leads to the next. The major disadvantage of the sceneline is that you can't tell at a glance how long a clip is—they all look the same.

The **timeline** gives you a more traditional, video-editor's view of your project. The time scale at the top gives you a reference for your entire movie and for each clip. It's easy to look at any clip and determine its length and relationship to the rest of your movie. Every bit of media in your project appears in a track, and you can even see visual representations of transitions and volume changes in your audio tracks. When you dig deep, the timeline offers a slew of tools for tweaking your movie.

If you're an old hand at video editing, you may be inclined to use only the timeline. There's nothing wrong with that. If you're a fan of the quick-and-easy approach to editing, you may want to stick with the sceneline.

If you're like most Premiere Elements editors, you'll probably jump back and forth, depending on the chore you're tackling at the moment. For example, the sceneline is great for your first crack at assembling clips in a sequence, while the timeline is the tool for fine-tuning transitions, audio, and complex visual effects. So, don't hesitate to explore both tools before you get set in your video editing ways.

Assemble Your Movie

You can put your movie together using either the sceneline or the timeline. Whether you use the sceneline's boxes or the timeline's tracks, the act of putting one clip after another is easy; choosing the *best* sequence is a little more challenging, and that's where the art of movie editing comes in. That means you won't necessarily get it right the first time. So you'll spend some time editing In and Out points, rearranging clips, and swapping one for another as you work.

Assemble Your Movie in the Sceneline

In the sceneline, you build your movie by dragging clips and scenes into the boxes (Figure 5-16). To see the current state of your movie, press the Home button to automatically go to the beginning of your movie, and then press the space bar or click the monitor's Play button. You change the order of clips simply by dragging them to different boxes. When you drag a clip to a box that already holds a clip, Premiere pushes the existing clip (and all its neighbors) toward the beginning or the end of the sceneline and replaces the resident clip with the one you drop in. As you do so, Premiere displays a blue vertical line showing you where in the sceneline the new clip will end up.

Here's a short list of what you can do in the sceneline:

- **Add your first clip to the sceneline.** Drag a clip to the first box, and you've started assembling your movie. You can get the clip from Premiere's Media or Project View. The box displays the first frame of the clip. If the clip was smart-tagged and divided into scenes (as described on page 124), each scene occupies its own box in the sceneline.

- **Add a clip to the end of the movie.** To add the next scene in your movie, drag another clip to the next empty box. When you play back your movie-in-progress, they play in sequence without time gaps between clips.

- **Add a scene from a clip.** If you want to add a single scene from a clip that Auto-Analyzer divvied up into multiple scenes, in Media View, click the button on the right edge of the stacked clips to display each scene. Drag the scene you want to a box in the sceneline.

- **Review clips or scenes in the sceneline.** Click on the clip in the sceneline and press the space bar. Your clip plays in the monitor and if you let it, it continues to play the rest of the clips to the end of the movie. You can use any of the monitor tools to move around and review the scenes you're assembling, including the shortcut keys described on page 155.

- **Remove a clip or scene from the sceneline.** Select the scene you want to remove and press the Delete key, or right-click the scene and click "Delete just scene" from the drop-down menu. Premiere removes the clip and any overlays it has, such as titles or superimposed pictures (more on those fancy features on pages 267 and 261). The other clips move to close the gap left by the deleted scene. (Remember, you're not really deleting the clip from your project, it's still sitting in your catalog in the Project Panel.)

- **Reposition a clip in the sceneline.** Select the clip in the sceneline and drag it in front of another scene. The scene and its overlays move to the new spot. If you Shift-drag, a menu asks if you want to "Move Scene and its objects" or "Move just scene".

- **Insert a clip in the middle of a movie.** To place a clip in front of another clip that's already in the sceneline, drag the new clip on top of the clip in the sceneline. Again, the blue vertical bar shows you the clip's destination.

- **Insert a clip in the middle of another clip or scene.** In the monitor, position the playhead where you want to divide a clip that's in the sceneline. Shift-drag the new clip you want to insert onto the monitor (not the sceneline or timeline). There are several special effects you can create by Shift-dragging one clip onto another in the monitor, so a pop-up menu asks which you want. Choose "Split and Insert".

Tip: Don't forget the ever-faithful Undo key (Ctrl+Z). It's often the quickest way to fix a mistake or backtrack as you edit and assemble a movie. It works in both the sceneline and the timeline. If you undo too much, use Redo (Ctrl+Shift+Z) to, ahem, undo your Undo.

Figure 5-16:
Drag clips into the large boxes in the sceneline to assemble your movie. You use the small boxes for transitions between the scenes. You can drag clips from the Media View or from the Project View.

Video clip   Drag to zoom the mini-timeline   Boxes for transition

Assemble Your Movie in the Timeline

Assembling your movie in the timeline is similar to doing so in the sceneline, but the view's entirely different. Drag a clip from the Media or Project panel onto the timeline, and video and audio tracks pop into place instead of a thumbnail. The scale at the top of the timeline displays the movie's timecode (in *hours;minutes;seconds;frames* format). Hold your cursor over a clip, and a tooltip shows you the exact moment it begins and ends.

Just above the scale, you find the set of buttons shown in Figure 5-17; they help you select clips and zoom in and out on the timeline.

In the timeline, you can "link" clips, meaning you can lock the video and audio tracks together so they act as one. When you move linked tracks around the timeline they stay together unless you use an explicit command that unlinks them. Other times, you may add video- and audio-only tracks to the timeline.

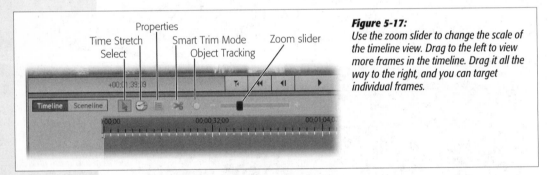

Figure 5-17:
Use the zoom slider to change the scale of the timeline view. Drag to the left to view more frames in the timeline. Drag it all the way to the right, and you can target individual frames.

- **Add your first clip to the timeline.** Drag a clip from Media or Project View to the 00;00;00;00 position in the timeline. When you first create a project, Premiere gives it several video tracks. You main movie is built on the tracks Video 1 and Audio 1. You use the tracks above that, Video 2 and Audio 2, for special effects and overlays like picture-in-picture (see page 261 for a full description).

- **Add a clip to the end of the movie.** Drag another clip to the timeline and put it right after the first clip. As your cursor gets close to the end of the first clip, the second clip automatically snaps to the end of the first, making a snug fit. When you first install Premiere, it enables a feature called Snap (Timeline → Snap). This makes it easy to butt one clip against another without a high degree of mouse marksmanship. Press S to toggle Snap on and off. With Snap off, it's easy to place a clip in the middle of another clip, splitting it into two parts in the process, as described below.

- **Add a scene from a clip.** Premiere's Auto-Analyzer divides some clips into individual scenes, as explained on page 124. In the Organize tab, clips holding multiple scenes appear with a thick, light-gray border, an icon in the upper-right corner, and a Group Open button on the right edge of the frame. Click the Group Open button to expand the clip into its multiple scenes, and then drag the scene you want to the timeline.

- **Review clips or scenes in the timeline.** To move the playhead to a particular point in your movie, click on the timescale. The playhead jumps to the spot you click. Then press the space bar or click the Play button to watch your video at normal speed. You can use any of the video transport buttons under the monitor to go to a specific spot in your video. When you work in the timeline, you'll find the Go To Previous Edit Point and Go To Next Edit Point buttons and the shuttle particularly helpful (see Figure 5-18). You can also use the keyboard shortcuts mentioned on page 155.

Figure 5-18:
The buttons under the monitor help you move quickly or slowly through your movie. Use the "Go to" buttons to jump to edit points. Use the "Step" buttons to move a frame at a time. The shuttle let's you move at variable speed.

Go to Previous Edit Point
Rewind
Step Back
Play/Pause
Step Forward
Fast Forward
Go to next Edit Point
Shuttle

- **Remove a clip from the timeline.** Click on a clip you want to remove and press Delete (or right-click and press Delete and Close Gap). Premiere removes the clip from the timeline and closes the resulting gap. Press Shift-Delete to remove the clip without closing the gap (in case you want to insert a different clip in that space.

- **Move a clip in the timeline.** Drag a clip from the middle of the timeline to a new location, and the other clips shift to accommodate the new clip. But a gap remains in the original location. To move a clip without leaving a gap, hold down Ctrl as you move the clip.

- **Insert a clip between other clips.** Drag a clip from the Media or Project View of the Organize tab to the timeline, and it displays a vertical white line. Use the line to find the precise spot between two clips, and then release the mouse. The clip wedges itself into the edit point between the two clips, which move to accommodate the insertion.

- **Insert a clip in the middle of another clip or scene.** Follow the same steps used above, but instead of finding an existing edit point, place the clip in the middle of another clip. The clip automatically splits into two, with your new clip in the middle. To position a clip with precision, you may have to zoom in on the timeline as described in Figure 5-17. As an alternative, you can move the playhead to the point where you want to split a clip, and then Shift-drag the new clip onto the monitor. When the pop-up menu appears, choose "Split and Insert".

- **Remove frames from the middle of a clip or scene.** Drag the playhead to the first frame of a clip you want to split. Under the monitor, click the Split Clip button (which looks like a pair of scissors) or press Ctrl+K. The clip splits into two segments. Then, with the Select tool (V), trim the clip as described on page 158. If a gap results, right-click in the gap and select "Delete and Close Gap".

- **Select just the video or audio part of a clip.** Most clips that come from your camcorder have their video and audio tracks linked together so they play in sync. Occasionally, you want to break this duo apart. For example, you may want to add a music track to a video, so you want to keep the video track but replace the audio track. Right-click on the clip and select "Delete Audio" from the menu. Alternatively, to move the audio track to another part of your movie, Alt-click it and drag the audio to its destination. The video track stays put.

- **Synchronize linked clips.** If you move clips out of sync using the Alt-drag method described above, you can bring them back into sync with a single command. Right-click one of the offset numbers shown in Figure 5-19 and choose "Move Into Sync" from the menu.

Customize the Timeline

When you edit your project using the handcrafted approach, the timeline is where all the action is. If you've got the computer screen real estate, you can enhance your view of the timeline. To see more timeline tracks, drag the bar between the timeline and the monitor. To adjust the size of the tracks themselves, right-click on an empty part of the timeline and choose "Track Size". Like a theater snack bar, you have three choices: Small, Medium, and Large. Want to customize even more? On the left side of the timeline, drag the horizontal track boundaries to change the size of individual tracks. You can make the video tracks larger, for example, which gives you easy-to-see thumbnails in the timeline.

Better yet, if you have two monitors (or one really big monitor), you can move the timeline so that it stands on its own, giving you more room to increase the track sizes or other panels (Figure 5-20).

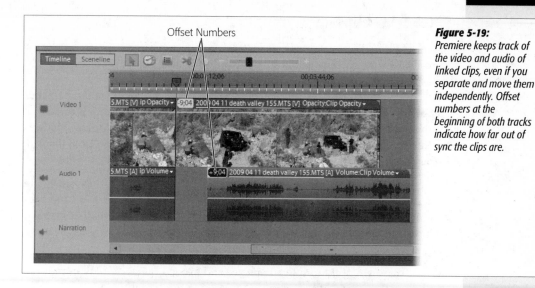

Figure 5-19:
Premiere keeps track of
the video and audio of
linked clips, even if you
separate and move them
independently. Offset
numbers at the
beginning of both tracks
indicate how far out of
sync the clips are.

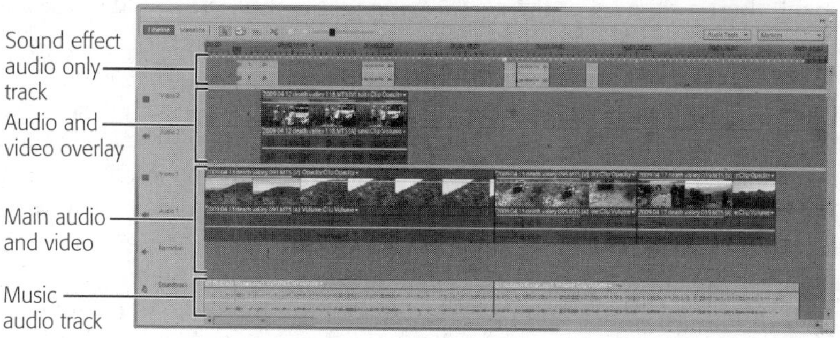

Figure 5-20:
If you have two monitors
or one large monitor,
you can expand the
timeline for a better
view. Here you see two
audio-only tracks: Audio,
used for SFX, and
Soundtrack, used for
Music. Video with
synched audio is on
Video 1/Audio 1(main),
and Video 2/Audio 2
(overlay).

To separate the timeline from the rest of Premiere's panels, choose Window →
Show Docking Headers. A new bar appears at the top of the timeline (on the left
side it says "My Project", and on the right there are two triangle buttons that open
the panel menu). Click the middle of the docking header and drag the timeline to a
new spot. Once you separate it from the Premiere window, you can resize the
timeline by dragging any edge.

Whenever you want to put all Premiere's parts and panels back the way they were
when you first installed the program, go to Window → Restore Workspace.

On the left side of the timeline, there are little icons next to the words Video,
Audio, Narration, and Soundtrack. These are actually buttons in disguise. Click
them to change the way Premiere shows clips in that track. For example, click a
video track button to change the video thumbnails that identify that clip. You can
have thumbnails the whole length of the clip, a thumbnail on each end or a single
thumbnail at the beginning of a clip. For audio tracks, the button shows and hides
the waveform representation of the sound.

Final-Trim Clips

Listen to film editors talk, and you'd think they were jazz musicians—you hear words like tempo, rhythm, and beat. A good editor knows exactly how long to hold a close-up of someone's face and when to cut away to a long shot. Inevitably, someone will ask, "Shouldn't we stay on that for another beat?" If you're taking the hand-crafted approach to your project, you probably want to take another pass through it after you complete the rough assembly work. If you're adding a music soundtrack, as covered in Chapter 10, you may want to hold off on your final trim until that's in place. Then you can use the soundtrack's beat to guide your final trim.

In the final trim, look for ways to make your movie more interesting visually. In most cases, final trimming makes your movie shorter. You trim the front and back ends of clips so that you end up with only the needed and best parts. The monitor automatically shows you two clips at once as you trim the point where they meet, as shown in Figure 5-21.

In some cases, you want to split a sequence and insert a "cutaway." For example, if you have a long scene of two grandfathers talking to each other in a living room, you might insert a cutaway of the dog sleeping by the fire. The sound of the conversation continues, even though the image changes. While the dog might not be vital to the scene, it contributes to the mood and atmosphere. The cutaway provides visual interest both when it cuts to the dog and when it cuts back to the grandfathers. There are plenty of technical reasons to use a cutaway, too. It gives you a smooth way to trim out bad bits of film. For example, suppose at one point in the grandfather's conversation, the shot was ruined by a reflection off of one of their glasses. You could use a cutaway to remove that segment of video without disrupting the flow of the conversation. Or you could use the cutaway as a transition shot, letting you change from a close two-shot to a longer shot. Often, jumping from one view of a subject to another seems jarring. A cutaway can help smooth the transition.

In your final trim, you use the same review and trim tools described earlier: the monitor, the In and Out points, and all the video transport tools. It's important to watch your video at normal speed when you make final-trim decisions, and you may want to watch the video in full-screen mode to approximate what it would look like on a TV. Just click the Full Screen icon in the upper right-hand corner of Premiere's menu bar. Premiere has a few additional tools to help when it comes to the final trim. If you're looking for a little guidance and some automation, try Smart Trim and the Auto-Analyzer, both described next.

Famous Movie Moment: Early filmmakers shot movies like stage plays. They set the camera up at distance and turned it on. Filmmakers like Edwin S. Porter, D.W. Griffith, and Sergei Eisenstein, among others, invented the film language we use today. They learned how to use multiple shots to tell a story and communicate, whether the action was taking place simultaneously or at some other point in time. Like any language, the language of the moving picture became more complex and poetic. "Meanwhile, back at the ranch…"

Figure 5-21:
When you trim with multiple clips in the timeline, the monitor displays the Out point for one clip and the In point for the next. This helpful feature gives you a great way to fine-tune your transitions.

Get Guidance from Smart Trim

Smart Trim is a new Premiere feature that marks areas of your clip that may not be up to snuff. Choose Timeline → Smart Trim Mode, and the Auto Analyzer begins examining the clip in the timeline. It marks questionable sections of your video with the diagonal highlights shown in Figure 5-22. As long as you keep Smart Trim toggled on, it analyzes and marks clips as you add them to the timeline.

Tip: Smart Trim has two modes: Manual and Automatic. In Manual mode, it highlights (with diagonal lines) parts of your clips that have problems. In Automatic mode, Smart Trim takes the initiative and trims out those bad bits. Until you get a feeling for Smart Trim's taste and decision-making process, it's probably best to work in Manual mode. If Smart Trim isn't behaving the way you expect it to, check out the Smart Trim options: Go to Timeline → Smart Trim Options. You may have to click "Mode" to see the Manual and Automatic buttons.

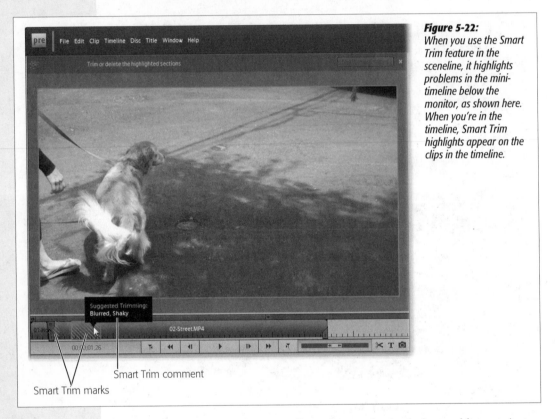

Figure 5-22:
When you use the Smart Trim feature in the sceneline, it highlights problems in the mini-timeline below the monitor, as shown here. When you're in the timeline, Smart Trim highlights appear on the clips in the timeline.

Once Smart Trim highlights your clips, you can play back the trouble spots just as you would any other portion of your movie (Figure 5-23). As it analyzes, Smart Trim splits your clips into good and bad shots, so you can work with highlighted segments just as you do regular scenes in a clip. That makes it easy to remove or trim the highlighted segment. Use the Selection tool (V) to select a segment marked by Smart Trim. The selection works like a toggle—click once and the marked segment is selected; click again, and it's deselected. This makes it easy to select different segments along the timeline. Press Delete, and Premiere cuts selected segments from the clip.

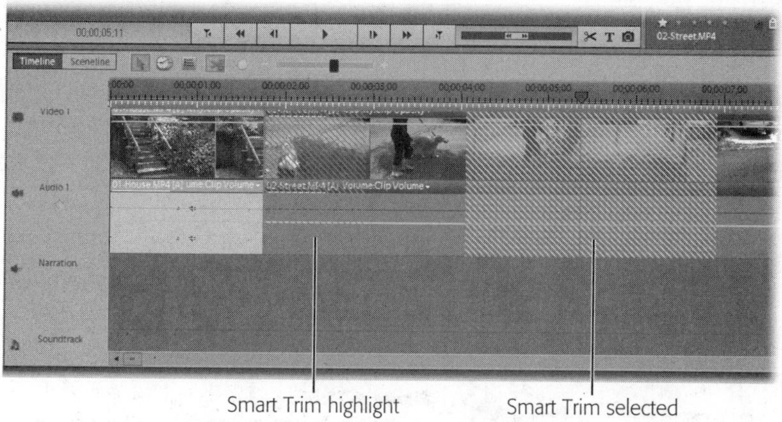

Figure 5-23:
Areas marked by Smart Trim show as a checkerboard highlight in this timeline. When selected, the highlighted areas turn orange.

Smart Trim highlight   Smart Trim selected

To determine your video offense, move your cursor over one of the marked sections and Smart Trim pops up a tooltip. Right-click on a marked area and a shortcut menu appears with a few options (Figure 5-24):

- Click **Trim** to remove the marked and selected segments. Of course, trimming out a section in your clip creates a cut. Premiere automatically puts a dissolve transition at the cut. If you want to change that, go to Edit → Preferences → General and turn off the checkbox labeled "Apply Dissolve on Smart Trim". Keep in mind that Smart Trim edits only affect the clip on the timeline. The master clip from which it's taken remains in your media catalog and can be used in other projects.

- Use **Keep** when you disagree with Smart Trim. The diagonal stripes disappear, and the segment is no longer branded.

- The **Select All** option selects all the segments Smart Trim marked. At this point you can Trim or Keep them.

- Choose **Smart Trim Options** to fine-tune the way Smart Trim analyzes your clips (below it includes two settings, one for what it calls "Quality Level" and one for "Interest Level").

- **Undo Smart Trim** restores sections you deleted.

Figure 5-24:
Right-click on a Smart Trim highlight to see this menu, where you can edit the highlighted segments.

Adjust Smart Trim options

If you consistently disagree with the way Smart Trim tags your clips, you can fine-tune its options (Figure 5-25). Right-click on a highlighted clip or go to Timeline → Smart Trim Options to open a panel where you can make changes. Sliders let you adjust how rigorously Smart Trim evaluates your clips in two (rather obscure) categories: Quality Level and Interest Level. Quality Level looks at a clip's brightness, contrast, and focus; Interest Level considers faces, voice, and motion (presumably how much of each there is, on the assumption that more is better).

Drag the sliders to the right to emphasize the characteristics measured in the two levels. Under Mode, you can choose Manual or Automatic Smart Trimming.

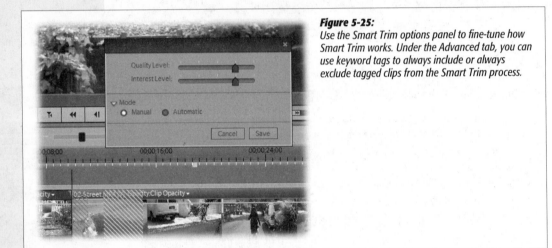

Figure 5-25:
Use the Smart Trim options panel to fine-tune how Smart Trim works. Under the Advanced tab, you can use keyword tags to always include or always exclude tagged clips from the Smart Trim process.

Group Clips for Protection

Once you get a sequence of clips just the way you want them in the timeline, you don't want to inadvertently mess them up by inserting new clips or moving one to another spot. You can protect your work by grouping clips together. In either the sceneline or timeline, select the clips you want to group, then right-click one of them and choose Group. The clips now behave as if they were a single clip. You can trim the ends of the group, but not the individual clips without an extra step or two. To break up the group into individual clips again, right-click the group and choose Ungroup.

Use Markers to Locate Edit Points

As your movie grows larger and more complex, your timeline gets longer and longer. At some point, you're going to find yourself scrolling around looking for a specific spot in the timeline and wasting time. Premiere lets you add markers to the timeline so you can pinpoint important spots and provide additional details. Think of them as electronic sticky notes.

You can choose from a few different types of markers:

- **Timeline markers** can be numbered or unnumbered, as shown in Figure 5-26. You can have a total of 100 timeline markers.

- **Clip markers** are much like timeline markers, except that you view and create clip markers in the Preview window. You can have 100 markers in any clip, in addition to Timeline or other markers.

- **Beat markers** help you edit your video to a music soundtrack. More on that in the chapter on sound, beginning on page 308.

- **Menu markers** identify chapters (and other elements) in your video for use with DVD menus. See the details on page 338.

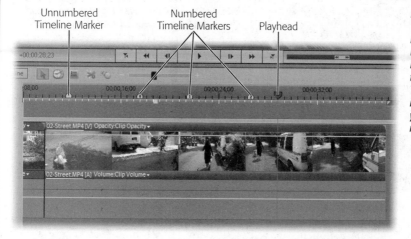

Figure 5-26:
You can use either numbered or unnumbered timeline markers, as shown here, to a maximum of 100. That's not as limiting as it might seem because you can attach up to 100 markers to each clip.

To add a marker to your timeline, drag the playhead to the point of interest, right-click anywhere on the time scale, and choose Set Timeline Marker. A submenu gives you three choices: "Unnumbered", "Next Available Number", or "Other Numbered". Use the Other Numbered option when you want to create a numbered marker that's out of sequence.

Once you have a marker in the timeline, you can drag it to a new location if need be. You don't have to keep numbered markers in sequence in the timeline. For example, marker 7 could be to the left of marker 6. Double-click a marker in the timeline to open the Marker panel where you can type in details about that spot in your movie (Figure 5-27).

To move through the markers, right-click the time scale and choose "Go To Time-line Markers". A submenu lets you choose the next marker, a previous marker, or a numbered marker.

To delete a marker, use the Go To commands to find the marker, right click the time scale and then choose "Clear Timeline Marker". You can also choose the option "Clear All Timeline Markers".

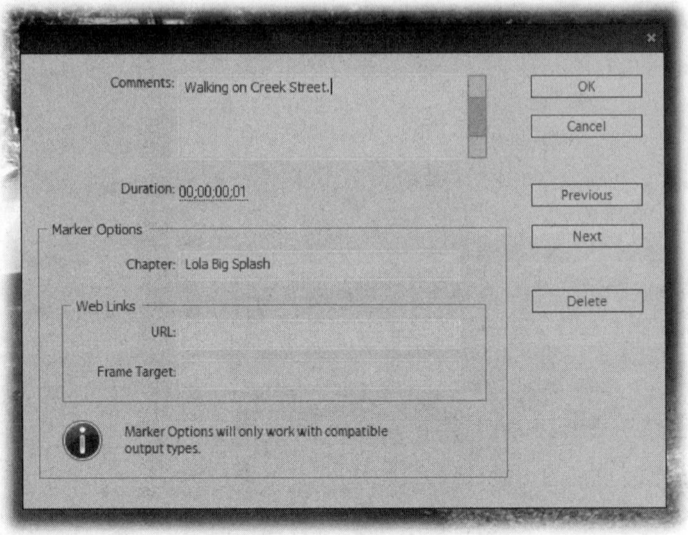

Figure 5-27:
You can add a lot of additional information to each timeline or clip marker, including comments, chapter points for use with Adobe Encore (a DVD production tool), and even links to websites when the video output format supports linking. Use the Next and Previous buttons to navigate through your markers.

Clip markers work like timeline markers, with a few exceptions. Clip markers don't support comments, chapter numbers, or web addresses. Those are only available in timeline markers. And you create Clip markers in the Preview window. To open the Preview window, double-click a clip in Media View, the Project panel, or the timeline. Drag the playhead to the point where you want to add a marker, then right-click on the video image or the mini-timeline and choose Set Clip Marker. The pop-up menu gives you several options for different types of In and Out points. At the bottom of the menu, there are options for creating numbered and unnumbered markers.

FREQUENTLY ASKED QUESTION

Render Your Movie Automatically or Manually

Why Does Premiere Need to "Render" Video?

As you assemble video clips and, later, add transitions and special effects, displaying all that razzle-dazzle as it will appear in the final movie saps your system's processing resources. If it's too much for your computer to handle, playback becomes herky-jerky. To resolve the problem, Premiere creates previews of your movie that do a lot of this intensive processing up front, before playback. That way, your movie plays back more smoothly as you edit. The process that does this is called "rendering." Premiere uses two rendering modes: background rendering and manual rendering.

Background rendering, introduced in Premiere Elements 8, relieves you of the chore of manually rendering, provided your computer has enough horsepower to do it. With background rendering, when your PC isn't busy doing other tasks, Premiere automatically renders the video in your timeline. That way, when you want to preview your film, the rendering is already done.

In computers that have powerful dual- or quad-core processors, this feature works well. However, if you're using an older system and find everything runs too slowly, you may want to work with background rendering turned off (Premiere automatically turns this feature on during installation). Go to Preferences → General and turn off the checkbox next to Enable Background Rendering, then click OK.

If you turn off background rendering, you need to manually render your video to get smooth playback. When you add a clip to the timeline, you may notice a thin, red horizontal line above the frames. That means that the clip hasn't been rendered. Once a clip *is* rendered, the line turns green (Figure 5-28).

You can manually render the video in your timeline by pressing the Enter key. A dialog box appears with a progress bar and other details about the rendering process.

Rendering may take some time, depending on the complexity and length of your clip. You can't do anything in Premiere while it manually renders, so it's a good time to check your email or the baseball scores. You can preselect the area that Premiere should manually render by positioning the WorkArea bar, the adjustable gray bar just above the timeline. You can drag the entire bar to move it, and you can adjust it by dragging the ends to a new position. When you press the enter key to manually render your video, Premiere renders the portion below the bar.

Unrendered clip   Rendered clip   WorkArea bar

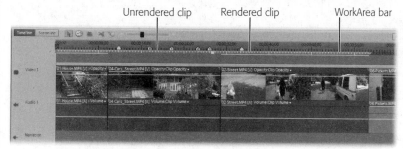

Figure 5-28:
The timeline displays a red line above unrendered video frames. After you render a video, the line turns green. Press Enter to manually render video.

LOLA'S BIG SPLASH PROJECT

Assemble Your Movie

If you're following along with the exercises for "Lola's Big Splash," this is a good time to practice your assembly and trimming skills:

- View clips in the Media View and Project View.

- Use Auto-Analyzer to smart tag your clips.

- Preview and rough trim clips in the Preview window.

- Add clips to the timeline or sceneline.

- Practice trimming clips in both the sceneline and timeline.

- In the timeline, practice trimming clips at a cut where two clips meet.

- Turn on Smart Trim to see Auto-Analyzer results and Smart Trim suggestions.

You can assemble your movie however you want, but each of the Lola video clips are numbered, like *01-House.MP4, 02-Street.MP4.* If you preview, trim, and place the clips in the sceneline or timeline according to their numbers, your movie will be similar to the finished video shown at *http:// missingmanuals.com/cds/premelements8tmm/.* Keep in mind the duration for the soundtrack and the final movie as shown is a little under two minutes, so trim your clips accordingly.

CHAPTER 6

Add Transitions

Filmmakers use transitions in a movie to switch from one scene to another. Transitions between scenes can smooth the narrative flow of a film or add to its emotional impact. In Premiere terms, adding transitions means you insert an effect where the end of one clip meets the beginning of another.

You've seen these effects—they include everything from a simple dissolve between scenes to the more elaborate turning page or spinning cube. Some transitions subtly bridge the visual jump from one scene to another, while others end up calling attention to themselves and taking the viewer's attention away from the content— witness the infamous Star Wipe.

Premiere gives you dozens upon dozens of between-scene transitions to work with, as you can see in Figure 6-1. That's more than enough to make a really cheesy movie.

This chapter explains how to use and customize transitions, along with advice on how to keep a tight reign on them so you don't overdo it. But if you're just experimenting and having fun, go crazy.

Choose a Stock Transition

Watch most feature films, and you may be surprised at how few transitions they use and how unobtrusive they are. Transitions are part of the language of film and, for the most part, they communicate a message about time. For example:

Fade in from black (page 179). Most movies start off by fading in from a black background. This is the filmmaker's version of "Once upon a time…." You understand that things happened to the characters before this moment, but this is where the

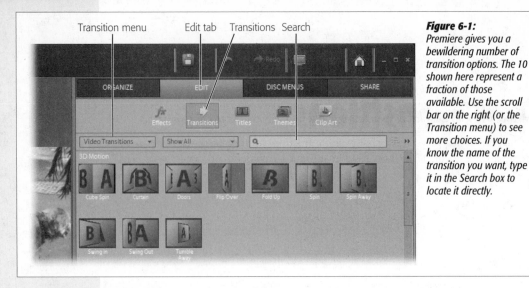

Transition menu   Edit tab   Transitions   Search

Figure 6-1:
Premiere gives you a bewildering number of transition options. The 10 shown here represent a fraction of those available. Use the scroll bar on the right (or the Transition menu) to see more choices. If you know the name of the transition you want, type it in the Search box to locate it directly.

filmmaker wants to begin to tell her story. It's a fine film convention and works well whether you're making an indie film or editing a video of your cousin's wedding.

Fade to black (page 179). The other bookend for most movies is the fade to black at the end of the story. The transition elegantly implies that the story the film-maker wants to tell ends here, even though the story and characters continue. Some-times, filmmakers use the fade-to-black transition to break their movie into segments, similar to the way a rising and falling curtain demarcates acts in a play.

Straight cut. The most common transition in most movies is a cut from one shot to another, without any transition at all. Why? Because in the language of film, a straight cut signals to the viewer the normal flow of time. More elaborate transi-tions almost always imply a break in the flow of time—taking the viewer forward in time or back to the past.

Actually, a good straight cut is deceptively simple. Some viewers take the straight cut for granted, while filmmakers sweat over it. That's because good filmmakers use a specific visual grammar that prevents a straight cut from being jarring—a film faux pas known as a jump cut. For example, suppose the subject of your movie sits in a café wearing sunglasses, elbows on the table, talking earnestly to a companion. If the next shot shows the same person leaning back, holding their sunglasses in their hand, that's a jump cut. Your audience will feel that they missed something in between. On the other hand, a smooth straight cut would be a close-up of the same person in the café, with their hands, glasses, and everything else in the same position as the previous shot. Alternatively, if you want to imply that the person has been sitting at the table talking for hours, that's the perfect opportunity for a transition.

Dissolve (page 179). The second-most-common transition is the dissolve, which you've seen many times. One clip fades out as another fades in. For a moment, one scene is superimposed over the other.

Dissolves can be short or long. Longer fades are more dramatic and often imply a longer passage of time or some extraordinary change over time. (Keep in mind that a "long" transition is something like three seconds; anything much longer and your audience will lean forward in their seats wondering why the video has seized up.)

On the flip side, very short dissolves—a fraction of a second—can soften or smooth a straight cut. The actual dissolve only affects a handful of frames; it happens so quickly that it doesn't necessarily imply the passage of time.

Since the 1940s, the great majority of feature films used these four transitions, seldom venturing into more exotic territory. When a filmmaker uses a fancy transition, she tends to call attention to the effect rather than the narrative, to the point of disrupting the flow of the film. For example, see Figure 6-2. If, as you use transitions or other effects, your audience spends more time thinking about a transition, they may not be paying attention to the narrative of the film.

Famous Movie Moment: In Martin Scorsese's *The Departed,* he uses an iris effect to frame Matt Damon on the streets of Boston. Most of the screen is stark black. Finally, the lens opens to full-frame, and you see that Damon is in front of a government building, about to start his new job.

The transition jumps out in the movie. It's such an artificial and manipulative effect that it makes you wonder why Scorsese chose it for that moment in the film. Is it an homage to Hitchcock or D.W. Griffith? Did the cameraman forget to bring his zoom lens? Or is Scorsese effectively portraying the apprehension and sense of isolation one feels at the start of a new job, particularly one fraught with danger?

Needless to say, Scorsese knows filmmaking (*The Departed* won Best Picture and Best Director Oscars) and uses every element in his movies for a reason. You need to follow the same rationale.

Apply a Transition

In Premiere, it's as easy to apply a transition as it is to add a clip to your movie. You simply find the right transition and drag it into place. You can apply transitions from the sceneline or the timeline. The next couple of exercises show you how to add a traditional set of transitions to a short movie. You probably have your own clips to work with, but if not, download the three short clips of a flower garden from this book's Missing CD (download the file *transitions_begin_ch06.zip* at *http://missingmanuals.com/cds*).

Apply Transitions in the Sceneline

To apply a transition, start at the sceneline with your clips in place. If you're interested in seeing how transitions affect the runtime of your movie, you may want to note the clip lengths and the overall movie length. For example if you use the flower clips from the Missing CD, you can trim each one to run 5 seconds, making

---

Figure 6-2:
Fancy transitions, like the oval iris shown here, may detract from your movie if they call more attention to themselves than the subject.

the entire movie 15 seconds long. (If you need a refresher on adding clips to the sceneline, see page 164. For trimming clips, see page 156.) After you add these transitions, you can compare the new movie length with the old.

The following steps show you how to apply *cross-dissolve* transitions between your clips and a dip-to-black transition at the beginning and end of your video. You'll end up with a brief movie that has a traditional set of transitions.

1. **Click the Edit tab.**

   The Tasks panel displays your editing tools. Buttons at the top lead to Effects, Transitions, Titles, Themes, and Clip Art. Initially, the panel displays Effects.

2. **Click the Transitions button (it looks like an arrow).**

   The Tasks panel displays dozens of transitions, grouped into categories like 3D Motion, Dissolve, Iris, and GPU Transitions. (GPU stands for "graphics processor unit"—the brain behind fancier video cards. Some of Premiere's transitions and special effects require one of these cards.)

   If you haven't decided which transition to use, you can get a mini-preview. Each thumbnail displays the letters A and B. The A represents the first clip in the transition and the B the second. Move your cursor over one of the transitions, and the animated thumbnail previews the transition as it goes from A to B.

3. **Drag the cross-dissolve transition to the small box between the first and second clips in the sceneline.**

   An icon representing the transition fills the box between the two clips, as shown in Figure 6-3. Premiere works hard to make sure that the addition of a transition doesn't change the overall length of your movie—check its duration by opening the Info window (Window → Info) and then selecting all the clips. For more details on transitions and movie length, see the box on page 181.

4. **Right-click the empty transition box between the second and third clips and then choose Dissolve → Cross Dissolve.**

   The Cross Dissolve transition appears between the two clips, just as it did when you manually dragged it from the Tasks panel. You can use whichever method works best for you.

5. **Now go back to the first transition in the sceneline and click it.**

   Premiere moves the playhead to a point just before the transition. To preview the transition in all its glory, you need to see at least a few seconds of your clip before and after the transition—which is why Premiere positions the playhead a little ahead of the effect. If you want to see more of the lead-in clip, drag the playhead a little more to the left. If all you want to see is the transition, you can double-click the transition itself.

6. **Press the space bar.**

   Your movie plays back in the monitor. The clip images dissolve from one to the next. If the playback is rough or choppy, press the Enter key to render the movie before you view it.

7. **Drag the Dip to Black transition to the boxes at the beginning and end of your movie.**

   The Dip to Black transition makes your movie fade in from a black screen and fade out to a black one.

8. **Click the first Dip to Black transition.**

   The playhead moves to the first frame of your movie.

9. **Press the space bar.**

   Your movie plays back in the monitor. When the movie ends, Premiere displays the movie's running time in the lower-left corner of the sceneline. Note that adding transitions didn't change the duration.

The cross-dissolve is such a popular transition that it's one Premiere uses by default. To change the default transitions, go to Window → Transitions and select a new transition from the Tasks panel. Right-click the transition and choose Set Selected as Default Transition.

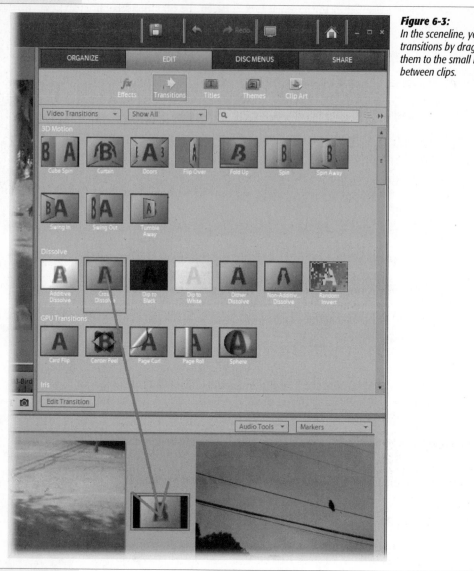

Figure 6-3:
In the sceneline, you apply transitions by dragging them to the small boxes between clips.

Swap and Delete Transitions in the Sceneline

If you decide to use a different transition from the one you originally added, drag the new transition from the Tasks panel and drop it on top of the existing one. The new transition takes the place of the old one. To remove a transition entirely, select it and then press Delete.

How Transitions Affect the Length of Your Movie

Most transitions display images from two adjacent clips at the same time. You'd think that all this overlapping would shorten the running time of your movie. Normally, that would be the case, but Premiere goes to near-heroic lengths to preserve your movie's running time and the cuts you've made from one clip to another.

Remember that you trimmed frames from the beginning and end of many of your clips. Premiere uses those trimmed ends to create the transition. If you haven't trimmed an end, Premiere duplicates the last frame on clip A and/or the first frame on clip B. This solution works well most of the time. But there are times when Premiere's solution doesn't work with your clips. In those cases, you need to jump in and manually adjust the transition, as explained below.

Edit Transitions in the Timeline

Click the timeline button, and you see a different view of the Transitions work area. As usual, the timeline gives you a bit more information about your movie than the sceneline does, and more editing control, too. In the timeline, the transitions you added appear above the video portion of your clips, as shown in Figure 6-4. (You may have to expand the video track horizontally to reproduce this look.) Right-click on an empty spot in the timeline and choose Track Size → Large or use the Zoom slider above the timeline.

Transitions

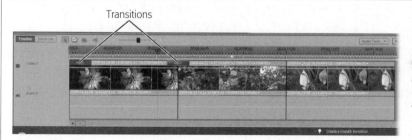

Figure 6-4:
Premiere represents transitions using a rectangle with arrows. Here, the transition between the second and third clip is selected and shows a purple highlight.

You work with transitions in the timeline as if they were video clips. Using the Selection tool (V), click a transition to highlight it. Move a transition by dragging it to a new location. Delete it by selecting it and pressing Delete. Change the timing by trimming its ends, as shown later in Figure 6-6.

Tip: You can change a transition's alignment so that it's before the cut, after the cut, or centered on the cut. You do that by editing the transition as explained on page 186.

The steps below continue the transition exercise started on page 177. If you followed those steps, you now have a three-clip movie with transitions in place.

1. **Click the Timeline button.**

   The timeline shows your movie with Dip to Black transitions at the beginning and end. Cross-dissolve transitions are in place where two clips meet.

2. **Select the cross-dissolve transition between the first and second clip and then press Delete.**

   Premiere removes the transition. At this point, there's a straight cut between the first and second clip.

3. **If necessary, go to Window → Transitions to view the full list of transitions.**

   As an alternative, you can click the Tasks panel's Edit tab and then click the Transition button.

4. **Drag the Spin Away transition from the Transitions panel to the point where the first and second clips meet.**

   The transition snaps to one of three places over the splice, depending on where you had it when you let go of the mouse: It ends up at the end of clip one, the beginning of clip two, or straddles both. As explained in the box on page 181, Premiere creates a transition using frames you trimmed from the clip earlier or, if you haven't done any trimming, by duplicating existing end frames.

5. **Click the timeline in front of the new transition and then press the space bar.**

   Premiere previews the transition in the monitor. If the effect appears choppy, press the Enter key to render the transition.

6. **OK, go ahead and test a bunch of the goofy transitions.**

   You know you can't resist.

7. **Drag the transition to the timeline.**

   When you first drag a transition to the timeline, it snaps into position as described in Step 4. After it's in place, you can slide the transition to *any* position over the splice. As you place the transition, you can see where in your film it will end up because the monitor displays two side-by-side frames—the last frame of the first clip and the first frame of the second clip (Figure 6-5).

8. **Drag the front end of the transition toward the beginning of the timeline.**

   The duration of the transition increases as you resize it in the timeline. As you do so, a tooltip displays the change in the duration (Figure 6-6). For example, if you move the left end of the transition five frames to the left, the tooltip shows a negative time: *–00;00;00;05.* You can resize transitions from either end.

Figure 6-5:
Drag a transition on the timeline and you see the end of both clips displayed in the monitor. That gives you the opportunity to find the best fit for the cut and the transition.

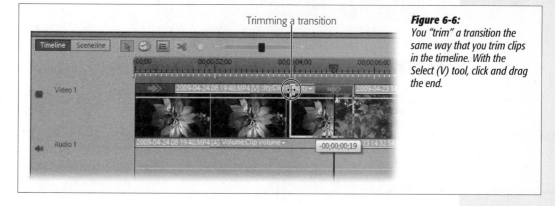

Trimming a transition

Figure 6-6:
You "trim" a transition the same way that you trim clips in the timeline. With the Select (V) tool, click and drag the end.

As you can see from Step 6, you can make some basic changes to the timing of any transition from the timeline. If you need to make more specific edits, see the techniques described on page 184.

Add Transitions to Favorites

If you're like most video editors, you have a few transitions you use most of the time. Premiere gives you a place to keep these favorites so you don't have to scroll through the entire list of transitions each time you want one. To add a transition to Premiere's Favorites panel, right-click the transition in the Tasks panel and then choose Add to Favorites from the shortcut menu. To view your favorites, choose Favorites from the transitions menu, as shown in Figure 6-7.

You can add as many transitions to the Favorites panel as you want. If you decide that a particular transition is no longer a fave, click on it and hit Delete. Premiere removes the transition from Favorites, though it's still available in the standard transitions panel.

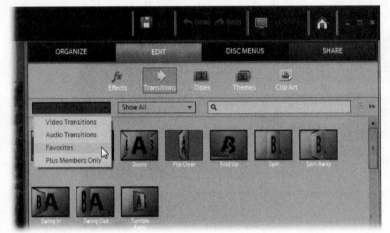

Figure 6-7:
Store your favorite video and audio transitions in your Favorites folder, and you can cut through the clutter of the Transitions panel. As shown here, the Favorites folder is another option on the Transitions menu.

Edit Transitions in the Tasks Panel

There may be times when you want to fine-tune a transition to your own satisfaction. You might, for example, find that a stock cross-dissolve transition overlays two frames more quickly than you like.

You can only edit a transition once it's in the timeline or sceneline—you can't right-click a transition in the Transitions panel and customize it. To edit a transition, select it in the timeline and click the Edit Transition button in the lower-left corner of the Transitions panel. When the Properties panel appears, tweak the transition as much as you want.

Tip: To edit a transition that's in the timeline, double-click it, or right-click it and choose Show Properties (Figure 6-8).

Preview a Transition While Editing

The top-right corner of the Properties panel displays the name of the transition you're customizing, along with a preview window. To see the effect of the changes you made, click the Play/Stop button to the right of the Preview window. At first, Premiere shows you the boring A and B frames for a transition. If your computer has the horsepower to display transitions smoothly, turn on the checkbox "Show Actual Sources" (you may have to scroll down to see it). This replaces the A and B frames with the actual frames from your movie. (With the Spin Away transition and some others, you can also change the direction of the transition's motion by clicking one of the small triangles surrounding the thumbnail.)

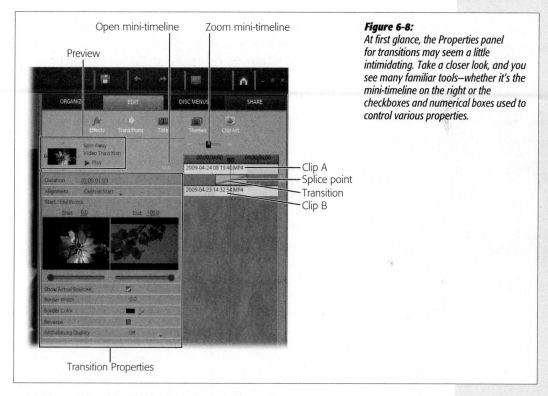

Open mini-timeline   Zoom mini-timeline

Preview

Clip A
Splice point
Transition
Clip B

Transition Properties

Figure 6-8:
At first glance, the Properties panel for transitions may seem a little intimidating. Take a closer look, and you see many familiar tools—whether it's the mini-timeline on the right or the checkboxes and numerical boxes used to control various properties.

Trim Transitions with the Mini-Timeline

Click the Show/Hide Timeline button on the right side of the Properties panel (it looks like a stopwatch) to display a mini-timeline that helps you visualize the three elements of a transition. The A clip (the first clip) appears at the top, the transition is in the middle, and the B clip sits at the bottom. A vertical line indicates the splice—the point of the straight cut between the two clips.

You drag the ends of the clips or the transition itself to change the timing of the transition. As you do, the monitor guides you in the edit by displaying the last frame of the first clip and the first frame of the second clip.

To reposition the transition, either drag the transition itself (the middle purple element) or, in the timeline, drag the splice point (the vertical line).

The mini-timeline is a true timeline, with a playhead and your movie's time scale at the top. If you don't see the playhead, click the time scale to move it into view. Move the playhead in front of the transition and press the space bar to preview your transition in the monitor—a larger and much better view than the one the tiny thumbnail gives you.

Change Transition Properties

On the left side of the Properties panel, you see a list of transition properties you control by checkboxes, number boxes, menus, and other selection tools. Some of these properties, such as duration, alignment, start/end points, and "Show Actual Sources", are common to all transitions. Others deal with a particular transition's effects.

As usual with numerical/time properties like Duration you can change these settings by clicking on them and typing in a new number, or you can click and drag to scrub to a new number.

The Alignment settings, which give you four options for positioning a transition, appear on a drop-down menu. Your options are Center at Cut, Start at Cut, End at Cut, and Custom Start. These are similar to the options available when you drag a transition to the timeline or drag it within the timeline.

The Start/End Points don't relate to the *movie's* timeline, they're relative to the *transition's* timeline. For example, you can change the start point of a Page Curl transition, so that it begins with the page already partly curled up.

Use the Reverse checkbox to play a transition backwards. For example, you can have a page-curl transition appear to curl *onto* the screen as opposed to having it curl off.

Tip: When you drop a transition into the timeline, Premiere sets the duration at 30 frames. To change this default setting, go to Edit → Preferences → General and change the value in Video Transition Default Duration.

Some transition properties, like the Border Color property found in the Page Peel transition, apply color to the transition (make sure you specify a border width for the transition to display this effect). A color chip and an eye dropper icon appear next to the property. Specify a color by clicking the eyedropper icon, and your cursor changes to an eyedropper. You can click any color in the Premiere window to have the page match that color. For example, you might want the transition color to reflect the predominant hue in the scene prior to the transition. You're not limited to the image in the monitor, either—you can click on Premiere's tabs, image frames, and even the purple *pre* icon in the menu bar. The selected color appears in the color chip, and Premiere uses it as the setting for the border color.

If you don't see the color you want in the Premiere window, or if you want more precision and control over your color selection, click the color chip. A color picker window opens, as shown in Figure 6-9. You can specify a color several ways. The easiest is to use the vertical slider to select a hue and then click somewhere within the large square to choose a specific shade.

There's another way to specify color, too. Graphic artists use a standardized set of numbers to represent specific colors. One standard is known as the color's RGB (Red, Green, Blue) value, which stands for the relative amount of the three primary colors (red, green, and blue) it takes to produce a specific color. The RGB value for royal blue, for example, is 51 red, 102 green, and 255 blue.

Premiere's color picker accommodates the RGB scale and several other standards: HSB (hue, saturation, brightness), HSL (hue, saturation, luminance), YUV (luminance, 2 chroma channels), and a hexadecimal number (for example, #FF0033).

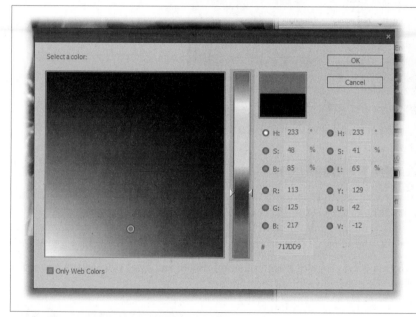

Figure 6-9:
No matter how you choose a color—by entering a number or by using the slider and color box—all the related color values are shown in the boxes for the different color systems. This shade of blue is RGB value 113,125,217, which has the hexadecimal number #717DD9.

Change a Transition's Center Point

Transitions with motion may make use of the *center point,* the point in a video frame around which the transition takes place. For example, the Tumble Away transition shows clip A flipping around and getting smaller until it disappears. Premiere initially centers this motion; however, you can move it off-center by dragging the center point to a new location, as shown in Figure 6-10.

As you edit a transition, Premiere only lists options for the properties that a transition uses. The old standby cross-dissolve, for example, doesn't move an image in any direction—it simply replaces one image with another—so there's no option to change the direction of the effect when you edit a cross dissolve.

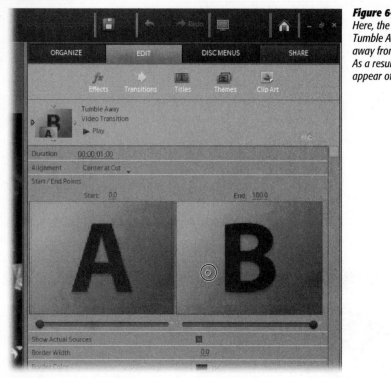

Figure 6-10:
Here, the center point (circled) for the Tumble Away transition is moved away from the middle of the frame. As a result, the tumbling motion will appear off-center.

Customize Iris Transitions

Iris transitions go from one frame to the next using a geometric shape as the medium for the transition—for example, the Iris Diamond transition starts off pinhead-size diamond in the center of the screen, which gradually gets larger until it takes over the screen, in the process replacing the initial frame with the new one.

The Iris transition provides several standard shapes and gives you tools to customize it. Follow these steps to explore the options:

1. **Choose Window → Transitions.**

   Premiere displays the transitions in the Tasks panel.

2. **Choose Video Transitions from the Transitions drop-down menu.**

3. **In the drop-down menu to the right, choose Iris.**

   Premiere displays the iris transitions. Most of them name the geometric shape they use, such as Iris Box, Iris Round, or Iris Star.

   The Group menu is to the right of the Transitions menu and limits the displayed transitions to specific groups such as 3D Motion, Dissolve, or Iris.

4. **Drag Iris Shapes to a point in the timeline where two clips meet.**

   If there's already a transition there, the Iris Shapes transition replaces it.

5. **Double-click the Iris Shapes transition in the timeline.**

   The Properties panel displays the settings for the Iris Shapes transition.

6. **At the bottom of the Properties panel, click the Custom button (you may have to scroll down to see it).**

   The Iris Shapes Settings panel appears over the Properties panel, as shown Figure 6-11.

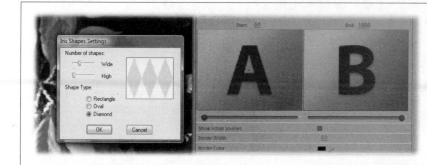

Figure 6-11:
As you work with transitions, you find different tools to help you customize the transition effects. Here, a special panel controls the features of the Iris Shapes transition.

7. **Select one of the radio buttons: Rectangle, Oval, or Diamond.**

   The shape changes based on your choice, and it becomes the basic shape for the iris effect. Initially, the Diamond shape is used for the effect, but you can change it to a rectangular shape, as shown in Figure 6-12.

   Use the "Wide" and "High" sliders to change the size and quantity of shapes used for the iris effect.

8. **Click OK.**

   The settings panel closes.

9. **Make adjustments to the transition properties.**

   Use the techniques described earlier in this chapter to customize and preview the Iris Shapes transition.

10. **Click Done.**

    The transition Properties panel closes.

Audio Transitions

Visuals aren't the only elements in your movie that make use of transitions—you can use transitions in the audio portion of your video, too. The offerings for audio

Figure 6-12:
You can customize the Iris Shapes transition to use Diamonds, Ovals, or Rectangles—the last is shown here. The "High" slider creates two rows of rectangles. You can choose as many as eight rows.

transitions are much leaner. In fact, you choose from only two: Constant Power and Constant Gain. Both work by changing the volume of the audio, making it seem to fade. The audio mechanics used to do the job differ for each effect, but the end result is that Constant Power provides a seemingly smoother fade, while Constant Gain seems more abrupt.

To apply an audio transition, go to the first pull-down menu in the Transitions panel and select Audio Transitions. Select either Constant Gain or Constant Power and drag it to the audio track in the timeline (it doesn't matter if the track is linked to or unlinked from a video clip). You can drop the audio transition only at the beginning or end of an audio clip and only on one side of a splice or the other. As with video transitions, you can change the transition's duration by dragging the end of it in the timeline, as shown in Figure 6-13.

Place a transition at the end of an audio clip to fade the volume down. Place it at the beginning of a clip to fade the volume up. It's easiest to change the duration in the timeline, but you can edit audio transitions in the Properties panel, too. Double-click the transition or right click it and then choose Show Properties.

Premiere uses Constant Power as the standard audio transition. To change that, go to Window → Transitions, select Audio Transitions from the left-most drop-down menu, right-click the Constant Gain transition (your only other choice), and choose "Set Selected as Default Transition".

Figure 6-13:
Change the duration of an audio transition by dragging the end of the transition in the timeline.

Transitions and Slideshows

Creating slideshows is a Premiere specialty. You assemble still images in the scene-line or timeline, along with various special effects, and then save the results in a video file or burn them to DVD. Transitions add visual interest to slideshows.

Premiere uses standard transitions for slideshows: Cross-dissolves for images and constant power for audio. To change either of them, drag a new transition on top of the old one.

Types of Transitions

Premiere offers dozens of transitions—some in good taste, some not so good.

3D Motion. These are some of Premiere's flashiest transitions—the type that call attention to the effect itself. Here you'll find spinning cubes, opening curtains, and opening doors. You can make clips fold up and disappear or spin away into oblivion.

Dissolve. The dissolve transitions include the classic cross-dissolve, one of the best known and least obtrusive of the genre. You can create different effects by changing its duration. The Dissolve category also includes Dip to Black and Dip to White, which are essentially dissolves and from black or white. Black is a standard effect, especially at the beginning and end of a movie or scene. White, on the other hand, has an eerie effect without getting too flashy. The Additive and Non-Additive dissolves play color tricks, while the Dither and Random Invert effects use dots and blocks of video.

GPU Transitions. These effects require a bit more video processing horsepower, so you can only use them if your computer has a video card with its own processor. The effects include Card Flip, Center Peel, Page Curl, Page Roll, and Sphere. Don't feel bad if you can't use these transitions, there are others that are similar.

Iris. Iris transitions are all based on geometric shapes that tend to look like cookie cutters. The term comes from the "iris" of a camera, the internal contraption that lets more or less light hit a piece of film. Early filmmakers (we're talking Buster Keaton and Charlie Chaplin here) opened and closed the camera's iris to create in-camera transitions for their movies.

Map. Premiere has only two map transitions, and they have nothing to do with geography. They use video color tricks to create special effects. For example, you can map one color to appear as a different color. So, during the effect, all reds can appear green, blue, or transparent. The Luminance transition plays off of the image's brightness and darkness.

NewBlue 3D Explosions Elements. Yep, these transitions do pretty much what you'd expect (Figure 6-14). You get nearly 10 ways to slice, dice, bounce, and blow up your images.

Figure 6-14:
Part of the NewBlue Explosion Elements group, the Confetti transition turns the first clip into lots of little pieces that blow away.

NewBlue 3D Transformations Elements. These transitions turn clips into folded boxes, checkerboards, magic carpets, and other distorted forms.

NewBlue Art Blends Elements. A little more subtle than the other NewBlue transitions, this group primarily uses color effects such as glow, halo, and metallic effects.

NewBlue Motion Blends Elements. These 2D effects include things like roll, shake, shear, spin, and wave.

Page Peel. This group boasts a variety of page-peel transitions, the main differences between them being the method of turning the page.

Picture Wipes. These transitions move cartoonish images, such as a road sign, across the frame to reveal the follow-on frame. Options include Stars, Travel, and Wedding.

Slide. If you want to slide your images on and off the screen every which way, take a look at this group. You'll find more than a dozen ways to create bars, bands, spins, swirls, and sliding boxes.

Special Effects. This group includes some video-intensive effects, including an Image Mask effect where you supply a custom shape for an iris-like effect.

Stretch. The Stretch transitions offer ways to stretch, squash, and otherwise distort your images.

Wipe. You have the tools to wipe images across the screen in every imaginable direction and shape. Wipe effects include transitions with names like Barn Doors, Checker Wipe, Gradient Wipe, Pinwheel, Venetian Blinds (Figure 6-15), and Zig-Zag Blocks.

Figure 6-15:
Part of the Wipe group, the Venetian Blinds transition simulates the effect of blinds opening. Your first clip is replaced by a window view of the second.

Zoom. These transitions simulate the effect of a camera zooming in and out on an image. Some include shapes such as boxes; others superimpose images where one clip zooms in while the other zooms out, as in the Cross Zoom.

Note: You can get additional transitions from Photoshop.com, though some effects and transitions are available to paid members only.

LOLA'S BIG SPLASH PROJECT

Add Transitions

If you're following along with the exercises for "Lola's Big Splash," this is the time to add transitions. Nothing fancy. Just put the Dip to Black at the beginning and end of the movie and add the Cross Dissolve to the edit points.

Add Effects and Themes

After you assemble the rough cut of your movie, it's time to think about effects that enhance it—make it look and sound better and give it a more polished look. Premiere gives you a toolbox full of video and audio effects (Figure 7-1)—in fact, you might be surprised at how many there are (and how useful they are). If you have footage with exposure problems, Premiere can adjust the brightness and increase the contrast. Have a clip with a green hue to it? Premiere's color-correction effects can fix it. Want to twist, twirl, and distort your image in any of a dozen different ways? Premiere can help you there, too.

Even though different effects perform entirely different tasks, you apply and edit the effects consistently—one of Premiere's smarter features. This chapter teaches you the basics of adding effects to your movie, and making first-level edits. Chapter 8 takes you to the next level, telling you how to control the timing of effects on a frame-by-frame basis.

In addition to the effects Premiere offers, you can create your own snazzy effects using Premiere's timeline tools. This chapter explains how to speed up or slow down your clips and how to play an entire clip in reverse. You'll also learn a few video magic tricks, such as picture-in-picture displays and "green screen" keying. So, if you're ready, roll up your sleeves and dig into effects and themes.

Choose an Effect

When it comes to video, an effect can be as subtle as a minor color adjustment or as dramatic as a hallucinatory distortion of someone's face. In many ways, effects

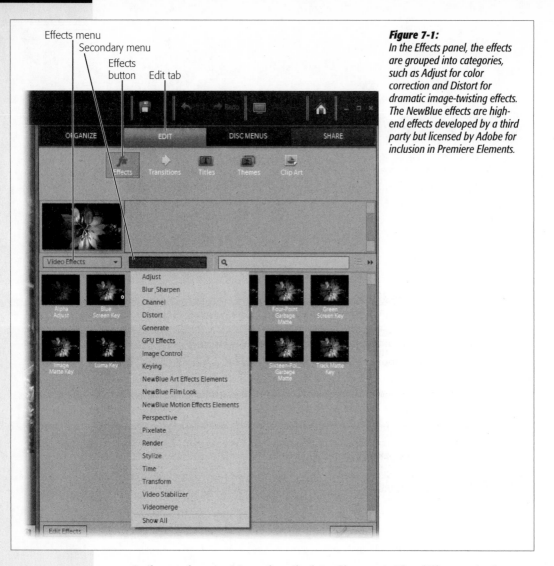

Effects menu
Secondary menu
Effects
button   Edit tab

Figure 7-1:
In the Effects panel, the effects are grouped into categories, such as Adjust for color correction and Distort for dramatic image-twisting effects. The NewBlue effects are high-end effects developed by a third party but licensed by Adobe for inclusion in Premiere Elements.

are similar to the transitions described in Chapter 6. The difference is that you always apply transitions to the ends of clips, while you can apply an effect to an entire clip.

Special effects are fun, but it's important to make sure they're as much fun for your audience as they are for you. As with the transitions discussed in Chapter 6, if you want people to take your film seriously, choose your effects carefully. If you're just having fun, that's a different story.

Fixed Versus Standard Effects

Premiere has two types of effects: fixed and standard. In many ways, the two are similar. For example, both types appear in the Properties panel of a clip, where you can edit the effect by adjusting its properties using sliders, checkboxes, and numbers. Still, understanding how fixed and standard effects differ can save you some video-editing aggravation.

Fixed Effects. Premiere embeds five fixed effects with every movie clip you add to the timeline; three of them are video effects (Image Control, Motion, and Opacity), and two are audio effects (Volume and Balance). Technically, these aren't really "effects," they're video and audio *properties*. But by grouping them in with effects, you can use a common set of tools to adjust both a clip's properties and its special effects. It's a smart move you'll come to appreciate.

Fixed effects are always present; you don't add them to your clips, and you can't delete them from your clips. For the most part, they're fairly subtle. If you don't make any adjustments to them, your video and audio looks and sounds the same as it did when you recorded it.

Standard Effects. Premiere comes with dozens of standard effects, and you can order more from companies that specialize in creating them. In the standard effects group, you find everything from understated color-correcting tricks to flashy Industrial Light and Magic kind of effects, like Blur, Ripple, and Twirl. Go to Window → Effects to see what Premiere has to offer.

You need to manually apply a standard effect to a clip by dragging it from the Effects panel to a clip in the sceneline or timeline (you can also drag an effect directly to the monitor). After you do, the effect appears in the Properties panel, where you can edit it.

You don't have to settle for a single effect per clip; Premiere lets you apply multiple effects to any clip. In addition, by changing the *order* of the effects, you can change the look of the clip. Finally, unlike fixed effects, you can reposition or delete standard effects.

Premiere's themes and its InstantMovie feature use standard effects, automatically applying them to your movie (in addition to applying other elements, such as transitions and titles). See page 233 for more on Premiere's themes.

Customize a Fixed Effect

Drag a clip to the timeline, and it automatically gets Image Control, Motion, and Opacity values. All you have to do is select a clip and then click the Properties button above the timeline (see Figure 7-2), and Premiere displays controls for these fixed effects. Initially, Premiere sets the properties so that it displays your clip just as you shot it. So, for example, Premiere sets a clip's opacity to 100 percent, making the clip fully visible, with no transparency applied to it. It also sets the clip's scale to 100 percent, so the clip takes up the full playback window. You can edit these properties as you go along to get different effects. Some of the examples in this chapter show you how.

> **Tip:** You can work with effects from the sceneline, but you'll have more options and get more out of the effects if you view your movie in the timeline. Through the rest of this chapter, the description and exercises assume you're in the Timeline View.

Properties

Selected clip

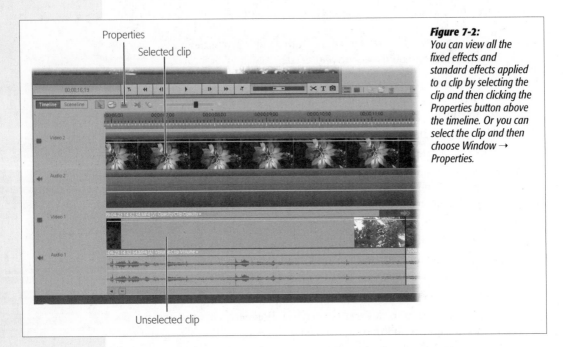

Unselected clip

Figure 7-2:
You can view all the fixed effects and standard effects applied to a clip by selecting the clip and then clicking the Properties button above the timeline. Or you can select the clip and then choose Window → Properties.

To see the fixed effects that are part of every clip and to make a few changes, follow these steps:

1. **In Premiere, choose File → New → Project.**

   If you already have a project open, Premiere asks if you want to save it. Once you're past that, a box appears where you provide a name and settings for your new project (see page 23). Once you do, click OK.

2. **Drag a clip from the Media panel (Organize tab → Media) to the timeline.**

   Your timeline holds a single, unaltered clip. You'll see a yellow horizontal line near the top that runs the length of the clip.

> **Tip:** If you need a better view of the timeline, right-click an empty part of it and choose Track Size → Large.

3. **Click Premiere's Edit tab.**

   When you first click the Edit tab, Premiere displays the Effects panel. You'll see an Edit Effects button at bottom-left side of the panel. It's grayed out because you haven't selected a clip to edit yet.

4. **Click the clip in the timeline and then click the Edit Effects button (or click the Properties button above the timeline).**

   Premiere displays the Properties panel, listing all the clip's effects. Even though you haven't added any effects to the clip, you see five of them listed already. These are the clip's fixed effects: the three fixed video effects (Image Control, Motion, and Opacity) and the two fixed audio effects (Volume and Balance).

5. **Click the triangle button next to Opacity.**

   The slider for clip opacity is set to 100 percent (Figure 7-3). Use the slider to change the opacity or click the *100.0%* number and scrub it to a different opacity, anywhere from 0 to 100 percent. You can also change the opacity by clicking the number to highlight it and then typing in a new number.

   Two buttons, labeled Fade In and Fade Out, sit below the slider.

6. **Drag the slider to about 50 percent.**

   The clip becomes half-transparent as you change its opacity. Note that as you drag the slider, the yellow line within the clip changes position—it moves down in this case. Think of that line as a graph line that reflects the value of a clip's properties, opacity in this example.

7. **Press the space bar.**

   Premiere previews the clip at its new opacity. Changes you make as you edit a clip's properties take effect immediately and appear in the monitor (so long as you position the playhead over the clip you're editing). You don't have to leave the Properties panel to preview your movie with the effect in place.

8. **Click the Fade In and the Fade Out buttons, then click Done.**

   Each end of the clip's yellow line dips down toward the bottom of the clip, indicating an even lower opacity at these points.

   When you click the Done button, the Tasks panel changes to the Effects View.

9. **Press the Home button and then press the space bar.**

   The Home button moves the playhead to the first frame of your video. The space bar toggles the Play button. After all these changes, your clip fades in until it reaches an opacity of 50 percent, then it fades to black at the end.

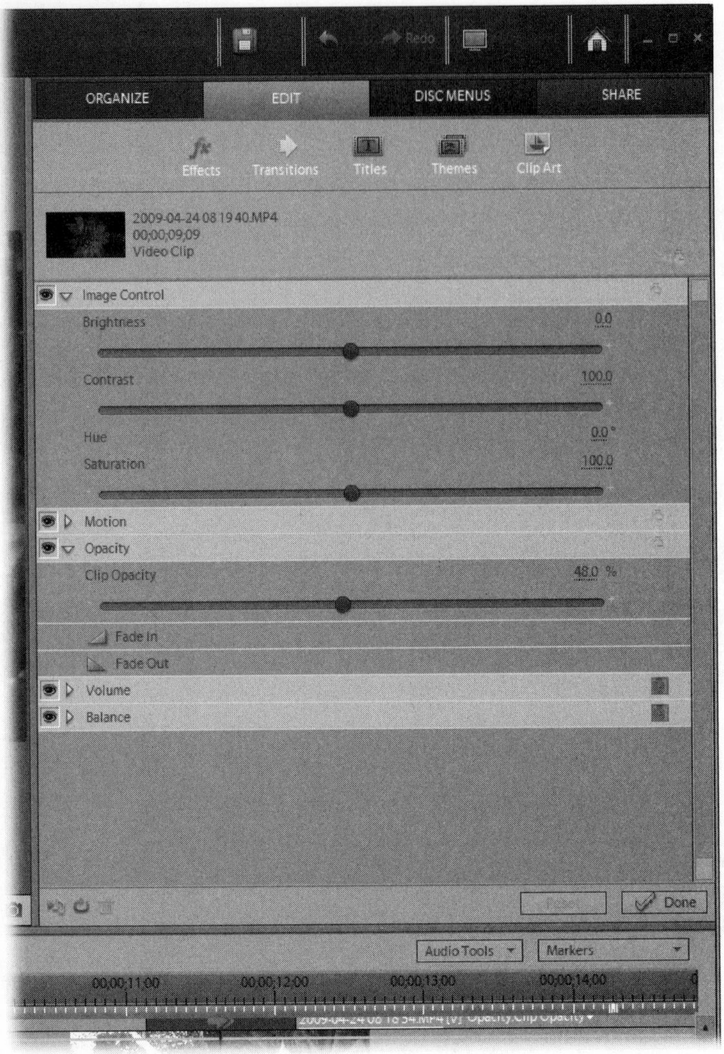

Figure 7-3:
Here, in the clip Properties panel, you see the fixed effects that are automatically part of every clip. Click the triangular expand/collapse button to see the settings that control each effect. Here, the Image Control and Opacity panels are expanded.

Apply and Customize a Standard Effect

To see Premiere's library of standard effects, choose Window → Effects. To apply a standard effect, drag it from the Tasks panel to a clip in the timeline. Once Premiere applies the effect, it appears in the clip's Properties list.

Follow these steps to add a standard effect to the clip in your timeline:

1. **Choose Window → Effects.**

   The Tasks panel shows all the available effects. You can use the drop-down menus at the top of the panel to filter the display, making it a little easier to find the effect you want. (On the other hand, if you know the name of the effect you want, type it into the Search box.)

2. **In the first Effects drop-down menu (at the top-left side of the panel), choose Video Effects.**

   Unless you used this menu before in the same work session, Video Effects appears when you first open the Effects panel.

3. **In the second drop-down menu, to the right of the first (which this book will call the secondary menu), choose Distort.**

   The Effects panel displays all the Distort effects available. The choices include Bend, Mirror, and Wave Warp.

4. **Drag the Mirror effect to the clip in your timeline.**

   The effect immediately changes the image in the monitor.

5. **Position the playhead just before the clip and press the space bar.**

   Premiere applies the Mirror effect to your clip, as shown in Figure 7-4, and you see the results during playback.

6. **Click on the clip and then click the Properties button.**

   The Mirror effect appears in the Properties panel, along with the fixed effects that are part of every clip.

   As you add effects to your project, you edit them here. For example, the Mirror effect has three settings. Two of them position the center point of the reflection and the third changes the angle of the reflection.

7. **Drag the number next to Reflection Angle to the left, then release the mouse button.**

   Dragging the number scrubs a new value into the number box. As you change the value, the angle of the image's reflection changes.

8. **Click the eyeball button next to "Mirror".**

   The eyeball button toggles an effect on and off. When you toggle an effect off, Premiere doesn't display it during playback (or include it when it exports a movie).

9. **Toggle the effect back on and click Done in the lower-right corner of the Tasks panel. The Properties panel closes and you return to the list of Distort effects.**

Usually, you apply standard effects one clip at a time; but you can apply an effect to several clips at once, using Shift-click to preselect the clips and then dragging the effect to any of the selected clips. Preview your movie and the effect shows up in all the clips.

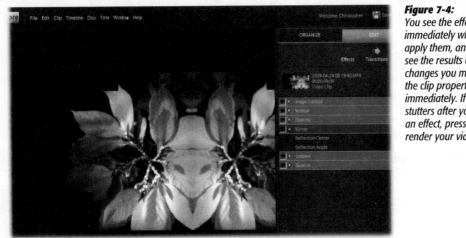

Figure 7-4:
You see the effects immediately when you apply them, and you can see the results of any changes you make in the clip properties immediately. If playback stutters after you apply an effect, press Enter to render your video.

Copy and Paste Effects

If you develop an effect you particularly like, you can copy it to other clips. If you plan to use it across many projects, create a preset effect as described on page 217. If you just want to copy an effect to another clip in the same timeline, you can execute a simple copy and paste operation, as you would in a word processor.

To copy and paste a single effect, select a clip that has the effect you want to copy. Click the Properties button (or right-click the clip and select Show Properties or choose Window → Properties). Then, from the Properties panel, right-click on the name of the effect and choose Copy from the shortcut menu. Click the target clip and, in the Properties panel, right-click in an empty spot and select Paste from the shortcut menu.

To copy and paste more than one effect, Ctrl+click or Shift+click the effects you want to copy. Then click the target clip and choose Paste from the shortcut menu.

To copy and paste *all* of a clip's effects, right-click a clip and choose Copy from the shortcut menu (it's a long menu; the standard Cut, Copy, and Paste commands are at the top). Then, right-click the target clip and choose Paste Attributes.

Using either method, you can paste effects to more than one clip at a time. Hold down the shift key to select multiple target clips (each clip highlights in purple when you select it). Right-click on one of the clips and choose the Paste Attributes command.

Apply an Effect to Part of Your Image

In graphics arts, a "mask" conceals (and protects) part of an image while you work on another part of it. Premiere lets you apply a mask to a clip so you can add an effect to just a portion of a clip. You can use this technique to produce a dramatic effect, like the Solarize effect shown in Figure 7-5. Or you can use it to subtly enhance part of your image. Here are the steps you take to add an effect using a mask:

1. **Start with a video clip in the timeline.**

   You can think of this initial clip as your background.

2. **Choose Stylize from the Video Effects' secondary menu, then drag Solarize to your clip.**

   When you first apply the effect, it covers the entire image.

3. **Right-click on the clip and choose Effects Mask → Apply from the shortcut menu.**

   The mask appears as a rectangle on top of your image, with the effect shown in the rectangle; the rest of the image is unaffected. You may notice that Premiere has added a duplicate video clip in the track above the background clip, as shown in Figure 7-5 (you may have to scroll up in the timeline to see it). The two clips are linked; when you select one clip, you automatically select the other one, too.

4. **On the monitor, drag the mask to reposition it.**

   Click the middle of the image to reposition the effect. You can drag the mask to any position over your background image.

   Notice that, as you reposition the mask, the effect changes only the portion of the image that's under the mask.

5. **Drag a handle on the mask's border to change its proportions.**

   As you drag, the mask changes shape, applying more or less of the effect to the underlying image. Unfortunately, masks are always rectangular.

Premiere isn't fussy about the order of the steps you take when you apply a mask. For example, you can apply the mask first (right-click a clip and choose Effects Mask → Apply from the shortcuts) and then add an effect. If you want to edit the mask after you apply it, click on your clip in the timeline and then choose Effects Mask → Edit. Premiere automatically selects the mask for you and you can move and reshape it as much as you want.

Figure 7-5:
When you "mask" an effect you can limit the effect to just a portion of your video image. Here the Solarize effect is applied to just a part of the image of a flower.

Remove an Effect

Premiere makes it easy to remove all the effects from a clip. Right-click the clip and then, from the shortcut menu, choose Remove Effect → All Effects. If you want to remove video effects only, choose Video Effects from the submenu. Likewise, choose Audio Effects to remove all the audio effects only.

You can apply more than one effect to a clip, so there will be times when you want to remove just one effect from the several you applied. Here are the steps to do so:

1. **In the timeline, right-click the clip with the effect you want to remove and choose Show Properties from the shortcut menu (shown earlier in Figure 7-2) or click the clip and choose Window → Properties.**

   The Properties panel shows all the fixed and standard effects for that clip.

2. **Right-click the effect you want to remove.**

   A shortcut menu displays several commands, including Cut, Copy, Paste, and Clear. Grayed-out options are unavailable for the clip at the moment. For example, you can't cut or clear fixed effects because, as mentioned earlier, you can't remove fixed effects from a clip.

3. **Choose Cut or Clear.**

   Choose Clear to remove the effect, but choose Cut if you want to paste the effect to another clip.

If you want to temporarily prevent an effect from…well, from having an effect, see the next section.

Disable an Effect

You can temporarily disable both fixed and standard effects. The effect remains in place, but you don't see it in the monitor or when you encode your movie.

To disable an effect, click the eyeball icon next to the effect's name (Figure 7-6). The icon box turns solid gray. Toggling the eyeball on and off gives you a great way to compare a clip with and without the effect.

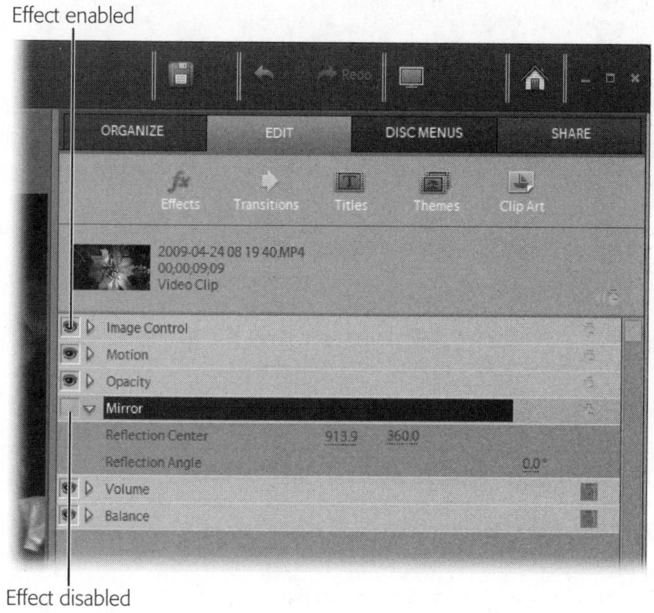

Effect enabled

Effect disabled

Figure 7-6:
When you want to compare a clip's image with and without an effect applied, click the eyeball icon. The button works like a toggle, making it easy to jump back and forth.

Color-Correct an Image

Video effects aren't always blockbuster attention-getters. Some of Premiere's effects simply fix problems in so-so clips. Color correction—making colors look natural, yet striking—is a huge task, part art and part science. In fact, color-correction is such a challenging undertaking that some people spend their whole career fixing color for both movies and still images.

Color correction for video is complex because you're not just correcting color for a single image; you're trying to fix hundreds of images. So if you're new to correcting color, think of it as a swimming pool and then decide whether you want to stick your toe in, wade in up to your waist, or take a swim in the deep end. If you're unfamiliar with some of the color-correction terms used here, see the box below.

So, how do you know when an image needs color correction? You have to trust your own eyeballs. Is it way too dark for a daytime shot? Does the whole image seem a little green? Do all the clips in a sequence (in film, a series of related scenes is called a sequence) have the same look, or does one seem out of place because of its color or exposure? Start your color-correction adventures working on the most obvious problems, and you'll gain skill and confidence over time.

UP TO SPEED

Color Correction Glossary

Like most professions, the color correction pros have a slew of words they use to describe their work. If you're familiar with still photography, some are familiar.

Brightness. Is an image light or dark overall? Often a single video clip may be too bright or too dark in some of the frames.

Contrast. How well do the colors separate from each other? Is it a muddy indistinguishable mess, or do different colors and shades pop out? Often, brightness and contrast need to be adjusted at the same time.

Hue. The same as tint, it refers to the overall color. An image may appear to have too much green or red. The type of light–morning light, interior lamp light–has a major effect on an image's hue.

Saturation. Vibrant, vivid colors are said to be saturated. Colors that are ghostly and faded are not.

Highlights, Shadows, and Midtones. Color pros often separate parts of an image into the light portion, the dark portion, and the midportion. In a black-and-white image, the hightlights are closer to white, the shadows are closer to black, and the midtones are neutral gray.

Apply Image Control Effects

For the simplest level of color correction, you can use Premiere's Image Control effect, which applies basic image settings—for brightness, contrast, and hue and saturation. Image Control is one of Premiere's fixed effects.

To work with Image Control, select an image in the timeline and choose Window → Properties. The Properties window displays the clip's fixed effects and any others you applied.

The brightness, contrast, and hue and saturation controls may remind you of the ones you use to adjust your TV set and computer monitor. For best results, adjust the settings working from the top (Brightness) down (Hue and Saturation). That way, you correct a clip's exposure first and then you make changes to its hue and saturation if necessary.

Tip: As you make adjustments, Premiere previews your changes in the thumbnail at the top of the Properties panel. But the thumbnail is so small that the changes are hard to see. Position the playhead on the clip so the preview appears in the much larger monitor window.

For example, if your clip is underexposed, increase its brightness first. Most of the time, you want to use a light hand when color-correcting an image. As explained in Figure 7-7, you can adjust these setting using the slider or by scrubbing in a value. Often, if you increase the brightness, the image looks a little washed out, so you may want to increase its contrast, too. Adjusting the contrast separates an image's colors from each other without changing the image brightness.

After you make exposure adjustments, you may or may not need to change an image's hue and saturation. If you do, make small, incremental changes. It's always helpful to compare the corrected image to the original. That's where the enable/disable toggle button (Figure 7-6) comes in handy. Click the eyeball icon next to the effect's name (Image Control here) to turn it on and off.

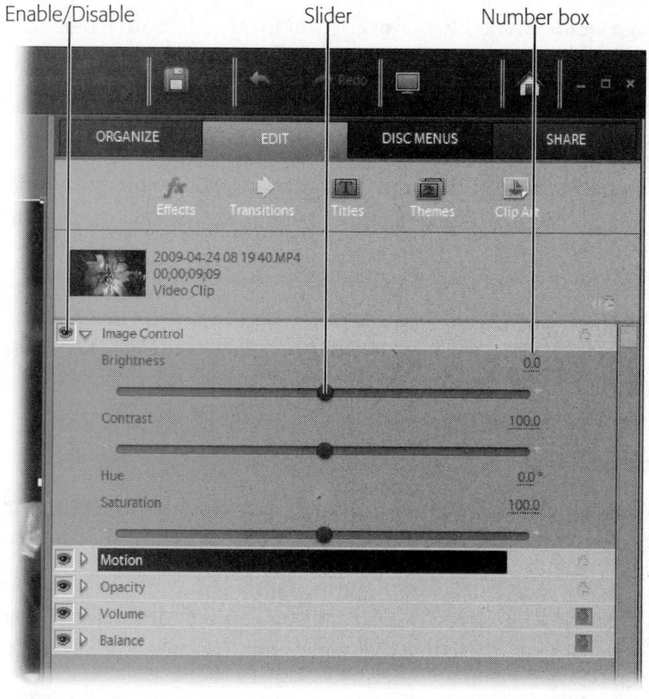

Figure 7-7:
When you color-correct, instead of using the slider to adjust brightness, try scrubbing in a new value by clicking and dragging a value in the number box. The value changes more slowly, making it easier to find just the right setting.

Apply Auto Color-Correction

Another easy way to improve a clip is to use Premiere's "auto" adjustment tools. They analyze your images and make adjustments based on built-in formulas. Go to the Edit tab and click the Effects button to see all the effects Premiere offers. Choose Video Effects from the left drop-down menu and Adjust from the secondary menu to see Premiere's auto tools. The group includes a huge range of effects, including those that make subtle changes, such as Auto Color and Brightness & Contrast, to effects that are far more conspicuous, like Extract (removes all the color in a clip) and Posterize (reduces the variety of tones in an image, making it appear "flat").

Use Auto Color when you want to apply a quick image-quality fix to an entire clip. Auto color changes a clip's contrast and hue. Color-correction pros usually divide an image into three parts: shadows, highlights, and midtones. Often, only one or two of these settings need help. For example, the shadowy areas of your image may be so dark that they have few or no details. The Auto Color effect analyzes these three characteristics in each clip and makes the needed changes. Other effects, such as Shadow Highlight, correct these attributes independently.

Use Auto Contrast if the image seems washed out and you want more separation between the lighter and darker colors.

Use Brightness & Contrast if your image is over- or under-exposed but you're happy with the colors. Premiere adjusts brightness and contrast in tandem since, if you change the brightness to fix exposure problems, you usually need to tweak the contrast. If the image seems overly blue or overly yellow, try the Auto Color effect.

Use Auto Levels when your image has brightness or hue problems (when an image takes on an unnatural color, or it's too bright or too dark). For example, video shot under fluorescent lights sometimes has a greenish cast.

Use Shadow Highlight when your image is well-exposed except for the shadowy areas. This effect brightens the shadows to reveal more detail, as shown in Figure 7-8.

Tip: Experiment with the "Auto" effects. Often, they'll give you the quick fix your clips need; but, double-check what they've done. Computers don't always see things the same as humans. Premiere may change something you don't want changed or it may be too heavy-handed in "fixing" your image.

Edit Auto Color-Correction

If you're ready to wade a little deeper into the color-correction pool, you can fine-tune the color-correction effects that appear under the Adjust menu.

The fact that an effect has the word "auto" in its name, like Auto Color or Auto Contrast, doesn't mean you can't edit it. In fact, you can edit auto effects just as you would any other. (And yes, it's ironic that you're fine-tuning an "auto" effect.)

Figure 7-8:
Top: In the original clip, the shadows are dark and missing some detail.

Bottom: With the Shadow Highlight effect applied, the shadowy areas are brightened without changing the midtones or highlights.

In the Effects secondary drop-down menu, choose "Adjust" and apply Auto Contrast to a clip. Select the clip and then click the Properties button above the timeline (or use the Window → Properties command). The Auto Contrast effect appears in the Properties panel. Click the triangle button next to it and you see its settings. At that point, you can go ahead and make your own changes.

Some of the effects in the Adjust group share the same settings and tools. If you understand how the settings work for Auto Color (Figure 7-9), you can apply that understanding to edit the other effects, too. Here are some of the common settings that need interpretation:

- **Temporal Smoothing** prevents effects from making abrupt changes from one frame to the next. When you color-correct a video clip, you change multiple images. After all, every frame is a separate image. When you apply an effect, such as Auto Color, Premiere analyzes the frame designated by the playhead. In some cases analyzing a single frame works just fine. Other times, you'd like Auto Color to examine some of the adjacent frames, too. If Temporal Smoothing is set to *0.00,* Premiere analyzes a single frame. If you set Temporal Smoothing to *2.00,* Premiere analyzes all the frames 2 seconds prior to the current frame.

- **Black Clip** limits how much Premiere applies the effect to the shadowy areas in your image. Larger values add more contrast.

- **White Clip** limits how much Premiere applies the effect to the highlights in your image. Larger values add more contrast.

- **Snap Neutral Midtones** fixes an image that has color problems, if it's too green or too red for example. Behind the scenes, Premiere identifies a color as middle gray and then adjusts the other colors accordingly.

- **Blend With Original** cranks up or turns down the intensity of an effect. Imagine that your original image is on a lightbox and the color-corrected image is a transparency. If you place the transparency over the original image, you see a composite of the original and the corrected images—part of the original shows through as does part of the corrected image. Adjusting the Blend With Original setting is like adjusting the influence of the original image—the higher the number, the more the original image shows through. Set Blend With Original to 100 percent, and the transparency has no effect at all.

Fix Shaky Video

Unless you use a tripod all the time, chances are you've got some shaky video in your media panel. Yes, some successful filmmakers use shaky video to great effect (witness *The Blair Witch Project*), but most of the time a shaky image screams "amateur filmmaker" to a seasick audience. Many camcorders have built-in stabilizers, which help minimize the problem.

If, after you import clips into Premiere, you see some shakiness, you can use Premiere's Stabilizer effect. It analyzes an image and identifies its subject. Then it shifts the individual frames in an attempt to keep the subject centered and moving smoothly. To make the process work, the effect zooms in on your image a bit, so that the Stabilizer effect has some room to play with as it tries to keep the subject centered.

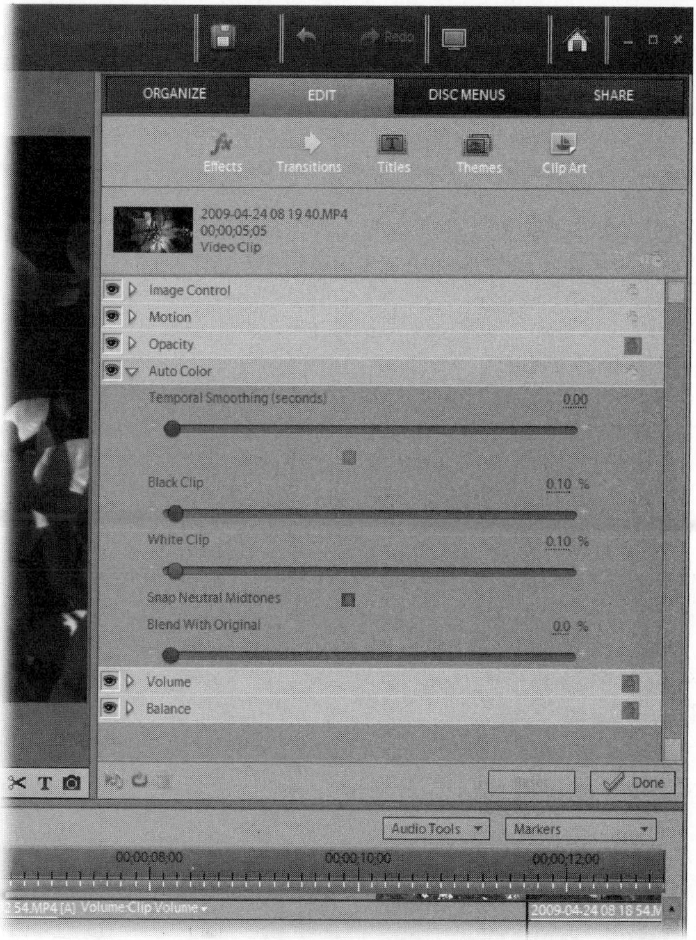

Figure 7-9:
Want to make some adjustments to Auto Color's image-correction efforts? Just open the clip Properties window (Window → Properties), and you can tweak the settings to your heart's content.

As you might expect, the results are sometimes pretty good and sometimes not so good. If you've got shaky video that you need to use, it's worth a try. Go to Window → Effects and choose Video Effects from the drop-down menu, and then choose Video Stabilizer in the secondary menu. Drag Stablizer onto your shaky clip and then press Enter to preview it.

Select your clip and then click the Properties button to examine the Stabilizer settings. There are a couple:

Use the **Smoothing** slider to increase or decrease how much stabilizing Premiere applies to the clip. When you have scenes with intentional camera movement, you need to experiment with this setting. If Premiere cranks smoothing up too high, it can remove movement you want in the clip.

The **Zoom** slider controls how much the Stabilizer zooms in on your image. If you're correcting a very shaky image, the Stabilizer will need to zoom in quite a bit. If it doesn't zoom in enough to compensate for the shifting subject, you end up with no picture in part of the frame.

Click the checkbox labeled "Background—Use Original" to fill in the parts of the frame left empty when Stabilizer zooms in on the subject. Whether or not this works well depends on the subject and how much shaking's going on.

Use the **Correction-Limit to Zoom** check box to ensure that the Stabilizer leaves no empty space in the frame. This may result in a shakier image.

Apply an Audio Effect

You apply audio effects the same way you do video effects—by dragging the effect to the timeline. But this time, make sure you add the effect to your project's *audio* track, not the video track you've been working with until now.

Premiere automatically adds two audio fixed effects to every clip: Volume and Balance. These work pretty much the way they do on your home music system. In addition to a slider control, Volume has two buttons (Fade In and Fade Out) that you can click to fade the volume in and out at the ends of a clip.

Premiere's standard audio effects—the ones you apply yourself—work primarily as filters, letting you remove or enhance sound at certain frequencies. From the Edit panel, choose Audio Effects in the first pull-down menu and Show All in the second.

The effects include the DeNoiser, which does just what you think it does—removes static from clips. Reverb creates an echo-like effect. PitchShifter helps you to make low-pitched tones sound like high-pitched tones and vice-versa. Maybe you could make Bob Dylan sing like Alison Krauss.

If you want to preview a clip's audio without viewing its video, click the "Play only the audio for this clip" button. Next to that button, another button lets you loop the audio—play it over and over until you stop it.

Famous Movie Moment: In Francis Ford Coppola's film *The Conversation,* Walter Murch, the sound editor, used a number of audio effects to distort the surreptitious recordings made by Harry Caul (Gene Hackman) and his crew. Bit by bit, the recordings became more understandable and the secret twist of the film was revealed.

Edit Effects in the Timeline

You don't have to travel to the Properties panel to make small changes to an effect applied to a clip. Remember that a yellow line running horizontally through your clips represents the setting for a specific effect. How do you know which effect it represents? The answer is in a mini-menu attached to each clip. Look to the right of a video or audio clip's name, and you see a small triangle indicating there's a menu hidden there. Click on the triangle, and you see the drop-down menu. The menu for a video clip includes its fixed effects (Motion, Image, and Opacity, as shown in Figure 7-10), and the names of any effects you added to it. In a sound clip, you see Volume and Balance, along with the name of any audio effect you added.

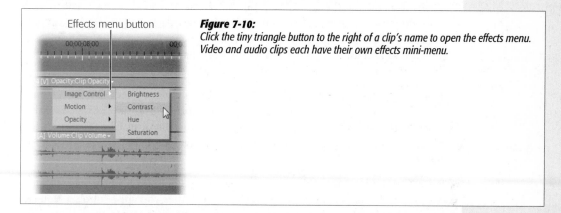

Figure 7-10:
Click the tiny triangle button to the right of a clip's name to open the effects menu. Video and audio clips each have their own effects mini-menu.

Each effect has a submenu where you see the properties for that effect (they're the same properties you'd see in the clip's Properties panel). For example, the Motion effect includes properties such as Position, Scale, and Rotate. Click a property on the submenu, such as Scale, and the yellow graph line in the clip changes to represent the setting for that property. A check mark appears beside the graphed property, Scale in this case. To edit the property once you select it, drag the graph line. As you do, you can see that the scale of the clip changes in the monitor panel (Figure 7-11). Just make sure the playhead is over the clip, or you won't see the changes.

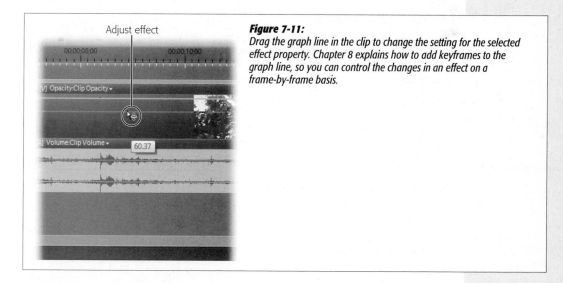

Figure 7-11:
Drag the graph line in the clip to change the setting for the selected effect property. Chapter 8 explains how to add keyframes to the graph line, so you can control the changes in an effect on a frame-by-frame basis.

Apply an Effect Preset

If you followed the exercises in this chapter so far, you can see that some effects are complicated and you can spend a lot of time tweaking the settings. Fortunately, you don't have to. Premiere includes *presets*—a bunch of effects already tuned up to perform specific tasks. For example, there are picture-in-picture effects designed to shrink a clip and then position it on the screen—great when you want to place multiple images over a background image, à la news shows that tap three experts simultaneously. Other presets create drop shadows and beveled edges. Some presets zoom in on an image and pan across it—an action sometimes called the Ken Burns effect, after the popular documentary filmmaker.

To find Premiere's preset effects, open the Effects panel (Window → Effects) and choose Presets from the menu in the upper-left corner. You can use the secondary menu to choose a category of presets or you can use the search box if you know a preset's name. You apply a preset the same way you apply any effect—drag it to a clip in the timeline.

Presets are nothing more than your run-of-the-mill effects with their characteristics already set and a new name. That means that after you apply a preset, you can go into the clip's Properties panel and tweak the settings. Preset effects give you a head start if they're even close to the effect you want.

The only trick is to know which fixed or standard effect the preset uses—and that's not always apparent by the name. Often, if you click the Properties button or choose Window → Properties immediately after you apply a preset, you see the effect properties selected and open. Otherwise, refer to the list below for the name of the effect.

Table 7-1 describes some of the presets Premiere provides.

Table 7-1. *Premiere's effect presets*

Preset name	Original effect name	Fixed or standard?	Description
Bevel Edges	Bevel Edges	Standard	These effects alter the edges of an image, giving it a 3D feel. You can choose thick or thin edges. You can apply this effect to any clip in your movie, but it works best for a clip that's superimposed on another image and scaled down so it doesn't fill the entire frame. Consider using one of these effects when you apply a picture-in-picture effect.

Table 7-1. Premiere's effect presets (continued)

Preset name	Original effect name	Fixed or standard?	Description
Blurs	Fast Blur	Standard	These effects are a bit like transitions because they affect the ends of your clips. For example, Blur In looks a little like you started rolling film before you focused on the subject (filmmakers refer to this effect as "racking focus"). When you want something more dramatic than a simple dissolve or fade-in, this is a tasteful option.
Color Effects	Tint	Standard	These presets change the hue of a clip or image. For the most part, they make very dramatic color shifts. In most cases, you wouldn't want to use an effect like Hyper-Tint Blue/Green on your entire image for a long period of time. On the other hand, you could use it to simplify a background clip if you place multiple images on top of it.
Drop Shadows	Drop Shadow	Standard	Similar to the bevel effects, Drop Shadows works best when you place one image on top of another. The shadow makes it appear as if one image is floating over another.
Horizontal Image Pans	Motion	Fixed	Makes an entire video clip or still image move horizontally across the screen. L-R means the image moves from the left to the right. Each preset has a dimension, such as 640×480 or 2048×1536, that defines how much of your image is used in the effect. So, if the frame size of your image is 1280×720, then the 640×480 setting crops your image. This is handy if you don't want the edges of the image to appear during the pan.
Horizontal Image Zooms	Motion	Fixed	Zooms in and out of an image. The dimensions work as they do with a pan. If you use an effect with smaller dimensions, you're less likely to see the edges of the clip's frame on the screen.
Mosaics	Mosaic	Standard	The mosaic effects break an image into little chunks, giving it a blocky appearance. This is another one of those effects that are applied to either the beginning (Mosaic In) or the end (Mosaic Out) of a clip.

Table 7-1. Premiere's effect presets (continued)

Preset name	Original effect name	Fixed or standard?	Description
PIPs	Motion	Fixed	There are quite a few different PIP (picture-in-picture) presets and they come in quite handy when you want to place smaller images over a background. These presets change the settings for the Motion fixed effect, like Position, Scale, and Anchor Point. You could spend a lot of time tweaking PIPs to come up when an effect setting such as *PIP 25% LL Scale In*. Perhaps a little decoding is in order. You already know PIP stands for picture-in-picture. "25%" means that Premiere reduces the overlay image to 25 percent of its original size. "LL" means the image will be in the lower left corner of the frame. "Scale In" means that at the beginning of the clip, the image starts very tiny and grows to be 25% of its original size. "Scale Out" means that the image shrinks at the end of the clip.
Solarizes	Solarize	Standard	This dramatic effect makes your image look as though a piece of film got snagged in a projector and it's burning and changing the color of the image as it does so. You can use it as a transition at the beginning or end of a clip.
Twirls	Twirl	Standard	Another dramatic effect that distorts an image and is designed for the beginning or end of a clip.
Vertical Image Pans	Motion	Fixed	Similar to the Horizontal Image Pans described above. The only difference is that the movement is vertical instead of horizontal.
Vertical Image Zooms	Motion	Fixed	Similar to the Horizontal Image Zooms described above. The only difference is that the movement is vertical instead of horizontal.

As you use presets, remember that you can make changes after you apply the effect.

Remove an Effect Preset

If a preset doesn't live up to your expectations, remove it as you would any other effect. If you haven't done anything since you applied the preset except preview it, click Undo or press Ctrl+Z to undo it. If you used other commands in the interim, you're in for a little more work. If the preset uses a standard effect like Drop Shadow or Tint, right-click the clip and then choose Properties from the shortcut menu. Then, right-click the effect in the Properties panel and choose Remove Effects → Video. If the preset is one of the many effects that use the Motion fixed effect, select the Motion effect in the clip's properties panel and then click Reset, in the lower right corner of the Effects view.

Save Your Custom Effects as Presets

If you use a lot of effects in your videos, chances are you've got some favorites. You'll be happy to know that after you fine-tune an effect, you can save it for reuse and apply it just as you would any other effect.

There are plenty of reasons why you'd want to save a customized effect. For example, applying a certain effect throughout your movie gives it a certain continuity. Even if an effect corrects a technical issue, like color or exposure problems, you may want to make it a favorite.

To keep a custom effect, you save it as a preset. Your saved effects end up in the My Presets panel (Figure 7-12).

Tip: Premiere gives you a lot of effects to choose from. If you want to cut through the clutter, there are two effects folders where you choose the contents. When you save a custom effect, it shows up in your My Presets panel. Go to Window → Effects and choose My Presets from the menu. There's another item on that menu called Favorites. You can store any effect here, whether you customized it or not. In the Effects view, just right-click on an effect and choose Add to Favorites.

Figure 7-12:
Use the Effects menu to choose one of the main groups: Video Effects, Audio Effects, Presets, My Presets, Favorites, or Plus Members Only. Then, you can use the secondary menu on the right to zero in on the effects within that group.

As with any preset, your own preset starts with either a fixed or standard effect. Once you customize an effect, you can go to the clip's Properties panel and save the effect as a preset. Here are the steps involved:

1. **Apply one of the standard effects, like Lens Distortion, to a clip in the timeline.**

   If you're creating a preset from one of the fixed effects described on page 197, you can skip this step. Premiere automatically applies fixed effects to every clip, so they always appear in a clip's Properties panel.

2. **With your clip selected, choose Window → Properties.**

   All the effects applied to the clip appear in the Properties panel.

3. **Customize the effect.**

   Fine-tune the settings in the effect. If you don't see the settings, click the triangle button to expand the effect's menu. Each effect uses different settings to create its magic. There are more details on customizing effects on page 200.

4. **In the Properties panel, right-click the effect name and choose "Save Preset".**

   The Save Preset window opens (Figure 7-13).

5. **Type in a name and description for your Preset.**

   Give your preset a good descriptive name that you'll understand three years from now. For an example of a descriptive name, see the paragraph on PIP presets on page 216. You don't have to fill in the description box, but you may appreciate additional detail later on when you're trying to figure out how your preset works.

6. **Choose how Premiere should apply the preset to clips. The choices are Scale, Anchor To In Point, and Anchor to Out Point.**

   You can apply a preset to the beginning of a clip, the end of a clip, or proportionately throughout a clip. Remember, when you create a preset, you want it to be versatile enough so you can use it on different clips. Effects anchored to the beginning or end of a clip are similar to transitions. Premiere's Blur presets are good examples of anchored effects.

7. **Click OK.**

   Premiere saves your preset in the My Presets panel.

Once you create a preset, you can apply it to any clip in your timeline by dragging it from the My Presets view onto a clip. If you really, really like to keep all your tools in one spot, you can add your presets to your Favorites panel. Right click on a preset and choose Add to Favorites from the shortcut menu.

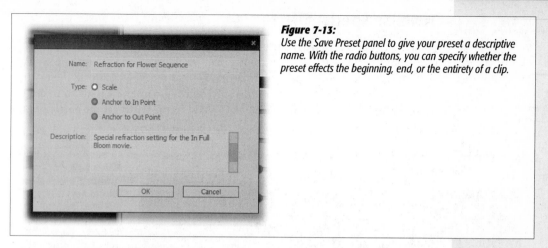

Figure 7-13:
Use the Save Preset panel to give your preset a descriptive name. With the radio buttons, you can specify whether the preset effects the beginning, end, or the entirety of a clip.

Use a Third-Party Effect

If you don't find the special effect you need in Premiere's Effects panel, you can hunt down effects from companies other than Adobe. Lots of them develop effects packages as plug-ins for Adobe's professional video-editing program, Premiere CS4, and many of them work in Premiere Elements as well. In some cases you may suffer a little sticker shock. Professional plug-ins often cost more than the Premiere Elements program itself.

Premiere loads plug-ins whenever you launch the program, and they work as though they were a part of Premiere all along.

You can find audio plug-ins as well as video plug-ins. For example, there's a popular plug-in standard for audio programs called VST (Virtual Studio Technology) that works with Premiere.

Here are some places to start your hunt for effects plug-ins:

- ABsoft (*www.neatvideo.com*) publishes a video noise-reduction plug-in.

- Boris FX (*www.borisfx.com*) develops professional graphics effects plug-ins.

- Red Giant Software (*www.redgiantsoftware.com*) publishes tools that give video a stylized look.

- SyntheticAperture (*www.synthetic-ap.com*) publishes video plug-ins and other tools of interest to filmmakers.

- Bias (*www.bias-inc.com*) offers several audio products, including audio noise-reduction tools.

- Voxengo (*www.voxengo.com*) offers a variety of VST audio plug-ins.

Timeline Special Effects

Some special effects don't require a trip to Premiere's Effects panel. Want to make a car move backward? Or make clouds rush across the sky? Perhaps you want to show a basketball player's perfect move in slow motion. You can do all these things using Premiere's Time Stretch command (Figure 7-14). If you want to freeze the action entirely, you can do that using the Freeze Frame button at the bottom of the monitor.

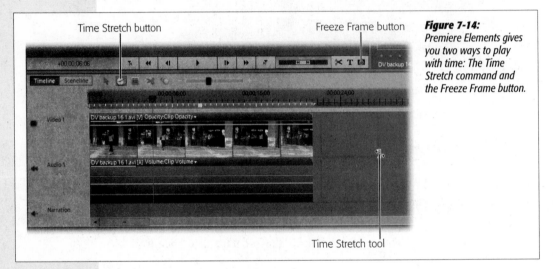

Figure 7-14:
Premiere Elements gives you two ways to play with time: The Time Stretch command and the Freeze Frame button.

Play Your Movie Backward

It's easy to make any clip play in reverse. All you need is the modestly named Time Stretch tool (Figure 7-15). When you explore Time Stretch, you'll see that it does a lot more than its name implies. You can open this handy tool several ways:

- Select a clip and then press Ctrl+R.

- Select a clip and then click the Time Stretch button above the timeline (it looks like a clock).

- Right-click a clip in the timeline and then choose Time Stretch from the shortcut menu.

- Select a clip and then choose Clip → Time Stretch.

The tiny Time Stretch panel provides a few settings, some of which may seem a little puzzling at first. For example, there's a checkbox labeled Reverse Speed. Click it and preview your clip—the entire clip plays in reverse. In fact, Adobe could have called the command Reverse Frames, because that's just what it does—it reverses the order of the frames when you play back a clip. With some clips, the effect is hardly noticeable; for example, flowers blowing in the wind. For others, ones with people or cars moving, for example, the change is pretty dramatic.

You can use Reverse Speed along with some of Time Stretch's other tricks for unique effects. For example, if you want to show your basketball star perform a real reverse dunk in slow-mo, you've got the tools to do it.

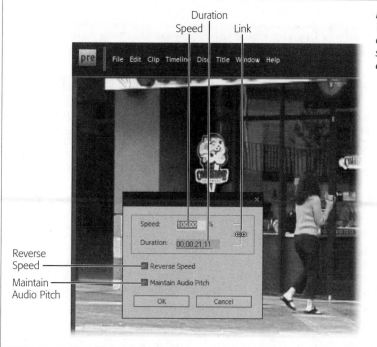

Figure 7-15:
The Time Stretch panel puts you in control of dramatic special effects such as slow motion, fast motion, and reverse motion.

Change the Speed of Playback

Again using the Time Stretch tool (Figure 7-14), you can make a clip run faster or slower. Click the Time Stretch button, and your cursor changes to the time stretch cursor. With this handy time-bending device, you can drag the end of a clip to the right, creating a slow motion effect. Or you can drag the end to the left, creating a fast-motion effect. If you want to do the same thing with a little more precision, follow these steps:

1. **Select a clip in the timeline and then press Ctrl+R.**

   The Time Stretch panel opens. The two top settings are Speed (shown as a percentage) and Duration (shown as time).

2. **Click on the number next to Speed and type in "400".**

   When you change a clip's speed, its duration automatically changes to accommodate that change. Use numbers over 100 percent to speed up a clip and numbers below 100 percent to slow it down.

3. **Click OK and preview your movie.**

A speed increase of 400 percent is, with the right footage, pretty dramatic. If you have people in your clip, they'll take on Charlie Chaplin-esque movement. Use slow motion and your characters look like they're in one of Sam Peckinpah's films from the '70s—bullets and blood optional.

If people are talking in a clip you speed up, the pitch of their voices changes to something like that of Alvin the chipmunk. Too fast, like 400 percent in the previous example, and you may not be able to understand them at all. If you want to speed up a clip and keep the words intelligible, try speeds between 130 and 200 percent. If you want to speed up a clip beyond that and get rid of the resulting chipmunk voice, check the Maintain Audio Pitch box in the Time Stretch panel (Figure 7-15). The pitch of the voices sounds better, but overall the sound may remind you of a bad wiretap from a cop show.

When you go in the other direction and slow down a clip, similar audio aberrations occur. Without the Maintain Audio Pitch box checked, people's voices get very low. When you check the box, the pitch sounds fine. In fact, the audio is much more intelligible than it was when you speeded up a clip. That's because you're not *losing* any audio data, you're actually *repeating* it. The overall effect is that people speak very, very slowly.

Another way to control the speed of a clip is to change its duration. As usual, Premiere displays time in timecode format, *hours;minutes;seconds;frames*. Type in "20;00" if you want a clip 20 seconds in length (Premiere automatically fills in the other numbers), or "1;20;00" if you want a clip of 1 minute and 20 seconds.

Changing a clip's duration automatically changes it speed, unless you unlink the two. To do so, click on the Link icon in the Time Stretch window and the icon changes to a broken link. When you break the link between Speed and Duration, Time Stretch doesn't really produce a time-bending effect. Instead, it's an alternative way to trim a clip. That's because, when you change a clip's duration with the Speed and Duration settings unlinked, Premiere adds or removes frames from the end of the clip.

Add a Freeze Frame

Freeze frames are a dramatic form of punctuation in video. Perhaps you'd like to freeze the "You may now kiss the bride" moment at a wedding and then slowly dissolve to the couple's walk back down the aisle. In most cases, you want to insert your freeze frame for what playwrights call a dramatic pause. Here are the steps to add a freeze frame to your movie:

1. **Place the playhead on the image you want to freeze**

The image in the monitor is the one you'll ice.

2. **In the lower corner of the monitor, click the Freeze Frame button (it looks like a camera, as shown in Figure 7-16).**

The Freeze Frame panel opens. At the top, you control the Freeze Frame Duration setting via a number box. Unless you've made changes to Premiere's preferences, the duration is automatically set to 5 seconds.

3. **Click the number 5 and type in a new duration.**

You can also click and drag the number to scrub in a new one.

4. **(Optional) Check the box "Edit in Photoshop Elements after inserting".**

Use this option to edit the image in Photoshop. Perhaps you'd like to tweak the color, add a special effect, or a title.

5. **Click Insert in Movie.**

Premiere inserts the freeze frame image into your movie as a video clip and adds the single frame to your media catalog as a still image. As with all still images, there's no audio track. Unless the freeze frame was at the end of a clip, Premiere splits the source clip in the timeline into two parts, with the freeze frame clip in the middle.

If you checked the "Edit in Photoshop Elements" box, that program starts up and opens the still image for a little photo magic.

Figure 7-16:
Position the playhead on the frame you want to freeze and then click the Freeze Frame button. Change the Freeze Frame Duration setting to match the time you want to freeze the image on screen.

Freeze Frame Duration   Freeze Frame button

If you want to change the duration of a freeze frame after you insert it in your timeline, use the Select tool (V) to drag the end of the clip to trim it as you would any other video clip. To use the freeze frame elsewhere in your movie, drag it from the Media view (Organize tab → Media).

Famous Movie Moment: In *Butch Cassidy and the Sundance Kid,* the last moment of the movie uses a freeze frame. Paul Newman and Robert Redford race through a doorway, greeted by a hail of gunfire. The frame freezes on their running figures before the bullets arrive. The legends are frozen in time—a much better ending than seeing the aftermath.

Change a Clip's Frame Size

Want to place a clip in a small window over another clip? It's a popular effect for music videos and fast-moving TV shows like *24*. The easiest way to achieve this effect is to use one of the PIP (picture-in-picture) presets described on page 216. If the preset sizes don't work for you, you can always create your own PIP effect.

1. **Place two video clips on the timeline, one above the other.**

   For example, put your background clip in the Video 1 track and the clip destined for the small window in Video 2. In Premiere, the clip in the top track always hides the clip below. As for audio, you'll hear both tracks in equal volume. You can adjust this using the Audio Mixer (Window → Audio Mixer). See page 309 for details.

2. **Click on the image in the monitor.**

   When you select the image, you see a border around the clip and handles on the edges and corners.

3. **Drag any of the handles to resize the clip.**

   As you drag a handle, the clip changes size but keeps its relative proportions.

4. **Drag the image to position it on the screen.**

   Click anywhere within the image (but away from the border) to select it so you can drag it around the screen.

5. **Render the effect and play it back.**

Tip: If you want, you can place the image partially outside the frame of your movie. When you render the movie, Premiere lops off the part that's out of frame.

If you want to make additional changes to your PIP clip, you need to open the Properties panel and edit the Motion settings. Select the clip and then click the Properties button above the timeline, or choose Window → Properties. Click the triangle button next to the name Motion to open the panel, where you see the settings shown in Figure 7-17, which, because you altered the clip's default size and position, now include settings for scale and position. With these additional settings, you can change the width and height of the clip independently. Just remove the check mark in the Uniform Scale box and then make adjustments to the Scale and Scale Width sliders. Use the Rotate buttons to spin your clip around.

Tip: Want to move your PIP window around the screen? See the chapter on effects and keyframes, page 261.

Figure 7-17:
The tools to create a good picture-in-picture effect are tucked in the Motion effect panel. Using these settings you can change the size, position, and rotation of any clip in your timeline.

Adventures in Transparency

Every clip you add to the sceneline or timeline starts off 100 percent opaque—at its full exposure, with no transparency. So if you add a clip to the Video 2 track, it hides the clip on Video 1. If you want to make parts of the clip underneath visible, you have to resize the top clip (see page 224) or make parts of it transparent.

Premiere gives you several ways to change the transparency of a clip. When you understand how the different techniques work, you can choose the right method for the job at hand. For example, you can:

- **Change an entire clip's transparency.** It's easy to make an entire clip semitransparent. If the semitransparent clip sits over another clip in the timeline, you see both images simultaneously, like a double exposure.

- **Cut a whole in the top image to reveal part of the bottom image.** Using a mask or a matte, you can tell Premiere to make a certain region in the top clip transparent. For example, you can snip a heart shape out of the top image, and you have the effect shown later in Figure 7-18.

• **Make a certain color transparent in the top image to reveal part of the bottom image.** This works great for a constantly moving image, like the classic example: the meteorologist standing in front of a weather map as an animated storm system moves across the screen. The weather person is standing in front of a blue background—that's the top image. The weather map is the bottom image. By electronically removing the blue background from the image that has the meteorologist in it, you see the moving weather map underneath.

Change a Clip's Transparency

The main reason to make a scene semitransparent is to superimpose one video clip over another. Usually, you leave the underlying clip set to an opacity of 100 percent and you put the other clip above it and make it partially opaque.

1. **Place a clip in the Video 1 track.**

   The video track at the bottom of the timeline has the name Video 1 (unless you renamed it).

2. **Place a second clip in the Video 2 track as shown in Figure 7-19.**

   The new clip hides the clip in Video 1 because it's 100 percent opaque. You need to change this clip's opacity or size so that the first clip shows through.

3. **Click the Properties button above the timeline.**

   The Properties panel shows the clip's fixed effects: Image Control, Motion, and Opacity.

4. **Click the triangle button to open the Opacity settings and then drag the Clip Opacity slider to *50%*.**

   Once you adjust the Opacity, the image from the Video 1 track shows through. Experiment a little to find just the right degree of opacity for the effect you want. The sweet spot varies depending on the complexity of the images and their relative brightness and contrast.

There are many ways to use transparency as a special effect. You can use it with moving video or still images. In some cases, you may want to remove the background of an image. Suppose your film has a young man wandering the city haunted by the memory of his lost love. You could use a transparent close-up of his loved one filling the frame as the underlying image shows his travels through the streets.

Transparency is one effect that requires a hefty amount of video-processing muscle. You may need to render the effect to see a smooth preview (see page 173). If you render manually, drag the center of the work area bar over your effect as shown in Figure 7-19. Drag the ends of the bar to match the area you want rendered and then press the enter key. There's more on rendering on page 173.

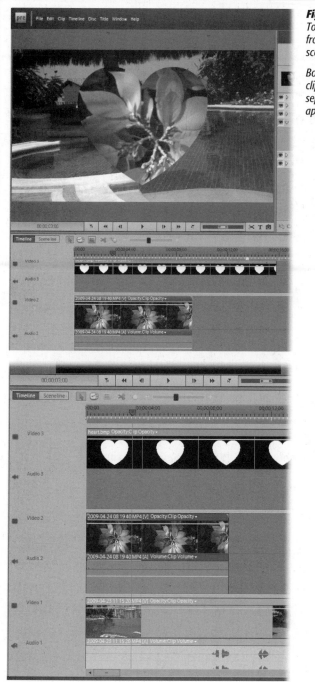

Figure 7-18:

Top: This matte effect cuts a heart shaped image from a clip of a flower and places it over the night scene of a city.

Bottom: The matte effect is created with two video clips and a black and white still image, each on separate tracks. The Track Matte Key effect is applied to the top video clip.

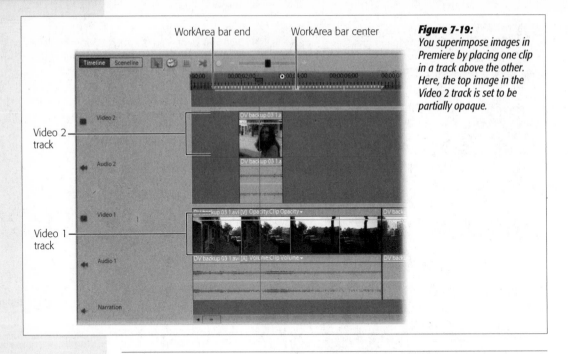

Figure 7-19:
*You superimpose images in
Premiere by placing one clip
in a track above the other.
Here, the top image in the
Video 2 track is set to be
partially opaque.*

Famous Movie Moment: In *Raiders of the Lost Ark,* the original Indiana Jones movie, Steven Spielberg superimposes the image of a map and an airplane. The map shows the globetrotting journey and sets the audience up for the next adventure. The effect adds to the sense of the period (the 1930s) and is an homage to earlier films that used the same visual shorthand.

Make Part of a Clip Transparent

Sometimes you want to show two clips on the screen at the same time, but you don't want either image to be semitransparent. If you just want a rectangular picture-in-picture effect, you can use one PIP presets (page 216) or the manual PIP technique described on page 261. But if you want to put a dancing wedding couple in a heart-shaped frame with a background image that shows the gardens where they were married, read on. The method discussed here works best for non-rectangular shapes, such as flowers, stars, or hearts. Most of the time, you don't want to use an overly complex shape with lots of corners and edges.

To get started, you need a couple of video clips and a still image to serve as a mask. Your mask should be a single opaque shape, such as a white heart on a black background. Follow these steps to apply what the pros call a "mask" effect:

1. **Place a clip in the Video 1 track.**

2. **Place a second clip in the Video 2 track.**

    The new clip hides the clip in the Video 1 track because it's 100 percent opaque.

3. **Place the mask image in the Video 3 track.**

   At this point, the mask image obscures the clips on the other two tracks.

Tip: You can find some black-and-white art in Premiere—click the Edit tab and then click the Clip Art button. If you're adventurous and have a photo-editing program like Photoshop Elements, you can cut some the colored part out of some of the other Clip Art shapes to create masks. Also, if you have Photoshop Elements installed, you'll find some more black and white shapes by clicking the Cookie Cutter tool (Q) on the toolbar.

---

4. **Choose Window → Effects.**

   The Effects panel opens.

5. **Choose "Video Effects" in the menu and "Keying" in the secondary menu.**

   The Effects view displays a variety of Keying effects, like Blue Screen Key, Chroma Key, and Track Matte Key.

6. **Drag Track Matte Key onto the clip in the Video 2 track.**

   You want to apply the matte effect to the clip that will appear *over* the background.

7. **Click the Properties button.**

   The Track Matte Key effect shows up in the clip Properties panel.

8. **Set the Matte menu to Video 3 and set the Composite Using menu to Matte Luma.**

   The matted image appears on the screen and the image in Video 1 shows as the background. Why use Matt Luma? Premiere uses the clip's luminance, or relative brightness, to identify the transparent areas. You could use this same technique with a photo that has very bright and very dark areas.

Tip: If you want to reverse the role of clips used in one of the Matte effects, open the clip Properties and the effect. Then, check the Reverse box in the matte properties.

Superimpose Part of a Clip Over Another Clip

The snazziest transparency trick of all is where you place one moving image over another. For example, if you've got some spare footage of Neil Armstrong's stroll on the moon, you could add an image of your best friend walking alongside him. This video trick goes by a few different names. You may hear people talk about green-screening or blue-screening. Or perhaps they'll call it blue-keying.

Whatever name you use, here's how it works: For the moonwalk, film your friend walking around in front of an all-blue or all-green background (just make sure his clothes don't have the same color as the background, or part of him will disappear when you apply the effect). Then you assemble your timeline as you did in the two previous exercises. Put the background moon footage on the Video 1, or the bottom-most track. Put your friend, walking in front of the blue screen on the track above the background. Then, use the Blue Screen Key effect to tell Premiere to make anything that's blue in the top image transparent. When the blue background disappears, your friend walks on the moon with Armstrong. The Green Screen Key works the same way, except it makes anything *green* transparent.

The Chroma Key effect uses the brightness or luminance to create a mask. VideoMerge is an effect that automatically does a lot of the work of a Chroma Key. It even automatically selects the color Premiere removes. Sometimes, when you add a clip to the timeline above another clip, you see a dialog box asking if you want to use the VideoMerge effect. Answer yes and VideoMerge attempts to do all the work for you. If you don't get the results you want, open the clip Properties as shown in Figure 7-20, and make adjustments by manually selecting a color and setting the tolerance.

If you want to VideoMerge two images and Premiere doesn't show a dialog box when you add a clip to the second track, just apply VideoMerge as you would any effect. Go to Window → Effects and drag the VideoMerge effect on top of the second image.

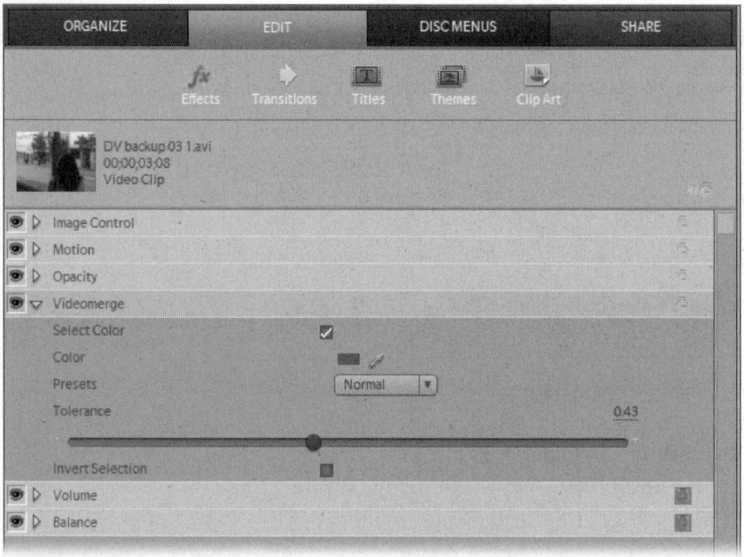

Figure 7-20:
The VideoMerge effect is designed to be as automatic as possible. However, if you don't get exactly what you want, you can always open the clip Properties panel and tweak the VideoMerge settings.

Premiere Elements' Themes

As mentioned in Chapter 1, Premiere comes with a selection of prepackaged visuals (titles and transitions, for example) and background music that you can apply to your movie. These themes, as they're called, give you an easy way to apply professionally designed components to your project.

When it comes to Premiere's themes, you either love 'em or hate 'em. They can be a bit on the corny side and if you like to micro-manage your video projects, you're probably in the "hate 'em" camp. On the other hand, if you want to take the fast and easy track to videos that come complete with titles, transitions, special effects, and menus, you may be interested. Adobe has developed themes based on common types of video projects, like road trips, birthdays, and holidays. Premiere's InstantMovie feature (described on page 28) uses themes as a cornerstone of the movies it creates.

Tip: Confused trying to figure out where Themes end and InstantMovie begins? You're not the only one. As Premiere has evolved, these features have become intertwined; in fact, they tap the same reservoir of preformatted titles and graphics, soun clips, video effects, and transitions. The real difference is in the way you select one or the other. When you click Themes, Premiere uses all the clips currently in the timeline or sceneline in your themed movie. When you click InstantMovie, Premiere asks which of the clips in the Media panel you want to include, and then it moves on to the Themes panel; from that point forward, the two features work exactly the same.

Here are some of the elements that themes automatically add to your movie:

- **Preformatted opening and closing titles and graphics.** You get to type in your own words, but Premiere provides the graphics and formats the type, as shown in Figure 7-22. Many of the themes use animation to zoom the type in and off the screen.

- **Royalty-free music.** Themes come with music. It may not be the latest pop song, but you don't have to pay for it.

- **Automated effects and transitions.** Most themes combine PIP (picture-in-picture) effects with motion- and clipart-style backgrounds.

- **Automatic editing.** When you use themes along with InstantMovie, Premiere analyzes your footage and makes decisions about what parts to use and what parts to leave out. InstantMovie can also choose the order of the clips. You get to choose whether you want the movie to run the same length as the music or whether you want to repeat or trim the music to match the movie.

Stock Themes

Premiere themes come in categories such as Style and Events (Figure 7-22). The Style themes, for example, are based on seasons and activities such as a school yearbook. Event themes focus on holidays and family events such as birthdays and weddings.

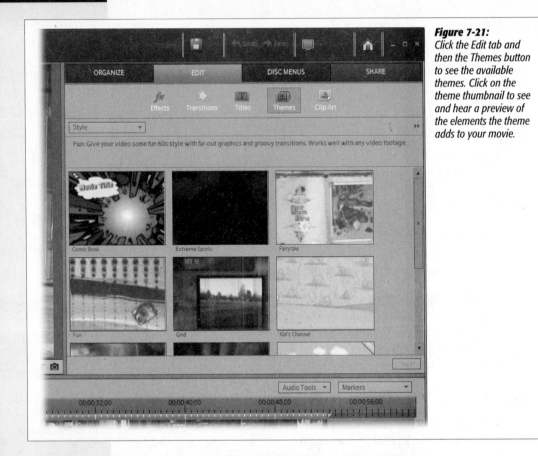

Figure 7-21:
Click the Edit tab and then the Themes button to see the available themes. Click on the theme thumbnail to see and hear a preview of the elements the theme adds to your movie.

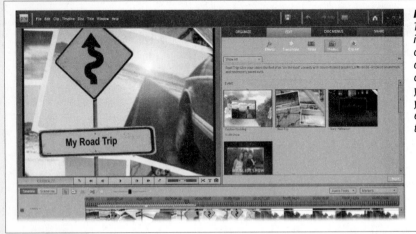

Figure 7-22:
The Road Trip theme includes stock footage, clip art graphics and lots of special effects. You can choose which elements you want to apply to your project and you can edit a themed move after the fact.

Here are some examples of what you find in the themes collection.

- **Outdoor Wedding** has background images with gardens and flowers. Slow zooms are applied to the clips and the music has a nice, solemn feeling to it—Pachelbel Canon in D.

- **Road Trip** uses a map as the background, along with street-sign clipart. The soundtrack includes car engine sounds and slashing guitar riffs. See Figure 7-22.

- **Slideshow Pan and Zoom**, as you might guess, is designed to work with still images and uses motion guided by Premiere's ability to guess the points of interest in your movie. The background audio has a world music kind of sound with woodblock percussion, thumb-organ harmonies, and flute melody.

- **Comic Book** has colorful graphics and "KAPOW!" and "WHACK!" title callouts, along with lots of synthesizer music with a strong drum beat.

- **Extreme Sports** gives you fast-changing effects with a variety of background stills. Premiere edits your clips using scale, zoom, and pan effects. The music includes lots of rock-and-roll power chords.

- **Fairytale** has an old-fashioned feeling with book pages flipping, lots of calligraphic type, and dreamy harp music.

- **Fun** brings a strong '50s/'60s rock drumbeat to your clips and uses the timing to add transitions and zoom effects.

- **Grid** adds a techy feel to your movie. Lots of grid lines in the graphics and it uses the mosaic effect to break your clips into blocky elements. The background music is a synthesized orchestra.

- **Kid's Channel** is designed to look like a children's television program. Cartoonish graphics, sound effects, and kind of snappy music.

- **Music Video** puts your movie to the beat of rock-and-roll. Graphics include lots of effects, clipart of stereo speakers, and other musical icons.

- **Secret Agent** lets you turn your stars into James Bond. The background music and sound effects give you the impression something exciting and dangerous is about to happen. Graphic images include crosshairs, surveillance maps, and plans for something that a spy might want to get their hands on.

Adobe continues to develop themes, so you're likely to see new ones as time goes on. Some themes are only available when you opt for a premium Photoshop.com account.

Apply a Theme

Themes are tied to Premiere's InstantMovie tools. So when you apply a theme, you take advantage of tools like the Auto-Analyzer, Auto Edit, and many other settings that automate video editing. You'd think that themes and InstantMovie would be an all-or-nothing proposition for your movies, but that's not really the case. Premiere lets you choose which theme elements it uses in your movie and gives you some options to fine-tune those features (Figure 7-23). That way, after you pre-view your movie with the theme applied, you can go ahead and make additional edits as you would with a movie you assembled from scratch.

The first important decision you need to make is whether you want to apply a theme and the InstantMovie magic to an entire movie or just to clips you select before you choose the theme. If don't select any clips, and there are no clips in the timeline, Premiere chooses clips from your project and adds them to the timeline. If you already have clips in the timeline, Premiere uses those. Otherwise, you can tell Premiere which clips to use by Shift-clicking or Ctrl-clicking the clips in either the timeline or the Media panel.

- **Add text for your titles.** Premiere provides the text boxes for the opening and closing titles. Click in a box and type away. Use Ctrl+Enter to add new lines. Each theme handles titling a little differently. In some cases, your titles may scroll up the screen, in others they may zoom in and out.

- **Choose "Auto" edit options for your movie.** These options are key to the way Premiere assembles your clips in a movie and how long it takes Premiere to build that movie. Click Auto Edit and Auto-Analyzer if you want Premiere to decide which bits of clips to use. You can choose to apply the theme to your entire movie or to just clips you select in the sceneline or timeline (Shift-click to select multiple clips).

- **Use theme music or choose your own.** Premiere gives you stock music and sound effects to match each theme, but you're not limited to those. You can choose your own music by clicking the Browse button, or you can choose to have no music at all. Use the slider to set the balance between the soundtrack music and the audio on your clips. Check the Smart Mix button and Premiere automatically drops the volume of the music when it identifies voices or other sounds in your video clips.

- **Set the speed and intensity for your movie.** Movie editing is all about timing. Certain subjects, like sports, deserve fast cutting and lots of movement and special effects. Other subjects, such as weddings, deserve a slower, more romantic sense of timing. Premiere's themes do a pretty good job of setting the beat, but you can use the sliders in the Speed and Intensity panel to fine-tune these settings. Sliders give you control over the use of effects and the speed of the cutting. Faster cuts means your clips are chopped into shorter pieces with fewer frames.

- **Set the duration for your movie.** Another timing aspect of your movie is the runtime, or duration. What's most important—the soundtrack music or your video clips? Often, you want the movie to run just as long as the background music, usually around 4 minutes. You can change this to a time of your own choosing, in which case the music will fade out or repeat. Another radio button, "Use All Clips", ensures that Premiere uses all the clips in a project in your movie. The music is adjusted accordingly.

- **Choose a sequence for selecting and assembling clips in the timeline.** Even if you let Premiere choose which clips to use and how to order them, you can still provide a little guidance. Most themes have their own ideas about how to order clips. They may look for a long shot at one point and want a closeup of a face at another. If you want to override the theme order, click the button Time/Date and Premiere organizes the clips according the clip's time/date stamp.

- **Choose whether or not to render your movie.** Depending on the options you've chosen, your movie may include lots of special effects. The best way to preview your themed movie in all its glory is to let Premiere render the effects, titles, and other elements first.

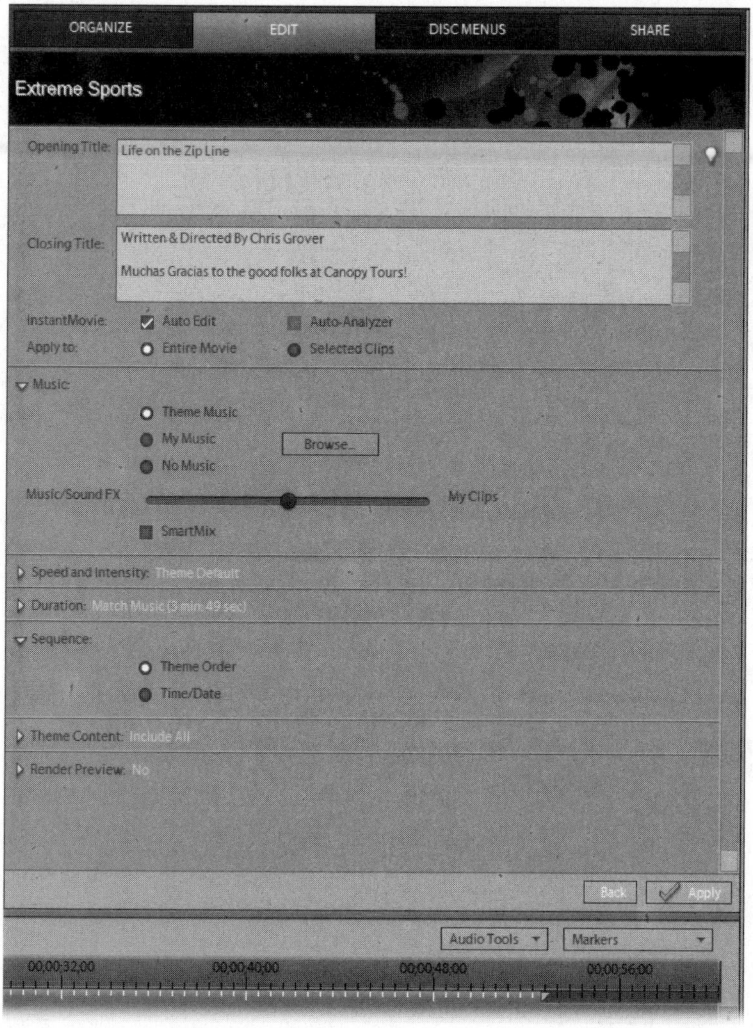

Figure 7-23:
You actually have a lot of control over InstantMovie and the theme elements that are applied to your project. For example you can choose to use the theme music, music from your own library, or to dispense with music altogether.

Edit a Themed Video

You may have creative differences with your theme or InstantMovie editor. No problem! You're still the movie mogul. You can jump in and edit a themed movie or InstantMovie just as you'd edit any other video.

After Premiere adds all the theme elements to a movie, it places the results on the timeline as a single grouped clip. If you want to replace clips, change effects, or otherwise edit your movie, you need to break the single clip back into multiple clips. Right-click the clip in the timeline and then choose Break Apart Instant-Movie from the shortcut menu. Once the InstantMovie appears on your timeline as separate clips, you can select the individual clips and add or remove effects. You can also replace or rearrange the clips on the timeline.

LOLA'S BIG SPLASH PROJECT

Add Effects to Your Movie

If you're working on the "Lola's Big Splash" project as you go through the chapters in this book, there are two special effects you can apply at this point.

Add the Zoom Blur effect to the final clip in the movie, then adjust the Blend With Original setting to get just the right look. In the next chapter, you'll learn how to make this effect change over time.

For the first clip, use the Time Stretch tool to reverse the way the movie plays. If the camera pan moves from the house to the street, it implies that Lola and her dog-walker leave the house, walk down the stairs and then show up on the street in the next clip.

CHAPTER 8

Create Animated Effects

When you edit video, the fourth dimension—time—is all-important. You want to control the pacing of your movies. You want voices in sync with images. Music should reflect the action on the screen and the mood you want to create. And effects should occur at just the right moment. In Chapter 7, you learned how to apply effects to an entire clip, while Chapter 6 focused on transitions (which are really effects at the beginnings and ends of clips). This chapter explains how to control the timing of those effects.

Premiere gives you frame-by-frame control over your effects. You'll learn how to make effects fade in and fade out at exactly the right moment and how to make pictures, clipart, and titles move around the screen.

What Is an Animated Effect?

An animated effect is one that changes over time. Consider these two animated effects:

- You want an object to start out perfectly visible and then to slowly fade away.

- You want a small picture-in-picture window to move around a static background.

Even though these two examples will look very different in your movie, they have something in common: the tool that Premiere uses to control the effect's timing. That tool is called a *keyframe*, and it's a type of marker you place in your movie's timeline. For example, in the first effect listed above, you want to control the degree of transparency of an object (Figure 8-1). By adding a keyframe, you tell Premiere, "At this frame, I want this object to be exactly this transparent." In the case of the mini-picture moving over the background, you can specify exactly where that picture-in-picture window is at a particular moment.

Figure 8-1:
By placing keyframes in your timeline, you can animate special effects. Here are three frames from an Opacity effect.

Top: A keyframe specifies 100 percent opacity.

Middle: Premiere automatically sets the opacity for all the frames in between. The result is a smooth, linear decrease in the opacity effect.

Bottom: Another keyframe specifies 35 percent opacity.

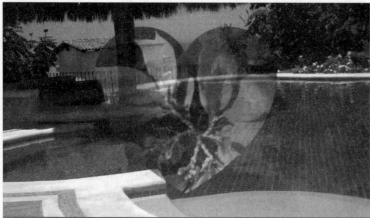

If you've ever used an animation program such as Adobe Flash, you may already be familiar with keyframes. Keyframes let you control changes in your movie on a frame-by-frame basis. But, thanks to technology, you don't have to fiddle with every single frame. Premiere does most of the heavy lifting for you. For example, 2 minutes into a clip on the timeline, you can create a keyframe for an effect called Gaussian Blur that specifies 100 percent opacity ("opacity" refers to how visible an object is; it's the opposite of transparency). Then, 4 minutes and 21 frames into the film, you can create another keyframe that specifies an opacity of 35 percent. Premiere takes care of all the frames in between, with each image a little more ghostly than the last.

Learn Keyframing

Keyframes are markers you pop into your timeline (or into the mini-timeline in a clip's Properties panel). The markers themselves don't appear when you preview your movie nor in your final video—they just control the action behind the scenes. Chapter 7 explained that the yellow line running horizontally through video and audio clips actually represents the value for an effect's property. Keyframe values show up as part of that graph. For example, Figure 8-2 shows the keyframes and graph line for the opacity effect shown in Figure 8-1.

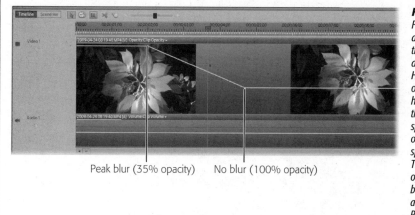

Peak blur (35% opacity)   No blur (100% opacity)

Figure 8-2:
Figure 8-1 showed an animated effect where the opacity of an image decreased over time. Here, the timeline's orange graph line shows how Premiere created that effect. One keyframe specified 100 percent opacity. Another specified the 35 percent. The graph line shows the opacity levels for the in-between frames, automatically set by Premiere.

Don't be intimidated by all this talk about keyframes and graph lines. The animation process is easy to understand, and you get instant feedback as you work. This chapter helps you master all the techniques you need to work with keyframes. Keyframe tasks include:

- **Add keyframes.** You can add keyframes at any point in your timeline with the push of a button. Drag the playhead to a spot in your film and click the Add/Remove Keyframe button shown in Figure 8-3 (see page 241 for more details).

- **Set effect properties at keyframes** (page 246). Keyframes lock in specific property and values for the effect paired with them. Some effects have only one property, while others have several. Using keyframes, you can control those properties individually.

- **Navigate between keyframes** (page 246). It's easy to jump back and forth from one keyframe to the next using the keyframe navigation buttons (Figure 8-3).

- **Copy and paste keyframes** (page 247). Once keyframes are in your timeline, you can copy and paste them as if they were words in a word processing document.

- **Move keyframes** (page 248). Moving keyframes to a different point in time is a simple click-and-drag operation.

- **Remove keyframes** (page 248). Yanking keyframes out of the timeline is a simple select-and-delete operation.

- **Fine-tune or smooth effect animation** (page 252). Premiere gives you tools to adjust the rate of change in your animations. You can make the changes abrupt, or you can make them ease in and out gradually.

- **Move objects around the screen** (page 256). When you move objects on the screen, you use the Motion fixed effect. Set the start and end points for a move using keyframes, and Premiere handles all the in-between positions.

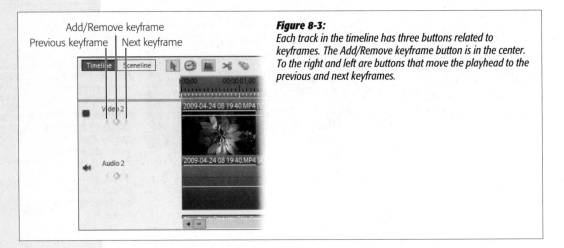

Figure 8-3:
Each track in the timeline has three buttons related to keyframes. The Add/Remove keyframe button is in the center. To the right and left are buttons that move the playhead to the previous and next keyframes.

Learn how to use keyframes in Premiere, and you have a head start should you learn other programs, like Adobe After Effects or Adobe Flash. The tools and techniques used in the three programs are quite similar. However, keyframes aren't an exclusive Adobe feature; nearly any program that animates objects has some form of keyframing. (To get a larger view of the timeline, find an empty spot on it, right-click and select Track Size → Large. For other tips on getting a better view of your timeline, see the box on page 245.)

Use Keyframes to Create Your Own Effect

Ready to animate an effect? Here's the place to start. Suppose you want to use the dramatic Find Edges effect on a picture of a flower. When you crank up the effect to full force, Find Edges makes your video image look like a drawing made with color markers. As the effect's name implies, it uses color change to find the edges in an image. Then it emphasizes the color on the edges and de-emphasizes it in the middle.

As with many effects, Find Edges has a slider that lets you specify how much the effect influences the original image. At half strength, it looks as if someone traced the image edges with a color marker (Figure 8-4). For your flower clip, say you want to start with a realistic image and then have the Find Edges effect gradually increase until it reaches full strength. Then, you want to fade it out so that by the end of the clip, the image is back to normal.

You create this effect by putting three keyframes in the timeline. Using these keyframes, you set the value for Find Edges' Blend With Original property.

Show Keyframes

Toggle Animation   Blend With Original slider

Figure 8-4:
The Find Edges effect makes a video image look like a drawing. A slider controls the Blend With Original property, which adjusts the intensity of the effect. You control the property using keyframes.

Add Keyframes to Set Effect Properties

Here are the steps you follow to change the intensity of the Find Edges effect. If you start with a single, short clip in your timeline, it makes the lesson quicker and easier:

1. **In the Tasks panel, click the Edit tab.**

    When you first open it, the Edit tab displays all of Premiere's effects. Use the two menus near the top of the panel to zero in on the effect you want.

2. **Set the first Effects menu to Video Effects and the secondary menu to Stylize.**

    The panel shows several effects that dramatically change the appearance of an image, including Alpha Glow, Emboss, Replicate, Strobe Light, and Find Edges.

3. **Drag the Find Edges effect onto the video clip in the timeline.**

   The Find Edges effect immediately changes the image.

4. **In the Effects panel, click the Edit Effects button and then click the triangle button next to the Find Edges effect.**

   When the Properties panel opens, you see the clip's fixed effects, along with the Find Edges effect you just applied. Click the triangle buttons to open the individual Effect panels, where you see the properties for each effect. Find Edges has two properties: Invert (a checkbox) and Blend With Original (a slider).

   The Blend With Original property is set to zero, meaning that Premiere isn't mixing any of the original image into the effect, so the effect will appear at full strength for the clip's duration unless you change this property's value.

5. **In the Properties panel, click the Show Keyframes button (the stopwatch in the upper right-hand corner).**

   Clicking the stopwatch button opens and closes the mini-timeline in the Properties panel, as shown in Figure 8-5.

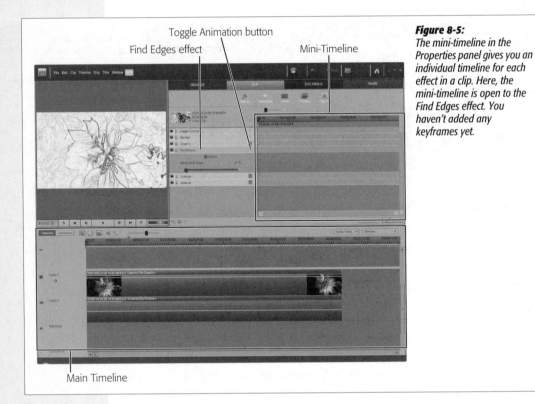

Toggle Animation button

Find Edges effect

Mini-Timeline

Main Timeline

Figure 8-5:
The mini-timeline in the Properties panel gives you an individual timeline for each effect in a clip. Here, the mini-timeline is open to the Find Edges effect. You haven't added any keyframes yet.

6. In the mini-timeline, drag the playhead back and forth, and then move it all the way to the left.

Note that as you move the playhead in the mini-timeline, the playhead in the main timeline moves, too.

Moving the playhead all the way to the left in the mini-timeline places the playhead on frame 1 of your clip.

7. Click the **Toggle Animation button in the effect's title panel.**

The Toggle Animation button looks like a stopwatch, too (see Figure 8-5)—what is it with Adobe and stopwatches?

When you toggle animation on, you activate Premiere's keyframe tools. In fact, when you toggle animation on for the Find Edges effect, Premiere creates two keyframes, one for each of the two properties associated with the effect (Invert and Blend With Original). In addition, each keyframe specifies that property's value. Here, Invert is turned off and Blend With Original is set to zero, so the top keyframe sets the Invert value to *deselected,* or off (because the checkbox is turned off), and the bottom keyframe sets the Blend With Original value to zero.

The keyframes appear at frame 1 (to the far left) in the mini-timeline, and they may be a little hard to see—look for two right-pointing solid arrows (they're actually diamonds, Premiere's shorthand for keyframes, but the edge of the mini-timeline has cut them in half).

8. Click the **Toggle Animation button (a stopwatch yet again) next to Invert and then click OK in the Warning box.**

The warning message explains that when you toggle animation off for a property, you remove any keyframes associated with that property. When you click OK, the keyframe for the Invert property disappears. At this point there's a single keyframe in the mini-timeline next to the Blend With Original property, as shown in Figure 8-6.

9. **Drag the Blend With Original slider to 100 percent.**

The video image is restored to its original appearance.

10. **Drag the playhead to the middle of the clip and then click the Add/Remove Keyframe button (it's the diamond-shaped button beside the Blend With Original property slider).**

Premiere creates a new keyframe for the Blend With Original property with a property value of 100 percent.

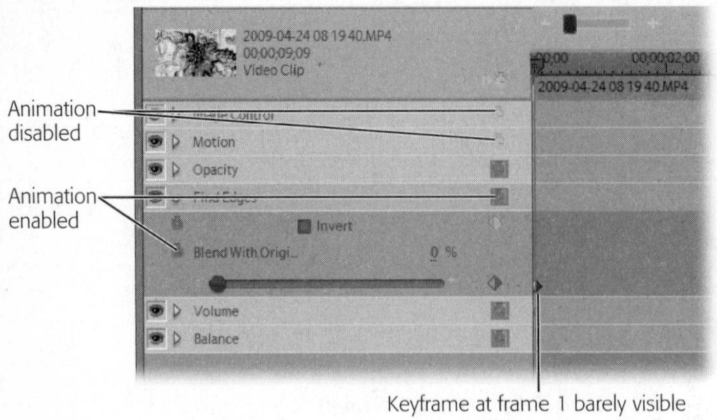

Figure 8-6:
Click the stopwatch toggle buttons to turn animation on and off for specific effects and properties. When you enable an effect or property, Premiere highlights the stopwatch icon in blue.

Animation disabled

Animation enabled

Keyframe at frame 1 barely visible

11. **Drag the Blend With Original slider back to 0 percent.**

    As you make the changes in this exercise, the image in the monitor changes, too. When you change the Blend With Original setting, you automatically create a new keyframe that stores the new value, and the keyframe appears in the mini-timeline (now as the full diamond shape). There's no graph line in the mini-timeline as there is in the main timeline, so all you see are diamond-shaped keyframes.

12. **Drag the playhead all the way to the right in the mini-timeline.**

    You can also press the End key to move the playhead to the last frame of the clip.

13. **Drag the Blend With Original slider to 100 percent.**

    The monitor shows the original image without the special effect. When you change a property's value, Premiere automatically creates a new keyframe in the timeline, which stores the changed value. Premiere adds the keyframe right where the playhead is.

14. **Press the Home button and then the space bar.**

    The preview in the monitor shows the Find Edges effect grow in intensity, reach a peak, and then fade back to the original image. The mini-timeline shows three diamond-shaped keyframes: one at each end (cut in half by the display) and one in the middle.

In this exercise, you created three keyframes. Each keyframe sets the Blend With Original property to a specific value. When you previewed the clip, you saw that Premiere automatically adjusted the values for the effect's Blend With Original property for all the frames in between.

UP TO SPEED

Get a Good View of Keyframes

Keyframes, graph lines, and some of the other tools you use to animate effects are pretty small. You can help yourself out by making some adjustments to your workspace.

Timeline View Adjustments: First of all, right-click in the timeline and then choose Track Size → Large from the shortcut menu. This increases the vertical height of the track in the timeline, which makes it easier to see keyframes and make adjustments to the graph line. If it's still hard to see your work, you can change the track height manually, as shown in Figure 8-7.

Use the Zoom slider above the timeline to make sure you've got a close-up view of the frames you want to animate. Drag to the right to make each visible frame larger. The tradeoff, of course, is that you see a smaller portion of the timeline as a whole. If the thumbnail images in the video track make it hard to see the graph line, click the video icon to the left of the track name.

Mini-Timeline View Adjustments: You can make similar changes when you work in the mini-timeline. There's a Zoom slider above the mini-timeline that lets you get a closer look at individual frames in the timeline. It also helps to drag the left border of the Properties panel and then the left border of the mini-timeline.

You can drag the bottom border of the Properties panel to give the Effects properties more room, but Premiere doesn't let you change the vertical height of the tracks in the Properties panel.

Both timelines have vertical and horizontal scrollbars you can use to zero in on particular frames, tracks, and properties. With a little fiddling, you can find the perfect view for the job at hand.

If you've got a big, beautiful wide-screen monitor or a dual-monitor system, choose Window → Show Docking Headers. Then you can drag the timeline or the monitor to a new location and expand your Premiere workspace.

When you want to put everything back the way it was, choose Window → Restore Workspace, and all Premiere's work panels return to their right-out-of-the-box proportions.

Adjust Track Height cursor

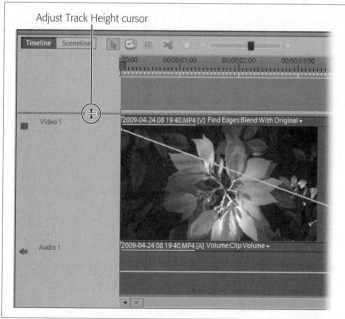

Figure 8-7:
Move your cursor over the top line on a track and you can drag the line to resize the track's height. This comes in handy when you want to fine-tune the effects graph line in a video or audio track.

Navigate Among Keyframes

It's often helpful to jump from one keyframe to the next, especially when you want to examine the different settings for an effect's properties. When you enable an effect, each property displays three buttons next to the mini-timeline, which are the same three buttons shown in Figure 8-3.The diamond-shaped button in the middle of the trio adds and removes keyframes. Drag the playhead to a frame and click this button to add a new keyframe, then set the value you want the property to have. The pointed arrows on either side of the Add/Remove Keyframe button move the playhead to the previous or next keyframe for that specific property. So if you examine the Blend With Original settings in the previous exercise, you can click the Previous Keyframe button to have the playhead jump to the left and display the value of the effect's property in that keyframe.

You can examine the values for any frame in the mini-timeline, even the values that Premiere automatically sets. Drag the playhead back and forth across the mini-timeline and you see the Blend With Original value rise and fall.

Note: When Premiere changes the property values for the frames in between keyframes, the process is called *interpolation.* You may hear editors talk about interpolation or "interpolated frames."

Set Effect Properties Independently

Using keyframes, you can animate certain effects, such as the Find Edges effect, and leave other effects, such as the Motion effect, unanimated. You can also pick and choose to animate specific properties within an effect. For example, Find Edges has two properties: Invert and Blend With Original. In the exercise on page 241, you animated the Blend With Original property and turned off the animation for the Invert property. That doesn't mean the Invert property doesn't have any effect on the clip; it just means that the Invert property isn't set to *change over time.* Go ahead and click the Invert checkbox. Immediately, you see in the monitor that Premiere reverses the image's color values. Drag the mini-timeline playhead, and you see that the Invert property has the same value (On) for the entire clip. There are no keyframes because you haven't turned Invert's *animation*—its change over time—on (you haven't clicked the stopwatch beside Invert yet, in other words).

With the playhead somewhere in the middle of the mini-timeline, click the Toggle Animation button next to Invert. Premiere inserts a new keyframe for the Invert property and stores the current Invert value (Animation On) in that keyframe. Drag the playhead to a new location and click the Invert checkbox again. Premiere adds a second keyframe in the Invert timeline, changing the value of the Invert property (to Animation Off).

Preview the clip, and you see that the Invert property is on from the beginning of the clip, and remains on as it passes the first Invert keyframe. At the second Invert keyframe, the Invert effect is turned off because it was at that point that you deselected the Invert button.

Move, Copy, Paste, and Delete Keyframes

Keyframes provide visual cues that help you animate a clip. The cues are subtle and, because keyframes are small, easy to overlook. The first and last keyframes in a timeline have shading on half of the icon, while keyframes in the middle have a solid color. In the mini-timeline, selected keyframes show a blue highlight, so they're a different color than unselected keyframes (light gray). For some examples of the different visual cues, see Figure 8-8.

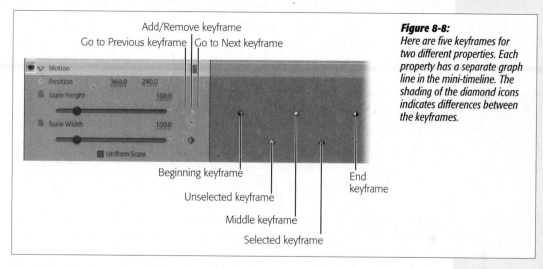

Figure 8-8:
Here are five keyframes for two different properties. Each property has a separate graph line in the mini-timeline. The shading of the diamond icons indicates differences between the keyframes.

Working with keyframes in the mini-timeline isn't that different from working with words in your word processor. You can select, move, copy, and paste them at different points along the timeline.

- **Select keyframes.** Click on a keyframe to select it. If you want to select more than one keyframe, hold down the Ctrl key as you click additional keyframes. If you want to select a bunch of keyframes that are close together, click and drag a selection box around them (Figure 8-9).

- **Deselect keyframes.** The easiest way to deselect all keyframes in the mini-timeline is to click an empty place in the timeline. If you select multiple keyframes with the Ctrl-click method, you can also Ctrl-click to deselect individual keyframes.

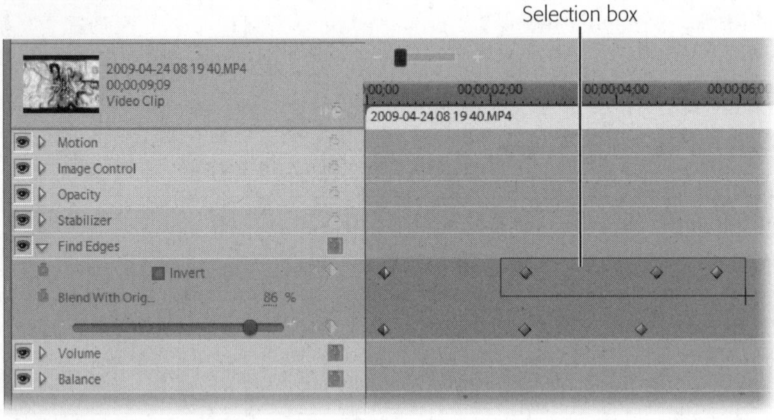

Figure 8-9:
To select several adjacent keyframes, drag a selection box around the group. Here, you're selecting the three top-right keyframes.

- **Move keyframes.** It's easy to move keyframes in the mini-timeline. Just drag the keyframe to a new location. You can even drag a keyframe past another one on the timeline—they don't bump into each other; they just pass on through like good neighbors on a trail. If you select several keyframes, they all move when you drag one of them.

- **Copy keyframes.** No big surprise here. You can copy selected keyframes using the usual Ctrl+C command, or you can right-click a selected keyframe and choose Copy from the shortcut menu. Premiere stores copied keyframes in its clipboard (its temporary memory) until you copy something else. You can paste the contents of the clipboard as described next.

- **Paste keyframes.** Press Ctrl+V to paste keyframes in the clipboard into the mini-timeline or right-click and choose Paste from the shortcut menu. Newly pasted keyframes appear at the position of the playhead. If you want, you can paste more than once—copying the same properties to different places in the mini-timeline.

- **Delete keyframes.** There are a couple of ways to delete keyframes. If you want to remove a single keyframe, the quickest way is to right-click the keyframe and choose Cut or Clear from the shortcut menu. The Cut command places a copy of the keyframe in Premiere's clipboard, and you can paste it into the mini-timeline later. The Clear command simply deletes the keyframe.

To delete multiple keyframes, shift-click to select the bunch and then press the Delete key. Alternatively, you can drag a box around several keyframes and then delete them.

- **Delete all keyframes.** Click the stopwatch to remove all the keyframes from a property or click the Effect stopwatch to remove all the keyframes in an effect. A box pops up to warn you that Premiere will remove the keyframes.

Suppose you want to create a strobe effect using Find Edge's Invert property. By turning the Invert property on and off rapidly, you create a flicker effect as you swap colors. Creating the strobe effect gives you a great way to practice moving, copying, and pasting keyframes.

Famous Movie Moment: In keeping with its 1960s origins, Peter Fonda's *Easy Rider* used lots of color-shifts and strobe-like special effects.

---

1. **Drag the playhead to a position near the middle of the mini-timeline.**

   Starting in the middle makes it easier to see and select keyframes.

2. **If necessary, click the Toggle Animation button for Find Edges and its Invert property.**

   The stopwatch icons display a blue highlight when you toggle animation on. When you first toggle the Invert property, it creates a keyframe.

3. **Drag the playhead to the right and then click the Invert checkbox.**

   Clicking the checkbox changes the Invert property and creates a new keyframe in the mini-timeline.

4. **Preview the effect.**

   The first keyframe sets the Invert property for the entire first portion of the clip. The second keyframe changes the Invert property.

5. **Click and drag the keyframes to adjust the timing.**

   Drag the keyframes closer together if you want to shorten the duration of the strobe effect.

6. **Ctrl-click to select the two key frames and then press Ctrl+C.**

   As you Ctrl-click the keyframes, they display a "selected" blue highlight. When you press Ctrl+C, Premiere stores the keyframes and their property settings in its clipboard.

7. **Drag the playhead to a new position to the right of the keyframes and then press Ctrl+V.**

   Premiere pastes two new keyframes into the mini-timeline. Each has the same values as the original keyframes.

8. **Repeat Step 7 to create multiple strobe flashes in the timeline.**

   You can paste the same copied keyframes into the timeline as many times as you want, as shown in Figure 8-10.

CHAPTER 8: CREATE ANIMATED EFFECTS

9. Press the Home button and then the space bar to preview the effect.

When you do, you see the image's colors reverse completely with each keyframe. If you move the keyframes on the timeline, you can change the timing of the strobe effect.

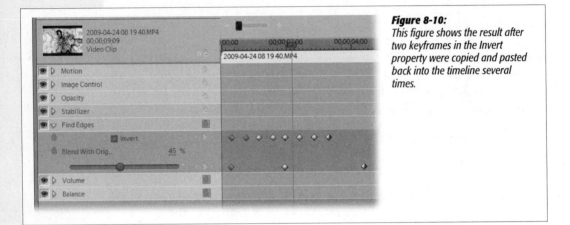

Figure 8-10:
This figure shows the result after two keyframes in the Invert property were copied and pasted back into the timeline several times.

Edit Keyframes in the Main Timeline

You can see keyframes in the main timeline, too. But there are some differences between this view and the view in the mini-timeline. In the main timeline, you can only see the value of keyframe properties one property at a time. Chapter 7 explained that the yellow line running horizontally through clips in the timeline reflect the value of a particular property in an effect. The name of the property that Premiere graphs appears at the top of the timeline. For example, Figure 8-11 shows that the graph line is displaying the value of the Find Edges:Blend With Original property. To display a different property in the clip, click anywhere on the property name and a menu appears where you can choose a different property.

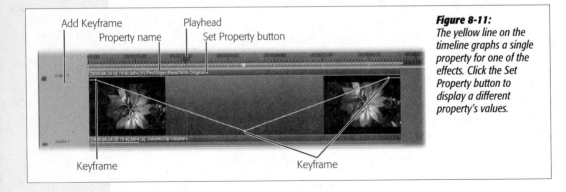

Figure 8-11:
The yellow line on the timeline graphs a single property for one of the effects. Click the Set Property button to display a different property's values.

Different types of properties have a different look in the timeline. Properties that are set with sliders and number boxes tend to change gradually over time, so their graph line looks smooth and consistent, like the Find Edges:Blend With Original line in Figure 8-11. On the other hand, a property like Find Edges:Invert is controlled by a checkbox, so it can only have one of two values, either On or Off. Figure 8-12 shows how different the graph line for the strobe effect looks as you turn Invert on and off using keyframes.

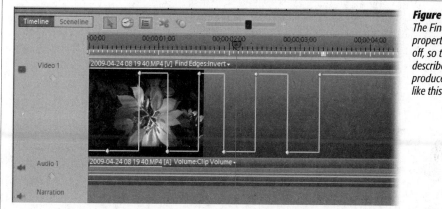

Figure 8-12:
The Find Edges:Invert property is either on or off, so the strobe effect described abovefs produces a graph line like this.

You can drag a keyframe in the main timeline to change a property's timing or value. As you do, a tooltip displays the time and the property value. That makes the timeline a great place to edit effect properties.

To change the timing of an effect, drag the keyframe horizontally along the timeline. To change the value for an effect's property, drag the keyframe vertically. As you make these changes, the yellow graph line adjusts to reflect the new values. Figure 8-13 shows the Find Edges: Blend With Original property as it's being changed.

You can use the same technique to change keyframe timing in the Properties panel's mini-timeline, but the main timeline is larger and gives you more information as you edit.

As in the mini-timeline, each video and audio track on the timeline has three keyframe control buttons—they mimic the Jump To and Add/Remove Keyframe buttons in the mini-timeline. Use the middle diamond-shaped button to add and remove keyframes. Use the left- and right-arrow buttons to jump to the previous or next keyframe. You can use the same techniques described on page 247 to select, copy, paste, and delete keyframes in the main timeline.

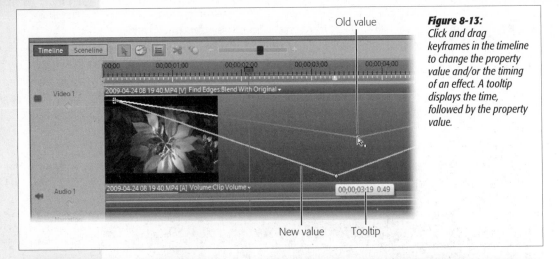

Old value

Figure 8-13:
*Click and drag
keyframes in the timeline
to change the property
value and/or the timing
of an effect. A tooltip
displays the time,
followed by the property
value.*

New value   Tooltip

Timeline vs. Mini-Timeline

Which is better, the timeline or the mini-timeline?

If you can edit keyframes in both the main timeline and the Properties panel's mini-timeline, how do you know which one works better? The answer is: You'll probably end up using both. Though they do many of the same chores, the tools and the views work differently. The mini-timeline makes it easy to see all the effects applied to a clip and easy to jump around and make changes to multiple effects and properties. The main timeline's graph makes it easy to see how a single property changes over time, but it's a little bit more cumbersome to jump around and compare different properties.

As you work with animated effects, you'll settle into your own rhythm for choosing the main timeline or the mini-timeline. Here are some general guidelines to get you started:

• **Use the mini-timeline** when you want to change multiple properties. It's quick and easy to jump around to different effects and properties in the Properties panel.

• **Use the main timeline** when you want to work primarily with a single property. The graph line makes it easy to visualize the changes of a single property over time. If you want to manually control the rate of change in an animated effect, you have to use the main timeline.

Control Change Between Keyframes

As any school kid knows, the shortest distance between two points is a straight line, and that's the method Premiere uses to create values between keyframes, as you can see by the yellow graph lines. For example, the straight line in Figure 8-11 shows the value for the Find Edges:Blend With Original property. But what if you don't want those values to take the shortest route to the next keyframe? Perhaps you'd like the Blend With Original property to change rapidly at first and then more slowly later on, and you want to display the Find Edges effect for a longer period of time? You could make those changes by adding keyframes, but you can do the same thing—and create a smoother effect—by changing the *type* of keyframe you apply to the effect. Right-click a keyframe in the main timeline, and the shortcut menu lists different types of keyframes (Figure 8-14).

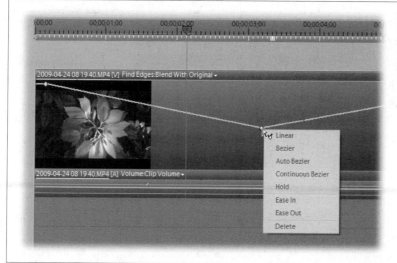

Figure 8-14:
Right-click a keyframe to change the keyframe type. There are five options. Use the Bezier options to create curved or more complex graph lines.

- **Linear** is the standard, shortest-distance-between-two-points keyframe that Premiere uses unless you change it.

- **Bezier** creates smooth curves around a keyframe. You can control the arc of the curve using Bezier control handles as shown in Figure 8-16. Unlike the Bezier options below, this option lets you change the position of the two control handles independently.

- **Auto Bezier** creates a consistent rate of change as the graph line passes through a keyframe; there are no abrupt changes of direction. When you change a keyframe to Auto Bezier, Premiere automatically positions the two handles to create the smoothest curves possible on both sides of the keyframe. If you manually move the handles, the keyframe changes to a Continuous Bezier.

- **Continuous Bezier** also creates a smooth curve, the difference being that you can manually adjust the handles so that the segments on either side of the keyframe are dramatically different. Even so, Continuous Bezier keeps the transition smooth. When you move one handle, the opposite handle moves automatically, too, and the two control lines always form a curve with a smooth form.

- **Hold** sets a property value and keeps that value constant. There may be a curve in front of the keyframe, but there's no curve following a Hold keyframe. In fact, the property value remains unchanged until the next keyframe or the end of the clip.

Tip: When you work with keyframes and Bezier curves, the clip background showing frames can be distracting. Click the Set Video Display Track Style button (Figure 8-15) to choose a simpler background for your curves and keyframes.

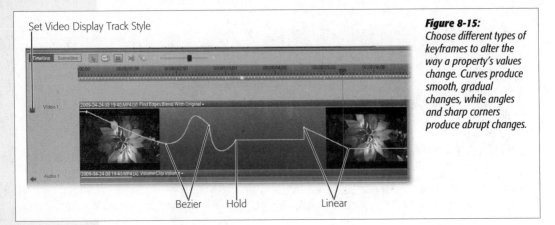

Set Video Display Track Style

Bezier   Hold   Linear

Figure 8-15:
Choose different types of keyframes to alter the way a property's values change. Curves produce smooth, gradual changes, while angles and sharp corners produce abrupt changes.

Adjust Bezier Curves

You find Bezier curves in all sorts of computer graphics programs because they're an easy way to define curves. In those programs, two grabbable lines with handles sprout from points along the Bezier curve. The lines don't appear in the final graphic—they're just there so you can easily adjust the curve. You, the artist, drag the handles to different positions, changing the shape of the curve.

Adobe includes Bezier curves in programs like Illustrator and Photoshop. In Premiere, it uses Bezier curves to control the shape of the Effects graph line. The graph line, in turn, charts the rate of change of an effect's property. If you're happy with the straight lines that Premiere automatically uses when you create a keyframe, you don't have to do anything. If you want to fine-tune the rate of change to create a smoother effect, right-click on a keyframe and choose Bezier or Continuous Bezier. Adjust the shape of the curve by dragging the handles (Figure 8-16). (The only way to manually control the curve of a graph line is via the main timeline; you can't edit a curve in the mini-timeline.)

If you haven't worked with Bezier curves in other programs, the easiest way to understand them is to jump in and work with them.

The biggest hassle with the Bezier curves in the timeline is that everything is so small: the keyframe markers, the Bezier control lines, and the handles. As a reminder, to get a larger view of the timeline, find an empty spot on in the timeline, right-click, and select Track Size → Large.

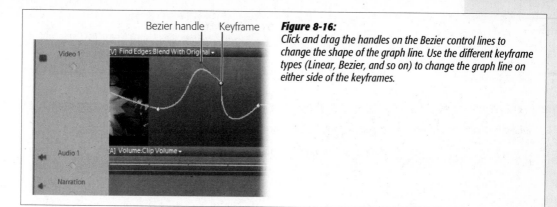

Bezier handle   Keyframe

Figure 8-16:
Click and drag the handles on the Bezier control lines to change the shape of the graph line. Use the different keyframe types (Linear, Bezier, and so on) to change the graph line on either side of the keyframes.

With all the different types of keyframes, how do you know exactly what type Premiere uses at a given point? When you work in the timeline, right click a keyframe and you see a list of keyframe types, one of which has a checkmark beside it. That checkmark identifies the type of keyframe it is, as you can see in Figure 8-17.

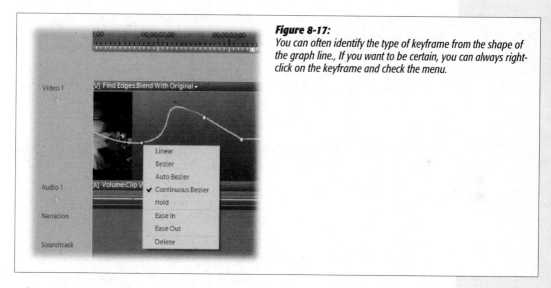

Figure 8-17:
You can often identify the type of keyframe from the shape of the graph line., If you want to be certain, you can always right-click on the keyframe and check the menu.

When you work in the Properties panel's mini-timeline, you won't see a graph line, but different types of keyframes have different icons. Figure 8-18 gives you a reference for Premiere's five types of keyframe. To convert a keyframe from one type to another—for example, from Linear to Bezier—right-click the keyframe and choose the new keyframe type from the shortcut menu.

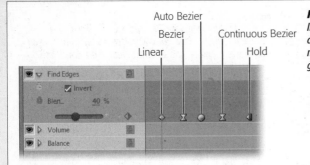

Auto Bezier

Bezier   Continuous Bezier

Linear   Hold

Figure 8-18:
In the Properties panel, each type of keyframe has a different icon. As you can see, you can mix and match different types of keyframes within the same graph line.

Animate Clips on the Screen

Every video clip has a fixed effect called Motion that controls the dimensions of a clip and its position on the screen. You use Motion effects when you want to zoom in on part of a clip. When you zoom in, you can pan and tilt the "camera" to see different parts of an image. (It's not really a camera, of course; you create the illusion of a camera by moving the clip so the video frame shows the good parts.)

When you create a picture-in-picture (PIP) effect, you shrink the size of a clip and then position it on top of another clip (Figure 8-19). With Motion effects, you can move the smaller images around the screen. Master the Position and Scale controls, and you can perform just about any multi-image effect in the book, from a *24*-style split-screen to a Ken Burns–style documentary shot.

There are only a handful of Motion effect properties you need to learn:

• The **Position** setting has two properties. They aren't labeled, but you can think of them as *horizontal* and *vertical* positions (or as *X* and *Y* coordinates if you're used to dealing with X-Y coordinates). The coordinate 0,0 is the upper-left corner of an image.

The Position setting defines the position of a clip's *anchor point*. Initially, an image's anchor point is the center of a clip, but you can change that using the Anchor Point setting, as described below.

• Use the **Scale** property to change the size of the playback window. All clips start out at 100% (full-frame). Use a setting smaller than 100 percent for picture-in-picture effects. Use a larger number to zoom in on and view a small portion of a clip. Premiere automatically keeps your image properly proportioned unless you turn off the Uniform Scale checkbox.

• **Scale Width** is grayed out and unavailable until you turn off the Uniform Scale checkbox. Then you can use Scale Width to distort your video image by changing its width and height independently.

- **Uniform Scale** controls whether the image stays in proportion. With the box checked, the image maintains the proportions of the original clip if you resize it.

- **Rotation** controls the rotation of a clip using degrees as the unit of measure. Clips rotate around the anchor point, which starts out in the center of the clip unless you change it with the Anchor Point settings below.

- **Rotate Left** spins your clip counter clockwise in 90-degree increments.

- **Rotate Right** spins your clip clockwise in 90-degree increments.

- **Anchor Point** sets the anchor point in your clip—the point used as the reference point for positioning and rotating clips. You define the anchor point using two numbers, which represent the horizontal and vertical coordinates of the image. The coordinate 0,0 is the upper-left corner of the image. Try it; click on each of the two anchor-point coordinates to highlight them and type "0" into each. The upper-left corner of your image becomes the center point on the screen.

- The **Anti-Flicker Filter** helps minimize flicker when interlaced video is shown on computer monitors and the new high-definition TVs. If you have flicker-prone images, experiment with this setting. Use it just enough to remove the flicker problem. If you use it at too high a setting, it can cause blurring.

Figure 8-19:
Use the Motion fixed effect to change the size of a clip and move it around on the screen. You can find everything you need when you go to Window → Properties and open the Motion panel.

FREQUENTLY ASKED QUESTION

Get Centered Again

I accidentally moved a video clip off-frame. I tried to undo it with Ctrl+Z, but it was too late. How do I get centered again?

It's not too hard to put your video back in the middle of the screen. Here's the solution.

Premiere puts the "anchor" for each image smack dab in the middle of each frame, so it's a matter of positioning the anchor in the middle of the frame again. Click the Properties button above the timeline and then open the Motion panel. The item at the top is the Position setting. If your video isn't centered, you've got some screwy numbers in there.

Next, choose Edit → Project Settings → General to open a dialog box with your project settings. Next to Frame Size, you'll see a horizontal number and a vertical number. Divide the horizontal number in half and replace the first number in the Properties panel Motion:Position setting with it. Then, divide the vertical number in half and put that in place of the second number. That's right: Because Premiere makes the center of your clip the anchor point, the proper horizontal position for the anchor is half the frame width, and the perfect vertical position is half the frame height.

Create Custom Zooms and Pans

Using the Scale settings, you can zoom in on a clip to view just a portion of an image. You can zoom in as much as 600 percent, but there's a cost to such a dramatic zoom: your image is likely to get fuzzy, as explained in the box on page 259.

Once you zoom in on a clip, you can choose which portion of the image to view. If you want to move the "camera" to view different parts of a clip while it plays back, that's called panning, which is explained on page 256.

Begin with a clip in the timeline and then follow these steps. The easiest way to see how Motion effects work is to use a still image or a clip where the camera isn't zooming, panning, or moving.

1. **Select the clip and choose Window → Properties.**

   The clip Properties panel opens, displaying the fixed effects, including Motion.

2. **Click the triangle button next to Motion.**

   The Motion effects panel opens, showing several settings, including Scale.

3. **Click Scale and type in a new number, as shown in Figure 8-20.**

   Like most number boxes in Premiere, you can also click and drag to scrub in a new value.

4. **In the monitor, drag the image to reposition it.**

   As you reposition the clip in the frame, the Motion:Position properties change automatically.

When you preview the clip, the entire clip plays at the new Zoom setting. The clip is now anchored to a single position in the frame.

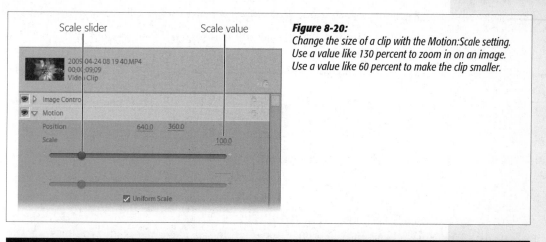

Scale slider | Scale value

Figure 8-20:
Change the size of a clip with the Motion:Scale setting.
Use a value like 130 percent to zoom in on an image.
Use a value like 60 percent to make the clip smaller.

Overcome Zoom-Size Issues

The major drawback to zooming in on a video clip is that it lowers the clip's resolution. Often, zooming in produces an image that's blurry or blocky. When you scale an image beyond 150 percent, it definitely starts looking scraggly. There are some ways to work around this problem. The easiest fix is to use a clip with an image that's larger than your video frame size. For example, if you create a video slide show from still images, you can use still images with a higher resolution than your video's frame size. That gives you plenty of room to zoom in and pan around your image. You can do the same thing with video if you shoot in high definition (1980x1080) and then render your movie at a lower resolution, such as standard DV (720 × 480).

Create an Animated Pan-Zoom Effect

The previous steps don't really create an animated Zoom effect. To do that, you need to create two keyframes with different zoom settings. Here are the steps to add a gradual zoom that also pans to a particular part of the image.

1. **In the main timeline, move the playhead to a position near the beginning of a clip.**

   Use either a still image or a clip with minimal motion.

2. **Click the Add/Remove keyframe button.**

   Premiere creates a keyframe in the main timeline at the position of the playhead.

3. **Click the Properties button in the timeline (or go to Window → Effects).**

   The clip Properties panel shows the fixed effects and any other effects you applied to the selected clip.

4. **Set the Motion:Scale property to 100 percent.**

   The zoom effect starts off displaying the full frame.

5. Click the Toggle Animation button beside Motion and make sure the button next to Position toggles on, too (in fact, all the effects should toggle on, which is fine for this exercise).

The keyframe stores the Position properties.

6. Move the playhead 5 to 10 seconds down the mini-timeline.

This is enough time to preview the zoom, but not so long that it puts you to sleep. Your mileage may vary.

7. Click the Add/Remove keyframe button beside the Scale property.

A second keyframe appears in the mini-timeline.

8. Set the Motion:Scale property to a value between 100 and 140 percent.

If you begin with a high-resolution image, like a hi-res still, you may want to zoom in even more.

9. Click the image in the monitor and drag it to reposition it.

Once you're zoomed in, you can reposition the image to find the most interesting part of it. A new keyframe for Motion:Position stores the value of the new position. When you move an image with animation toggled on, a line appears on the image in the monitor (Figure 8-21). This line won't appear in the final video—it's an animation tool called a "motion path."

Figure 8-21:
If you move an image with Motion:Position animation toggled on, Premiere creates a "motion path" that shows how the clip's anchor position changes over time. The circled crosshairs show the current frame in the path.

Path endpoint

Motion path   Current frame

When you preview the clip this time, the "camera" zooms in and moves to focus on the portion of the image you selected in the last step. Technically, this is called a Pan-Zoom effect. When you shoot video with a camcorder, you create a "pan" by pivoting the camera in a horizontal direction. Pivot in a vertical direction, and that's called a "tilt." To create a similar effect in Premiere, you move the anchor point for a clip. In the exercise above, you established the anchor point in Step 5 and repositioned it in Step 9. Dragging an image in the monitor is the same as changing the Motion:Position setting.

Tip: You can save any of the Motion effects for reuse by right-clicking the effect in the Properties panel and choosing Save Preset. See page 217 for all the details on creating presets.

Adjust a Clip's Motion Path

As shown in the previous example, you create a pan effect by creating two keyframes with different Motion:Position values. Unless you provide other instructions, Premiere creates a straight-line move. If you want to precisely control the motion of a pan or pan zoom, you use the "motion path" tool. It maps the position of an image's anchor point over time.

You sculpt and shape the motion path with keyframes and Bezier curve controls. Yep, those are the same tools you used to shape the Effects graph line, as described on page 254.

- **Move the start or end point of the motion path.** Place the playhead over the clip you used above and drag the X point to a new location.

- **Add a keyframe to the motion path.** First of all, make sure you have the Motion:Position property toggled on. Then drag the playhead to a new position. The frame marker, which looks like a circle with cross hairs, moves along the motion path as you do so. Drag the clip to a new position and Premiere automatically creates a new keyframe that stores the new Position property.

- **Change the shape of the motion path.** You change the shape of the motion path by repositioning the end points or the keyframes in the motion path (see Figure 8-22). You can create curves by right-clicking the keyframes and then choosing one of the Bezier options from the shortcut menu. See page 253 for a description of the different keyframe options.

Create Picture-in-Picture Effects

Premiere comes with a bunch of picture-in-picture preset effects. To check them out, open the Effects panel (Edit → Effects). Then, choose Presets from the first drop-down menu and choose PIPs in the secondary menu. Once there, you'll see dozens of presets that shrink clips to various sizes and make them scoot across the screen in various directions.

Tip: You can learn a few PIP tricks by adding one of the preset PIPs to your video and then analyzing how Premiere creates the effect. In the Properties panel, examine all the Motion properties as well as Opacity, Blur, and any other standard effects the preset uses.

Figure 8-22:
You can change the shape of a motion path using Bezier curves. It's just like changing the shape of an effect in the timeline.

Bezier control handle   Keyframe

Motion Path

If you prefer to roll your own PIP effect, it's not hard to do. You need to start out with two clips in different tracks in the Timeline—for example, in Video 1 and Video 2. Here are the steps to create a stationary picture-in-picture in the lower corner of the frame:

1. **Click the clip in the Video 2 track and then click the Properties button in the timeline.**

   The clip Properties panel shows the fixed effects, including Motion.

2. **In the properties panel, click the triangle next to Motion.**

   The Motion effect panel opens, showing the settings for different Motion properties.

3. **Click the Scale number box and type in *30*.**

   Naturally, you can scale your image down to any size that works for your project, but 25 to 30 percent works well for a lot of situations. It's similar to the PIP effect used for TVs.

4. **Drag the small clip to the lower left corner of screen.**

   As you reposition the picture, the Position settings change to show the new anchor point.

When you preview the movie, both clips play back, remaining in the same position. Using the Position settings, you can move the little picture around the screen, including having it pop in, play for a while, and then pop out of view.

Animate a Picture-in-Picture

To animate the PIP effect, all you need to do is add keyframes to control the Motion:Position property value for the smaller picture. Here are the steps to make the small picture from the previous exercise fly onto the screen from the left, hang around for a while, and then go off the right side of the screen.

1. **Drag the playhead all the way to the left of the clip.**

   This puts the playhead at frame 1.

2. **Change the Motion:Position value for the first position to a negative number, like −1,600.**

   The small picture should be completely out of view. The first number in the Position settings controls the image's horizontal position.

3. **Click the Toggle Animation button for Motion:Position.**

   This creates a keyframe at frame1 and stores the Position value.

4. **Drag the playhead to a position 2 or 3 seconds into the clip.**

   You'll make this point in time the place where your clip will pause on the screen.

5. **Change the first Position value to center the small window on the screen.**

   Try using the first anchor point value here. If your clip started at the same size as your project setting, this centers the clip horizontally.

6. **Drag the playhead down the timeline a few more seconds and click the Add/Remove Keyframe button.**

   Premiere creates a new keyframe and stores the same "centered" Position value once more but at a different point in the timeline.

7. **Drag the playhead to the end of the clip.**

   You're ready to create the final keyframe by specifying a position where the small picture is completely out of frame.

8. **Change the first Position value to a number that's greater than the width of your frame. For example, if your video frame size is 1,280 pixels, a value of 1,600 will do the trick, as shown in Figure 8-23.**

When you preview the PIP animation, it starts off with a single image. Then the small picture moves in from the left. It stops at the center of the screen for a few beats and then moves off the right side. Naturally, you can change the timing by moving any of the timeline keyframes horizontally. You can edit the motion path for the small picture as described on page 261. But first you've got to select the small picture. Move the playhead so the small picture is displayed on the screen, then double-click the small picture. Premiere adds a selection box around it and displays its motion path over the larger picture.

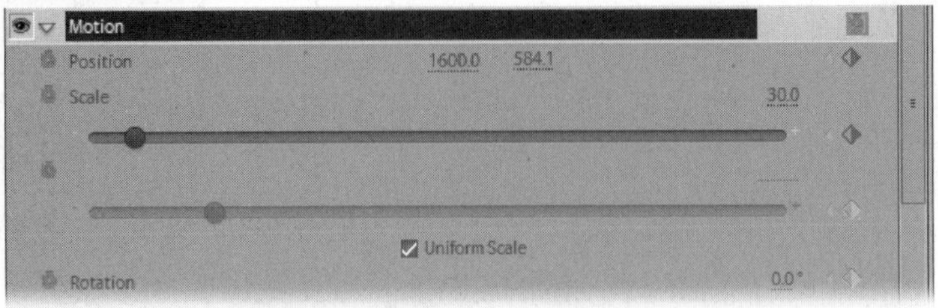

Figure 8-23:
You can move a window or other object right out of the frame of a movie by changing one of the position settings to a negative number or a number that's much greater than the frame size. Here, a horizontal setting of 1,600 puts the small picture's anchor point well out of 1280 × 720 frame.

Animate an Effects Mask

Chapter 7 explained how to create an effects mask (page 203), which is basically a small window that shows an effect. The part of the image outside of that window doesn't display the effect. To add an Effects mask to your clip, in the timeline (not the monitor) right-click on the clip and then choose Effects Mask → Apply from the shortcut menu. Then apply an effect like Find Edges to the clip. The effect only appears inside the mask. Click the Properties button in the timeline to see the Mask effect (Figure 8-24). The settings for it position the corners of the mask. You can animate the positions, the same way you moved the window in the exercise on page 261.

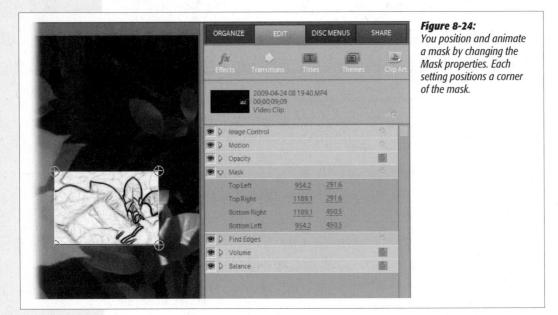

Figure 8-24:
You position and animate a mask by changing the Mask properties. Each setting positions a corner of the mask.

Split the Playback Screen

Splitting the playback screen for a *24*-style, multiple-screen effect is simply a matter of positioning more than one screen in the monitor. You can have many screens visible at a time, but when you get beyond four, it's hard for your audience to know where to look. Here are the steps for creating a three-screen movie, where all three images are the same size:

1. **Drag three clips to the Timeline, placing each on a separate track, as shown in Figure 8-25.**

   The clips should be on the Video 1, Video 2, and Video 3 tracks. While they're scaled at 100 percent, the top clip hides the clips underneath.

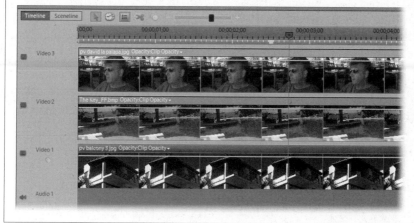

Figure 8-25:
These three clips play simultaneously because they're in the same position on the timeline. You have to scale to a smaller size for the clips in the lower tracks to be visible.

2. **Select the clip in the top track and click the Properties button in the timeline.**

   The Properties panel displays all the fixed effects and any standard effects you applied.

3. **Open the Motion panel and then change the Scale property to 50.**

   When you scale the clip to a size smaller than the playback window, you see the clip on the track below.

4. **Drag the clip to the top center of the screen.**

   If you want to be precise, you can change the values in the Motion:Position settings.

5. **Select the clip on the second track and then, in Properties, change Motion: Scale to 50.**

   When you change the size of this second clip, the bottom clip shows through.

6. **Drag the second clip to one of the lower corners.**

   Again, if you want to be precise, you can change the values in the Motion:Position settings.

7. **Repeat Steps 5 and 6 for the final clip.**

   With the clips scaled to 50 percent, you should be able to see all of each clip on the screen (Figure 8-26). Of course, you can scale and position the clip frames however you want.

Figure 8-26:
After placing three clips on different tracks as shown in Figure 8-25, you can resize and position the images for split-screen playback, as seen here.

Add Titles

You work hard to make your movies look good, but if you really want to give them a professional polish, don't stop after you edit your last frame. Consider adding titles.

You might think of titles as simply beginning and end credits, but they're useful in the middle of your movie, too. Think of all the times you've read "Six Years Earlier" or "Meanwhile, back at Alamogordo…" News shows and documentaries identify interviewees with banners at the bottom of the screen. And then, of course, there's Stephen Colbert's nightly segment "The Word," where titles mock him throughout his presentation.

This chapter covers titles from opening frame to closing credits. It starts off with guidelines for good titles, then explains how you can use predesigned title templates that come with Premiere. You'll learn how to tweak those templates for your own nefarious purposes and how to create your own custom titles. You'll even learn how to create a "crawl," the line of text that runs across the bottom of the screen during newscasts.

The Rules of Good Titles

The first rule of titles is: Use titles to tell your audience something they wouldn't know by just watching your movie. The second rule is: Titles need to be readable if you're going to accomplish the first rule.

What makes titles unreadable? Bad design decisions, like:

- Type that's too small.

- Type that gets lost on a busy background.

- Poor type/background color choices.

- Text that doesn't stay on the screen long enough.

You want all your viewers to benefit from your title's words of wisdom, so remember that not everyone has perfect vision or reads at the same speed you do.

If you use Premiere's title templates without any changes (except for the words, of course), you don't have to remember these rules, because the template designers know them forward and backward, and they followed the rules as they created the templates. But if you want to make changes to a template or if you want to create your own titles, consider the following tips:

- **Choose a readable font size.** Font size isn't usually a problem for opening titles, which tend to loom large in the center of the screen. But you want to make sure that your credit and caption titles are large enough to read, too. What's readable on your computer screen looks a lot smaller on a TV screen that's across the room, and even worse after your entire video's been compressed for the Web.

- **Choose a readable typeface.** Not all typefaces (a.k.a. fonts) are created equal, especially when it comes to video. Thin, spindly, delicate typefaces don't work very well for video. In general, you want your type fairly thick and bold, especially if you use it against a busy background. You can use a serif typeface, one that has little feet and adornments at the edge of the letters (the type in this paragraph is serif, for example), but if you do, use a heftier serif, like this one, called "**Bookman Old Style Bold**."

Mixing fonts on the same screen can be tricky business. If you're unsure which typefaces work well together, study or steal some of the combinations used in the title templates. You shouldn't need more than a couple of typefaces for your whole project—maybe a fancy one for your movie's title and something simpler and bolder for the smaller credits and captions.

- **Separate text from the background.** There are oh-so-many ways your type can get lost in a background image, many of which you learn through trial and error. If you overlay type on a busy or animated image, your titles are going to be hard to read. The solution? Use a solid background or still image. The best solution of all is to shoot footage specifically for your titles as shown in Figure 9-1. Usually, it's best to put light-colored type on dark backgrounds (as shown in Figure 9-2) or vice-versa. In a pinch, you can dial down the opacity of the background video clip; this helps make the text stand out.

- **Choose the right colors.** You want your text to contrast with its background without clashing with it. It's fine to coordinate colors, just make sure there's enough difference between them so that the text stands out. Drop shadows and outlines can help "lift" text off a page.

Figure 9-1:
This title appears over a still image selected specifically for the title sequence. The text is large, making it easy to read. Even though the colors of the text and wall are tonally similar, the heavy drop shadow does a good job of separating the text from the background.

Selection tool

Figure 9-2:
Here, you changed the main title to "London," while the subtitle still needs some editing. The Title Toolbar appears to the right of the monitor.

Title toolbar

Beyond that, some colors cause trouble when it comes to playback. For example, bright reds can create an unsightly smear on the screen because the color tends to bleed beyond the outlines of the letters. If you find colors bleeding when you preview your video, try making the color a bit darker. What's the best color for video? Most videographers feel yellows work best for type. Next to that, white characters on a dark background work well.

- **Stay within the frame.** When you work with titles, Premiere automatically displays two white rectangles on the screen, called "safe" areas. The larger rectangle represents the video-safe area. To make sure all TVs and playback windows display your video properly, keep your image within this frame. The inner frame is the title-safe area. Keep your titles inside this rectangle.

- **Control the scroll.** It's important to keep words on the screen long enough for people to read them. Most pros feel that you should be able to read the text two or three times at a decent clip before your video moves on, and that's true whether you use static or scrolling text. You don't want to err too much in the other direction, either. Nothing's gained by leaving text on the screen long enough to bore your audience.

In addition to these basic rules, consider aesthetics. A typeface like the one in the subtitle in Figure 9-1 might work great for a movie about horses or the Wild West, but it's a little old-fashioned for a film about marauding robots. If you use tinted text, keep the text color in line with your film's theme, too. You wouldn't use red and green for a Halloween movie, for example.

If you follow the rules for good titles and consider the aesthetics as you make design decisions, your titles will give your video a professional touch.

Use a Title Template

The fastest and easiest way to add well-designed titles to your project is to use Premiere's title templates. Drag an opening title template into your movie timeline, change the text to reflect your project, and you're done. It's easy and looks great. And the templates come with matching closing credits and smaller bottom-of-the-screen banners (which the pros call "lower-third" titles).

A big advantage to these templates is that professional designers created them, so they have some design flair to them (in the Drive-In template, for example, a half-circle of cars sit in front of a drive-in movie screen, which displays the title of your movie) and they include coordinated fonts. In addition, the templates respect the technical issues of titling; they use video-safe colors and have text boxes positioned within the safezones. Finally, if you apply one of Premiere's themes to your video (such as Extreme Sports or Music Video), the theme's title templates match the theme aesthetics.

The bottom line is that if you find a title template that works well with your project, you've saved yourself a ton of work. Even if you find a template that's close to what you want, you're ahead of the game because you can edit it using the techniques described on page 274.

Here are the steps for creating an opening title for a film called *London at Night*. You don't need any clips in the timeline for this first step, so start with a brand-new project.

1. **In the Tasks panel, click the Edit tab.**

   It displays five buttons for the major editing tasks: Effects, Transitions, Titles, Themes, and Clip Art.

2. **Click Titles.**

   Premiere displays its title templates, as shown in Figure 9-3. Two drop-down menus help you find the template you want: the Titles menu on the left and a secondary menu to the right of that.

3. **Click the Titles menu and then choose Entertainment.**

   The titles panel displays several templates that fit this category.

4. **Click the secondary menu and then choose NightVision.**

   Premiere displays three title templates. Their names describe their purpose: NightVision_title (for your movie's title), NightVision_credit (for end credits), and NightVision_left3rd (for captions). As you mouse over each title, it displays a Play button. Click one of them to see a thumbnail preview. For example, click NightVision_credit and closing credits roll off the screen.

   Click either of the other two clips' Play button, and the button disappears, giving you a clear view of the thumbnail—but, oddly, there's no animation, just a static title screen. In reality, these clips, like all title clips, have a duration of 5 seconds; it's just that it "plays" a static image.

5. **Drag the NightVision_title clip to the first frame in the timeline's Video 1 track.**

   NightVision_title is a static clip. It sports eerie green text and a background designed to look like an overhead shot of a town seen through a nightscope.

   The Title Toolbar appears next to the monitor. The arrow icon at the top represents the Selection tool. Use it to select a new font or text box in the monitor. The tool second from the top, called the Type tool, lets you edit text—just what you need to change this template for your project.

6. **Click the Select tool and then click the words "Night Vision" in the monitor.**

   When you do, a rectangular frame and control handles appear around the words. You've selected a text box.

7. **In the Title Toolbar, click the Type tool and then drag the text cursor (it looks like an I-beam) over the words "Night Vision" to highlight them.**

   Once you select the text box to edit a title, you can use many of the standard word-editing tricks you find in word processors. For example, double-click a word to select the entire word. When you start typing after you highlight text, new text replaces the selected text. You can use arrow keys to move the cursor within the text. Be patient though, even on a fast computer there's a bit of a lag when you work with titles.

8. **Replace "Night Vision" with the word *London*, as shown in Figure 9-2.**

   Then choose the Selection tool and click anywhere on the screen. When you do, you see the words in the title clip in the timeline change from "Night Vision" to "London" (this template automatically capitalizes all words, by the way). Keep in mind that any changes you make to the title in the monitor merely change the *clip*, not the template itself. Back in the Titles Template panel, NightVision_title looks just as it did when you started.

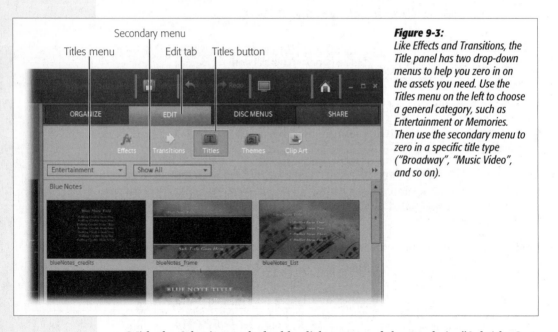

Figure 9-3:
Like Effects and Transitions, the Title panel has two drop-down menus to help you zero in on the assets you need. Use the Titles menu on the left to choose a general category, such as Entertainment or Memories. Then use the secondary menu to zero in a specific title type ("Broadway", "Music Video", and so on).

9. **With the Selection tool, double-click on any of the words in "Subtitle Goes Here."**

   When you double-click text in a title, Premiere automatically opens the text box for editing and changes your cursor to the Type tool.

10. **Replace "Subtitle Goes Here" with "At Night".**

    The complete title now reads "London" in big type, and, below that in smaller type and with a different but complementary typeface, "At Night." Even after you changed the text, the titles retain the template's style.

You edit all the title templates the same way. It doesn't matter if they're for opening titles, credits, or captions. To use a title, drag it onto your timeline. If you want to change the running time for a title, trim it just the way you would any clip—drag the end of the clip in the timeline.

When you put a title on an empty part of the timeline, Premiere automatically gives it a black background. If you drag a title to a track above an existing clip, Premiere usually makes the title transparent so the title appears over the clip underneath, as you can see in the Night Vision credits in Figure 9-4.

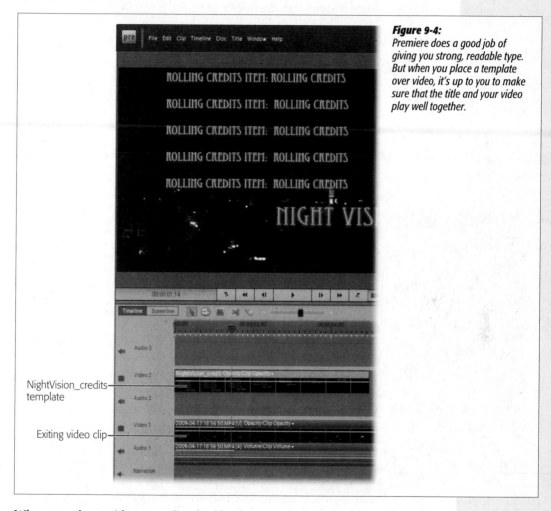

Figure 9-4:
Premiere does a good job of giving you strong, readable type. But when you place a template over video, it's up to you to make sure that the title and your video play well together.

NightVision_credits template

Exiting video clip

When you place a title over a clip, double-check it against the Rules of Good Titles explained on page 267. In particular, make sure there's enough contrast between the text color and your background colors. Most of Premiere's templates use effects like drop shadows to help separate the type from the background. If you overlay a title and find that background movement detracts too much from the text, you can always use a still image instead. Page 222 explains how to create a still image from any frame in a video clip.

Edit a Title Template

The example above explains how to add a title from a template and how to change the title's text to match your project. Sometimes, you need to tweak a title a little more to make it work. For example, what if your movie was named "Puerto Vallarta at Night" instead of "London at Night"? Can you shoehorn the longer title into the NightVision template? Sure. Here's how:

1. **Double-click the main title—the one that reads "London"—and change it to "Puerto Vallarta."**

   When you finish, the title looks something like Figure 9-5, with the text stretching outside of the title-safe area (and even outside the video-safe area).

Note: The figures for this example were created with HDV 720-pixel project settings. Your mileage may vary if your project has a different frame size.

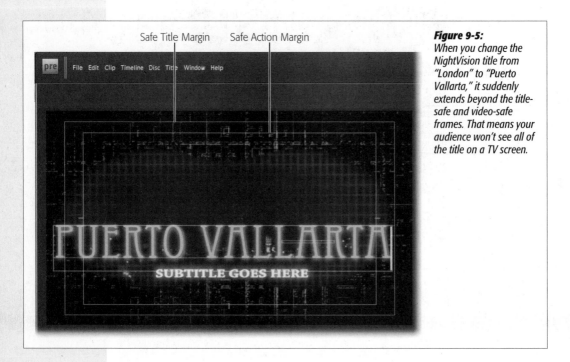

Safe Title Margin   Safe Action Margin

Figure 9-5:
When you change the NightVision title from "London" to "Puerto Vallarta," it suddenly extends beyond the title-safe and video-safe frames. That means your audience won't see all of the title on a TV screen.

2. **Move the text cursor to the beginning of the word "Vallarta" and press the Enter key.**

That creates a new line in the text box (just as pressing the Enter key in a word processing document would). Now the two words fit horizontally on the screen, but "Vallarta" covers up "At Night", and it goes beyond both safe frames at the bottom, too. (Next time, go to Aruba.)

3. **Click the Selection tool and then drag the Puerto Vallarta text box up.**

The Selection tool lets you drag text boxes to any position on the screen. (You can drag graphics objects, too, like the clip art discussed below.)

You can make lots of other changes to title templates. In fact, you can change everything about a template—Premiere doesn't lock any of it down. So you have control over the typeface, text boxes, background image, the works. And you can add new elements, too, like clipart or an additional text box. That's why templates are such timesavers.

The Title Toolbar

Chances are, you'll use the tools in the Title Toolbar (Figure 9-6) whether you use Premiere's templates or you create your own. These tools are the same kind you find in most graphics programs. They let you select and edit text, geometric shapes, and lines. If you know other Adobe programs, you'll feel right at home. If not, the learning curve is shallow.

Here's a rundown of the Title Toolbar:

- The **Selection** tool looks like an arrow. Click it and then click objects in the monitor to select them and start editing. Use Shift-click to select more than one object. Remember, a clip is an object; sometimes you have to select the clip before you can select objects within the clip (like text boxes).

- The **Type** tool looks like an I-beam. Click on it, and you can then click anywhere in the monitor to create a new text box. If you click on an existing text box, you can edit the words there just as you would with a word processor. Keep in mind that you can edit text boxes, but you can't edit text that's embedded in a still image or imported graphic.

- The **Shape** tools, which include the **Rectangle, Ellipse,** and **Rounded Rectangle** tools, are handy for making backgrounds for type. You can make these shapes look snazzy with Premiere's color, gradient, and transparency tools.

- The **Line** tool is like the Shape tools—it gives you a way to draw on the monitor. You can use the same color, gradient, and transparency features on lines.

- The **Vertical Center** and **Horizontal Center** buttons move a selected object to the center of the screen.

• The **Color Properties** icon opens a color palette with lots of options to add style to text, shapes, and lines. For more details, see page 277.

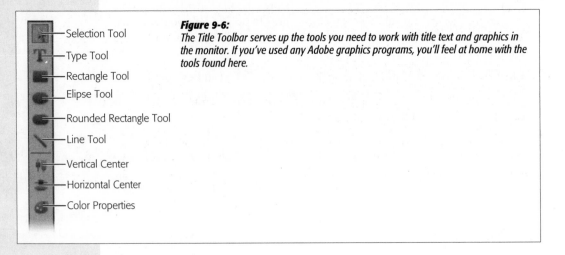

Selection Tool
Type Tool
Rectangle Tool
Elipse Tool
Rounded Rectangle Tool
Line Tool
Vertical Center
Horizontal Center
Color Properties

Figure 9-6:
The Title Toolbar serves up the tools you need to work with title text and graphics in the monitor. If you've used any Adobe graphics programs, you'll feel at home with the tools found here.

Create a Still Opening Title

This section explains how to create your own title from scratch. It starts with the simplest of title designs—white type on a black background—and then, in the following examples, shows you how to edit it and add new features using different titling tools.

Tip: For most movies, the opening title is the most important one. If it's not the first thing that appears on the screen, it's pretty close. Opening titles usually contribute to the overall tone of a movie, so they should match your content in feeling.

Opening titles often express a little more artistic flair than other titles, too. With fewer words on the screen, an opening title is usually larger, so you don't have some of the readability issues you might have with ending credits or captions.

You can perform this little experiment on a brand-new project:

1. **Move the playhead to an empty position in the timeline.**

   You can use any position, but if you're creating an opening title, you might as will begin at frame 1.

2. **Choose Title → New Title → Default Still.**

   Premiere adds a new 5-second clip to the timeline—it has a black background and white type that says "Add Text" (Figure 9-7). That's just a little hint, in case you don't know what to do next.

   The Title Toolbar sits to the right of the monitor (Figure 9-6).

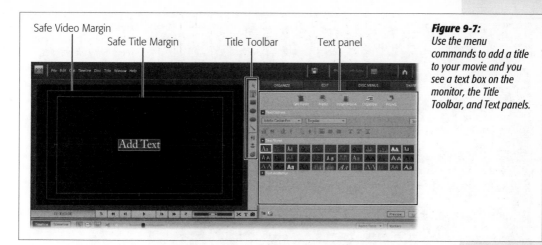

Safe Video Margin
Safe Title Margin   Title Toolbar   Text panel

Figure 9-7:
Use the menu commands to add a title to your movie and you see a text box on the monitor, the Title Toolbar, and Text panels.

3. Click the Type tool and then click the text box and highlight "Add Text". Then type in your title. Something like *Annie Hall* might be suitable.

   If you want to create a multiline title, press the Enter key at the end of each line.

4. With the text block still selected, click the Vertical Center and then the Horizontal Center buttons in the Title Toolbar (they look like transistors oriented 90 degrees from each other).

   With two clicks you've got yourself a perfectly centered title, as shown in Figure 9-8. Don't want it perfectly centered? Use the Selection tool to drag your text anywhere on the screen.

Famous Movie Moment: Titles for most Woody Allen movies use white text with a serif typeface on a black background. He began using that style in 1977 with *Annie Hall,* winner of multiple Academy Awards, including Best Picture. Since then, he's only varied from the white-on-black style a couple of times, most notably in *Manhattan,* where he used the neon sign on the side of a building (customized to read "Manhattan") for the movie's title.

Change Text and Background Colors

If you're not a fan of the Woody Allen School of Movie Titles, you can add color to the text or the background of your opening title. Changing the text to a different solid color is a cinch. Here are the steps:

1. Use the Selection tool to select the text box.

   The selected box displays an outline and handles around the text.

2. In the Title Toolbar, click Color Properties, which is the palette icon down at the bottom.

   The Color Properties palette opens, as shown in Figure 9-9. It gives you all the tools you need to pick a color or create a gradient (a color that subtly changes).

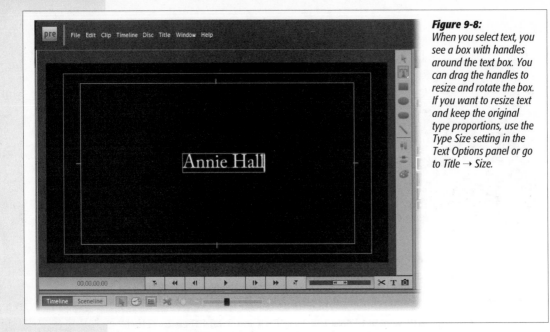

Figure 9-8:
When you select text, you see a box with handles around the text box. You can drag the handles to resize and rotate the box. If you want to resize text and keep the original type proportions, use the Type Size setting in the Text Options panel or go to Title → Size.

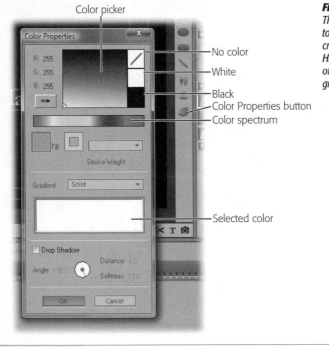

Figure 9-9:
The Color Properties panel combines the tools to pick any color in the rainbow with tools to create a few different gradient effects, too. Hidden under the Gradient menu are a couple of options for effects that aren't necessarily gradients: Bevel, Eliminate, and Ghost.

3. In the color spectrum bar, choose a hue.

The spectrum bar lets you pick a basic shade, such blue, red, green, or yellow.

4. To choose a specific shade, click in the color picker box above the bar.

A circle marks the spot you click; you can move it around with your cursor to choose just the shade you want.

The letters in the title text box change to match your selection, and Premiere displays the selected color in the gradient box near the bottom of the Color Properties palette.

Create a Solid-Color Background

When you add a title using the method described on page 276, Premiere automatically gives you a black background for the clip. (If you place the title on a track above an existing clip, the black area becomes transparent and the underlying clip shows through.) If you want to put your title on any color other than black, you need to create a background using one of the Shape tools.

1. In the Title Toolbar, click the Rectangle tool.

The cursor changes to a cross.

2. In the monitor, drag the cursor to create a rectangle.

With the rectangle tool, you can create a rectangle of any dimensions. If you want the rectangle to cover the entire screen, it's best to make the rectangle extend beyond the edges of the frame, as explained in Figure 9-10. Because you create the rectangle *after* Premiere creates the text box, the rectangle layer hides the text underneath. You need to change the stacking order of the layers to put the text back on top.

3. Right-click the rectangle and then choose Arrange → Send to Back.

Sending the rectangle to the back (behind the text-box layer) ensures that the text will show over it.

If you left your title white, you won't notice when you send the white rectangle to the back. Follow Steps 4 and 5 below to give the rectangle a color, and you'll see the white title overlay the now-tinted rectangle.

4. With the rectangle still selected, click the Color Properties icon.

The Color Properties palette opens.

5. Click a shade in the Color Spectrum and then choose a specific color with the Color Picker.

You see the rectangle's color change immediately in the monitor, making it easy to try different colors until you find the one that works best with your title.

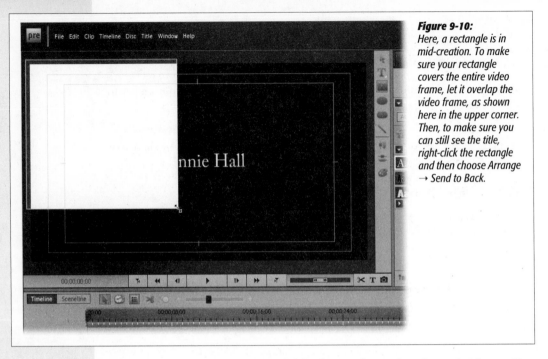

Figure 9-10:
Here, a rectangle is in mid-creation. To make sure your rectangle covers the entire video frame, let it overlap the video frame, as shown here in the upper corner. Then, to make sure you can still see the title, right-click the rectangle and then choose Arrange → Send to Back.

In this example you created a solid background covering the entire frame. You could just as easily create a strip of color in the lower third of the screen for a caption-style title, like the one in Figure 9-11.

Create a Color Gradient

When you first open Color Properties, Premiere sets the gradient menu to Solid, which produces the solid color described in the two previous examples. If you want to create a more complex color effect, you can apply a gradient, where one color gradually blends into another. Here are the steps to do that:

Note: This exercise uses the project begun on page 276. It includes a text box over a solid-color rectangle.

1. **Select the solid background rectangle.**

   You need to select the rectangle (and any object you want to edit) before you open the Color Properties panel. If it's hard to select the rectangle simply by clicking on it, right-click in the monitor and choose Select → Next Object Below as many time as it takes to highlight the rectangle.

2. **In the Title Toolbar, click Color Properties.**

   The Color Properties palette opens, displaying the current settings for the rectangle.

Figure 9-11:
*When you use lots of
titles in your video, it's a
good idea to use the
same background colors
and fonts throughout.*

3. **Click the gradient drop-down menu and choose Linear Gradient.**

   The Color Properties palette displays a gradient bar with two square "color stops," as shown in Figure 9-12.

4. **Click one of the color stops and then choose a new color.**

   When you select a color stop, a gray highlight appears on the small triangle above it to confirm that you selected it. The current color appears highlighted in the Color Picker. You can use either the Color Spectrum bar or the Color Picker to choose a new color. Part of the rectangle's color changes to the new color. Sometimes there's a little bit of a delay, so be patient.

5. **Click the other color stop and set its color.**

   Repeat the process in Step 4 for this color stop.

   Note the three boxes to the right of the Color Picker. The top one gives your selection transparency, the middle one is a shortcut for a white background, and the bottom one is a shortcut for a black background.

6. **Drag the color stops.**

   Dragging the color stops along the horizontal bar changes the coverage of each color. To increase a color's coverage, drag it away from the edge.

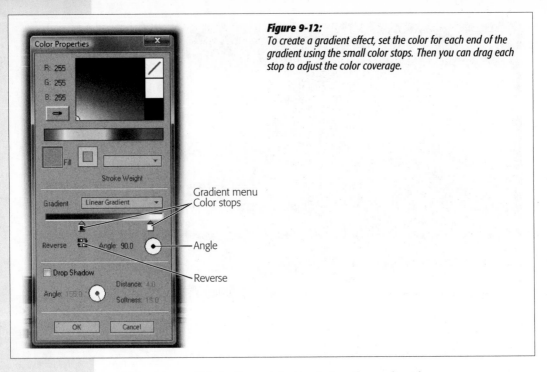

Figure 9-12:
To create a gradient effect, set the color for each end of the gradient using the small color stops. Then you can drag each stop to adjust the color coverage.

7. **If necessary, click the Reverse button below the gradient bar.**

   If the colors are in exactly the wrong spots, click Reverse. The colors in the color stops swap places and the change appears in the monitor.

8. **If necessary, type a new value in the Angle box or click on the Angle circle.**

   By adjusting the angle, you change the direction of the gradient. For example, you can make a gradient flow diagonally across the rectangle.

There are three color gradient options in all:

- **Linear.** One solid color blends into another solid color (or fades to transparency). The effect moves along a straight line, as shown in Figure 9-12.

- **Radial.** Similar to the linear gradient, except that one color begins as a single point on the screen and a circular blend radiates out from that point.

- **4-Color Gradient.** The gradient is made up of four colors, each starting from a different corner of the rectangle.

In addition to the color gradients, you can choose three other gradient effects:

- **Bevel.** The bevel option gives your rectangle a simulated 3D beveled edge (see Figure 9-13). You can specify the gradient's background color (use the left box under the drop-down menu) and set the edge color with the right box. The size property sets the thickness of the bevel (in pixels), and the balance box specifies how "fuzzy" the bevel edge is.

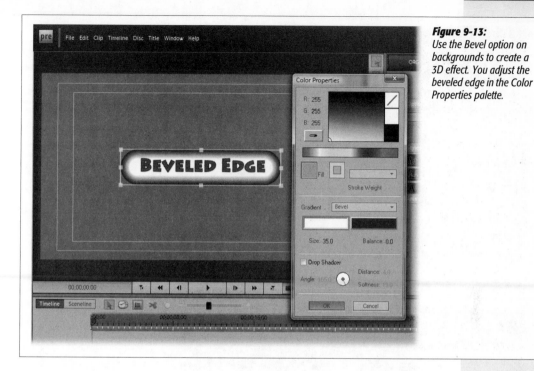

Figure 9-13:
Use the Bevel option on backgrounds to create a 3D effect. You adjust the beveled edge in the Color Properties palette.

- **Eliminate.** Makes the innards of text characters (or a shape) transparent so the letters have an outline (so you can read them), but no "fill" color, meaning no color within the letter itself. This effect is good for creating an outline of text or an outline of a shape. Unlike Ghost, below, the Eliminate option doesn't cast shadows.

- **Ghost.** Ghost is similar to Eliminate, creating a transparent fill; however, it adds a shadow to the characters within the shape, as shown in Figure 9-14. You can use the Color Properties palette to set the distance, angle, and softness of the shadow.

Format Title Text

After you add a title to the timeline, you may notice several new options over in the Tasks panel. The panels shown in Figure 9-15 appear whenever you work with Text.

- The **Text Options** (Figure 9-16) panel provides standard tools for changing the characteristics of text: its typeface, size, spacing, alignment, and style. If you're not sure what a setting does, hold your cursor over it and a tooltip identifies the characteristic. To use these tools, select the text you want to format and the characteristic you want to change. Here's what you can do:

  — *Change Font.* The drop-down menu under Text Options lists every font installed on your computer, but that doesn't mean they all work well for video titles. See page 268 for guidelines on choosing a good font (also known as a typeface).

Figure 9-14:
Ghost, another effect under the Gradient menu, creates interesting type effects, some of which appear in 3D. Here, you see a thin black stroke on the letters in combination with a drop shadow.

— *Change Font Style.* Many typefaces have alternate styles, such as Bold, Bold Italic, and SemiBold. Select them with this drop-down menu, to the right of the font menu.

— *Save Style.* If you create a custom text style and want to use it for other titles or other projects, click the Save Style button and give your style a name. After you save it, it appears in the Text Styles panel, where you can apply it to text with a single click.

— *Change Text Size.* Select text in the monitor and then change the number next to the two Ts. Simpler, bolder fonts are more readable at smaller sizes. With most fonts, you probably don't want to use a font size smaller than 60.

— *Leading.* The distance between two lines of text is known as leading, because in the old days printers used lead slugs to separate lines of type. You don't need any metal here; all you have to do is change this number.

— *Kerning.* With large type, like that in titles, designers often customize the distance between the letters that make up a word. For example, it's not unusual to close the gap between the letters A and V. Other times, designers will deliberately change the spacing to create a style.

Text with exaggerated spacing is called letter-spaced text. Text that's packed tightly together is called condensed. You can adjust the distance between the

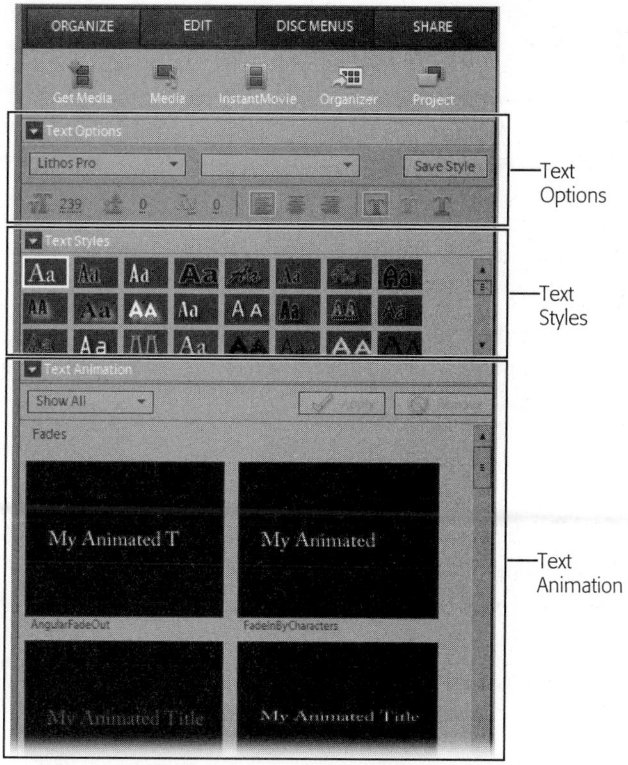

Figure 9-15:
Select a text box in the monitor, and the Tasks panel shows three text panels. Using the Text Options panel, you can choose font typefaces, sizes, and format options like bold or italic. Text Styles shows lots of styles predesigned for video. Text Animation gives you prebuilt effects for type that moves.

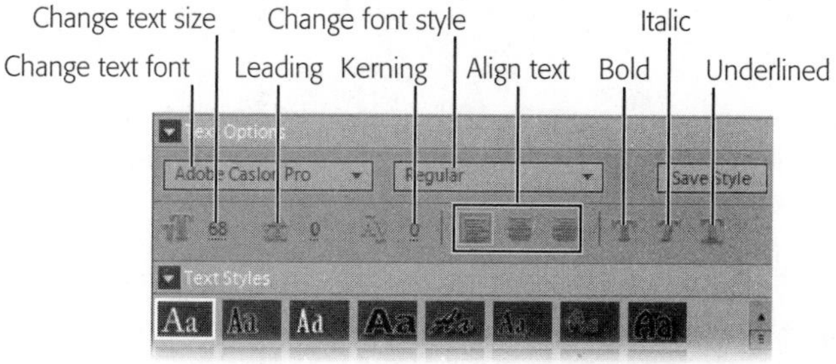

Text Options

Text Styles

Text Animation

Figure 9-16:
The Text Options panel packs a bunch of text-formatting tools into a very small space.

letters in your titles en masse or a couple at a time. Just select the letters you want to adjust. Negative numbers scrunch letters together, positive numbers spread them apart.

— *Change Paragraph Alignment.* You've got the usual suspects here: Left Align Text, Right Align Text, and Center Text.

— *Bold, Italic, Underline.* Use these buttons as a shortcut to change the style of your text. Depending on the font, some options might not be available. For a complete list of the styles available for a specific font, use the Change Font Style menu described above.

- The **Text Styles** panel offers styled type designed specifically for video's special requirements. To use any of these styles, click on a text box and then click on a style. Use the scroll bar on the right to see all your choices. There's quite a variety, so it may not be hard to find one you want for your project.

  Many of the styles use drop shadows and outlines to increase their readability. In fact, if you want a brief tutorial on designing text for video, study the elements the Adobe designers used in this library. Once you're an expert, you can add one of your own designs. Just select text formatted with your style and then click the Save Style button in the upper-right corner.

- The **Text Animation** panel provides predesigned animation effects for your text. Click one of the animation thumbnails to see a preview. As with other special effects and transitions, you probably want to use discretion when you animate text. There's a fine line between an amusing text effect and one that's boring after the first couple of seconds. To apply animation to text, drag the effect onto the text box in the monitor.

Place a Title Over a Still Image

Reading a title over a moving image can be difficult and distracting. One solution is to use a freeze frame from your video clip as the background. If you want the image to change along with different titles, use a series of stills.

1. **Position the playhead on a frame whose image you want to capture.**

   Simpler backgrounds work better.

2. **Click the Freeze Frame button.**

   The Freeze Frame window opens, as shown in Figure 9-17.

3. **Click Insert in Movie.**

   Premiere inserts a 5-second clip of the still image into the timeline. At this point, it's like any old clip. You can move it, drag it to another track, or trim it by dragging the end of the clip.

4. **If necessary, apply video effects to enhance the image.**

   You can often make titles more readable by applying one or more of the Adjust effects to the background image. Go to Window → Effects. Then, in the Tasks panel, go to Video Effects → Adjust. Experiment with Auto Color, Auto Contrast, and Auto Levels.

   More dramatic, stylized effects work well with titles, too. For example, you can de-saturate the color in an image, making it almost-but-not-quite black-and-white. Then use a strong color for the title text over it.

   To control color saturation, select the clip and go to Window → Properties. You find the Saturation slider under Image Control. Some other effects that work well for opening titles include Posterize, Tint, Pastel Sketch, and Duochrome. If you're in a creative mood, there are many possibilities. For example, Figure 9-18 uses Lighting Effects to shine a spotlight on the title.

Figure 9-17:
Click the Freeze Frame button to make a still image out of any frame in your movie. The Freeze Frame window displays the image you're saving and gives you options to insert the still into the timeline or to export (save) it in one of your computer folders.

Freeze Frame window

Freeze Frame button

Figure 9-18:
This effect was created using a freeze frame, modified with Auto Color and Lighting Effects. The type format is one of Premiere's predesigned styles. The effects are applied to the freeze frame clip on the Video 1 track. The title was created using Title → New Title → Default Still on Video 2.

5. Choose Title → New Title → Default Still.

The new title appears in the track above the freeze-frame image. The words "Add Text" appear in the monitor, with the text selected and your tools awaiting you in the Title Toolbar.

6. **Use the Type tool to select the words "Add Text" and then type in your title.**

Press the Enter key if you need to split your title into more than one line.

7. **Format the Title Text.**

You can use any of the predesigned styles on the Text Styles panel (page 285). Or you can create your own style from scratch, as explained on page 283.

Import Still Images for Titles

Still images don't have to come from your video clips. You can use just about any image as a background. If you've got Photoshop Elements installed on your computer, you've probably got a whole library of stills. Click Premiere's Organize tab and then click Organizer. Elements Organizer opens. To add a photo to your project, drag it from the Organizer onto the Tasks panel. After you import it, it appears in your Project panel and in the Media panel.

If you want to use a still image that isn't in the Organizer, bring it into your project using the Organize → Get Media tools. Click on PC Files and Folders and grab the image. For more on importing media into Premiere, see page 86.

Mix Artwork and Titles

You're certainly not limited to freeze frames and still photos when it comes to artwork for your titles. Premiere comes with a clipart library (go to Edit → ClipArt). It divides the images into groups like Baby, Food, and Nature (Figure 9-19). To use a clip, drag the image onto the timeline. Usually, you want to drag it to a track above your title. That way, the black area in the clipart becomes transparent and you can see the title beneath, as shown in Figure 9-20.

If you can't find what you want in the ClipArt panel, you can import line art and other graphics from computer files. The process is just like bringing in a photo. Click the Organize tab and choose Get Media. Then, click on PC Files and Folders. At that point, you can navigate to any folder on your computer and import graphics files into your project. For more details on importing files into Premiere, see page 86.

Famous Movie Moment: In 1967, the documentary filmmaker D.A. Pennebaker used some creative titles in *Dont Look Back,* his film about Bob Dylan. With the recording of Subterranean Homesick Blues playing in the background, Dylan holds up pieces of cardboard with the lyrics.

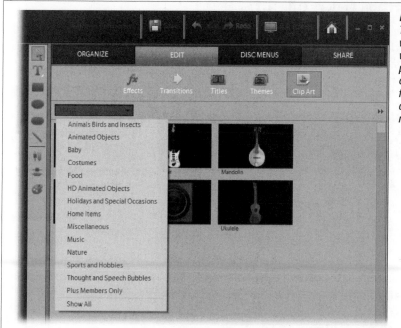

Figure 9-19:
The ClipArt panel provides a variety of art. The quality varies. Some are photorealistic and others are cartoon-style. If you don't find what you need, check online at Photoshop.com, more may be available.

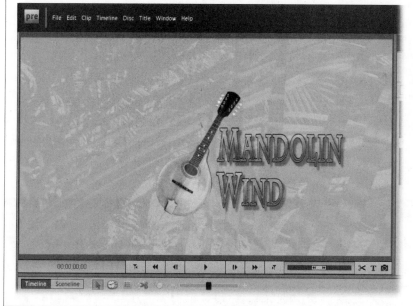

Figure 9-20:
This title uses three clips. A still image on Video 1 provides texture. The title text and a light yellow rectangle are on Video 2. The rectangle's opacity is set to about 85 percent. The mandolin clipart was placed on Video 3, then resized and rotated, so that it appears to be leaning on the text.

Export and Import Title Art

In your timeline, clips with title text usually have imaginative names like "Title 01." That's the name Premiere assigns to a clip when you create it. The same clip has a spot in your Project panel. To see your title, click the Organize tab and then click the Project button or go to Window → Project (Figure 9-21).

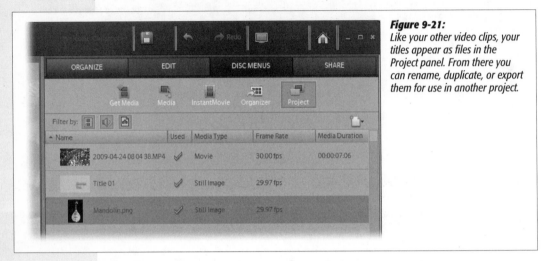

Figure 9-21:
Like your other video clips, your titles appear as files in the Project panel. From there you can rename, duplicate, or export them for use in another project.

Once you create a title you like, you may want to export it—to give it to another Premiere editor for use in their projects, for example. To do that, select the title in the Projects panel and then go to File → Export → Title. The Save Title window opens, and you can save your file in any folder on your computer. Premiere saves titles with a filename that ends in *.prtl*.

It's no good exporting Premiere titles unless you can import them, too. You can import titles saved in the .prtl format. The technique for importing titles is just like the technique for importing stills and graphics files. Go to the Organize tab and click Get Media or go to Window → Get Media. Then click PC Files and Folders. The Add Media window opens, where you can browse to any file or folder connected to your computer.

LOLA'S BIG SPLASH PROJECT

Create Titles and Credits

If you're following along with Lola the golden retriever, you may want to create your own title and closing credits for the video. Some of the techniques you can play with include:

• Use a title template

• Modify the type and graphics in a title template

• Create your own title from scratch

• Use a freeze-frame as a background image for your title

• Create rolling ending credits

Edit Your Sound Track

If you stay in the theater at the end of a movie as everyone else heads for the door, you may get a glimpse of seemingly endless credits. Somewhere in there, along with the drivers, caterers, publicists, assistants, and accountants, you'll see a credit for the sound designer. What a great description for the art of making a movie sound as good as it looks. Just as you build the visuals in your movie by layering video clips, special effects, and titles on top of each other, so you build its audio portion, with multiple tracks that may include music, sound effects, and narration.

Chapter 3 explained how to get sound files into your computer. This chapter explains how you craft a Hollywood-style soundtrack by layering dialog, sound effects, music, and narration, and then fine-tuning those tracks using volume settings and all kinds of effects for sound that Premiere provides.

When a soundtrack is done right, your audience is moved emotionally. They may not realize how much the sound affected them, but they'll feel its influence.

Design Sound from the Start

The first rule of sound design is to treat your audio as an equal partner to your video. That means you need to plan on capturing sound just as you planned on capturing video. Before you start shooting, you identify and organize all your visual elements: You decide where you want your actors, where to put the camera, and what's visible in the background.

When you capture sound, you should go through a similar checklist:

- **Choose your mic.** Today, nearly every camcorder has a built-in mic, but that might not always be your best choice for capturing the sound you want. Onboard microphones have limited capabilities.

  Adding another mic to a shoot complicates things quite a bit. In most cases, you need a person to hold a boom-based mic, monitor the sound, and keep the mic out of the picture. (For tips on choosing among the many different types of microphones, see the box on page 75.)

- **Position your mic.** You want to get your mic as close to your sound source as possible. That way, you capture sound with good fidelity and volume and minimize extraneous noise. That's why camcorder mics aren't always the best option—they're fixed on the camcorder. They may even pick up noise from the camcorder's motor. In addition, they always point in one direction and that direction might not be close enough to the sound you want to capture.

- **Consider using more than one mic.** Depending on your video equipment, there are a few ways to use more than one mic on a shoot. You can plug two mics into your camcorder so they both record perfectly synced sound. That lets you position the mics in different locations—one for each person in a scene, for example.

  If you can't plug two mics into your camera, you can use a separate recorder to capture sound while you shoot (though you'll need to take steps to synchronize this sound with the picture; more on that in the box on page 293).

- **Consider sound effects.** If you can't capture the sound you want while the camera is rolling, consider recording sound effects independently. You can record vital sounds, like the slam of a door or the rattle of a tin can, on your own time and add them to your movie later. You can even use your camcorder to record that sound (just delete the video track when you import the clip into your timeline). Alternatively, you can capture sound effects on a separate audio recorder (see the note on page 302 for more on audio-only recorders).

- **Plan your "synced sound" and your "non-synced" sound.** You've probably seen cheesy movies where the movement of characters' lips doesn't match the dialog, and the results always make you laugh. Your camcorder records sound in sync with the image, so you don't need to worry about that (unless you deliberately unlink the audio and video tracks as you edit, as described on page 303). But if you use an independent sound recorder, you need to sync your sound to the video, as described in the box on page 293. If you know you're going to record non-synced sound, you need to plan ahead.

- **Eliminate background noise.** The person responsible for sound may be you, a one-person video crew, or an actor not in the current scene. Whatever the case, before a shoot, the person who records your audio should listen carefully for sources of unwanted noise and eliminate them. Noise from outside traffic?

Close a couple of windows. Sound of the dishwasher running? Turn it off. Phones? Turn 'em off, too.

In a perfect world, sound designers listen to the audio they record after every take to make sure they captured the best possible audio. If you're in a room that produces a lot of boomy echoes, you may want to drape blankets over the outside-of-frame walls to keep the sound from bouncing around. And as mentioned earlier, one of the best ways to eliminate unwanted noise is to get the mic close to the sound you want.

• **Consider multiple takes.** Sure, if you're shooting a wedding or a birthday party or some other event that occurs only once in the real world, you can't do a second take. In many other instances, however, you can. For example, if you shoot an interview or training video, you can usually call for another take if the lighting's bad. You should be equally prepared to do multiple takes if the sound isn't clear. If you take the time to watch a scene after you shoot it, you should listen to the playback through a set of headphones.

SOUND ADVICE

Sync Sound Recorded Separately

When you watch one of those old-time movies about making movies, someone always yells "Quiet on the set." That's followed by the command "Roll film" and the response "Rolling." Then, some production assistant clacks a slate. In those old films, the slate was like a mini-chalkboard, with a hinged arm on the top that would come down with an audible "thwack." The board included the name of the movie, scene, and take. The purpose of the whole slate exercise was to identify a common point in both the picture and the sound. That way, the editor could synchronize the film with the recording tape. At least, that's the way it was in the old days. When you shoot with your camcorder today, the camera records the picture and sound together and timestamps both.

But if you capture sound on an independent recorder, it's up to you to synchronize the sound and picture. For short, obvious sounds, like a door closing or a thunder clap, it's pretty easy to find the frame where you want to drop the audio in your timeline. Usually, the toughest thing to sync is conversation, especially when you can see the characters' lips. The solution is to "slate" your video clips whenever you start and stop the camera and the recorder. You can actually buy a film slate for the job, or you can slate your films the low-rent way: Have someone stand in front of the camera with their arms outstretched. Once you get the camera and sound rolling, have them bring their arms together to make a loud clap. When you edit your film in Premiere, you align the frame where the hands meet with the sound of the clap on the audio track. In fact, you probably want to place a marker in the timeline called "slate." (For details on creating timeline markers, see page 170.)

If you want to take slating to the next step, visually identify the scene and take (a large chalkboard or piece of paper or cardboard can do the trick). Repeat the same identifying words for the sound recorder.

In the hubbub of a shoot, it's easy to forget to slate a shot—especially if it's not something you do on every shot. If you remember before you finish up your shot, you can "back-slate" it. That is, do the slate routine at the end of the shot rather than the beginning. It's not quite as handy as having all that info at the beginning of a clip, but it does the job.

Build a Soundtrack

Drag a video clip to the timeline, and a sound track goes along with it in most cases. The timeline displays both the video and audio track. For example, Figure 10-1 shows a video clip on Video 1 and a linked audio clip on Audio 1. In the soundtrack, waveforms represent the relative volume in the clip. Once you get a feel for waveforms, you can use their bumps and squiggles to identify points in your soundtrack without having to listen to every moment in a clip.

Tip: While you can work with audio in the sceneline, in many ways it's easier to understand what's going on in the timeline. For example, if you try to synchronize a sound effect with a particular event in your movie, the timeline is definitely the way to go because it gives you precise, frame-by-frame control. So this chapter uses the Timeline view for most examples.

Video 1

Set Audio Track
Display Style

Audio 1

Figure 10-1:
Most video clips include two audio tracks, one for the left channel of a stereo recording (which you hear through the left speaker during playback) and one for the right channel. Initially, Premiere displays sound waves in each track, but if you find that distracting you can hide the waves by clicking the Set Audio Track Style button.

Use Multiple Audio Tracks

When you first fire up Premiere, the empty timeline shows tracks labeled Video 1 and Audio 1. Scroll up in the timeline, and you see a couple more linked tracks, numbered 2 and 3. Premiere automatically provides these tracks on the assumption that, at least in some cases, you'll layer images and sounds to enhance your film.

Some of those sounds will be sound effects. Sound effects come in different shapes and sizes. A car crash or gunshot take just a moment, but the sound of waves crashing on-shore or birds chattering in the jungle might run through an entire scene. Your job as sound designer is to make sure the sounds occur at just the right moment and, in the final mix, at just the right volume, especially in relationship to other sounds. Placing sound effects in individual tracks gives you the ability to fine-tune each of your movie's audio components independently.

Note: For a full discussion of recording and importing sound effects, see page 73 in Chapter 3.

Premiere isn't stingy about additional tracks. You can add as many as you like, which is handy if you're adding multiple sound effects.

Think about a scene with two people walking the mean streets of a big city. You capture their voices as they walk, so that's on Audio 1. You have music on the "Soundtrack" track and Narration on its eponymous track. But you also want to give the scene some atmosphere, some of that constant background rumble of a city. The audience will notice if it's missing. So you record cars going up and down the street and voices from the crowded sidewalks and storefronts. Occasionally, there's a car honking or a cabby cursing. A bus stops and opens its door. The driver urges someone to hurry off. All these sounds have a place on your timeline. Some should be subtle background sounds and others, like your actors' voices, need to be in the foreground. Put the clips on different tracks, as shown in Figure 10-2, and you can adjust the volume and timing for each of the tracks.

Figure 10-2:
The audio files shown in this timeline were designed to capture the multilayered sounds of a city street. Separate tracks hold the audio for car motors, horns, and bus-stop hustle and bustle. The audio for characters' dialog and the video are linked in the Audio 1 and Video 1 tracks.

Below the Audio 1 track, Premiere provides two additional, special-purpose audio tracks, called Soundtrack and Narration. Figure 10-3 shows what the timeline looks like after you fill these tracks with clips. You drop background music in the track labeled "Soundtrack". Like narration, music communicates with your audience—its emotion and tempo have a remarkable effect on viewers. Your choice of music can also say something about your movie's time period or season. Tips for adding music to your Soundtrack start on page 308.

By narrating a movie, you can give your audience lots of information they may not glean from the images. Done well, narration adds to the mood of a movie. Narration can be nostalgic (*A Christmas Story*) or ominous (*Apocalypse Now*). You'll find more on recording narration on page 81.

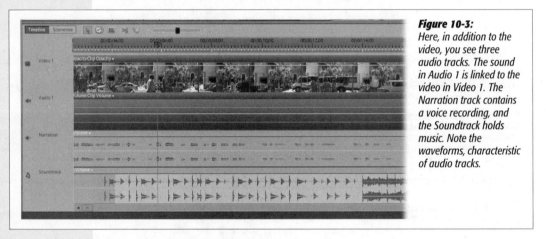

Figure 10-3:
Here, in addition to the video, you see three audio tracks. The sound in Audio 1 is linked to the video in Video 1. The Narration track contains a voice recording, and the Soundtrack holds music. Note the waveforms, characteristic of audio tracks.

Trim and Split Audio Clips

Once you put audio clips in the timeline, you can trim them just as you would a video clip; by dragging one or both of the ends. If you want to split a clip into separate parts, drag the playhead to the point where you want the split and then press Ctrl+K or click the Split Clip button (the scissors icon) at the bottom right of the monitor.

Cut, Copy, Paste, and Clear Clips

You have all the usual editing suspects at your disposal for editing audio tracks. For example, if you want to duplicate a clip that's already in the timeline, select it and press Ctrl+C (Copy). Move the playhead to the destination and then press Ctrl+V (Paste). In addition to these keyboard shortcuts, you can see a list of editing commands by right-clicking a clip in the timeline. At the top of the shortcut menu, you see commands like the ones shown in Figure 10-4.

Figure 10-4:
Right-click any clip in the timeline, be it audio or video, and a shortcut menu appears. As shown here, the standard Cut, Copy, Paste, and Clear (delete) commands appear at the top.

Remove Unused Tracks

If you need to add a lot of audio tracks to a timeline, you end up with a bunch of unused video tracks, too. That's because, when you use Premiere's Add Tracks command (right-click an empty part of the timeline and choose Add Tracks from the shortcut menu), it adds tracks in *pairs*, one for audio and one for video. It's easy to remove all those unused tracks at once. Right-click on an empty spot in the timeline and then choose Delete Empty Tracks from the shortcut menu. Premiere cleans up the timeline. Don't worry, you can always add new audio and video tracks as needed. To create new tracks, drag a clip to the top part of the timeline—that space between the topmost clip and the ruler—or right-click an empty place in the timeline and then choose Add Tracks from the shortcut menu.

Tip: If you need to add several audio tracks at once, choose Timeline → Add Tracks. A window opens where you can specify how many video or audio tracks you want to add. Use the Placement menu to position the tracks. Numbered tracks start with "1" at the bottom, so if you choose After Last Track, your new tracks appear at the top of the timeline.

Preview Audio Clips

You may want to listen to your audio before you add it to the timeline, and as you build multiple tracks in the timeline, you'll want to listen to the combined effect, too. You can preview audio clips just as you would video clips:

1. **Go to Window → Available Media.**

   The Tasks panel displays the media for your project, including video and audio clips.

2. **Double-click a clip.**

   Premiere's Preview window opens. If you double-click a clip that has audio and video linked, you see the video image in the window. If it's an audio-only clip, you see a waveform like the one in Figure 10-5.

3. **Click the Play button.**

   You've got all the standard controls to navigate and preview your clip.

4. **If necessary, adjust the In and Out points for the clip.**

   You can drag the In and Out markers or position the playhead and click the Set In and Set Out buttons. Once you set In and Out points, you can jump from one to another by right-clicking in the Preview window and then choosing Go to Clip Marker → In (or Out).

5. **Drag the clip from the Preview window to the timeline.**

   The trimmed clip appears in the timeline. Some clips, like the audio for a car horn, may not be synced to a video clip. You can control those clips' timing by moving them up and down the timeline.

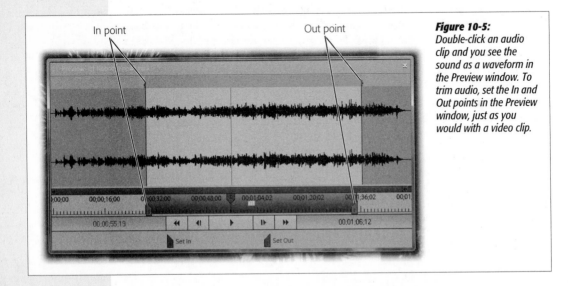

Figure 10-5:
Double-click an audio clip and you see the sound as a waveform in the Preview window. To trim audio, set the In and Out points in the Preview window, just as you would with a video clip.

Preview Layered Audio

You design the sound for your movie by layering audio clips. For big projects, you usually have some audio tracks linked to video clips and some unlinked. To preview the combined effect of the audio tracks, click somewhere in the timeline and then press the space bar. All the audio clips (as well as any video clips) play back.

Watch the playhead's red line as it passes over the soundtrack to get a feel for the way the waveform represents the recorded sounds. Larger waves indicate louder sounds.

What are you looking and listening for as you design your sound? Volume and clarity are the two most important qualities. Just like your video image, which you can overexpose or underexpose, you may record your sound at too high or too low a volume.

Keep in mind that, at this point, you want to focus on the volume of the initial recording—this is a sound-quality issue, which is different from how loud the clip will be in your final movie. Many camcorders automatically control the audio volume as they record. Sometimes, that provides the results you want, and sometimes it doesn't.

To see your recording displayed using the standard scale for audio (where sound is measured in decibels), go to Window → Audio Meters. The Audio Meters (shown in Figure 10-6) give you information about the quality of your recording. As the sound plays, you see the green bars jump up and down. Little gold lines sit at the top of the bar. And each time the green bar reaches a new height, the gold line marks the spot. At the end of the clip, that line represents the peak volume for the track.

Ideally, you want that peak volume to be between –6dB (decibels) and 0. If your audio falls in this sweet spot, you'll see gold lines in the meter. If your peak falls below –6dB (too low a volume), green lines mark the peak. And if the peak goes above 0dB, the boxes above the scale turn red, which means you recorded the sound at too high a volume, causing distortion. We're not talking cool Jimi Hendrix or White Stripes distortion here—digital audio distortion is usually unpleasant.

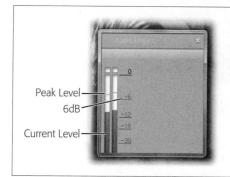

Peak Level
6dB
Current Level

Figure 10-6:
Go to Window → Audio Meters to display this little guy. As you preview your clip, the green lines indicate the volume of recorded sound. The gold lines show the peak volume of the audio. If the meters hit the box above the 0 line that means the audio is distorted.

Tip: There aren't many great fixes for really unpleasant digital distortion. If possible, you should try to re-record the clip. Alternatively, you can try to edit out the offending noise (see page 303).

Disable (Mute) Timeline Tracks

After you add several tracks to the timeline, you may want to hear some of those tracks with the other ones turned off. You can enable and disable audio or video clips in the timeline. If you disable a video clip, it doesn't play back in the monitor. If you disable an audio clip, you won't hear it when you preview your movie.

Premiere automatically enables clips when you add them to the timeline. To disable a clip, right-click it. The shortcut menu pops up, and you see a checkmark next to the Enable command, as shown in Figure 10-7. Click Enable, and the checkmark disappears. When you want to put the clip back in action, toggle Enable back on.

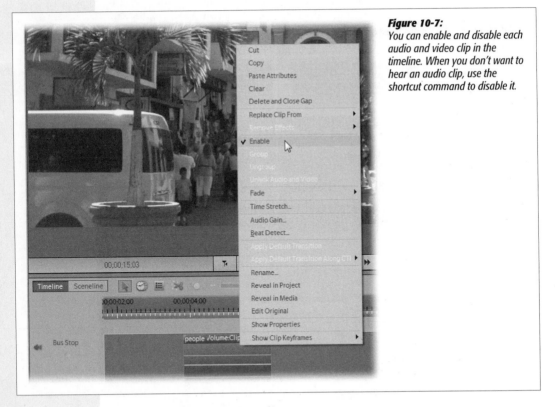

Figure 10-7:
You can enable and disable each audio and video clip in the timeline. When you don't want to hear an audio clip, use the shortcut command to disable it.

Fix Poorly Recorded Audio

If you record your soundtrack at too low a volume, its waveform looks flat, and the audio meter's lines (Window → Audio Meters) will never pass the –6dB mark. If you record the audio at too high a volume, the waveform gets cut off at the top of the audio track (as in Figure 10-8). In the audio meters, the levels hit the ceiling, leaving red marks in the small boxes at the top of the meters.

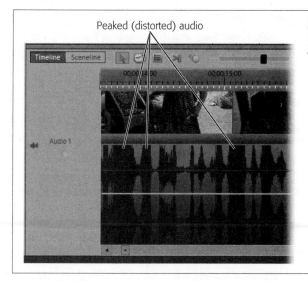

Peaked (distorted) audio

Figure 10-8:
Tracks recorded at too high a volume show flat spots instead of nice, curved waveforms, as shown here.

To fix audio problems, follow these steps:

1. **In the timeline, right-click the clip and then choose Audio Gain.**

   The Clip Gain panel opens, as shown in Figure 10-9.

2. **Click the Normalize button and then click OK.**

   Premiere adjusts the gain (volume) so that the quietest parts of a clip are louder, and the too-loud parts are quieter. The Clip Gain panel closes and the waveform takes on a new shape.

3. **Review the changes by playing back the audio.**

   It's a good idea to listen to the entire clip after you normalize it. You may or may not be happy with the changes. If you're not, press Ctrl+Z (or click Undo in the menu bar at the top of the screen) to undo it.

Figure 10-9:
You can try to fix poorly recorded audio automatically by clicking the Normalize button in the Clip Gain window shown here. If you're not happy with the results, you can try to fix it manually by changing the dB (decibel) number. Type in a negative value, like –1.5, to reduce the volume or a positive value to increase it.

Remove Noise from Analog Recordings

These days, you should record your audio with digital equipment (instead of old analog cassette-based recorders, for example). Analog recordings pick up background hiss, and, what's worse, each time you copy an analog recording (such as when you import it into Premiere), the embedded background noise becomes more pronounced. What's more, your camcorder records crisp digital audio, so mixing the two types of recording gives you unsatisfying results. If you use a separate recorder for sound, you can find a variety of digital recorders from companies like Alesis, Sony, Tascam, and Zoom.

That said, if you've got a noisy analog recording you *have* to use, Premiere can help remove some of the background hiss. It's an audio effect called, appropriately enough, the DeNoiser. Here's how it works: Analog background noise is lower in volume than the foreground sound you actually want. Using the DeNoiser, you set what's called a NoiseFloor, another way of saying you remove sounds on an audio track that fall below a certain level, a level the DeNoiser sets.

1. **Go Window → Effects and then type DeNoiser in the Search box.**

2. **Drag DeNoiser onto the offending audio clip.**

Adobe designed the DeNoiser to automatically find and remove noise from your clips. You should notice a difference when you listen to the clip.

If you think the DeNoiser needs some human intervention, click the Properties button above the timeline. In the Tasks panel, open the DeNoiser effect and choose Custom Setup. Then, adjust the controls that identify noise in your clip (see Figure 10-10). Click Custom Setup and then, at the bottom-left of the Properties window, click "Play only the audio for this clip".

The DeNoiser graphs your audio in its own little monitor. It displays the Noise-Floor setting as a green line during playback, and as a numeric value in decibels (dB) just below the monitor window. Change the Reduction setting to increase or decrease the amount of noise the DeNoiser removes. The Offset value represents a range between the sound you want to get rid of and the sound you want to keep. You can manually adjust that number, too. The Freeze checkbox locks the Noise-Floor to the current value; when you check it, the DeNoiser stops automatically adjusting the NoiseFloor.

Note: Most digital audio recorders save your audio on memory cards, but you can find recorders that store it on CDs or MiniDiscs. There's nothing wrong with using these recorders, it's just that the newer memory-based recorders are a little easier to use; CD recorders are bigger and slower. Mini-discs use great technology developed by Sony, but they never caught on with the general public.

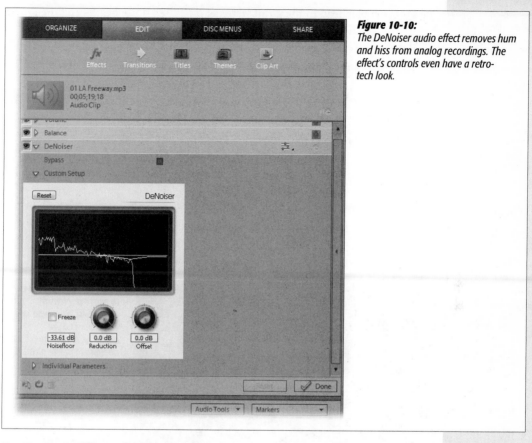

Figure 10-10:
The DeNoiser audio effect removes hum and hiss from analog recordings. The effect's controls even have a retro-tech look.

Separate Audio and Video Tracks

Sometimes, you may only be interested in the audio portion of a camcorder clip, or you may use your camcorder as a sound recorder at one point when you don't need the video and just want the sound. After you drop the clip in the timeline, right-click it and then choose Delete Video from the shortcut menu. The video clip disappears and the audio track remains. (You can do the opposite, too—delete the audio track and keep the picture. Just choose Delete Audio from the shortcut menu.) This only affects the instance of the clip in the timeline; your original clip (which you can see in the Media panel and the Organizer) remains unaffected—it still has both audio and video tracks.

What if you want to edit an audio track separately from the video track? Perhaps you want to cut out an annoying bit of distortion or a sound that shouldn't be there. You want to keep the picture, but you want to delete a chunk of the audio track, too. That, of course, will make the clips unequal. Here's what you do:

1. **Select the clip in the timeline and then go to Clip → Unlink Audio and Video.**

   Premiere unlinks the two clips. At this point, you can select each separately.

2. Drag the playhead to the point were the offending noise begins and then press Ctrl+K or click the Split Clip button (the scissors) in the lower-right corner of the monitor.

Note that this splits *both* the audio and video clips.

3. Click the right-hand edge of the audio clip and then drag the edge to the right.

Dragging the edge trims the clip, letting you trim out the distortion.

4. Move the playhead before the edited audio and press Space.

Listen to make sure you removed the offending noise. You can re-trim the audio clip if necessary.

When you play the clip, the poor-sounding audio portion is missing, as shown in Figure 10-11.

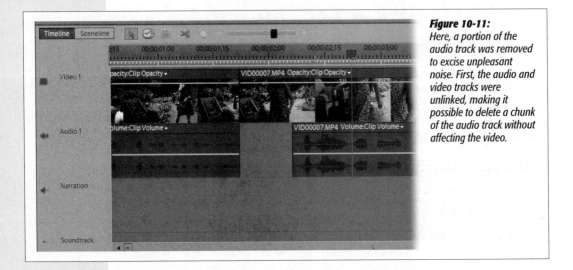

Figure 10-11:
Here, a portion of the audio track was removed to excise unpleasant noise. First, the audio and video tracks were unlinked, making it possible to delete a chunk of the audio track without affecting the video.

Tip: Another, even easier way to eliminate sound in the middle of a clip is to set beginning and ending audio keyframes and then reduce the volume in between the two. Figure 10-12 shows you this technique in action.

Linked but Not Synced

Most of the time, when video and audio tracks are linked to each other, you want them to play in sync, so that the sounds and the pictures match up. If you want to use the sound separately, you *unlink* the tracks as described on page 303. For those rare occasions when you want the tracks linked but you want to shift the sound, hold down the Alt key and drag the audio track. As the audio track moves, the video stays put, as shown in Figure 10-13, and a tooltip displays the time difference between the two tracks. When audio and video are out of sync, you see a red

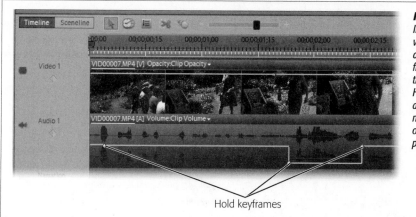

Figure 10-12:
In this timeline, the volume property for the audio clip is changed from normal to zero and then back to normal. Hold keyframes maintain a specific value until the next keyframe (for more on Hold keyframes, see page 253).

Hold keyframes

tag with numbers in the upper-right corner of the clip. After you move the clips out of sync, Premiere still keeps them linked. Drag the audio or video part of the clip and both move together. If you want to put them back in sync, Alt-drag either the audio or video until the numbers in the red tags disappear.

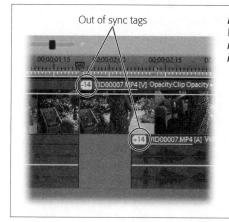

Out of sync tags

Figure 10-13:
When your audio and video clips are out of sync, Premiere displays a red number at the beginning of the clips. The number tag (circled) indicates, in frames, how far out of sync the clips are.

Adjust Volume and Balance

All audio clips have two fixed effects: Volume and Balance. To see them, select a clip and then click the Properties button (see Figure 10-14). Volume is expressed in decibels, with 0.0 dB representing the volume at which you recorded the clip. Use the slider to increase or decrease the volume of the entire clip. To modify the volume at different points in time, use keyframes, which let you specify the value for Volume. Simply put, you can set the volume low at one point in a clip and high at another point. Then Premiere automatically sets the volume between those two points so that it gradually increases. There are a lot more details on using keyframes with effects on page 239. That discussion focuses on visual effects, but the concepts apply to audio effects, too.

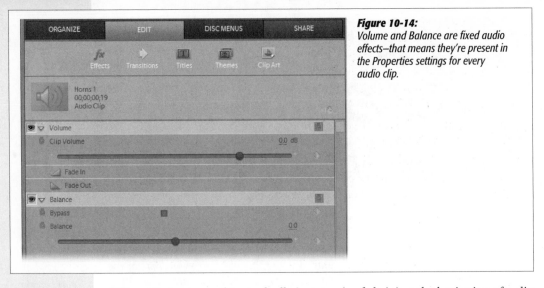

Figure 10-14:
Volume and Balance are fixed audio effects–that means they're present in the Properties settings for every audio clip.

Often, you want sound to gradually increase (or fade in) at the beginning of a clip and gradually decrease (fade out) at the end. The Volume effect has two handy buttons that do just that automatically. If you click Fade In, Premiere automatically creates a keyframe at the beginning of a clip with the volume set low. At the end of the fade-in, it sets a second keyframe with the volume at the normal, or recorded, level. You can see the results in Figure 10-15. If you click the Fade Out button, Premiere mirrors these settings at the end of a clip.

Premiere's Balance effect works just like it does on your home theater system or car stereo. You use Balance to send sound to the left or right speaker. This is particularly effective in video, because it gives you an opportunity to direct the sound so that it matches an image. For example, if your characters walk along a sidewalk on the right side of the screen while a car goes by on the left, you want the sound of their footsteps to come from the right speaker and the sound of the car to come from the left speaker. Use the Balance slider to direct the sound in each of these clips to different speakers. As with Volume, you can adjust an entire clip or you can set keyframes to change the balance over the course of a clip.

Add Audio Effects

Premiere comes with a bunch of audio effects. Not to be confused with recorded sound effects, these effects alter your recordings. Volume and Balance, discussed in the previous section, are fixed effects that are part of every audio clip. Other effects change the way a clip *sounds*. For example, the Delay effect adds an echo to an audio clip. The DeNoiser effect, discussed on page 302, removes hiss and hum from an analog recording.

You apply effects by dragging them onto an audio clip. You can make adjustments to the effects in the Properties panel (Window → Properties).

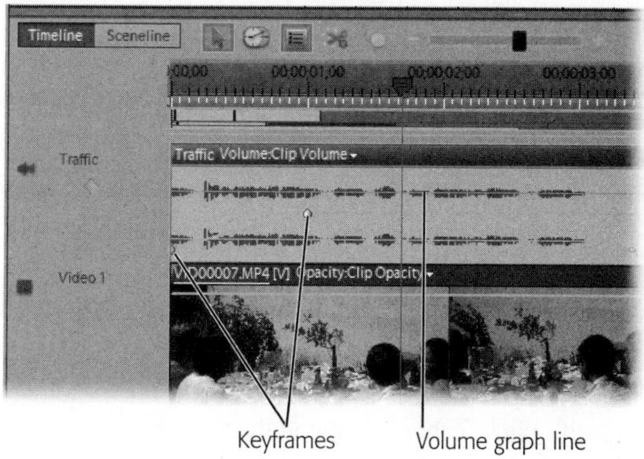

Figure 10-15:
The yellow graph line displays the volume for this clip. A keyframe at the beginning of the clip sets the volume low. The second keyframe brings the volume up to the normal, recorded level (0.0 dB). You can create your own keyframes to control volume and other audio effects.

Keyframes   Volume graph line

Tip: Most of Premiere's audio effects include a Bypass option, where you can click the Bypass checkbox to temporarily disable the effect. This gives you an easy way to compare a clip with and without an effect.

Here's a brief introduction to some of Premiere's other sound effects:

• **Bass** and **Treble** boost either the low (bass) or high notes (treble) in a clip. Works just like your car stereo.

• **Channel Volume** lets you control the volume for the right and left speakers independently. Unlike the Balance effect, increasing the volume of one channel doesn't automatically reduce the volume in the other.

• **Delay** adds an echo effect to a clip. You can control the timing of the echo and mix it with the original sound.

• **Dynamics** works kind of like the DeNoiser described on page 302, but Dynamics removes noise from *digital* audio rather than from analog audio. To remove low-volume noise, set AutoGate to a specific decibel value. The Limiter sets the maximum level for sound—if a sound exceeds the limit you set here, Dynamics doesn't eliminate it, it just reduces the sound to the maximum level.

Use the Compressor to increase soft sounds and reduce loud ones. Sound engineers often use this effect when recording voices. If you don't overuse it, the result is a smoother, but still natural, sound. Expander reduces all signals below a certain threshold to a ratio you specify. The effect is similar to AutoGate, but Expander gives you more settings, so you can fine-tune the effect a little better.

• **Fill Left** and **Fill Right** copy one stereo audio track to the other. Fill Left, for example, copies the sound in the left track to the right track (Premiere dumps the sound previously in the right track). This effect comes in handy when you have a monaural clip and you want the sound to come out of both the left and right speakers of a stereo setup.

- **Highpass** and **Lowpass** filter specific frequencies out of a sound clip. For example, apply the Lowpass filter to a clip, and it lets the low frequencies pass through while removing those high-pitched frequencies that make your dog put her paws over her ears.

- **Invert** changes the "phase" of the sound channels. Sometimes, if you record the same event with two different devices and play both recordings at the same time, the waveforms have a way of canceling each other out, resulting in weak or lifeless sound. The Invert effect helps by coordinating the two recordings.

- **Notch** removes certain frequencies, similar to the Highpass and Lowpass filters. Those filters remove sound from the ends of the sound spectrum, while Notch removes it from the middle.

- **PitchShifter** adjusts a sound's pitch without changing the timing of a clip. Create your own chipmunks.

- **Reverb** adds what audio technicians call "ambiance." Using these settings, you can make a recording sound as though you recorded it in a cathedral—or a phone booth.

- **Swap Channels**—you guessed it, the right and left channels do a do-si-do.

Add a Music Track

You may need to use the scroll bar on the right of the timeline to see the Soundtrack tucked away at the bottom of your timeline. You can put any audio clip you want in this track, but its intended purpose is for music. Drag a music clip (to which you have attained all legal rights from parties of the first part) to the Soundtrack. You can adjust the volume and balance as explained on page 305, and the Volume property's Fade In and Fade Out effects are particularly handy for music tracks (page 306).

You can use any of the audio editing techniques or special effects discussed here on your music track, but there's one special trick that's unique to music tracks. You can have Premiere analyze the audio and place markers in the timeline that match the beat of the music. Then you can edit your video to the beat of its soundtrack—that is, position your cuts and transitions to match the beat of the soundtrack. It's very effective, as you know if you've ever watched MTV.

Select an audio clip in the timeline and then choose one of three ways to get Premiere to analyze the clip:

- Select Detect Beats from the Audio Tools menu (Figure 10-17) in the upper-right corner of the timeline.

- Right-click a clip in the timeline and choose Beat Detect from the shortcut menu.

- Select a clip and choose Clip → Beat Detect.

No matter how you get there, you see the Detect Beat Settings panel (Figure 10-16), where you can fine-tune the detection process. It's probably best to use the initial settings first, and then, if necessary, go ahead and make adjustments, as indicated in Figure 10-16.

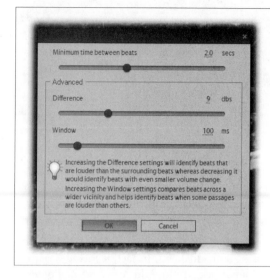

Figure 10-16:
Use the "Minimum time between beats" setting to make sure the detector doesn't become too staccato. As the helpful note in the panel explains: Increase the Difference settings to identify beats that are louder than the rest of the clip. Increase the Window value to make that comparison over a wider range of time.

Once Premiere detects the beats in your sound clip, it identifies them with cheery little musical-note markers in the timeline (see Figure 10-17).

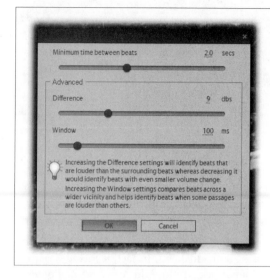

Figure 10-17:
Beat markers look like musical notes, so it's easy to tell them apart from regular timeline markers. You can find the Detect Beats command in the Audio Tools menu.

Mix the Audio Track

Sound mixing is serious work. It's more easily done on a physical mixing board than it is on a computer screen using a mouse. And even then, it helps if you have as many hands as an octopus has tentacles. The concept is this: As your movie and multiple soundtracks play, adjust the level sliders for each track so that the sounds you want in the foreground have the proper volume and the sounds you want in the background don't distract. Everything needs to be balanced just right, but sometimes, when you change one level, it seems to discombobulate the others.

Edit the Soundtrack

If you're editing the "Lola's Big Splash" project, this is a good time to edit the soundtrack. In the first clip showing the house there's some wind noise. See if you can remove it. Here are some audio techniques you can practice once you add the music clip *01 Nobody Knows.mp3* from the Project panel to the soundtrack in the timeline:

1. Select the clip and then choose Audio Tools → Detect Beats.

2. Adjust some of the cuts to match the beat in the music.

3. Manually, adjust the volume and balance, or…

4. Use SmartMix to automatically adjust the soundtrack volume.

Mix the Level or Balance

You can change the level (volume) or balance for an entire clip or for just a single clip. As mentioned on page 305, Volume and Balance are both fixed effects. That means they're properties of every audio clip, and you can view them in the Properties panel (Window → Properties).

The Audio Mixer (Figure 10-18) lets you adjust Volume and Balance, but it operates on entire tracks as opposed to an individual clip. In fact, it includes settings labeled Audio 1, Narration, and Soundtrack. If you add a second audio track, Audio Mixer displays a set of Audio 2 control buttons, too, and so on. (If you've used Digidesign's ProTools, Adobe's Soundbooth, or a hardware mixing board, the controls will look familiar.)

Each track has a level meter, a level slider, a balance control, and a mute checkbox. When a track's level is set to 0.0, the track's volume is unchanged from the original recording. A positive number makes it louder than the original and a negative number makes it quieter. When you set the Balance to 0.0, it, too, is unchanged from the original recording. Turn the dial, and you can shift the balance from one channel to the other.

Automate Sound Mixing with SmartMixer

Premiere offers one quick-and-easy way to mix your sound, which just may work for some of your projects. It's called SmartMixer, and it uses Premiere's AutoAnalyzer to examine the audio clips in your timeline. It knows the difference between voice-over in the Narration track and music in the Soundtrack, and it automatically adjusts the levels so that it lowers the music when people talk. When there aren't any voices, the music comes up a bit.

Give SmartMixer a few moments to do its analysis and you might be able to save yourself a lot of time. Even if you're not 100 percent happy with the results, you can go in and make changes after SmartMixer does its thing.

Figure 10-18:
The Audio Mixer (Window → Audio Mixer) gives you two controls for each audio track: a level slider to control the volume and a balance dial to direct sound. To temporarily disable a track, click the Mute checkbox at the bottom.

SmartMixer assumes that you want certain audio tracks, including Narration and Audio 1, linked to Video 1 clips, and that these tracks take precedence over any other audio tracks. At the same time, it assumes that music on the Soundtrack and audio tracks above Audio 1 are secondary and should be in the background of the mix. If your sound design doesn't work that way, you can change the general guidelines before you fire up SmartMix. Click the timeline's Audio Tools menu and then choose SmartMix → Options. The SmartMixer panel opens, where you can choose which tracks should be foreground and which should be background, as shown in Figure 10-19.

To have SmartMix analyze and automatically mix the audio levels for your project, click the timeline's Audio Tools menu (in the upper-right corner), and then choose SmartMix → Apply.

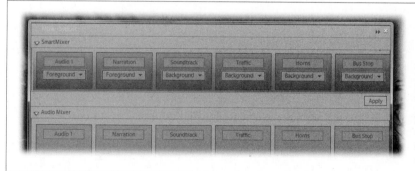

Figure 10-19:
Go to Audio Tools → SmartMix → Options to open this panel, where you can give the SmartMix tool some guidance. You have three choices for each track: Foreground, Background, or Disabled. Click the Apply button to start the SmartMix AutoAnalyzer.

Manual Sound-Mixing with the Audio Mixer

If you want to mix your audio manually, start with the most important tracks. That's probably the sound that's linked to your video clips. If necessary, mute some of the tracks so you can focus on the first track you mix. Position the playhead at the beginning of a clip and then press the space bar or hit the Play button. Make adjustments to the Level and Volume controls as the audio plays. Premiere automatically creates keyframes that save the Level and Balance values when you make changes in the Audio Mixer. It only records changes to the Level and Balance controls *as you play back your audio*—if you stop playback and change the controls, Premiere pays no attention.

When you finish, you probably want to listen to the track one more time and make final adjustments. You can do that in the mixer, or you can manually make changes to the keyframes.

Once you finish mixing the first track, it's time to tackle the next one. This go-round, pick the next-most-important track and don't mute the track you just fine-tuned. Repeat this process until you work your way through all the tracks in your project.

Mixing audio is an art, and there are plenty of folks who spend their whole career learning how to do it for movies and music production. So be patient and take your time as you mix. Don't be afraid to go back over tracks you already mixed and make adjustments. It's all part of the sound-design process.

Tip: If your screen space is limited, you can show and hide Audio Mixer's track controls. Click the panel menu in the upper-right corner—the button looks like two triangles. Choose Show/Hide Tracks. Click the boxes to show and hide individual tracks.

Part Three: Share Your Movie

3

Choose a Video Format

Once you edit your video and polish it up with transitions, effects, and a great soundtrack, it's time to share it. So how are you going to show your epic to family, friends, and neighbors? That's the subject of the remaining chapters in this book. This chapter explores the mysteries of video files. You'll learn the different options for saving your film. You can create a finished video and save it to DVD, upload it to a video-sharing site like YouTube, export it to a mobile device like an iPhone or an iPod Touch, or save it and play it back on your PC.

This chapter introduces these options and describes why Premiere creates different files for different destinations. Then, in Chapters 12, 13, and 14, you'll learn the details for publishing your film on each of these devices and on the Web.

Video Formats and Premiere Elements

In broad strokes, the steps you take to create and share a movie are as follows (see Figure 11-1):

1. You and your camcorder produce a bunch of clips.

2. You store that bunch of clips (video, audio, and still images) on your computer.

3. With the help of Premiere, you assemble those clips into a movie with lots of snazzy effects and a soundtrack.

4. Premiere exports your edited movie in different formats, each designed to match a display device. This process is known as "encoding" or "rendering" your movie (though this rendering is different from the on-the-fly rendering Premiere does as you edit your movie).

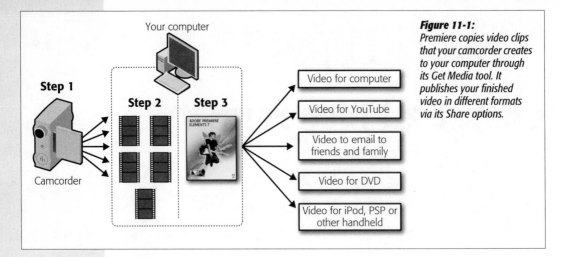

Figure 11-1:
Premiere copies video clips that your camcorder creates to your computer through its Get Media tool. It publishes your finished video in different formats via its Share options.

What Comes In

Your camcorder produces video clips in a specific digital format, but you're not limited to that format when it's time to share your movie. In fact, you *shouldn't* use the same format for every destination: DVD, YouTube, iPhone, and the file you email to Grandma should each have a different file format.

You made one decision about video formats when you bought your video camera. As the friendly salesperson probably explained, different camcorders record video in different formats. If you have an older, tape-based DV camcorder, Premiere captures your video clips and saves them to your computer in the AVI format (for a review of the different video file formats, see page 380). If you have one of the newer high-definition camcorders, Premiere may save your video in MTS format.

In fact, Premiere is great at reading and understanding all the common video file formats, so you don't have to worry about how your camcorder stores video. There's one camcorder characteristic that significantly affects the video you create, however, and that's aspect ratio.

Camcorder aspect ratio

Aspect ratio, in simple terms, is the shape—the width and the height—of your movie's playback window.

Here's an easy way to think of aspect ratio: Remember when everybody had TVs that were nearly square in shape. Those TVs had an aspect ratio of 4:3, meaning that, for every 4 horizontal inches your TV screen had, it had 3 vertical inches. Nowadays, TVs are shaped like the movie screens you see in theaters. Today's TVs, just like those movie screens, have an aspect ratio of 16:9.

Like television sets, camcorders, too, have evolved. If you have an older model camcorder, it probably shoots video in the 4:3 aspect ratio. If you have a new high-def model, it shoots in the 16:9 ratio. (A few cameras can shoot both.)

Tip: When you choose a preset for importing or exporting video, Premiere refers to video that's in the 16:9 aspect ratio as "widescreen." In some cases, it refers to video in the 4:3 format as "standard." In other cases, Premiere never specifies a format or doesn't let you select one. In those cases, the aspect ratio is probably the standard 4:3.

The shape of the video images in your raw clips is important to know, because if you change that shape when you export your finished movie—if you use a different aspect ratio, in other words—you'll end up with cartoon-like distortions—heads that look like footballs, for example, or dachshunds that look like mastiffs.

You told Premiere what your camcorder's aspect ratio is when you imported your clips—that's why you chose a camcorder type when you filled out Premiere's New Projects screen at the beginning of your project (see page 23). For example, if you have an AVCHD camcorder, you chose an AVCHD setting in Premiere's New Project window. Once you did that, Premiere knew how to handle your raw video, audio clips, and still images when you imported them.

It's just as important that you tell Premiere what aspect ratio to use when it *exports* your file—when it creates your final film. Fortunately, just as Premiere prompted you with a list of predefined specifications when it imported your files, it does the same thing when you create your final film file, except this time it lets you select from a list of *destination devices* instead of source devices.

What Goes Out

How and where will people view your video? That's the question you need to answer before you can save and share your movie. Put another way, the answer to that question determines the format you want for your final movie file to be in.

Are you going to show it to friends on your brand-new, high-def TV? Are you going to upload it to YouTube? Are you showing it off on an iPod at lunch or sending it out via email?

The good news is that you can do all of these things. In fact, you can save copies for each of these situations; just tell Premiere what you want. That copy for your high-def TV gets saved as a high-resolution (1920×1080 pixels) video, while the copy you email gets scrunched down to low resolution (maybe as small as 320×240 pixels). In terms of file size, the video for your high-definition TV will be huge, but it looks great. The one you email doesn't look as sharp, but it emails quickly and won't clog up someone's inbox.

Note: The term pixel is a contraction of "picture" and "element." Think of it as a little dot on your TV screen or computer monitor (though it's actually a tiny square or rectangle).

Now, here's the really, really good news: When it comes time to export your video, you don't have to sweat the details. Premiere anticipates just about every destination for your movie (DVD, website, Sony PSP, and so on) and lists them in plain English (Figure 11-2). You simply choose the device and Premiere spits out the proper file.

If your video is headed to YouTube, for example, you choose "YouTube" from Premiere's Share tab. The program then applies the proper settings and creates a video file perfectly suited to the file-sharing service. Behind the scenes, Premiere has set the right technical specifications (compression level, frame size, number of frames per minute, and so on) for YouTube (Premiere calls these predefined specifications "presets").

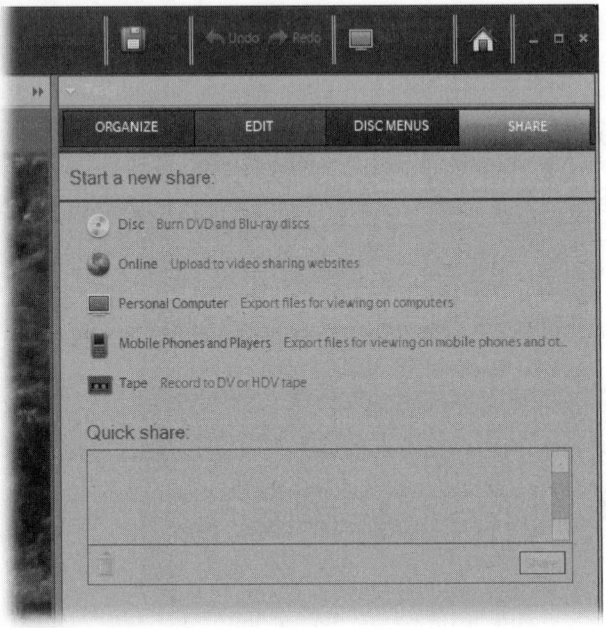

Figure 11-2:
At the first stop on the Share tab, you choose the destination for your video: DVD, online, a computer, a mobile device, or a DV or HDV tape.

Why So Many Formats?

At this point in our program, you may be scratching your head wondering why there are so many video formats to begin with. It's all about size and speed. As you know by now, video files are huge. That's not a problem when you store all of a movie's 1s and 0s on a Blu-ray disc, but it *is* an issue when you want to play it back over the Web or tuck a video into an email message. That Blu-ray disc can play your movie in all its glory, while the video you send over the Internet needs to be squashed down to a smaller file size.

How do the video wizards come up with ways to make video files smaller? They use some pretty ingenious techniques. Even so, in most cases, the tradeoff is almost always the same: If you want great video quality, you've got to deal with big files. If you want a smaller file, you've got to sacrifice video and audio quality. The trick is to find the right balance.

While you don't have to worry about the nitty-gritty technical details when you choose a preset from Premiere's Share tab, it helps to know how Premiere shrinks your video files for different media—and it almost always shrinks files. Except for high-definition video formats like Blu-ray discs or DVDs, Premiere usually needs to make your video more compact. Here's how it does that. It:

- **Lowers the resolution.** Each video frame is made up of a grid of pixels. The number of pixels used to create an image is called its *resolution*. When Premiere knows a video is destined for an iPod, it uses a resolution of 640 pixels × 480 pixels (640×480). If a video is destined for a Blu-ray disc connected to a high-definition TV, Premiere uses a resolution of 1920×1080 pixels.

- **Reduces the picture data in each frame.** Each frame of your move is essentially the same thing as a still photo. Premiere reduces file size by using techniques like those used to compact still photos—instead of defining the color for every single pixel in an image, Premiere uses a standardized shorthand to define large and repeating areas in an image.

- **Reduces the picture data from one frame to another.** With most video, only a portion of an image changes from frame to frame. Think of a long shot of a train moving through a mountain pass. The train moves, but everything else stays the same. One compression technique Premiere uses for video files is to update only the portion of the image that changes. The unchanged portion doesn't need to be stored in the video file again. Premiere can simply reference it: "Use the sky and mountain range from Frame 15 in this frame."

- **Reduces the frame rate.** In a movie theater, you see 24 frames of video every second. That's fast enough to fool your eye and brain into thinking you're seeing nice fluid movement rather than a bunch of still pictures. In a pinch, Premiere can reduce a video's file size by reducing the number of frames it displays per second (fps). So, if you choose one of the presets for email, Premiere may set the frame rate to 15 fps or even 10 fps.

It may seem like there are a bewildering number of ways to shrink video files and a bewildering number of video standards. But there *are* standards. The folks who manage the YouTube site expect you to send video using their standard, while the folks who developed DVDs use a different standard. Because Adobe did its homework, you don't have to worry about the minutiae; all you have to do is choose the video's preset from Premiere's Share tab.

Note: If you work with other videographers or production people, you may hear the term "codec" tossed around. Any program that scrunches a big video file into a smaller, more nimble file is called a *codec* (a contraction of the words "compressor" and "decompressor"). The video is compressed when it's written to a file and then it's decompressed when it's played. When you choose a preset, say for a DVD or iPod Touch, Premiere automatically knows what codec to use.

Choose a Preset

The next few chapters provide the step-by-step details for exporting movies for websites, video discs, and handheld devices like iPods and cellphones. Here's a preview of the steps you take when choose a preset to export your edited movie:

1. **Click the Share tab to see the options shown previously in Figure 11-2.**

2. **Choose from one of the following "share" categories:**

   - **Disc.** Choose this option to have Premiere burn (write) a copy of your movie onto a DVD or Blu-ray disc.

   - **Online.** Choose this option to send your video to YouTube or Photoshop. com. There's also a preset here for Podbean, a podcasting website.

   - **Mobile Phones and Players.** Choose this option to send your video to your iPod, Zune, or other handheld gadget.

   - **Personal Computer.** The presets here vary a little more than the others, but they all create a video file that's saved on your computer. There are file formats for video for web pages, your computer, and email attachments. In this category, you'll also find presets to save still images and audio clips.

   - **Tape.** If you have a tape-based video camera and like to archive your video on tape, you can use this option to record your finished movie.

   After you choose one of these categories, Premiere shows a new panel, like the one in Figure 11-3, where you choose a specific destination for your video and a preset.

3. **Choose your video's destination or device.**

   At the top of the panel, you see a scrolling list where you can choose the gadget, website, or other destination for your video. For example, the Discs list gives you a choice of DVD or Blu-ray disc. For mobile phones and players, you see a list that includes Apple iPods, Creative Zens, Microsoft Zunes, and Sony PSPs.

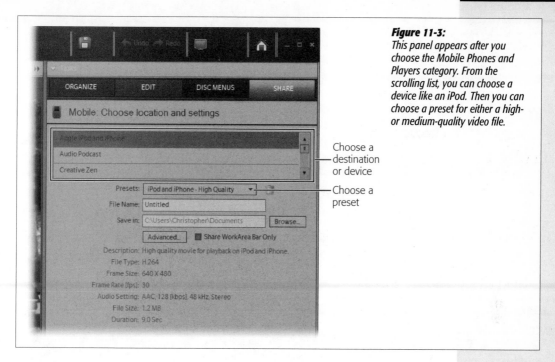

Figure 11-3:
This panel appears after you choose the Mobile Phones and Players category. From the scrolling list, you can choose a device like an iPod. Then you can choose a preset for either a high- or medium-quality video file.

Choose a destination or device

Choose a preset

4. **Choose a preset.**

   Here, you zero in on the characteristics of the video file that Premiere's going to create. Still, your choices aren't difficult. For example, if you're sending your movie to an iPod, you simply choose between High Quality (if you have plenty of room on your 'pod) or Medium Quality. In most case, you give the video file your own name. In some cases, you choose a folder where you want Premiere to save the file. Of course, that's not necessary when Premiere burns the movie to a disc or sends it off to YouTube.

5. **Click the Save button, and Premiere, with the help of the presets, does its stuff.**

That's all there is to it. Whether you burn a DVD, copy a movie to your cellphone, or send it off to YouTube, the steps are pretty much the same.

CHAPTER 12

Upload Videos to YouTube and the Web

If your videos are destined for the Web, you're in luck. Premiere presets make it easy to upload your videos to YouTube, Photoshop.com, Podbean, and your own website. Adobe, the company that publishes Premiere, also publishes a program called Flash. In the past few years, Flash files (whose file names end in *.flv* and *.f4v*) have become the video champs of the Internet. You find Flash-based videos on sites from YouTube to Hulu.

It wasn't long ago that a battle royale raged between Microsoft, Apple, and Real-Media for web video bragging rights. Back then, Flash seldom got mentioned in the contest; in those days, the only thing web designers used Flash for was creating little animations and annoying ads. But, like the Trojans with their famous horse, the Flash player managed to sneak onto about 90 percent of today's computers. And guess what? Flash now plays full-blown movie files, too. And before the competition could react, the Flash for Video format became a web standard because it provided a way to compress movies down to a reasonable size.

This chapter shows you how to prepare and send your videos to YouTube, Photoshop.com, Podbean, and other websites. Along the way, you'll get tips on creating Flash videos that are small and fast—perfect for websites.

Prepare Your Movie for YouTube

YouTube is an Internet phenomenon. People just like you put their movies on the video-sharing site, where anyone with an Internet connection can watch them. So what kind of things will you find on YouTube? You probably already know, but here are a couple random samples: Couples create YouTube wedding invitations.

Teenagers produce videos explaining why they love or hate a band. Musicians post performances in the hope that it will boost their career. Sports fans post their rants and raves.

In addition to the amateur content, there's plenty of professional content, too. You'll find everything from original Star Trek episodes to ABC World News broadcasts to technology posts from a *New York Times* columnist named David Pogue.

According to comScore, an organization that tracks all things web for marketing purposes, in January 2009, one out of every three web videos was viewed on You-Tube. Or, in other terms, 78.5 million viewers watched 3.25 *billion* YouTube videos. And all the while, your boss thought you were working on the quarterly report.

You've seen YouTube videos replayed on network television and news shows. You've probably had friends send you links to funny clips. You may have watched a YouTube tutorial to learn how to use a computer program or fix an appliance. It's obvious why YouTube is so popular; the site's designers made it easy to upload videos to the web. Oh yeah, they also made it free. You don't have to have a You-Tube account to watch videos on YouTube, but you do have to have an account to upload videos. It's an easy process—for the details, see the box on page 331.

YouTube offers guidelines for videos. It's helpful to understand what they think works best, but if you use Premiere's presets, it's not something you have to worry about. While they say they can handle almost any video format, here's what You-Tube recommends for different specifications:

- Video Format: H.264, MPEG-2, or MPEG-4.

- Aspect Ratio: Use native aspect ratio without letterboxing, either 16:9 or 4:3.

- Resolution: For 16:9 aspect ratios, use 640×360; for 4:3 aspect ratios, use 480×360.

- Audio format: Either AAC or MP3.

- Frames per second: 30.

- Maximum length: 10 minutes, though they recommend videos that are 2 to 3 minutes long.

- Maximum file size: 1 gigabyte.

Naturally, these specifications are likely to change over time. You can always double-check the current specs on YouTube's website (*www.youtube.com*).

After your movie is all edited and ready to go, follow these steps to encode it for the Web and upload it to YouTube.

1. **In Premiere, click the Share tab and then click Online.**

    The Tasks panel displays a scrolling list where you can choose different online services, including YouTube, Photohop.com, and Podbean.

Get a YouTube Account

You need to have a YouTube account to upload videos. The account is free, and it's easy to sign up, but be forewarned that the Terms of Use, Terms of Service, and Privacy Policy take what seems like an hour and a half to read. (You do read every word before you click the Accept button on websites, don't you?) As always, the details go on for several lawyerly pages with the caveat that they may change from time to time, and it's your responsibility to know when that happens. For the most part, Google (YouTube's owner) wants you to agree that the content you upload is yours and doesn't infringe on anyone else's copyrights. So, unless you're Mick Jagger or Keith Richards, your video probably shouldn't have a Rolling Stones soundtrack. Some other clauses make it sound like they'd prefer if you don't try to hack or attack the YouTube website for some reason.

If you already have a Google account for Gmail or for some other Google service, you can use your existing username and password to sign into YouTube. Go directly to YouTube (*youtube.com*) or sign into your Google service and then look for a link to the video-sharing site. In Gmail, there's a YouTube option at the top of each window, listed along with Calendar, Documents, and other tools (you may have to click "More" to see it). iGoogle provides a YouTube link in a panel on the home page.

Once you get to YouTube's home page, click Sign In at the top right, then type in your Google username and password.

Otherwise, you can create a new YouTube account, which amounts to this:

1. Go to *youtube.com*.

2. In the upper-right corner, click Sign Up.

3. Fill in the form with the name you want to be known by on YouTube (called a username) and other details, including a password.

4. YouTube gives you the option to let friends see your "channel," a standalone page that lists the videos you upload or that you mark as "favorites" as you browse YouTube. YouTube gives this page a unique web address (youtube.com/[your username here]) so you can pass it on to friends. To accept this option, check the box "Let others find my channel on YouTube if they have my email address".

5. Agree to the terms of service.

6. Click the "I accept" button.

After you accept, you see a new web page where you sign in using the userrname and password you just created.

---

2. **From the scrolling list, choose YouTube and then click Next.**

Premiere uses the Flash preset for YouTube. It sets the file format to FLV/F4V. Using the Medium setting, the frame size is set to a small but zippy 320×240 and the frame rate to 30 frames per second. Premiere displays the file size and duration of your video.

3. **Type in a title, description, and tags that describe your video (Figure 12-1), and then click Next.**

These words appear with your video on the YouTube website, so if you want the world to beat a path to your movie, put some thought into them, especially the tags. To see some good examples of tags, browse through a few YouTube videos to see how other people tag their movies.

Figure 12-1:
Before you send your video off to YouTube, fill out this form to give it a title, description, and keywords. That way, the YouTube universe can find your masterpiece.

4. **Next to "Allow public view of this share?", choose Yes.**

   This page also has links to YouTube's Copyright Tips and Terms of Use—helpful if you have questions about such things or if you have trouble falling asleep.

5. **Click the Share button.**

   A new panel displays a progress bar as Premiere encodes and uploads your film. On the right side of the bar, YouTube estimates how long the process will take. When it's complete, YouTube displays a confirmation panel like the one in Figure 12-2.

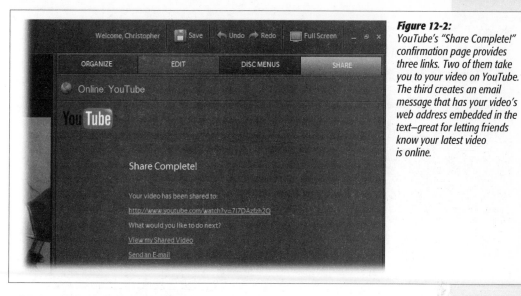

Figure 12-2:
YouTube's "Share Complete!" confirmation page provides three links. Two of them take you to your video on YouTube. The third creates an email message that has your video's web address embedded in the text—great for letting friends know your latest video is online.

After Your YouTube Premiere

So, now that your video is the star of YouTube, here are a couple of things you can do while you wait for that contract from Lorne Michaels. First, head over to your YouTube page, which looks something like Figure 12-3. Here are some of the things you can do to build traffic for your video:

- **Show off your video using MySpace, Facebook, Twitter, orkut, Live Spaces, or any other social site.** Under the video, click the word Share. Click any of the links, and YouTube helps you log into your account on the social site. Then you can either embed your video on the social site or create a link for it.

- **Email your friends links to your video.** Underneath the social site tools, there's a box that says: "Copy and paste this link into an email or instant message". Click the text box below and then press Ctrl+C to copy the link that goes to your video. Then you can type Ctrl+V to paste the link into an email or instant message (or anywhere else, for that matter). Even easier, YouTube provides a form where you can quickly type in email addresses and a message, then automatically send the link to the recipients.

- **Embed your video on your own website or blog.** If you have your own website or a blog where you can embed a little bit of HTML (webpage) code, you can add a YouTube playback window. In reality, it links back to the YouTube website, but it embeds the playback window on your site, complete with Play and Pause controls. Best of all, you don't have to be an HTML or JavaScript coder to perform this feat. It's a simple cut-and-paste operation. To the right of your video, find the box that says "Embed", as shown in Figure 12-4. Click the text box and then use Ctrl+C to copy the code. Then, use Ctrl+V to paste this code into the HTML code for your web page.

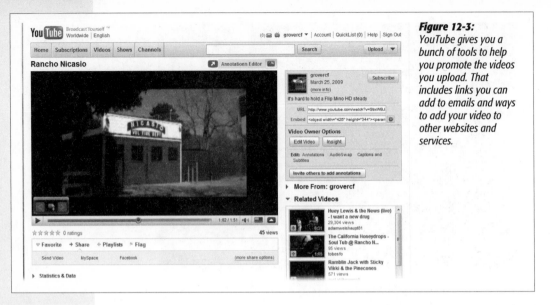

Figure 12-3:
YouTube gives you a bunch of tools to help you promote the videos you upload. That includes links you can add to emails and ways to add your video to other websites and services.

- **Change the music in your video with AudioSwap.** If you'd like to add a legal music soundtrack to your YouTube video, click the AudioSwap button. A new page opens where you can audition royalty-free music that generous YouTubers have uploaded. With a couple of clicks you can swap your soundtrack for a selected tune. Just bear in mind that this permanently changes the YouTube copy of your video.

Send Your Movie to Photoshop.com

Sending your movie to Photoshop.com isn't that much different from sending it to YouTube. You start on the Share tab and choose Online. Photoshop.com is the first option in the scrolling list, and it's already selected, so leave it that way. The drop-down menu under "Presets" gives you only one preset, for Photoshop.com, and it, too, is already selected. Click Next, sign in to Photoshop.com, and Photoshop displays a screen like the one in Figure 12-5. Click "Upload" to save your movie.

As mentioned earlier, you can also use Photoshop.com to back up your raw video, but that can be an expensive proposition because you pay for the space you use. It makes better sense to post copies of your finished videos to the site, because they won't take up quite so much room. Photoshop.com is another place where you can share movies (and stills) with your friends and family.

Tip: You don't have to fire up Premiere to load videos or photos to Photoshop.com. You can do it from the website itself. When you're on the site, click the "Upload Photos & Videos" button in the upper-right corner. A window opens where you can browse through the folders on your computer. Select one or more photos and/or videos to upload and then click Open. The window shown in Figure 12-6 appears to help with the upload and organization.

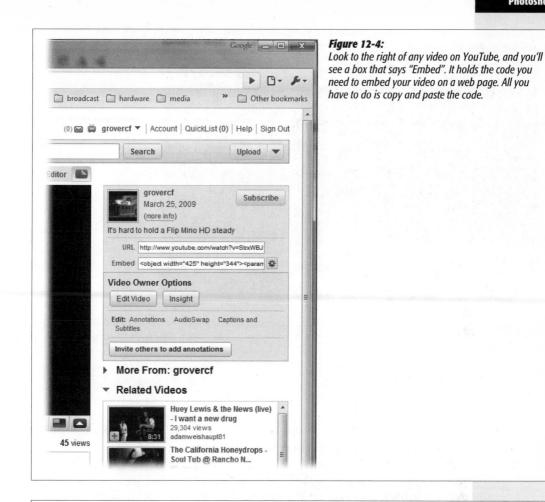

Figure 12-4:
Look to the right of any video on YouTube, and you'll see a box that says "Embed". It holds the code you need to embed your video on a web page. All you have to do is copy and paste the code.

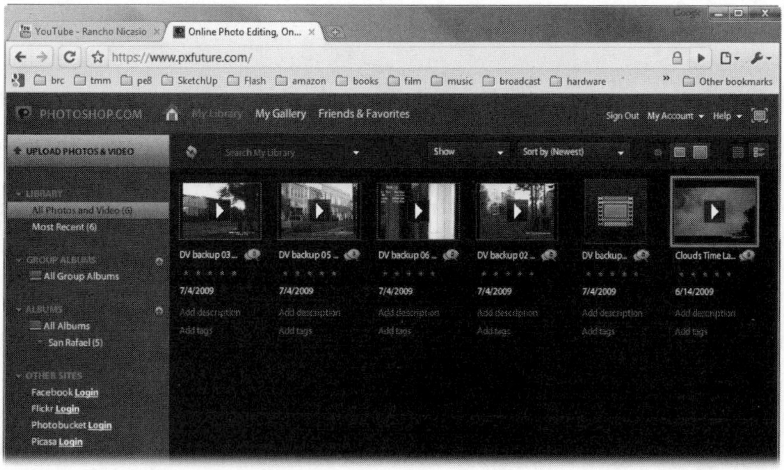

Figure 12-5:
You can upload movies to your Photoshop.com account from the Share tab in Premiere or while visiting the Photoshop.com site. Once you store videos in your Photoshop.com library, it's easy to share them with family, friends, and social networking sites like Facebook.

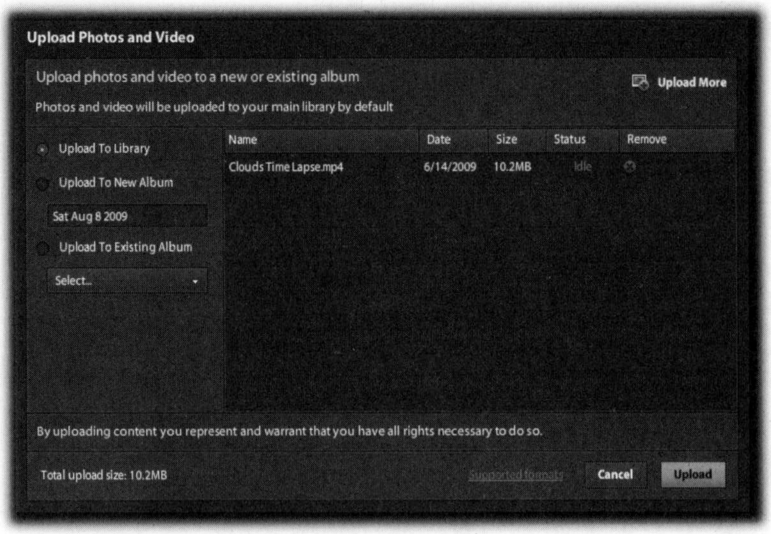

Figure 12-6:
You can upload videos and photos to the Photoshop.com website using web tools. As shown, here you can create a new album or add your media to an existing album.

One of the best things about having your videos on Photoshop.com is the ease with which you can manage the videos and photos you want to post to sites like Facebook and Flickr. Go to the Photoshop.com library with your videos. In the left column, click on the site you want to work with—Facebook, for example. A somewhat cryptic message appears that says: "Please click OK when you are done logging in". At that point, you're supposed to log into your Facebook account. Since you don't want to leave Photoshop.com, do this in another browser window or browser tab. Once you log into your Facebook account, come back and click the OK button in the message box. Then, Photoshop.com displays your videos and photos in the main part of the window, and, as shown in Figure 12-7, it displays your Facebook albums in the left column. To add a video to Facebook, just drag it to one of your Facebook albums.

Publish Your Movie to Podbean

Podbean is a site that hosts audio and video podcasts. There are four levels of membership, ranging from free to about $20 a month. At the free level, you get 100 megabytes of storage and you and your visitors are entitled to 5 gigabytes of traffic a month. That's enough to give you a taste of the podcasting experience if you're interested but haven't ever tried it. With a free account and Premiere, you're ready for broadcasting/podcasting business.

After you record and edit your podcast (see page 454), uploading it to Podbean is a cinch; it's just like uploading a video to YouTube or Photoshop.com. Go to Premiere's Share tab and then choose Online. Choose Podbean from the scrolling list of online sites. From the presets menu you can choose to upload a video or just the audio. You also have a choice of high or medium quality. Naturally, better quality always means bigger files.

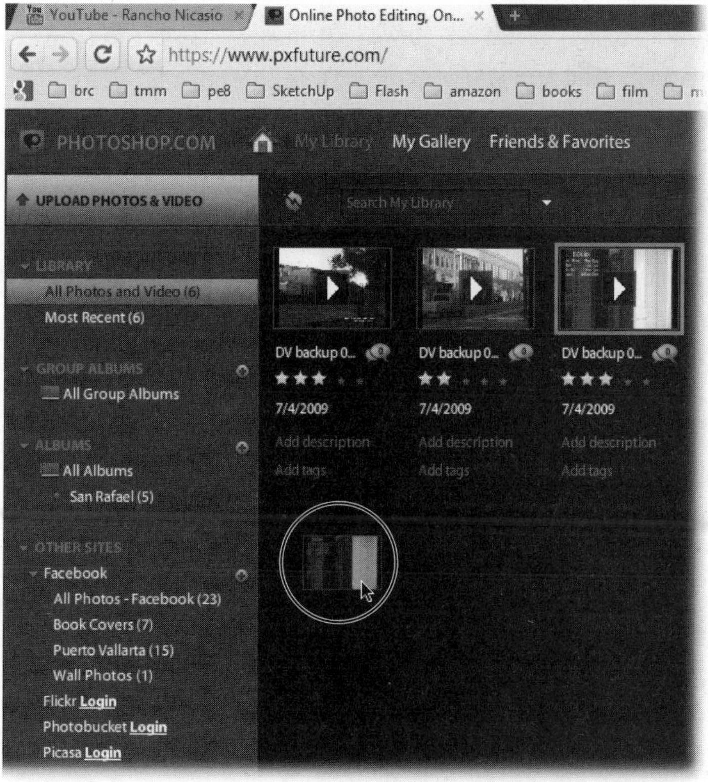

Figure 12-7:
You can use Photoshop.com to manage your videos and photos on social networking sites like Facebook or Flickr. Here, a video (circled) is dragged from the Photoshop.com library to a Facebook album.

Click the Next button to see a panel where you provide a name, description, and keywords for your podcast (Figure 12-8). Premiere encodes and then uploads your podcast to Podbean, where it's available to your audience. The site provides details if you want to embed your podcast into a blog or other website; it's similar to adding a YouTube movie to your site.

Make Your Movies Web-Friendly

When you send your videos off to YouTube, Photoshop.com, or Podbean, you use the presets provided by Premiere, so you don't have to worry too much about all the settings used to encode your movie. If you're posting videos on other sites, you need to pay a little more attention to the details. As mentioned before, smaller video files download and play faster, so if you know your movie is destined for the web, you want to keep the file size to a minimum. You'll lose half your audience if your video takes a long time to start playing or if it starts and stops instead of playing smoothly.

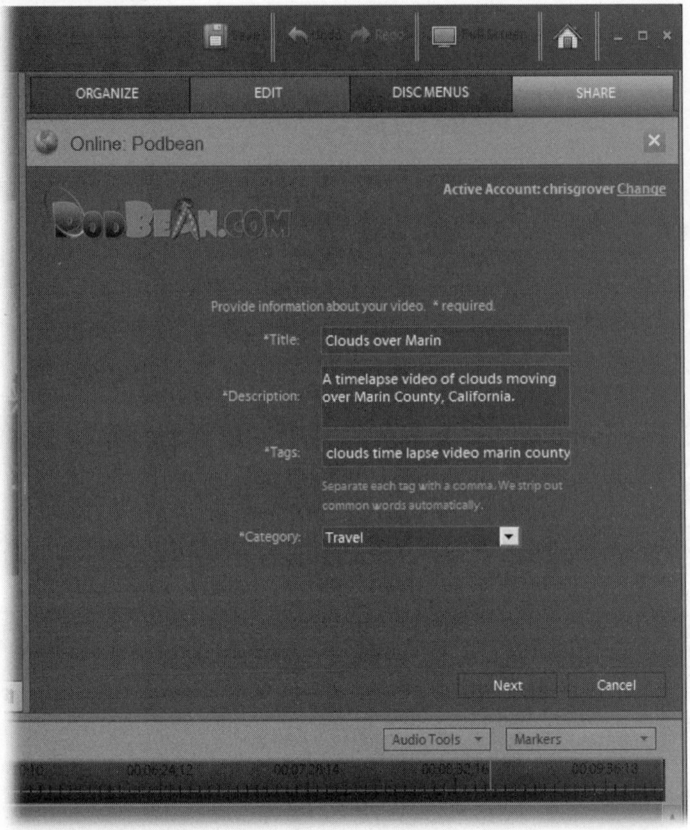

Figure 12-8:
Podbean is a website that hosts video and audio podcasts. Use the panel shown here to provide a name, description, and keywords for your podcast, and Premiere automatically uploads it to your account.

Decisions you make early on have a significant effect on the size of your video file. Sure, you can use a relatively small frame size and compress your movie. But you can also make your video files smaller by shooting video that compresses well. Camera motion and the visual qualities of your background dramatically affect how well your video compresses.

Here are some things to consider when you shoot video for the Web:

- **Use a tripod.** If the background doesn't constantly change, frame-to-frame compression is more effective. When you shoot video with shaky, hand-held camerawork, the background differs in every frame. But if you use a tripod, the background is often as static as a still image. If you don't have a tripod, perhaps you can fake it by setting your camera on a table or some other surface. If you're outside, try steadying your hand with the help of a street sign, a wall, or a tree.

- **Use pans, tilts, zooms, and dolly shots sparingly.** Again, frame-to-frame compression works better with an unchanging background. You probably don't want to avoid camera movement altogether, because it's an important part of moving pictures. So use it when there's dramatic need, but avoid it otherwise.

- **When possible, avoid backgrounds with complex patterns.** Plain, solid colors compress better than complicated random patterns. Multiply the intraframe compression benefit over multiple frames, and it makes a difference. You may not always have a choice, but when possible, put your subject in front of a painted wall instead of a brick wall or other complex background.

When you use the presets for YouTube and some of the other online services, Premiere handles the technical settings automatically. When you upload to a different website or email a video, here are some file-shrinking options to consider.

Some of these tips involve editing decisions. Other are encoding choices you make from Premiere's Share tab, after you choose a video preset like Adobe Flash Video. Click the Advanced button to open Premiere's Export Settings window, as shown in Figure 12-9:

- **Minimize effects such as dissolves.** A fancy transition, even your basic dissolve, makes video files bigger. In general, videos with fewer effects and fewer cuts compress better.

- **Lower the frame rate.** If your video is something static, like a talking head shot for a video blog or news show, reduce the frame rate to 15 fps to reduce file size. If there's a lot of action in your video, you probably want to keep your frame rate in the 24–30 fps range.

- **Use mono sound instead of stereo or multichannel sound.** Often, the benefits of stereo or multichannel sound are minimal for web-based video. Also, in many cases, camcorder mics don't separate sound well, so they record nearly identical sound on both tracks.

- **Reduce the audio bit rate.** If your movie's audio consists primarily of voices and sound effects, you may want to use an audio bit rate of 96 rather than 256 or 320.

- **Reduce the audio sampling frequency.** This is the audio equivalent of reducing the frame rate. Music CDs use a sampling frequency rate of 44.1 kHz. If your video doesn't demand that kind of high fidelity, you can lower the rate to 22.05 kHz or even 11.025 (about the equivalent of an AM radio).

When it comes to video compression, every little bit helps. Using any one of the techniques described here may not make a big difference, but if you use a few together, you'll see a difference in file size.

Put Video on Your Own Website

What if you want to send your video to a website other than one of those with the predesigned presets? Premiere has a generic My Website option in the scroll list. You can use this option to render your movie to one of Flash's compact video formats and then send it to the website of your choice. This doesn't create a page to display your video (that's up to whoever manages your site); it simply copies your edited movie to a web server.

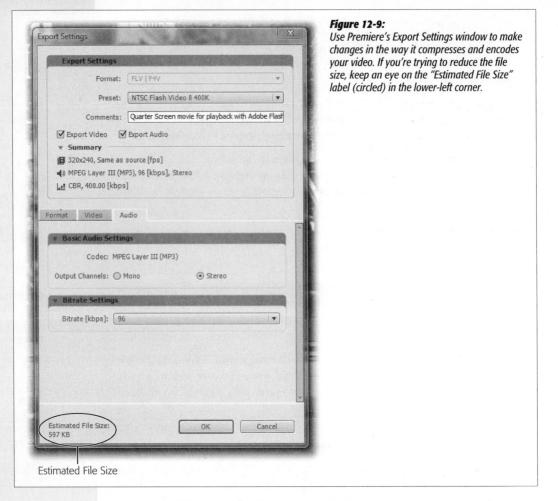

Figure 12-9:
Use Premiere's Export Settings window to make changes in the way it compresses and encodes your video. If you're trying to reduce the file size, keep an eye on the "Estimated File Size" label (circled) in the lower-left corner.

Once your video is ready for its web debut, follow these steps to make a Flash video file and send it on to a web server:

1. **Click Premiere's Share tab and then choose Online.**

   The Tasks panel displays a scrolling list where you can choose different online services, including YouTube, Photoshop.com, and My Website.

2. **Click "My Website".**

   The Share panel changes to show the My Website options (Figure 12-10), including a drop-down menu with different presets and text boxes where you provide information about your site's web server.

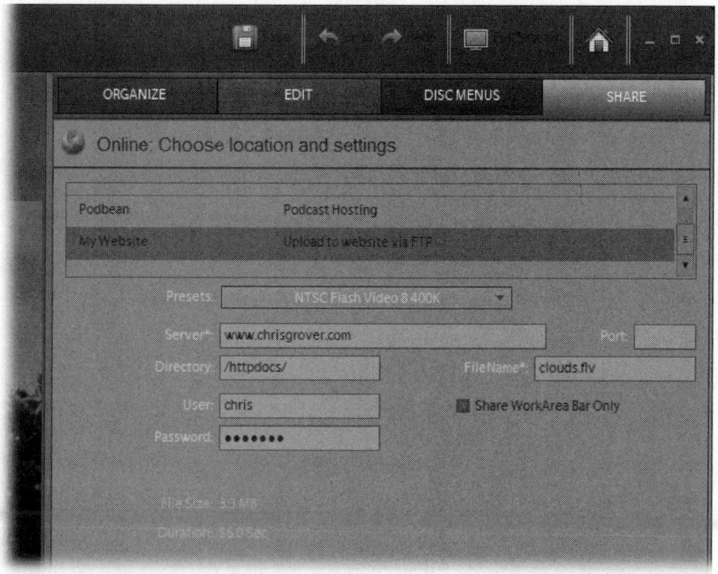

Figure 12-10:
Premiere's My Website panel seems to want a lot of information, but depending on the site, you may not need to fill in all the boxes. If you don't know the answers to the questions in this panel, you may have to contact the webmaster for your server.

3. **Choose one of the Flash video presets.**

   You have four options. First, decide whether you want to use the Flash Video 7 or the Flash Video 8 format. If you think the people visiting your site and viewing your video are likely to have older computers, it's safer to use the Flash Video 7 format. It's older and compatible with a greater number of computers. Otherwise, choose Flash 8, which uses the latest, greatest codec so it makes better-looking video in smaller files.

   The next choice has to do with the bit rate, or the Internet connection speed required to smoothly play the video. Larger numbers require more speed. The Flash 7 format offers two bit rates: 256K and 400K. Flash 8 offers two higher speeds: 400K and 800K. If your website visitors have a high-speed Internet connection (cable for example), they can view video at any of these speeds.

4. **Type a server address and a filename.**

   You may not need to fill in the rest of the boxes, but you have to supply these two details. If you don't know the server address, get it from your webmaster (in some cases, it may be the same as your website address). You may also need to supply a port number. In the "FileName" section, give your video the name you want it to have once Premiere copies it to your server. The person designing your web page will also need to know this name.

5. **If necessary, specify a destination directory, a username, and a password.**

   Here, the directory refers to the directory or folder on the web server where you want to store the file. Often, a server requires a username and password when you transfer files to it (using a technology called FTP, file transfer protocol; Premiere can handle an FTP transfer for you if you supply this information). Again, your webmaster is a good resource for this info.

6. **Click Next.**

   Premiere encodes your video to the Flash specification you provided and then sends it to your Web server (Figure 12-11). You see a progress bars for both procedures and an estimate of the time remaining.

   At the end of the process, you see a confirmation message.

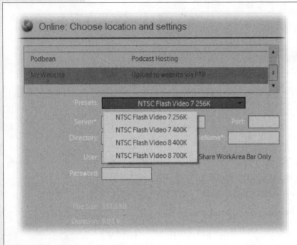

Figure 12-11:
Premiere has built-in tools so you can encode your movie to one of the compact Flash video formats and then send it to a website via a technology called FTP (file transfer protocol). If you're not familiar with FTP, you may need to get some details from the site's webmaster. You need an address, a file name and a directory.

CHAPTER 13

Create DVDs and Blu-ray Discs

Who ever thought that, one day, shiny little discs would change the way everyone watches movies? Shortly after the CD (compact disc) sparked a revolution in the audio world, DVDs (digital versatile discs) did the same in the video world. And just as audio made the transition from pop- and hiss-filled tape and vinyl recordings to the crisp, precise renderings of digital files when it jumped to CDs, video did the same when it moved from VHS tapes to DVDs. Great audio-visual quality. Durable enough to mail. Easy to store. What's not to love? And now, Blu-ray discs have emerged as the next standard in digital video, with enough capacity to hold feature-length movies in all their high-definition beauty.

This chapter shows you how to create pro-quality video discs, complete with menus that let your viewers jump to a specific scene on the disc (or, for multi-movie discs, to a specific movie on the disc). You'll also learn how to use use and edit the menu templates that come with Premiere. The first part of this chapter explains how to make menus. The last part gives you step-by-step details for burning your movies to DVD or Blu-ray discs.

Menu, Please!

If you don't create a menu for your movie before you burn it to disc, your video starts playing as soon as someone pops it into a player. Premiere calls these "Auto-Play" discs, and they're fine for short flicks. But if you fill a DVD or Blu-ray disc with video, your audience will appreciate some way to get around the disc, navigation tools like the one shown in Figure 13-1. That way, you can divide your movie into scenes (sometimes called chapters), and your audience can jump right to the scene they want to watch. Or, if you have several movies on a disc, they can select the movie they want to see.

You add menus to your disc using Premiere's predesigned templates. They automatically create two types of menus:

- The **Main menu** displays the title of your movie and has a Play Movie button. If your movie has separate scenes, there's also a link to a Scene menu (see below). When someone pops your disc into a player, the main menu is the first thing they see.

- The **Scene menu** provides links to individual scenes in your movie. (Hollywood DVDs sometimes call these "chapters.") The Scene menus also have a link back to the main menu. If you're movie isn't long or complicated, you don't have to create scene menus. In that case, your movie only has a main menu with a single link, which you click to play back your movie.

Note: It's easy to add Premiere's disc-menu templates to your project, but you can't change the way they *behave.* Premiere has preprogrammed them to create a main menu and a scene menu that work a certain way, so if you need a more complex menu structure, like one with submenus from the scenes menu or other bells and whistles, you'll have to use other video tools, like Adobe Encore, to create them. But for the majority of your projects, Premiere probably fits the bill.

Figure 13-1:
Premiere creates two menus for your discs: main menus and scene menus, the latter of which is shown here. After you use one of Premiere's predesigned templates, you can customize the text and images.

Set Menu Markers

So how does Premiere know where a scene, or, in the case of multiple-movie discs, a movie begins and ends? You gently point the way by placing markers in the timeline. Markers are a little like bookmarks: When Premiere gets down to the business of assembling your menus, it uses these "bookmarks" to build links from the disc's menus to a specific spot on your DVD or Blu-ray disc. As you explored time-line markers (page 170) and beat markers (page 308) in previous chapters, you may have noticed the Menu Marker option (Figure 13-2). (Each of these three markers has a different look, so you won't confuse one with the other as you work in the timeline.)

Think about the different ways you might want to present your movie and the way a DVD player needs to behave:

- **Discs with multiple scenes.** When you create menus for a movie that has multiple scenes, you want the movie to continue playing after each scene. No need to make your audience choose each scene from a menu.

- **Discs with multiple movies.** When you create menus for a disc with multiple movies, you want to play all the scenes for a movie and then, at the end, send the audience back to the main menu, where they can choose another movie. Wondering how to put multiple movies on a single disc? See the box on page 340.

You can create a disc with these kinds of navigational smarts with the help of just three types of color-coded menu markers that you place in your timeline:

- **Main Menu Marker** (blue). Use the main menu marker to signal the beginning of a movie. If you have more than one movie on a disc, use a main menu marker to flag the beginning of each one. When your audience clicks a link on the main menu, your movie starts to play at the point where you placed the main menu marker. The selected movie plays until it reaches a stop marker (see below), and then it sends the audience back to the main menu.

- **Scene Marker** (green). If you want to divide your movie into scenes, place a scene marker at the beginning of each one. Premiere displays links to the scenes in the Scenes submenu using the scene markers. When a movie is playing and it comes to a scene marker, it just keeps on playing. If your movie has more than three or four scenes, Premiere creates more than one scene menu to list them all.

- **Stop Marker** (red). Use a stop marker at the end of a movie to send your audience back to the main menu.

Set Menu Markers Automatically

Premiere offers a feature that automatically sets your menu markers, but most of the time, you'll be happier with the results if you set menu markers by hand. That way, you're sure they're in logical positions for the subject matter. However, there may be times when you're in a big rush or when it works to place scene markers at regular intervals, say every 3 minutes. This can be especially helpful if you're archiving some of your raw footage—automatically putting markers at regular intervals makes it easy to scan the footage as you search for specific material.

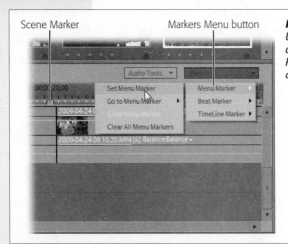

Scene Marker   Markers Menu button

Figure 13-2:
Use the Markers menu on the right side of the Timeline to add Main Menu, Scene, and Stop markers to your movie. Premiere uses these markers to create menus for DVDs and Blu-ray discs.

Create a Multiple Movie Disc

How do I put multiple movies on a single DVD or Blu-ray Disc?

First, you have to put all the movies on the same timeline. Then you mark the beginning and end of each movie. The last step is to use Premiere's Share tools to copy all the movies to a disc at one time. This leads to the next frequently asked question:

How to I put multiple movies on a single timeline?

If you plan ahead, you could build your movies that way—putting movies one after the other in a single project, on a single timeline. That's not always practical or possible. Another option is to export each edited movie as a single video file and then import those movies into a new Premiere project. For details on how to export movies to computer files, see page 380.

For those occasions when you want to automatically divvy up your movie:

1. **Click a clip in the timeline.**

   You don't have to select every clip—one does the trick.

2. **Choose Disc → Generate Menu Markers.**

   A window appears labeled "Automatically Set Menu Scene Markers" (Figure 13-3).

3. **Choose one of the three options for setting markers:**

   • **At Each Scene** tells Premiere to set markers at the beginning of each clip in the timeline. This is a good option if you have a lot of raw video in a project—for example, if you have an archive disc for raw clips.

   • **Every X Minutes** sets markers at regular intervals, a good option for long videos where you or your audience may want to jump around to sample different sections.

• **Total Markers** places markers at even intervals throughout your movie. You provide the number of markers you want and Premiere does the math.

4. **(Optional) Check Clear Existing Menu Markers.**

Premiere doesn't disturb any markers in the timeline when it creates new ones. It simply adds the newly generated markers. Check this option to remove existing markers before you generate the new ones. It clears all Main Menu, Scene, and Stop markers.

5. **Click OK.**

After you click OK, the Marker window closes and the scene markers appear in the timeline.

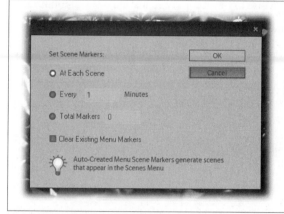

Figure 13-3:
Premiere can place a marker at the beginning of each clip, or it can put markers at regular intervals throughout your movie. If you want them at regular intervals, you can set the timing for the interval or type in the total number of markers you want Premiere to add and let it figure out the timing.

Create Markers Manually

Most of the time, you'll probably create menu markers manually. After all, you know exactly where one scene or movie ends and another begins.

To set markers manually, drag the playhead (or click the Previous and Next Edit Point button in the monitor) to a spot in the timeline where you want a marker. Then choose the type of marker you need. For main menu and scene markers, you can add text and a thumbnail image to the marker, which Premiere uses in the menus it creates. Here are the steps:

1. **In the timeline, position the playhead where you want a marker.**

Alternatively, you can type a specific time in the number box in the monitor.

2. **Click the Markers menu and then choose Menu Marker → Set Menu Marker.**

A window appears labeled "Menu Marker @" followed by the playhead's timeline position, as shown in Figure 13-4.

3. Click the Marker Type drop-down menu and choose one of the options.

You have three choices: Main Menu, Scene, and Stop.

If you're not dividing your disc into scenes, choose Stop marker. The only other thing you have to do is click OK, and Premiere adds a red Stop marker to the timeline. You can skip the rest of the steps below.

4. To place a main menu or scene marker, type in a name for it.

The name will appear on the disc menu Premiere creates, so it's best to keep them short—otherwise they won't fit on the menu screen. Premiere doesn't give marker names a whole lot of real estate in the menus.

5. (Optional) Click the Motion Menu button.

This option adds a moving picture to the Scene menu instead of a still thumbnail.

6. (Optional) Specify a timecode for the Thumbnail Offset.

The thumbnail offset designates which frame starts the moving image Premiere displays in the Scene menu. As you change the time in the thumbnail offset, the thumbnail picture changes. You can change the offset by typing in a new number or you can drag to scrub in a new time value.

7. Click OK.

Your manually created marker appears in the timeline, with a color that matches its purpose in life. Main menu markers are blue, scene markers green, and stop markers red.

Tip: Lots of times, you want to put markers at the very beginning of a clip. You can use the shortcut keys PageUp and PageDown to jump to the cuts between clips.

Add Stop Markers

When you burn single or multiple movies on a single disc, you want the audience to return to the main menu at the end of the movie. That little chore is the domain of the Stop marker. Whenever a DVD player encounters a stop marker, it stops playback and jumps to the disc's main menu. Follow these steps to insert a stop marker:

1. Position the playhead where you want the stop marker.

2. Click the Marker menu and then choose Menu Marker → Set Menu Marker.

3. Click the Marker Type drop-down menu and choose Stop Marker.

4. Click OK.

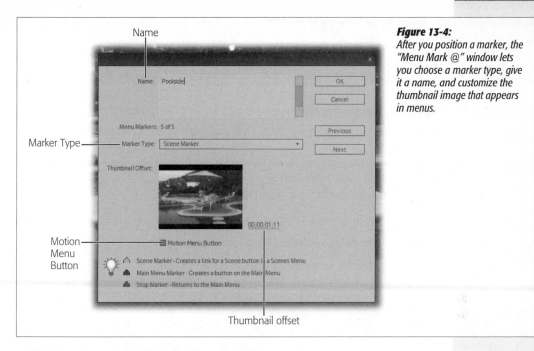

Name

Marker Type

Motion
Menu
Button

Thumbnail offset

Figure 13-4:
After you position a marker, the "Menu Mark @" window lets you choose a marker type, give it a name, and customize the thumbnail image that appears in menus.

Delete or Move Markers in the Timeline

If you decide you no longer need a menu marker, right-click it and then choose Clear Menu Marker from the shortcut menu (Figure 13-5). If the timing for your marker isn't quite right, you don't have to delete it and start over—you can simply drag it to a new location. When you delete or move menu markers, Premiere automatically renumbers them so they'll be properly ordered on the scene menus.

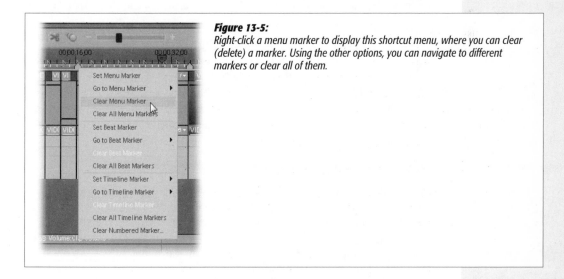

Figure 13-5:
Right-click a menu marker to display this shortcut menu, where you can clear (delete) a marker. Using the other options, you can navigate to different markers or clear all of them.

Use a Stock Menu

After you get your markers squared away, it's time to test out some menus. Premiere comes with a bunch of menu templates. The good news is that they're easy to use. Once you've placed markers in the timeline, the templates automatically use the markers to create scene menus (or movie menus if you create a multi-movie disc). The not-so-good news is that many of the menus are pretty hokey. At least in the initial package, most of them seem more appropriate for kid-vids rather than grownups. To be fair, Adobe promises to keep delivering additional menus and other content via Photoshop.com. Also, if you can't find a template that suits your project, you can apply a menu template and then customize it using your own graphics and music, as explained on page 345.

Applying a stock menu is a drag-and-drop operation:

1. **In the Tasks panel, click the Disc Menus tab.**

   The Disc Menus panel shows thumbnails of the available menu templates. Initially, you see all the templates in one long scrollable list. You can narrow that down using the two drop-down menus.

2. **Use the top-left menu to pick a general topic, such as** *Sports.*

   The menu offers other topics, including Entertainment, Happy Birthday, Kids Corner, and New Baby. Once you choose a topic, the secondary menu displays templates related to that topic.

3. **Use the secondary menu to choose a specific template, such as** *Extreme.*

   Each template comes with two screens, one for the main menu and the other for the Scenes menu.

4. **Click on the menu template and then, at the bottom of the Disc Menus panel, click Apply.**

   When you first apply a menu, the monitor displays the main menu, as shown in Figure 13-6. At the bottom of the monitor, you can choose between the individual main and scene menus that Premiere generates for your project. Each scene menu accommodates three or four scenes. Should your movie have more scenes than that, Premiere automatically creates additional scene menus. And if you added menu markers to your film, Premiere displays the thumbnails in the scene menu.

5. **In the lower-right corner of the monitor, click the Preview button.**

   A menu preview window opens, showing the same type of controls you find on most DVD or Blu-ray players. The background music plays and you can click any of the buttons to test-drive your disc menu system. This is a good time to check things out and make at least mental notes if you want to change the template. For example, there's boilerplate text in the menu titles ("Movie Title Here"). Perhaps the background music isn't right for your project, or you want to find better images for the scene thumbnails.

6. Click the X button in the upper-right corner of the Menu Preview window.

The window closes.

7. Press Ctrl+S.

Even if you're going to make changes to the menus, this is a good place to save your work.

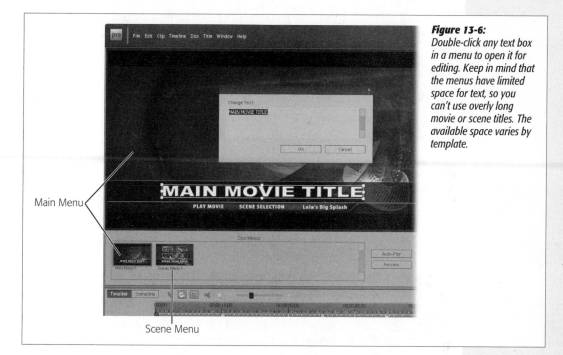

Figure 13-6:
Double-click any text box in a menu to open it for editing. Keep in mind that the menus have limited space for text, so you can't use overly long movie or scene titles. The available space varies by template.

Main Menu

Scene Menu

The menu preview window gives you a reasonable idea of how your DVD will look once you burn it. Don't forget that the video images may not be up to par because Premiere taps the same preview versions of clips (rather than the original footage) that it uses as you edit your movie. But don't worry—when you burn your disc, Premiere uses your original footage to create the high-quality clips that go into your menus (and your movie, of course).

Edit a Stock Menu

You almost always want to make some changes to Premiere's menu templates. If nothing else, you at least want to change the main text to reflect the title of your movie. Fortunately, it's easy to make some quick changes.

1. In the main menu, double-click the text box with the words "Main Movie Title."

The Change Text box, shown in Figure 13-6, opens, displaying the text currently in the box.

2. **Select the text and replace it with your title—something like** *Lola's Big Splash.* **Then click OK.**

When you click OK, your new text replaces the original title. It's always best to double-check to make sure the text fits in the menu.

3. **(Optional) Add a media file to a "drop zone."**

Some menus include drop zones where you can drag and drop video or still photos that will appear on the menu page. Examples include General → Fun, Entertainment → Music Video and Travel → Road Trip.

To add a still or video to a drop zone, click the Organize tab and then click the Project button. Drag a clip from the Project tab to the drop zone.

4. **(Optional) Change the position and formatting of the text box.**

As you change the words in a menu, you may want to move or modify the text font and style:

- **Move the text box.** Drag the text box to a new location to reposition it.

- **Change the text size.** With the text box selected, in the Disc Menus panel (Figure 13-7), change the value in Change Text Size box. When you change the point size for text, it keeps its proportions. You can distort the text using the next technique.

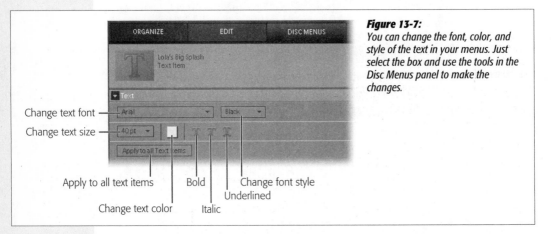

Figure 13-7:
You can change the font, color, and style of the text in your menus. Just select the box and use the tools in the Disc Menus panel to make the changes.

- **Distort text dimensions.** Drag one of the text-box handles to change the width or height of the text.

- **Change the typeface.** Choose a new typeface from the Change Text Font drop-down menu. Delicate fonts with lots of thin lines don't work well for video, so it's best to stick with bolder, simpler typefaces.

- **Change Font Style.** Use the drop-down menu next to the font names to choose a style such as Italic, Bold, or Black. In most cases, the thickest, boldest styles work best.

- **Change the text color.** Click the color chip and choose a new color from the menu. Make sure your text stands out from the background colors.

- **Change text style to Bold, Italic, or Underlined.** In most cases, it's best to use the Change Font Style drop-down menu to make style changes because they tap the fonts installed on your computer and provide the best font quality. If you don't see the option you want there, use one of these buttons.

  Adobe uses different terms for the different types of text in its menus. The categories include Text Items, Play Buttons, Scene Buttons, and Marker Buttons. If you want to change all the text boxes of a certain type, make the changes to one of the text boxes and then click the "Apply to all" button at the bottom. For example, you can apply changes to the Text Item boxes on the Main Menu and the Scene Menus.

5. **At the bottom of the monitor, click Scenes Menu 1.**

   Premiere displays the Scenes menu in the monitor, as shown in Figure 13-8. It includes four scenes that match the scene markers you added to the timeline. Each displays a thumbnail image and a title. As explained on page 342, when you create scene markers, you name them. Premiere uses those names to label the scenes in the menu.

Figure 13-8:
Premiere puts four scenes on each Extreme Sports scene menu. If you added more than four scene markers to your movie, Premiere creates additional scene menus. For the sake of symmetry, you may want to use an even number of scenes in your movie. That way, you won't end up with an additional scene menu with just a single scene on it.

6. **Edit the title for the Scenes page.**

Premiere's title for the scenes menu is something imaginative like "Scene Menu Title." You may want to change it to something that's more in tune with your movie, such as "Lola's Big Splash – Scenes." If your title is too big to fit on the screen, use one of the techniques described earlier to resize the text.

7. **Click the first scene thumbnail in the upper-left corner of the menu.**

The Disc Menu panel displays its properties, as you can see in Figure 13-9. Use the settings here to make changes.

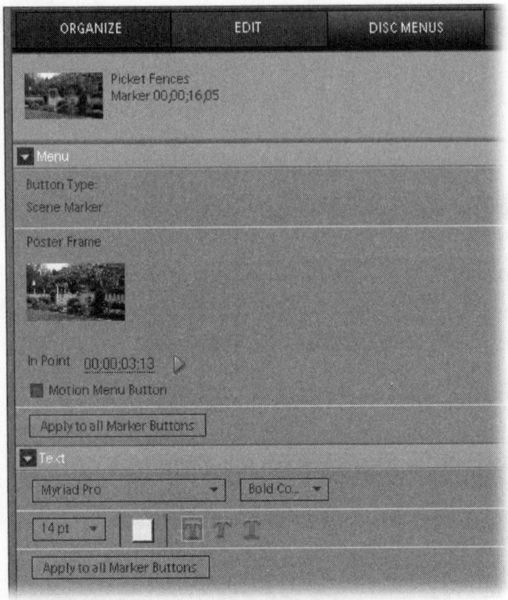

Figure 13-9:
Select any element in the menu and the Disc Menus panel displays its properties. Shown here are the properties for a scene marker. They include the button type, the poster frame, and the text format.

8. **Double-click the thumbnail in the Disc Menu Premiere uses for the first scene.**

The "Menu Mark @" window opens. This is the same old friend you used to create the menu marker in the first place. You can use this box to change the marker type, the name, and the thumbnail (Figure 13-10). That last option, changing the thumbnail, is the one you'll probably use most often. Premiere automatically uses the first frame after a marker as the thumbnail image. You can change it two ways:

• Create a Motion Menu Button.

• Change the thumbnail image or start point.

9. (Optional) Check the Motion Menu Button box.

   Check this box, and instead of using a still image for the thumbnail, Premiere plays a few seconds of the scene's video in the thumbnail. Sometimes this works great, but sometimes it creates a menu that's a little too busy. Use your own judgment.

10. (Optional) Change the time value in Thumbnail Offset.

   The time value to the right of the thumbnail image selects the frame for a still thumbnail or the starting point of a thumbnail video. Often, that first frame in a clip has some sort of "fade in" or "dissolve" effect, so it makes sense to choose a frame farther down the timeline. In other cases, you may want a better visual to define a scene.

Tip: You can change the Thumbnail Offset using the "Menu Marker @" window or the Poster Frame In Point in the Disc Menus panel. Both options have advantages and disadvantages. The Disc Menus panel has a handy Play button to help you find the perfect frame, while the "Menu Marker @" window gives you a bigger, better view of the thumbnail image.

---

11. Click OK.

   The scene menu button now reflects your changes.

12. Repeat these steps to edit the other scene buttons and then click Done.

   The Done button is hidden away in the lower-right corner of the Disc Menus panel.

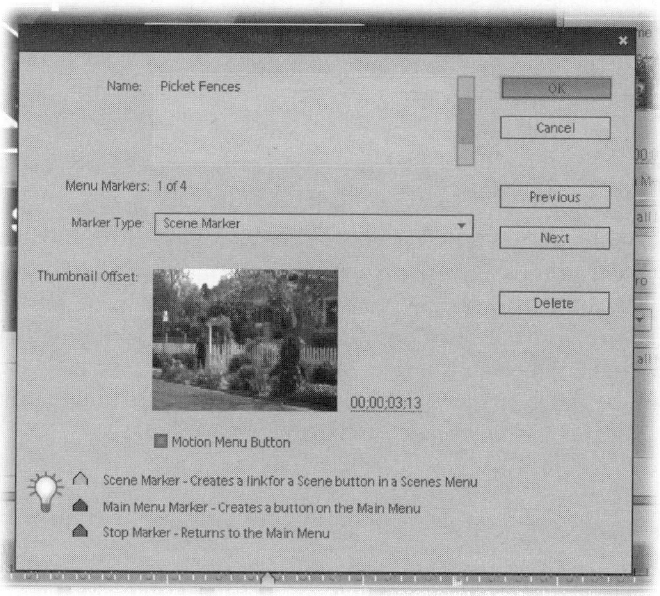

Figure 13-10:
Double-click one of the scene buttons in the menu or one of the markers in the timeline and you see this "Menu Mark @" window, where you can make changes. Premiere uses the name and thumbnail images here to create scene menus.

You can jump to any of the menus in your project by clicking the buttons at the bottom of the menu monitor. Often it takes some tweaking and previewing to get your menu just right. If you want to leave the menu monitor and go back to your movie in Premiere's regular monitor, go to Window → Monitor. To jump back to the menu monitor, click the Disc Menus tab.

Swap Menu Templates

Premiere's menu templates are pretty consistent in the way they look and work. They all use the menu markers in the timeline to build menus, for example. Title text may appear in different locations, and some scene menus have three scenes instead of four, but these are pretty minor differences. In most cases, you can swap one menu for another without a whole lot of work. Just go to the Disc Menus tab and use the two drop-down menus to choose a new template. Click on the template to select it and then click the Apply button. After you make changes, preview the results to make sure everything looks good. Look carefully for text that doesn't quite fit in the text boxes.

Remove a Menu from a Project

There may be times when you want to strip a menu from your project. In Premiere-speak a menu-less DVD project is known as an Auto-Play project. That's because discs without menus begin to play as soon as you put them in a player.

To remove a menu from your project, click the Disc Menus tab and then, in the lower-right corner of the Menu monitor, click the Auto-Play button. Without any fanfare or so much as an "Are you sure?", Premiere removes the menu from your project.

Tip: It's not hard to accidentally click the Auto-Play button when you mean to click the Preview button. As shown in Figure 13-11, they're right next to each other. Poof! All the hard work you just put in to create your menu disappears into the ether. Don't panic. Just press Ctrl+Z or click Edit → Undo and you're menu is back.

Create a Custom Menu

Premiere's templates don't work for every project. They're all pretty much in your face, and many might tickle a 12-year-old's fancy more than an adult's. Fortunately, you can change the background images and the accompanying music to create your own menus or templates. Often, you don't have to go any further than your own timeline to find some great images for your project. Remember, you can create a still from any video frame in your project. That's a large library of still images. You can even shoot some images with your menu in mind.

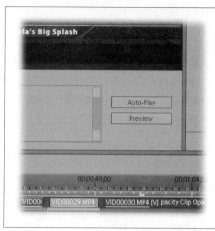

Figure 13-11:
*Click the Auto-Play button to remove the menu system from your project.
The result is a disc that automatically plays when you insert it in a DVD or
Blu-ray player.*

Create a Menu Background Image

For your menu background, you want an image that lets the text and scene thumbnails stand out. That means simple images work better. If the image is mostly light-
hued, you can use dark-colored text or vice-versa. Many images are too busy or
too colorful for menu backgrounds, but you can always use Premiere's effects to
modify an image to make it suitable as a menu background.

Note: You can't change the background image for templates that have "drop zones," areas in a template
menu to which you can drag-and-drop still or video images. Other menu templates use multiple graphics
files that are difficult to customize. Examples of easily customizable templates include Sports → Extreme
and Happy Birthday → Balloons.

Creating a new background image for a menu involves these steps:

- Find a frame in your video that you want to use as a background image.

- Modify the image using Premiere's effects or an image editor such as Photoshop Elements.

- Save the image as a file.

- Open your edited video project with a menu template already applied.

- Swap your saved image for the background image in the menu template.

If you're up for the challenge, follow these steps to create a new background image:

1. **Go to File → New → Project.**

   Creating a background still often involves a bit of experimentation with effects.
   If you do it as a new project, you're less likely to mess up your perfectly edited
   video.

2. **Drag the clip that has the image you want to use to the timeline.**

   The video appears in the monitor.

3. **Preview the clip until you find the right frame.**

   Use whatever means necessary to zero in on that perfect frame. The Shuttle button, shown in Figure 13-12, is a good tool for this job because it lets you vary the playback speed as you preview, and you can easily move forward and backward within a clip.

4. **In the lower-right corner of the monitor, click the Freeze Frame button (the camera icon).**

   The Freeze Frame window opens, and you can export a still or insert the still image back into the timeline.

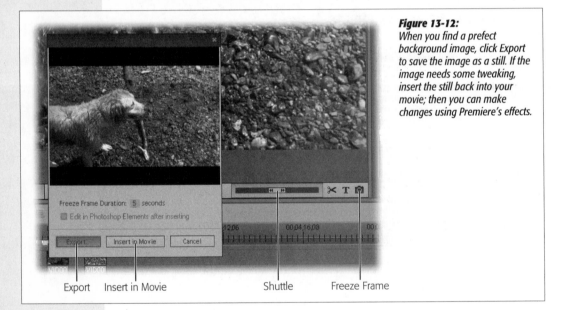

Figure 13-12:
When you find a prefect background image, click Export to save the image as a still. If the image needs some tweaking, insert the still back into your movie; then you can make changes using Premiere's effects.

Export Insert in Movie   Shuttle   Freeze Frame

5. **Click "Insert in Movie".**

   Most of the time, a still image can use the help of some effects, so pop the still back into the timeline and experiment with one of Premiere's effects.

6. **Click the Edit tab and then click the Effects button.**

   The Edit panel shows dozens of different effects.

7. **Experiment with different effects and combinations of effects.**

   The goal here is to create a background that won't fight with the menu text or scene thumbnails. That means you want to reduce the detail, contrast, and color differences between the background image and the menu elements. If you need a refresher on how to apply and edit Premiere effects, see page 197.

Here are some effects you may want to try, but don't be afraid to experiment with the others:

- **Image Control.** Every clip has the fixed effect "Image Control" applied to it. Used sparingly, you can tweak these settings to make an image look more realistic. In some cases, you may want to make more extreme changes to create non-photorealistic images. First, try moving the Saturation slider to the left to remove color from the image. By taking color out of the background image, the colorful menu text and thumbnail images stand out. If you completely desaturate the image, it becomes black and white. If you only go part way, the image becomes washed out. This isn't usually a good look for a photo, but it's not bad for a menu background. After you remove the color, try increasing the brightness and reducing the contrast. You can also adjust the hue, keeping in mind the colors you want to use for the menu text.

- **NewBlue Art Effects.** Several of the NewBlue art effects work well for menus. The *Air Brush* effect can make your photorealistic frame look like hand-drawn art—a great effect for menus. The *Line Drawing* effect removes color from an image, leaving lines at the edges, as shown in Figure 13-13. Using Edit Effects, you can change the line and background colors. Use the Density slider to add or remove line detail. *Pastel Sketch* softens colors while adding edge lines.

- **Emboss.** Initially, the Emboss effect (Stylize → Emboss) creates a mostly gray 3D image. Gray makes a good background because color type and thumbnails pop out in contrast. If you want, you can change the gray using the Blend With Original slider.

8. **With the modified frame selected, click Freeze Frame again.**

   Yes, you're freeze-framing a freeze frame—it's the best way to export a still image.

9. **Click Export.**

   The Export Frame window opens, where you name your image and choose a place to save it.

10. **Type a name such as** *background_embossed.bmp* **and then click Save.**

    Premiere saves freeze frames in Windows bitmap (.bmp) format. Make sure you save your freeze frame on your desktop or some other handy folder.

11. **Click the X button to close the Freeze Frame window and then choose File → Close to close your background image Premiere project.**

    That completes the first few steps of finding and customizing a background image.

You can give the main menu and the scenes menu unique backgrounds, so you may want to create a second freeze frame.

Figure 13-13:
*The NewBlue Line
Drawing effect creates a
two-color background.
You can use the Edit
Effects settings to change
the line and background
colors.*

Swap Menu Background Images

You can use any image file on your computer as a background image. That includes photos, hand-drawn art, or freeze frames from your movie. Once you store an image in a computer file, it's pretty easy to swap one menu background for another:

1. **Go to File → Open Project and then open your edited movie.**

   If you haven't already added menu markers and applied a menu to your project, you need to do that before you can move on with this exercise. See page 338.

2. **Click Disk Menus.**

   Select a menu template and drag it to the monitor. Premiere displays the Main Menu.

3. **Click within the Main Menu to select the Menu Background.**

   Once you select the Menu Background, the Menu Background properties appear in the Disc Menus panel.

4. **Under Menu Background, click the Browse button.**

   A file browser window opens. Locate the background image you created for your menu.

5. **Select your background image and then click Open.**

   Your background image appears in the monitor, as shown in Figure 13-14. Often, you won't know if an image works as a background until you see it in place.

Figure 13-14:
This main menu background was created using a freeze frame from a movie and the NewBlue Air Brush effect. The hand-drawn appearance gives the menu a handsome, artistic feel.

If you want to replace the background image for the Scenes menu, too, click Scene Menu 1 at the bottom of the monitor and repeat Steps 4 and 5.

Sometimes, you need to make a few changes for the background to work just right. For example, you may want to reposition the scene thumbnails to let part of a background image show through, as shown in Figure 13-15. In other cases, you may want to resize the text or scene thumbnails. Resist the temptation to make things so small that your audience can't see them on a TV screen. If necessary, go back and make more changes to the background image.

Premiere automatically forces background images to fit the video frame. You can't drag the image handles beyond the edges of the frame, so you can't zoom in on part of your image. The only way to do that is open the image in an editor like Photoshop Elements to resize and crop it.

Note: For details on how to edit images in Photoshop Elements, check out *Photoshop Elements 8: The Missing Manual* by Barbara Brundage.

Figure 13-15:
Here, the scene thumbnails were nudged slightly to the right so that the golden retriever in the menu background shows through. The color of the freeze frame captured from the video was desaturated to make the titles and thumbnails stand out.

Swap Menu Music

The other major element of Premiere's menu templates is their music. When you first add a menu to your project, Premiere uses a music loop that's related to the menu (and theme, if you applied one of Premiere's themes to your movie). The music Premiere applies to menus is professionally produced, and most of it is on the lively side of rock and roll. Whether this works for your movie is up to you. As the producer/director, you can take over for the music department and change the background score.

With your project open, follow these steps:

1. **Click the Disc Menus tab.**

    The main menu appears in the monitor.

2. **Click on the Main Menu background in the Monitor.**

    The Main Menu properties screen appears in the Disc Menus panel, and it includes an audio section.

3. **Under Audio, click the Browse button, as shown in Figure 13-16.**

    A file browser window opens, where you can navigate through the folders on your computer.

4. **Find an audio file you want to use for background music and then click Open.**

    Premiere swaps the soundtrack for the menus, but you may not be able to tell from the Disc Menus panel.

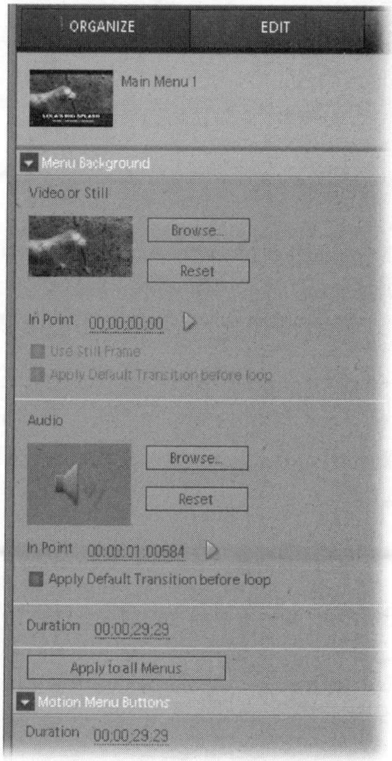

Figure 13-16:
Click the background of the Main (or Scene) Menu to see the audio settings. Use the Browse button to swap the background sound file. The other settings help you control the timing for the looped audio track.

5. Under the monitor, click the Preview button.

As you audition the new music, you may want to consider a different starting point for it.

6. (Optional) Change the In Point for the audio.

There are three ways to change the background music's starting point.

- Click the time value and type in a new time.
- Drag the time value to scrub in a new time.
- Click the Play button and then click Pause to set a new time.

7. (Optional) Check "Apply Default Transition before loop".

The menu audio loops—meaning that, when it gets to the end of the sound clip, it starts playing again at the beginning. You may want the music to fade out and then fade in at these points. Usually a fade-in is the default audio transition, so checking this box makes your menu audio fade out and then fade back in.

8. (Optional) Change the Duration.

Most menus are set up to play music for about 30 seconds before it loops. You can change the timing with this setting.

9. (Optional) Click the Apply to all Menus button.

   If you want the same background audio track on all your menus, go ahead and click this button.

10. **Click Done.**

   Premiere saves your audio changes.

Famous DVD Moment: You may not always want to use music as background audio for your movie. For example, the DVD for Rob Reiner's Rock and Roll mockumentary *This Is Spinal Tap* has some of the funniest dialog ever running behind menus. The somewhat deranged members of the band are critiquing how the DVD menu is designed.

Preview Your Movie and Menus

Before you commit your movie to a DVD or Blu-ray disc, it pays to give it a thorough review. That includes watching all the footage and giving the menu system a good workout. As explained earlier, the best way to test the menus is to click the Disc Menus tab and then click the Preview button below the monitor. The Preview Disc window opens, sporting the same controls you find on disc players. Use these controls to check all the links on the menus. Make sure the Scene links take you to the point in the video you expect. Double-check the stop markers by fast-forwarding to the end of your movie.

When it comes to previewing your video, you can do that in the Preview Disc window or in Premiere's main monitor.

Burn a DVD or Blu-ray Disc

While editing is a satisfying intellectual pastime, showing off your movie to friends and family is where you find glory. It's hard to find someone who can't watch a DVD on their computer or TV, making DVDs an excellent video distribution medium. If you've gone all-out with high-definition video, you likely shot your video with one of the new HD video camcorders, bought a Blu-ray disc burner for your computer, and hooked up a Blu-ray disc player to your home theater system. (If you're not up to speed on Blu-ray technology, see the box on page 359.)

As you learned earlier, you can create discs that display menus when they start up or you can create discs without menus, which start playing back as soon as you put them in a player.

If you want to create a menu and haven't done so already, go directly to the beginning of this chapter. Do not pass Go, and do not collect $200. Actually, creating a good menu system is more work than burning a disc.

DVD or Blu-ray?

When it comes to technology, time always marches on. The next stop on the disc-recording tech train is Blu-ray. If you don't have any Blu-ray equipment at the moment, odds are you will in the future. Blu-ray discs look just like CDs or DVDs, but they store five to 10 times the information. They were developed to deliver full high-definition movies and video to your HDTV—a standard DVD just doesn't have enough capacity. How do they manage to cram more data on those same-sized shiny discs? Instead of using a red laser, as CDs and DVDs do, Blu-ray discs use a violet laser, which uses a shorter wavelength of light—hence the name "Blu-ray". Somehow, this makes it easier to cram more 1s and 0s onto a shiny disc.

There was a relative short high-def format war, when Blu-ray and HD DVD technologies fought it out. The Blu-ray forces had a long list of heavyweights in their corner, including Apple, Dell, Hewlett Packard, Intel, Samsung, Sony, 20th Century Fox, Walt Disney Motion Pictures, and Warner Brothers. The combination of hardware and content providers won the day for Blu-ray. The HD DVD forces flew the white flag and surrendered in early 2008.

A single-layer Blu-ray disc holds 25 gigabytes of information, compared to a single-layer DVD's capacity of 4.7 gigabytes. *Double-layer* Blu-ray discs hold about 50 gigabytes of information, while double-layer DVDs hold about 8 gigabytes.

If you have trouble remembering how Blu-ray is spelled and capitalized, just think of it as a single word, "Blueray," where the "e" is replaced with a hyphen; the "r" is always lowercase.

Once you're sure your project is ready for distribution, follow these steps to burn a disc:

1. **Pop a blank disc into your computer's writable disc drive.**

   If you have questions about the different types of blank discs, see the box on page 362.

2. **Click the Share tab.**

   Premiere displays the different options for sharing your video.

3. **Click the Disc button.**

   The Share tab shows settings to create DVD or Blu-ray discs.

4. **Choose DVD or Blu-ray.**

   You lucky souls with Blu-ray disc burners and Blu-ray players can gloat a little as you click the Blu-ray option. On the other hand, if you're scratching your head and asking "What the heck's Blu-ray, and to I really care?", see the box on page 359.

5. **(Optional for DVDs) Set the "Burn to" menu to "Folder (4.6 GB)" or "Folder (8.5GB)" depending on the type of blank disc you'll be using, and choose a file location.**

   Today's fast computers are pretty good at rendering movies and burning them directly to a DVD, but that hasn't always been the case. With slower, older computers you may want to copy the movie file for a DVD to a folder on your computer and then use DVD burning software, like Nero BackItUp & Burn or Roxio Creator, to burn a disc.

What's the advantage? If Premiere fails to encode and burn a disc in one shot, you have to start all over from the beginning. However, if Premiere manages to copy your movie to a folder on your computer, you can exit Premiere and not have to worry about whether it can handle both assembling and burning your movie in the same step. Running by itself, a DVD burning program uses fewer computer resources than Premiere does as it creates a disc, so it may burn discs more successfully. In any case, you won't have to render all that video again before you try to burn another disc—you just use the encoded movie that's in the folder.

You can't use this option with Blu-ray discs.

6. **Type in a disc or folder name such as** *LOLA_SPLASH.*

   If you don't change the disc or folder name, Premiere uses a number. By tradition, people usually name discs with all capital letters and underscores in the place of spaces. You can do whatever you please.

7. **Check and set the Burner Location.**

   When you click the Disc button, Premiere scans your computer for drives capable of burning DVD or Blu-ray discs. Those names appear on the Burner Location drop-down menu. It also checks to see if you have a blank disc in the drive; if you don't, you'll notice the Burn button is grayed out. Put in a fresh disc and click the Rescan button to have Premiere check for drives and discs a second time.

8. **In the Copies box, enter the number of discs you want to create.**

   As you might guess, this option is deselected if you write your movie to a PC folder. If you know you want to create a bunch of DVDs, use this option because it only has to go through the time-consuming process of encoding your movie once. After that, burning multiple discs goes fairly quickly.

9. **Change the Presets menu to match your project.**

   The options includes standard and widescreen frames in NTSC or PAL formats.

10. **(Optional) Check the Fit Contents to available space box.**

    If you've got a really big video project, it may not fit on a DVD or Blu-ray disc. In that case, check this box and Premiere compresses the video as best it can to make it fit. Keep in mind that DVDs and Blu-ray discs have a tremendous amount of storage, as explained in the box on page 359.

11. **(Optional) Set the Video Quality slider to Highest Quality.**

    In most cases, your video will fit on a single disc. You can leave the quality box unchecked or you can set the slider to Highest Quality. The result is the same: Premiere burns uncompressed video to the disc. If you're curious about how much space your video takes, check the size estimate listed under the slider.

12. **Click the Burn button.**

Premiere encodes your video and then burns the files onto the DVD or Blu-ray disc (or saves it in a folder, if you chose that option). A message appears letting you know if the procedure was successful or (gulp) if it failed.

Once you burn your disc, you can take it out of your computer and pop it into a player. The video and the menus should look spectacular.

FREQUENTLY ASKED QUESTION

At the Disc Store

There are all these different types of discs, which ones should I buy?

You can buy DVDs and Blu-ray discs at computer or office-supply stores. You can also find some pretty good deals online. You may be surprised at the number of choices facing you, however.

First of all, DVDs and Blu-ray discs may look the same, but they're really different beasts, as explained in the box on page 359. Blu-ray discs use different machines and technology to read and write discs. Blu-ray players can read DVDs, but DVD players are stymied when you pop a Blu-ray disc in the tray.

The main trick to buying either DVD or Blu-ray blank discs is to make sure the blanks are compatible with your computer and with your player. In the PC/Windows world, most newer DVD burners are compatible with a wide range of discs. That's true with newer DVD players, too. Still, to avoid problems, double-check your computer and player manuals to see what discs are compatible. Here are the formats you'll find at the store for DVD discs:

- **DVD-R.** The most common type of blank DVD disc, these will play on the widest variety of DVD players. These discs are single-sided and hold about 4.7 gigabytes of information. You can write to them once, but you can't erase them and re-write them.

- **DVD+R.** Very similar to the DVD-R format, these are also single-sided, write-once discs. Occasionally, you may find older computers or DVD players that can't handle this format.

- **DVD-RW or DVD+RW.** These are much like the previously mentioned discs, except for one remarkable feature: You can erase these discs and reuse them. Again, there are some older DVD players that may not be able to read these discs (or they may prefer one of these two formats over another).

- **DVD+R DL.** Here, the "DL" stands for "double-layer," and that means these discs hold nearly twice as much information (8.5 gigs instead of 4.7) as the single-layer discs referred to above. You need to have a dual-layer DVD burner in your computer to make use of these high-capacity, write-once discs. Most newer DVD players can play these discs once you burn them.

Thankfully, Blu-ray discs haven't gone through the disc format battles that confused the blank DVD market. Here are your choices in Blu-ray blank discs. You must have a Blu-ray disc burner to create these discs—a DVD burner won't know what to do.

- **BD-R.** Your basic blank write-once Blu-ray disc holds 25 gigabytes.

- **BD-R DL.** A double-layer Blu-ray disc holds about 50 gigabytes.

- **BD-RE.** These are rewritable discs that hold 25 gigs of data.

If you're feeling smug because you've got a good handle on the three types of Blu-ray writable discs, be forewarned: Manufacturers are already considering ways to create Blu-ray discs with even higher capacities. Additions to the family are inevitable.

Archive Your Project

After you successfully create a video or shared your movie using one of other options in Chapters 12 or 14, you may want to archive your project. Sure, you've got your raw clips stored on your hard drive, but that doesn't back up your final project file and all its clips in a single location. By archiving your project, you're in better shape to recreate or make changes to your project. Once you save your project to an archive folder, you can copy it to an external hard drive, an online storage location, or to a DVD or Blu-ray disc. Best of all, archiving is pretty easy and painless.

With your project open in Premiere, choose File → Project Archiver. The two radio buttons at the top offer you a choice (Figure 13-17). Select the top button to archive the project and all the clips used in the timeline. Choose the second option, Copy Project, if you want to archive *all* the files in your project, in the timeline or not. Perhaps you imported a clip while the project was open or you tried a clip in the timeline and removed it. In that case, Premiere includes the clip in your project even if it isn't in your timeline.

The next decision is where you want to store the archive file. Click the Browse button to choose a folder. If necessary, you can create a new folder. The Disk Space box shows the available space on your drive, along with how much space the archive requires.

That's about all there is to it. Click the OK button, and Premiere saves the files in the designated folder. If you want to be ultra-safe, copy your archive files to a disc, an online storage location, or a removable hard drive.

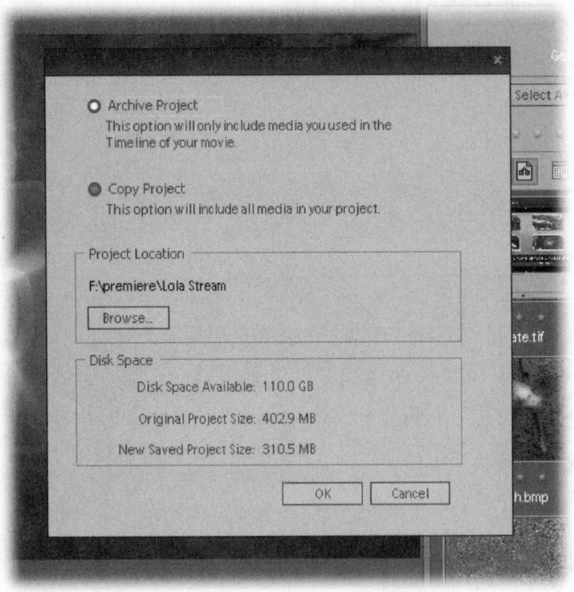

Figure 13-17:
The Project Archiver window, shown here, helps you copy your project file and media clips to a single location. Once you've got everything in one folder, it's a good idea to store a copy of this archive to a disc, online storage location, or a removable hard drive.

LOLA'S BIG SPLASH PROJECT

Make a Disc Menu System

If you've gone this far with the Lola Big Splash project, why not go ahead and create a menu system for movie. Here are some of the things you can do:

- Add menu markers to the timeline.

- Apply one of the stock disc menus.

- Modify the stock menu.

- Create a new menu background using a freeze-frame.

- Remove the menu by making an Auto-Play disc.

CHAPTER 14

Export to an iPod, Cellphone, or Other Device

Do you think Thomas Edison, the Lumière Brothers, or any other film pioneer ever imagined people would be walking around with movie projectors in their pockets? Not to mention the fact that portable devices like the iPod, Sony PSP, and Zune can hold not one, but dozens of movies.

If you have even a passing familiarity with consumer electronics, it probably doesn't surprise you that these movie machines, each from a different manufacturer, have different specs and play different types of video files. This chapter gives you the rundown for saving your video in the formats used by the myriad mobile gadgets out there. When you use Premiere's handy presets, the process is easy and the steps are pretty much the same regardless of the gadget. This chapter provides step-by-step process for a couple of popular units—Apple's iPhone, iPod, and iPod Touch, and Sony's PSP. You'll find out how to save movies for other hand-helds, including cellphones, too. If you have a tape-based camcorder, you may want to archive your project to tape, so this chapter explains how to export your edited video back to DV or HDV videotape.

And finally, you'll learn how to save your finished film to your PC. There are plenty of good reasons why you might want to do so. You may want to keep a copy to watch or review while you're at your desk, or you may want to put several movies on a DVD or Blu-ray disc and add each one to the timeline from your PC.

Export to Devices

In the old days, folks used to have pictures of their family in their wallet. With a little prompting, they'd bring them out to show you shots of Amy's birthday party or their vacation in the Bahamas. Today's version of that form of social interaction is to pull out your iPhone and show them a video. "It's hard to believe she's so grown up." "You wouldn't believe how blue the water is!"

When you want to export your edited video to a handheld device like an iPod, PSP, or other player, you have to jump two hurdles:

• **Encode your movie in the proper format.** Your Sony PSP doesn't want the video you encoded for your cellphone. Your iPod Touch expects a video that uses the H.264 codec and AAC audio. You get the point. These handhelds are persnickety about the video formats they're willing to play. As mentioned in Chapter 11 (page 320), "codec" is short for "compressor/decompressor". A codec is a program that *compresses* your video when you save it as a file and *decompresses* it when you play it on a device.

• **Copy your movie to the handheld device's memory.** Once you've gotten the video properly encoded, you need to copy it onto the device. Often, you can do that from inside of Premiere, but in some cases you may need (or want) to use the software that came with your device.

Encode Movies for Apple iPhone, iPod Touch, and iPod

Apple jumped into the video pool in a big way with its iPhone, iPod Touch, and iPod. If you have one of these devices, you're probably well aware of the video offerings in Apple's iTunes store. If you want to move your own features and featurettes onto one of them, the first thing you need to do is encode your movie using the codecs and settings that Apple's gadgets understand. As the steps below show, Premiere does most of the hard work for you. All you have to do is choose the right preset:

1. **Click the Share tab.**

   The "Start a new share" panel shows you five ways to share your movie. One of the options is Mobile Phones and Players.

2. **Click the Mobile Phones and Players button.**

   The Share tab changes to show a scrolling list of handheld devices at the top, as shown in Figure 14-1. Premiere changes the preset options and other settings it uses to encode a movie depending on your choice.

3. **In the scrolling list, choose "Apple iPod and iPhone".**

   The drop-down menu beside "Presets" gives you two options—one for high-quality video, the other for medium-quality.

4. Click "iPod and iPhone – High Quality".

   In most cases, you should choose the high-quality option. However, if you have an older iPod or need to conserve space on your current one, you may want to choose medium-quality.

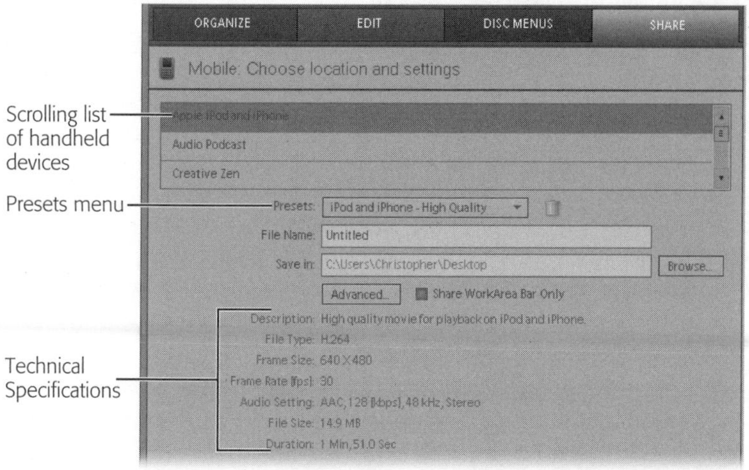

Scrolling list of handheld devices

Presets menu

Technical Specifications

Figure 14-1:
Choose your device in the scrolling list at the top of the screen and then choose a preset. As you make your choices, Premiere displays some of the techie details for the encoding process. Here you can see that Premiere will use the H.264 codec. The frame size is 640 × 480, and the frame rate is 30 fps. That's all iPod-perfect!

5. In the File Name box, type in a title, like *Lola's Big Splash*.

   Premiere makes sure you only use characters that are "legal" for filenames. For example, you can't use a question mark or an asterisk in a name.

6. Click the Browse button and then select the folder where you want to save the file.

   If you don't change anything, Premiere puts your movie in your Documents folder. That's not a bad location. It's easy to find when you're ready to import the file to iTunes or your iPod.

7. (Optional) Check the "Share WorkArea Bar Only" box.

   As with any of the Share methods, you can choose to export just a portion of your movie. To do that, adjust the WorkArea bar at the top of the timeline, as shown in Figure 14-2. It's a little hard to see because it, like most of the timeline, is gray.

8. Click Save.

   Premiere begins encoding your movie. A progress bar appears in the panel to entertain you while you wait. When Premiere finishes, you'll find your file saved in your Documents folder.

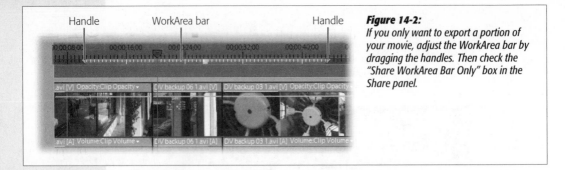

Handle WorkArea bar Handle

Figure 14-2:
If you only want to export a portion of your movie, adjust the WorkArea bar by dragging the handles. Then check the "Share WorkArea Bar Only" box in the Share panel.

Once Premiere encodes and saves your video as a file on your computer, you can view it using a media player such as Windows Media Player, QuickTime, or iTunes. You'll find that, like your gadgets, some media players won't read a certain type of file. For example, Apple's QuickTime Player might not like Microsoft's WMV files. When that happens, the simplest thing to do is use a different player.

Tip: If you'd like to have one media player that plays just about every type of video and audio file, including DVDs and their VOB files, you may want to download the free VideoLAN VLC media player (*www.videolan.org*). Versions are available for Windows PCs, Macs, and Linux computers.

Copy Video to an Apple iPhone, iPod Touch, or iPod

The encoding part of the process is complete. As explained earlier, the next hurdle is to move the video file from your Documents folder to your iPhone, iPod Touch, or iPod. Happily, all these devices use the handy iTunes program to move a file from computer to gadget.

1. **Connect your iPhone, iPod Touch, or iPod to your computer.**

   Depending on how you've got things set up, iTunes may start automatically when you plug in your device.

2. **If not, fire up iTunes.**

   Find your player listed in iTunes' "Devices" list and select it.

3. **Choose File → Add File to Library (or press the shortcut key Ctrl+O).**

   A file browser window opens. From there, navigate to the Documents folder (or any other location on you computer).

4. **Select the video file you want to import. For example,** *Lola's Big Splash.mp4.* **Then, click Open.**

   iTunes churns a little and then begins to import your video to the Movies folder in iTunes. A progress bar appears at the top of the iTunes window.

   If you see a warning saying that iTunes couldn't copy the file, that means iTunes and your device can't read the video file format you chose.

At this point, your iTunes experience may differ from these steps depending on your synchronization settings. If you've got a classic iPod with 120 gigabytes of storage, you may have set it up to automatically copy everything in the iTunes library to your iPod. If you have an iPhone or iPod Touch with more modest capacity, you may have it set up so that you manually copy items from the library to the gadget. (For some tips on using iTunes, see the box on page 370.) The next step explains how to manually copy a movie from the iTunes library to an Apple device.

5. Drag the movie from Library → Movies to Devices → [your device] → Movies (Figure 14-3).

A progress bar appears at the top of the iTunes window to report the status of the transfer. When you're done, you have a copy of the movie in both your iTunes library and on your Apple gadget. You can eject your iPod or continue to copy more items.

Figure 14-3:
If you don't use iTunes' AutoSync feature with your iPhone, iPod Touch, or other iPod, you have to copy media manually, by dragging it from the iTunes library to your device.

Audio Podcast for iPod Playback

If you're one of the many celebrities producing an audio podcast, you may want to consider using Premiere as your production studio. You can film your podcast and then post the video version on YouTube (or your own website). Then, using Premiere, you can create an audio-only version for distribution via iTunes. To do that, after you edit your podcast, go to the same Share tab that Premiere uses for exporting video. Click the Mobile Phones and Players button and then choose the Audio Podcast option. When you do so, Premiere creates an audio-only file. It displays the podcast settings in the Share tab, as shown in Figure 14-5.

iTunes Tips and Tricks

iTunes is a pretty complete media-management program and as such, it has quite a few tricks up its sleeve. If you want to learn all that things iTunes and your favorite gadget can do, get the book *iPod: The Missing Manual* by Jude Biersdorfer and David Pogue or *iPhone: The Missing Manual* by David Pogue.

As mentioned in the steps on page 369, iTunes can automatically copy movies from your Library → Movies folder to your Apple device if you have its AutoSync feature turned on, or you can move items manually. Select your iPhone, iPod Touch, or iPod under "Devices" in iTunes, then click the Summary tab. There are two check boxes that determine the way iTunes manages music and video:

- **Manually manage music and videos.** If you want to be in charge of what gets copied to your gadget, check this box. This option works well for a device with less storage space than high-capacity iPods, such as the iPhone or iPod Touch. Using this method, you copy movies to your iPod by dragging them

from the Library to the 'Pod (see Figure 14-3). To remove movies, right-click the movie and choose Delete.

Turn off the "Manually manage music and videos" checkbox, and iTunes automatically syncs the music and videos in iTunes with your iPod. This is great as long as everything that's on your computer will fit on your iPod. If you like the idea of iTunes automatically copying media to your iPod but have some space concerns, check out the next option.

- **Sync only checked songs and videos.** When you select this box, you control what files iTunes automatically copies to your iPod. Go to the Movies tab and then check the Sync Movies box. Using the radio buttons underneath, you can sync all your movies or you can pick and choose. When you're managing your own movies, *Selected* is a good choice. Then, just check the movies you want copied and leave the rest unchecked. When you're done, click Apply (see Figure 14-4).

You can choose from several different presets. The first two options produce MP4 files compatible with iTunes and Apple equipment. The last three create files in MP3 format, which, in addition to being compatible with Apple gear, also works for the whole wide MP3 world, including Windows-compatible products.

Here's the list of preset options:

- Audio Podcast – High Quality

- Audio Podcast – Medium Quality

- MP3 Audio Podcast – High Quality

- MP3 Audio Podcast – High Quality Mono

- MP3 Audio Podcast – Medium Quality

The rest of the screen displays file-saving and specification information similar to those you see when you share video files, as explained on page 368. You provide a name and choose where you want Premiere to store the file.

After you choose your settings, click Save. Watch the progress bar and, when it's complete, go get your file.

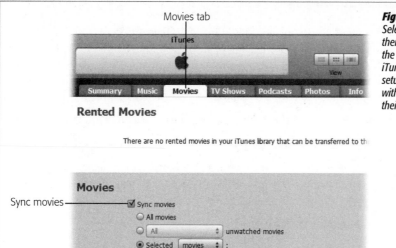

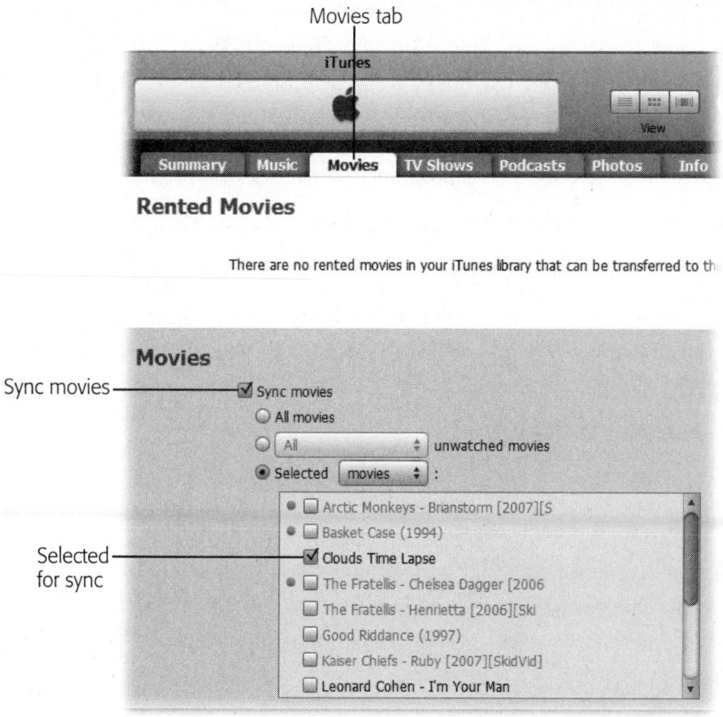

Figure 14-4:
Select your device in iTunes and then use the Summary tab and the Movies tab to control the iTunes autosync features. The setup shown here copies movies with checkmarks next to their names.

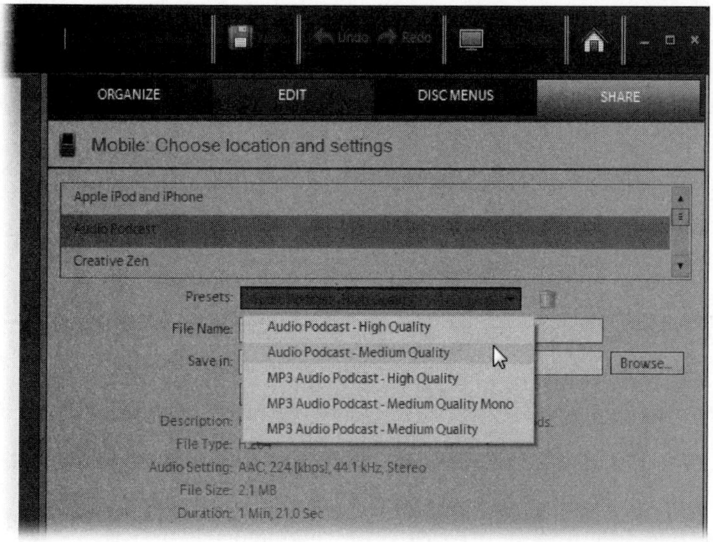

Rented Movies

There are no rented movies in your iTunes library that can be transferred to th

Movies

Sync movies —— ☑ Sync movies
○ All movies
○ [All ＋] unwatched movies
◉ Selected [movies ＋] :

Selected —— • ☐ Arctic Monkeys - Brainstorm [2007][S
for sync • ☐ Basket Case (1994)
☑ Clouds Time Lapse
• ☐ The Fratellis - Chelsea Dagger [2006
☐ The Fratellis - Henrietta [2006][Ski
☐ Good Riddance (1997)
☐ Kaiser Chiefs - Ruby [2007][SkidVid]
☐ Leonard Cohen - I'm Your Man

Figure 14-5:
Use the Audio Podcast option to produce an audio-only file in one of the official podcast file formats.

ORGANIZE   EDIT   DISC MENUS   SHARE

▤ Mobile: Choose location and settings

Apple iPod and iPhone
Audio Podcast
Creative Zen

Presets:
File Name: Audio Podcast - High Quality
Save in: Audio Podcast - Medium Quality   Browse...
              MP3 Audio Podcast - High Quality
              MP3 Audio Podcast - Medium Quality Mono
Description: MP3 Audio Podcast - Medium Quality   ds.
File Type: h.264
Audio Setting: AAC, 224 [kbps], 44.1 kHz, Stereo
File Size: 2.1 MB
Duration: 1 Min, 21.0 Sec

Export to Sony PSP (PlayStation Portable)

The general steps for exporting video to a handheld device are pretty much the same regardless of the device. Premiere simplifies the technical details by wrapping them up in a preset. Your job is only as tough as remembering the name of your gadget. You can use the software that came with your handheld, or in some cases you may be able to copy files directly as you encode them.

Here are the steps for encoding and copying a movie to a Sony PSP:

1. **Connect your PSP to your computer via the USB cable and turn it on.**

   When it's connected to your computer, Windows treats the PSP as if it were a removable hard drive. You can see it in Windows Explorer and other programs that list your available drives and storage devices.

2. **In Premiere, click the Share tab.**

   The "Start a new share" panel shows you five ways to share your movie. One of the options is Mobile Phones and Players.

3. **Click "Mobile Phones and Players".**

   The Share tab changes to show a scrolling list of handheld devices at the top. The preset options and other settings change depending on your choice (Figure 14-6).

4. **In the scrolling list, choose Sony PSP.**

   The Share panel displays the preset settings for the Sony PSP.

5. **Under Presets, choose "Sony PSP – High Quality".**

   At the bottom of the Share panel, you can see some of the technical details for this setting. Sony, like Apple, uses the H.264 codec, which creates good-quality video while keeping the file size to a minimum. The frame size is set to 320×240, and the frame rate is shown as 29.97, the standard for NTSC TV. You also see the settings for audio compression. At the bottom, Premiere displays a file size estimate and the duration of the video.

6. **Type in a filename for your video, such as *Lola's Big Splash.***

   You can use any characters that are legal for a Windows/PC file.

7. **Next to "Save in", click the Browse button.**

   The Browse for Folder window opens.

8. **Click "Computer" to expand the list underneath.**

   Your storage devices appear in the list (see Figure 14-7).

9. **Click the triangle next to the drive letter for your handheld device.**

   The folders in your handheld device appear in the list. If you don't know the drive letter for your device, see the box on page 374.

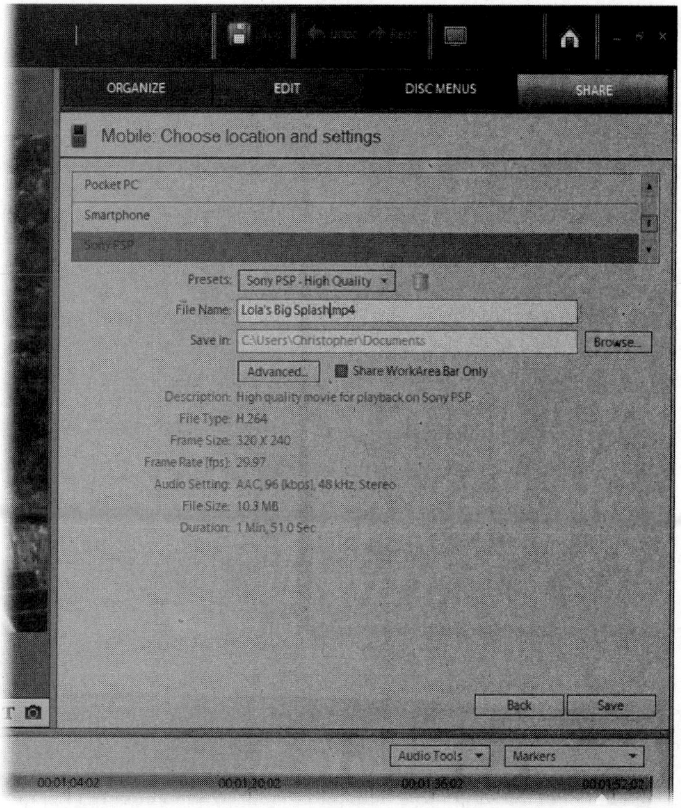

Figure 14-6:
Whether you're sharing to a mobile phone, an iPod, or a Zune, the Share tab looks pretty much the same. All you need to do is choose a preset and fill in the File Name and Save in location. Here, the Sony PSP is the selected device.

10. Select the Video folder and click OK.

This is where the Sony PSP stores video. You're likely to see a different name if you're copying video to another type of handheld.

Once you click OK, a new file path appears next to "Save in" in the Share panel.

11. Click Save.

Premiere encodes your video for the PSP and stores the file in the PSP's video folder. Next time you browse for videos on your PSP, you'll see it listed.

You can use these same steps for any device that shows up as removable storage device in Windows. The only thing you need to change is the preset.

Save Your Movie to Other Devices

If your handheld device is listed in the Share tab's scrolling panel, you're in great shape. All you have to do is select the device and one of the presets, and you won't have to fiddle with any other technical details related to codecs, frame sizes, or frame rates. As a matter of fact, you don't want to click that advanced button and

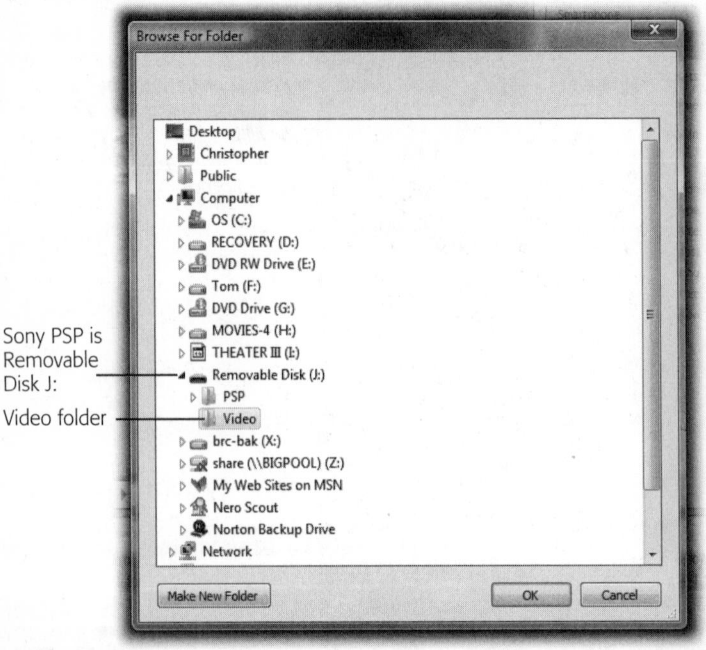

Figure 14-7:
Click the Browse button on the Share panel to display this window. If you can find your device in the list, you can copy a video file directly to your gadget and eliminate a couple of steps. The Sony PSP video directory is selected here.

Sony PSP is Removable Disk J:

Video folder

UP TO SPEED

How to Identify Your Portable Device

When you connect a device like a Sony PSP to your computer, Windows doesn't necessarily refer to it by name. In most cases, it identifies it as a drive letter, such as G:.

If you aren't sure what name Windows gives your device, try this: Before you connect, double-click the Computer icon on the Windows desktop, (or go to Start → My Computer). Windows Explorer opens, showing you all the drives connected to your PC, as you can see in Figure 14-5.

Make a quick note of the drives and then plug in your PSP or other gadget. You should hear a tone when Windows recognizes the device, and you should see a new item under the Removable Storage section in Explorer, labeled with a drive letter. If you don't see any changes in Windows Explorer, try pressing F5, the refresh key. Use the new drive letter when you want to Share video to the device.

---

start fiddling with the settings, because, chances are, you'll end up creating a video file that won't work in your Zune, iPod, Creative Zen, or whatever gadget.

The only case where you might have to make additional adjustments is when your device isn't listed in the panel. In that case, start off by digging out the manual for your handheld. Find the specifications for the video format. The most important details you need to look up include:

- **File container.** This is the file format that holds your movie's video and audio streams. Examples include DV AVI, Windows Media (.wmv), and Quick-Time (.mov).

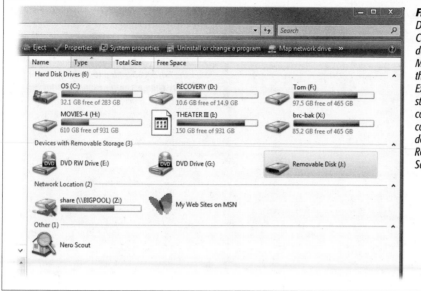

- **Video codec.** This is the video compression system your device is compatible with; it makes video streams smaller.

- **Audio codec.** This is the audio compression system your device is compatible with; it makes audio streams smaller.

- **Frame size.** For handhelds you're likely to see frame sizes from 176×144 (for mobile phones) up to 640×480 (for an iPod).

- **Frame rate.** A frame rate around 30 is common for devices that display video. Other devices that are merely video-capable may prefer a frame rate of around 15 fps.

So, if your manual explains that your handheld uses Windows Media files, then you use the scrolling list to choose one of the presets that write to that format, such as Creative Zen, Microsoft Zune, or Pocket PC. If you know you want an H.264 file type, choose the Mobile Phone or the Apple iPod and iPhone option.

Once you make a selection in the scrolling list, click the Advanced button, and the Export Settings window opens (Figure 14-9). At the top, you'll see Format, Preset, and Comments labels. The format is set to match the preset you selected a minute ago, and you may not be able to change that. Use the checkboxes to determine whether you're exporting video and/or audio.

Below these options, the Summary panel provides details on the export settings. For example, you might see something like: *NTSC, 320x240, 29.97 [fps] Progressive.* Translation: the video is NTSC (as opposed to PAL), the frame size is 320×240, and it uses the standard American TV frame rate of 29.97 fps. The video is progressive rather than interlaced (see page 380). Additional summary details give you info on the audio and other compression settings. As you make changes in the tabs and panels below, this summary reflects those changes.

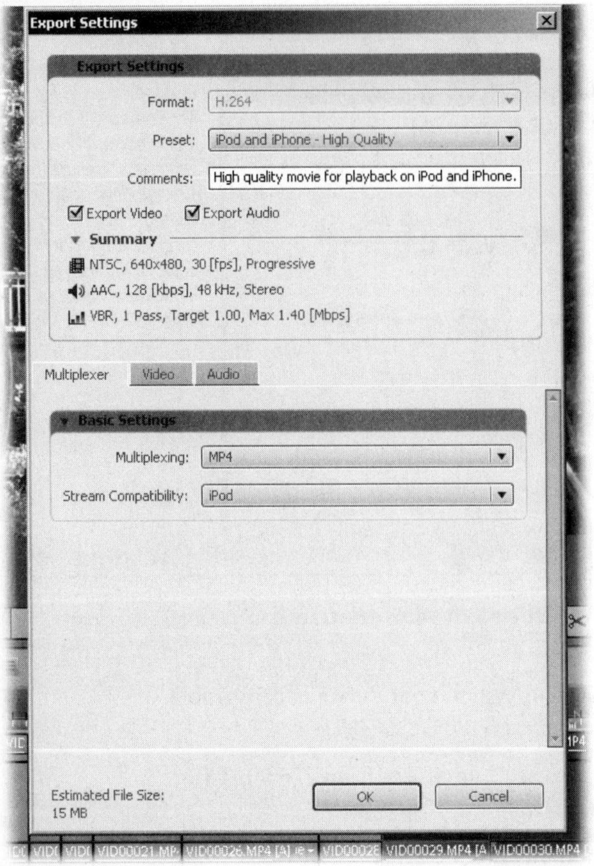

Figure 14-9:
If you're device doesn't have a ready-made preset, you have to roll your own. Start with a preset that's similar to your device's requirements (check the manual) and then click the Advanced button to make the necessary changes in this Export Settings window.

The settings and options shown on the three tabs underneath the Summary panel change depending on the preset you choose. For example, if you start off with the iPhone presets, you see different settings than you will if you start off with the Zune presets. Here's a general description of what you find on the tabs:

- **Multiplexer tab.** These setting affect the way audio and video is combined in the video file. You may see Multiplexing menus where you can choose between MP4 (for Apple gear) or 3GPP (for phones). In other cases, you may have options to create compressed or uncompressed video.

- **Video tab.** You can customize your video settings by choosing a codec, frame size, and frame rate. You'll also find options for adjusting the pixel aspect ratio. For more details on the differences in pixel aspect ratios, see page 316.

- **Audio tab.** Under the audio tab you can choose a codec for compressing audio and change some of the other settings that affect audio quality and file size. For example, you may be able to choose between stereo and mono audio tracks.

After you make changes in the Export settings window to match your device, click OK. The Choose Name box appears where you must give the new preset a name. After all, you don't want to mess up the perfectly good preset you started with. Click OK in the Choose Name box, and you've officially created your own preset. Premiere lists it with all the others. So, if you started off by modifying the generic Mobile Phone preset, you'll find your new preset listed with all the other Mobile Phone presets in the drop-down menu. It's no surprise that saving a video for your cellphone is like saving a video for other handhelds. Click the Share tab and choose the Mobile Phones and Players option. In the list, scroll down to Mobile Phones. Use the Presets menu to choose one of the Presets that came with Premiere or one that you created. At that point, all you have to do is give your video a name and choose where you want to save it.

It's probably no surprise that saving a video to your cell phone is like saving one to the other handhelds discussed here. Click the Share tab and choose the Mobile Phones and Players option. In the list, scroll down to Mobile Phones. Use the Presets menu to choose one of the Presets that came with Premiere or one that you created. At that point, all you have to do is give your video a name and choose a save location.

Export to Videotape

Exporting your movie to videotape is certainly not as common as exporting it to an iPod. But, if you've got a DV or HDV camcorder, there may be times when you want to copy your movie back to videotape. For example, you may use DV tapes to archive your projects. They're fairly inexpensive, they're small, and they're durable. In other cases, you may be working with a video production house that prefers working with DV or HDV tape.

Writing video to your camcorder reverses the workflow you used to get video *from* your camcorder into your computer. In fact, you can use the same "device control" feature discussed earlier to record to tape (see page 43). Connect your camcorder to your PC. Fire up Premiere and, with a couple of clicks, you can have Premiere control the recording features of your camera.

Before You Export to Tape

Sometimes when you export to tape, you want to make sure there's a little leader (a few black frames) at the beginning and the end of your movie. If a production house uses the tape to make copies, you may want to add color bars and tone at the beginning, so they can calibrate their copying device. As an example, here are the steps to add color bars and tone to your video:

1. **With your edited project open in Premiere, click the Organize tab and then click the Project button.**

   The Project panel displays all the media in your project. In the upper-right corner, you'll see a curled-page icon. Position your cursor over it, and a tool tip displays its name ("New Item") before a drop-down menu appears.

2. **Position the playhead where you want to insert the color bars and tone.**

   Most likely, you want the color bars to play for 30 seconds at the beginning of your movie, so press Home to move the playhead to frame 0.

3. **Click the New Item menu and choose "Bars and Tone".**

   Premiere inserts the bars and tone clip into the timeline, but it probably isn't set to run for 30 seconds.

4. **Drag the right edge of the Bars and Tone clip so that it runs at least 30 seconds.**

   This gives the production house enough time to use the signal to make their adjustments.

You use similar steps to add leader (black frames) or a universal countdown leader to your movie. Just position the playhead and choose the appropriate option (Black Video or Universal Counting Leader) from the New Item menu.

Copy to DV or HDV Tape

Once you have your movie edited with the leader in place, it's time to send it back to your camcorder:

1. **Connect your camcorder to your computer using the Firewire (IEEE 1394) cable.**

   Make sure you've got a tape in the camcorder and the tape is at a location where you want to start recording.

2. **Turn your camcorder on and set it to VTR, VCR, or Play mode.**

   If your computer didn't recognize your camcorder when you plugged it in, it should do so when you turn the power on.

3. **With your edited project open in Premiere, click the Share tab.**

   Premiere shows you several options for sharing video. The last item listed is Tape Record to DV or HDV tape.

4. **Click "Tape".**

   The Export to Tape window opens, as shown in Figure 14-10.

5. **Choose your export-to-tape options.**

   Premiere presets the most important one, "Activate Recording Device". This option gives Premiere control over your camcorder. You may not need to change any of the other settings, but here's a quick rundown:

   • **Assemble at timecode.** Use this option to start recording to a specific location on your videotape.

- **Delay movie start.** If you find that you're losing a few frames at the beginning of your movie, experiment with this setting by adding a few frames.

- **Preroll x Frames.** If you use the option to "Assemble at timecode", you may want to use this option to get your camcorder up to speed before it begins to record.

- **Abort After x Dropped Frames.** Recording back to tape isn't always a perfect operation. If your computer and camcorder aren't in harmony, you may experience dropped (unrecorded) frames. Use this option to tell Premiere the number of dropped frames you're willing to tolerate.

- **Report Dropped Frames.** Most likely, Premiere already checked this option, meaning that you'll see the number of dropped frames in the Export Status box during the recording process.

6. **Click Record.**

   Premiere starts off by rendering any unrendered video. Then, it starts up the camcorder, and your movie plays back while the camcorder records it. You can follow the progress on either your computer monitor or the camcorder screen. There's no way to speed up the process, so an hour-long movie takes an hour to record.

7. **Afterward, click Stop and then close the Export to Tape box.**

   When you're finished, you can review the tape on your camcorder using its playback controls.

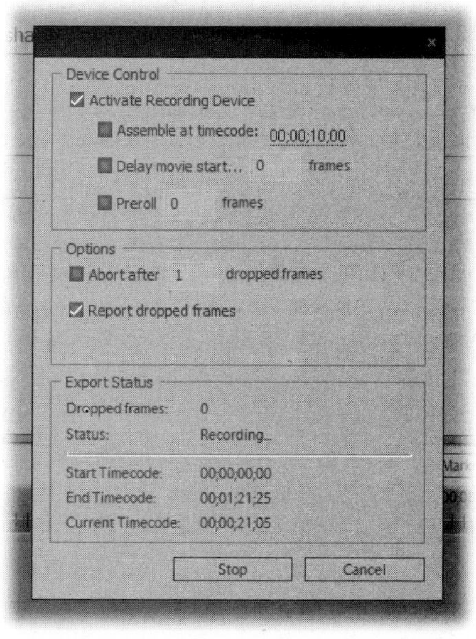

Figure 14-10:
Most of the time, the settings on the Export to Tape panel are ready to go. All you have to do is click Record to start the process and then Stop when you're through. The panel shown here is in the middle of a recording session, so the Record/Stop button is labeled Stop.

Save Movies to Your PC

As explained in this chapter and some of the earlier ones, if you're ready to send your video to DVD or Blu-ray disc, a website, or an iPod, your best bet is to choose those options in the Share tab and then use the presets Premiere provides. That way, you don't have to worry about all the technical details.

If you're not ready to send your video in one of those directions, you may want to save it as a computer file. You'll have a copy you can watch on your PC, and then later on maybe you'll burn it to a DVD, upload it to a website, or bring it back into Premiere to use for another movie. Once you save your movie as a computer file, you can move it and copy it just as you would any other file on your PC. For example, you could copy the file to a USB thumb drive to move it to another computer or take it to a friend's house.

The steps for exporting your movie as a PC file are similar to the other Share options. You click the Share tab, choose Personal Computer, and then choose one of the file formats and presets Premiere offers (Figure 14-11).

Knowing which file format to choose is the trickiest part of the process, because different file formats are better for different jobs. In fact, these are the same formats Premiere uses to create video for discs, the Web, and iPods. Here's a description of each, along with a note about where they shine:

- **Adobe Flash Video** is the format to choose if you want to put your video on a website at some point because it's become the de facto standard for delivering video over the Web. YouTube, Hulu, and CBS all use Flash to play video.

Tip: If you ever want to see if a website uses Flash video, right-click the video and look for a menu option that says something like "About Adobe Flash 10."

- **MPEG** (Motion Picture Experts Group) is a good option for making high-quality video files for a few destination devices. Choose this, and you'll see that there are several presets in the drop-down menu. That's due to the nature of ever-evolving standards. Choose one of the NTSC DVD presets to create a DVD-quality video file. Using this format, you have a choice of standard or widescreen. If you want a Blu-ray–quality file, choose H.264 1920 × 1080i 30. What do all those numbers mean? *H.264* is the codec used to compress the video. *1920 × 1080i* is the resolution or number of pixels used to create the image. The *i* at the end of the resolution indicates the video is interlaced—the video image is created in two passes, odd numbered lines then even numbered lines. The last number *30* is the frame rate, as in 30 frames per second.

- **AVI** is the file format Premiere uses as you edit your video. It's a good format to choose if you want to save your video to your computer because the video quality is good. It's also a good format if you plan to bring it back into Premiere to use in other projects.

- **Windows Media** files (.WMV) use Microsoft's video file format, designed for streaming video from a website or emailing videos. You can't edit .WMV files, but they are compact.

- **QuickTime** is a good format if you're planning on sharing video with friends who use Macs. Apple's format works well for all sorts of projects. The files are a little bigger than Windows Media files, but the image looks great. The snazzy QuickTime player comes preinstalled on every Mac. For PC users, the Quick-Time player is automatically installed if they have iTunes on their computer. For those few folks who don't have QuickTime already installed on their computer, it's a free download from *www.apple.com/quicktime/download/*.

- **Image** converts your movie into a series of still images or a single still.

- **Audio** is the option to choose when you want to save only a movie's sound, not its video.

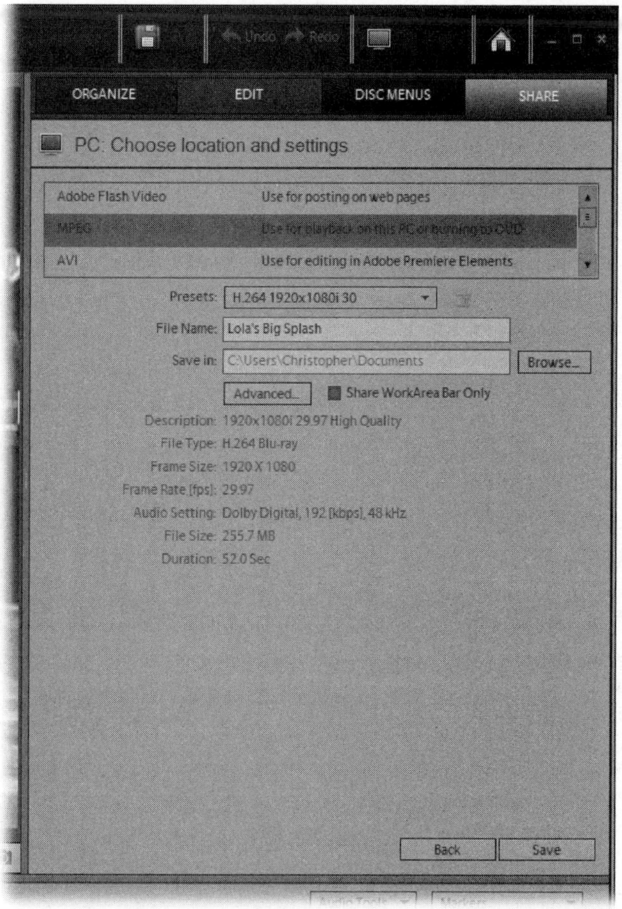

Figure 14-11:
To save an edited movie as a PC file, go to the Share tab and choose the Personal Computer option. This panel opens, where you choose a file format in the scrolling list and then a preset from the drop-down menu.

If you've used the Share tab to send your movie to a disc, website, or handheld gadget, you probably already know the drill. But just in case, here are the steps to save your movie as a file on your computer:

1. **Click the Share tab.**

   The "Start a new share" panel displays your options.

2. **Click Personal Computer.**

   The "PC: Choose location and settings" panel appears. The scrolling list at the top displays the PC file formats you can use.

3. **Choose one of the file formats listed on page 380.**

   When you click on any of the options in the scrolling list, the Presets menu displays different options. Once you choose a format, Premiere displays a description of it, along with other details, at the bottom of the panel.

4. **Choose a preset from the drop-down menu.**

   The presets vary depending on the file format, but usually you can zero in on a specific resolution and choose a widescreen or standard format.

5. **In the File Name text box, type in a catchy name like *Puerto Vallarta Days and Nights*.**

   Make sure it's a name that helps you identify the file three or four years from now.

6. **Click the Browse button and choose a folder where you want to save your file.**

   Initially, Premiere chooses your Documents folder. You may want to change that to your Videos or any other folder.

7. **(Optional) Click Share WorkArea Bar Only.**

   You can choose to make a file from just a portion of the video in the timeline. This is a handy way to test a file format to make sure it meets your needs. Adjust the work area bar over the portion of video you want to save, as shown in Figure 14-2. Then check the "Share WorkArea Bar Only" box.

8. **Click Save.**

   The panel displays a progress bar while it encodes the video according to your specifications. When it's done, Premiere displays the message "Save Complete". At this point, your movie is ready for your viewing pleasure.

Part Four: Appendixes

4

Install Premiere Elements 8

When you edit video, you make your computer work hard—really hard. Not only is its processor pushing around tons of information to put a picture on your screen 30 times a second, its hard drives juggle enormous video files, audio files, still images, titles, transitions, and effects. And every time you make an edit, Premiere has to update your project file, which keeps track of all the little pieces.

Fortunately, when it comes to video editing, today's computers are much more capable than their ancestors. Underpowered netbooks aside, PC manufacturers make the brains behind today's PCs (the *CPU,* or central processing unit) with video needs in mind. Hard drives are bigger and faster. Video display cards (sometimes called *GPUs,* or graphics processing units) do lots of their own processing, taking some of the load off of the CPU. And Premiere takes advantage of all these advances.

This appendix is all about getting Premiere up and running on your computer. You'll learn what kind of horsepower you need and find tips for making the program run smoothly. In the last part of this appendix are step-by-step instructions for installing Premiere.

Get Ready for Installation

Software publishers list the minimum system requirements for their programs on the package, but they tend to fudge them a little because they want to sell their program to as many customers as possible. Also, different people have different tolerances for the speed at which programs work.

With that caveat, here are Adobe's official Premiere Elements system requirements (you'll also find a mini-glossary below to help you translate a few technical terms):

- 2 GHz processor with SSE2 support; 3GHz processor required if you want to create files in high-definition video (HDV) format or to burn Blu-ray discs. You'll need a dual-core processor if you want to create video in the more rigorous AVCHD (Audio Video Compression for HD) format.

UP TO SPEED

Definitions for Premiere's System Requirements

Adobe may expect you to know all these terms, but your friendly Missing Manual doesn't:

- *SSE2* is a bit of video-processing smarts that Intel added to its processors starting with the Pentium 4. What does it stand for? Streaming SIMD Extensions 2. Aren't you sorry you asked?

- *HDV* is a high-definition video format.

- *AVCHD* is also a high-definition video format, though it uses different technology. It stands for Audio Video Compression for High Definition.

- Microsoft Windows XP with Service Pack 2, Windows Vista, or Windows 7.

- Memory requirements:

  — **For Windows XP:** 512MB of RAM (2GB if you want to create HDV, AVCHD, or Blu-ray video).

  — **For Windows Vista:** 1GB of RAM (2GB for HDV, AVCHD, or Blu-ray video).

  — **For Windows 7:** 1GB of RAM (2GB for HDV, AVCHD, or Blu-ray video).

  — 4.5 GB of available hard-disk space.

- Color monitor with 16-bit color video card.

- 1024×768 monitor with 16-bit color video card.

- Microsoft DirectX 9- or 10-compatible sound and display driver.

- DVD-ROM drive (you need a compatible DVD burner if you want to burn DVDs, and a compatible Blu-ray burner to burn Blu-ray discs).

- DV/i.LINK/FireWire/IEEE 1394 interface to connect a Digital 8 DV or HDV camcorder, or a USB2 interface to connect a DV-via-USB compatible DV camcorder (other video devices supported via the Media Downloader).

- QuickTime 7 software.

For a better Premiere Elements experience, here are a few hardware tips:

- **Faster processors (CPUs) and dual-core processors are better.** Surprising, huh? (Processor speed is measured in gigahertz, or GHz.) Most new computers come with dual- or quad-core processors, which is like having two (or four) brains working at the same time. That's good for video editing.

  If you have a single-core processor, all is not lost, though it's best if you have a 3GHz or better CPU. The speed rating on dual-core processors is often lower than that of single-core CPUs, but overall the dual-cores perform faster because the two brains split the workload and then work simultaneously. So, when you edit video, a 2.4GHz dual-core processor outperforms a 3GHz single-core processor.

- **The best operating system for video editing is Windows 7.** If upgrading to this latest version of Windows isn't an option, working with XP or Vista is fine. (Some folks are leery of constantly updating their operating systems as Microsoft pumps out fixes for this and that in Windows. Don't be. Keep Windows and Premiere up-to-date by installing any updates the companies publish.)

Tip: To see which version of Windows you have on your computer, right-click the Computer icon on your desktop and choose "Properties".

- **When you edit video, more memory makes everything go faster.** Measured in gigabytes, 2GB of computer memory is good, but 4GB is even better. If you use a 32-bit operating system (like Windows Vista Home Premium), you don't need more than 4GB. How do you know if you're using a 32-bit OS? If you're not sure what you have, it's probably 32-bit. The computer salesman would have made a big deal of it if you'd bought a 64-bit system.

- **Two big, fast internal hard drives are great for editing video.** Premiere requires 3GB or 4GB of hard drive space. But the issue really is all those big video files you import from your camcorder and the temporary files Premiere creates so you edit copies of your raw footage instead of the originals. All this means that Premiere is always reading from and writing to disks as you edit.

- **After you install Premiere, make sure you have at least 10GB of free space left on your hard drive.** It's better to have much more. Ideally, your drive should never use the last 10 percent of disk space. A good setup has Premiere and your project file on one drive (probably the *C:* drive), and your raw clips and the scratch disks (temporary files) on a separate internal hard drive (a 500GB or 1TB drive). Why an internal drive? They transfer files faster than USB-connected drives.

- **Video cards that come with their own processors take the video-processing load off of your computer's CPU.** You don't have to get the $500 card the kid down the block uses for video games, but an nVidia card with 128MB (megabytes) or more of memory can speed up processes like special effects without breaking the bank.

• Use two monitors—or one widescreen monitor—and you'll spend less time opening and closing windows and panels. You can undock Premiere's monitor and timeline, which means you can move them to a second monitor or to another spot on a widescreen monitor. This saves time and you get a bigger picture of your project.

Hard Drive Maintenance

As you edit in Premiere, your hard drives get a good workout. You can help them out a bit by regularly optimizing them. Yeah, this is a really geeky topic and it wouldn't matter much if all you used your computer for was word processing or browsing the Web. But when you edit video, keeping your drives in tip-top shape makes a difference.

Optimizing your hard drives is also know as *defragmenting* (or "defragging") them. When computers save files to a hard drive, they indiscriminately break up the file (with pointers to each piece) to use every available space—in other words, they scatter bits and pieces of files all over the place. This fragmentation slows down your computer when it reads and writes big files like videos because it has to do a lot of running around to gather the pieces.

You can optimize your drives a couple of ways. The easiest one is to let a program like Windows' Disk Defragmenter or Norton 360 do it on a regular basis during "quiet" periods when your PC isn't busy with other tasks.

If you don't want to do that, you can defrag your drives manually when you think it's necessary. One downside of optimizing drives manually is that you have to remember to do it. And by the time you *do* remember, the disk can be pretty fragmented, the digital equivalent of scrambled eggs, so defragging may take a long time (so long you might want to start the process at the end of the day and let it continue overnight).

In either case, it doesn't hurt to manually optimize your drives before you install Premiere. If your drives are in good shape, the process goes quickly. If your drives are a mess, it's well worth the time. Here are the steps to manually optimize your hard drives using Vista (the process is similar for XP and Windows 7).

Tip: Just got your copy of Premiere Elements and you don't want to waste time with hard drive maintenance now? You can go ahead and install the program and do the optimization later.

---

1. **Double-click the Computer icon on your desktop.**

   Windows Explorer opens, showing you the hard drives and other storage devices attached to your computer.

2. **Right-click drive *C:* (or any other drive you want to optimize).**

   Windows displays the Properties panel for the drive, which includes a graph showing how much used and free space your drive has.

3. **Click the Tools tab.**

Windows displays the tools it offers for hard drives, including "Defragmentation".

4. **Click the Defragment Now button.**

Windows opens the Disk Defragmenter panel and begins analyzing your drive. This panel also lets you set up a schedule to run the defragmenter automatically.

As the defragmenter examines your drives, it updates you with messages like "Analyzing disk 3 of 5 (F:)". After it's done, a message appears telling you whether you need to defragment your drives.

Note: Depending on how your computer is set up, Windows may display something called the User Account Control (UAC) window. If it does, click Continue. If you can't continue, you need to have someone with an administrator account help you with this project.

---

5. **If any of your drives need defragmenting, click the Defragment Now button.**

The Defragmenter runs until it optimizes all the drives. A message helpfully explains that "This may take from a few minutes to a few hours."

You can continue working while the Defragmenter runs. Most programs like the Defragmenter are smart enough to run in the background as you read web pages or ponder what to say next in the quarterly report. But if you find the Defragmenter interfering with your work, click the Cancel Defragmentation button. You can always run it again later.

As you work with Premiere, you'll constantly add new media files to your computer. So from time to time, check your disks using the steps above and manually defrag your disks when they get messy.

Install Premiere Elements

You can buy Premiere Elements as a boxed DVD or download it from the Adobe website (*www.adobe.com*). If you have a decent Internet connection, the program takes between a half hour and a couple of hours to download. If you've never used Premiere before and don't want to shell out the big bucks sight unseen, you can download a test-drive of the program. After 30 days, if you want to keep using it, you pony up for a serial number that makes your copy official and legal (you don't need to reinstall the program). If you get the boxed DVD, it includes a copy of Photoshop Elements you can test drive.

If you download Premiere, double-click the downloaded file to start installing the program. Premiere first unpacks all the setup files, meaning that it copies some temporary files to your computer that it needs for installation. Then it begins the installation, which is similar to the steps described below for installation from a DVD.

Adobe has been selling software for a long time and they've pretty much got the whole installation procedure down so that it's easy and there aren't many pitfalls for you or their product support people. Typical Adobe instructions say something like:

1. **Close any other programs currently running, including your anti-virus software.**

2. **Put the installation disc in your DVD drive and follow the instructions.**

And it's about that simple. The DVD automatically loads and starts the installation process. Adobe keeps its instructions brief because the installation procedure may change from time to time and it may be different in different parts of the world—they probably don't want to write a new set of installation instructions for every product and every release.

That said, here's a more detailed description of the installation process:

1. **Put the Premiere Elements disc into your computer.**

   In most cases, the disc starts the installation process automatically. If it doesn't, double-click the Computer icon on your desktop, double-click the DVD, and then double-click the file named Setup.exe.

2. **Choose a language/location and click OK.**

   Use the drop-down menu to choose a language/country. That way, when the program displays menus, help files, and other parts of the program, it does so in your language. You may see a progress bar as Premiere unpacks some files. Eventually, a new setup window opens.

3. **Click Next.**

   This panel and some of the others have Back, Next, and Cancel buttons, as shown in Figure A-1. You can use the Back and Next buttons to move back and forth through the installation process (to go back and change the installation location if you change your mind, for example). The Cancel button stops the installation. After you click Next, the License Agreement appears.

4. **Click Accept to agree to Adobe's license.**

   The Adobe agreement is similar to that of most consumer software. You agree that Adobe owns the program code (the digital instructions that make Premiere work) and you're only going to use it on one computer. Adobe gives you permission to install a copy on a second computer, like a laptop, as long as you use only one copy at a time.

5. **Type in your name, choose a country (again), type in Premiere's serial number, and then click Next.**

   Adobe uses your name and serial number to keep track of the legitimate copies of the program. If you downloaded the program, you were given a serial number with your receipt. If you have the DVD boxed version, the number is on the box.

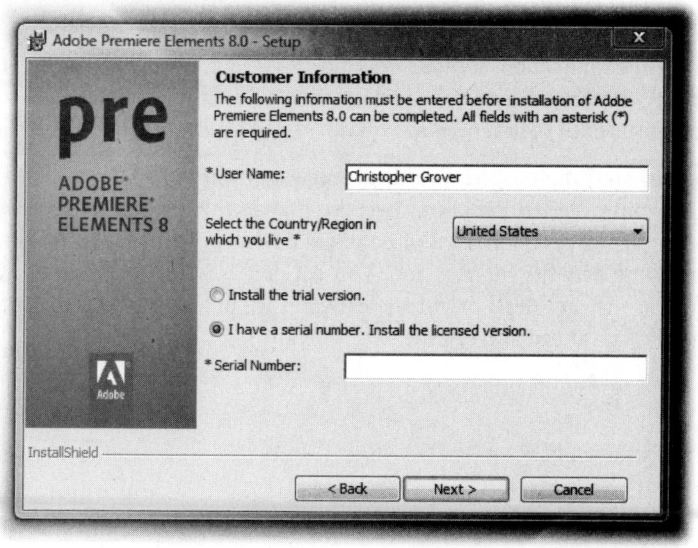

Figure A-1:
Adobe uses your name and serial number to track the legitimate copies of the program. If you download the program, Adobe gave you a serial number along with your receipt. If you bought Premiere on DVD, the serial number is on the DVD box.

6. **Choose your TV format (NTSC or PAL) and then click Next**

   In the Americas, the Caribbean, Japan, Taiwan, and South Korea, NTSC is the video standard for TVs. In Europe, Russia, Africa, the Middle East, and other parts of Asia, PAL is the standard.

7. **Choose a destination folder for Premiere and then click Next.**

   Most of the time when you install a new program, it's best to use the folder it suggests. That way, any add-ons you might buy for the program (like additional templates for Premiere) can easily find the program because the add-ons use the same default destination. Accepting Premiere's default location puts Premiere on your *C:* drive. After you click "Next", a panel appears with details about the Adobe License Activation.

8. **Read the Activation info and then click the Install button.**

   The activation details explain that the installer program contacts Adobe over the Internet to make sure it's a legal copy. When you click Install, the actual installation begins. A status bar keeps you apprised of the progress, which can take a few minutes. Once the program is installed, one last window appears with a couple of notes about QuickTime and other software components.

9. **Click Finish.**

   A warning box explains that you need to restart your computer before you fire up Premiere. Click the Yes button to restart, or click No to keep working and restart your computer later.

Register Premiere Elements 8

After you restart your computer, you can run Premiere Elements by clicking the Adobe Premiere Elements icon on your desktop. You may want to drag that icon to the Windows QuickStart bar (or, depending on your version of Windows, to the Taskbar) at the bottom of your screen so you can start Premiere with a single click.

The first time you start the program, Adobe encourages you to register it. Software publishers like you to register programs because it gives them a way to keep track of legal copies. It also gives them a list of potential customers for sibling programs. Still, there are some benefits for you, too. You get details when they update your program, and you may get deals on future software. So, unless you're dedicated to a life "off the grid," go ahead and register.

Get Help for Premiere Elements 8

Take a look at the credits at the end of a movie and you get an idea how many pros it takes to make a Hollywood blockbuster. You probably won't need quite that much help when you work with your camcorder and Premiere, but it's still good to know where to turn when you need a second opinion. This appendix has two parts: help you can get from Adobe, and help you can get from other sources.

Help from Adobe

You're working along in Premiere and you have a question about a menu command, a preference setting, or the timeline. As with many Windows programs, you can get help by pressing the F1 key (or clicking Help → Adobe Premiere Elements Help). Premiere opens your browser and displays the help files shown in Figure B-1. Unlike some other help systems, Premiere doesn't show you help related to what you were doing at that moment. Instead, when you press F1, it takes you to the first page of Premiere Elements' help. It's up to you to find the topic you need. The next section explains how.

Search Adobe's Help Files

When you have Premiere's help documents open, you can find the information you need in a couple of ways. Adobe organizes the help files like a book, with a table of contents on the left. Click the + buttons to expand the topics listed so you can see their subtopics.

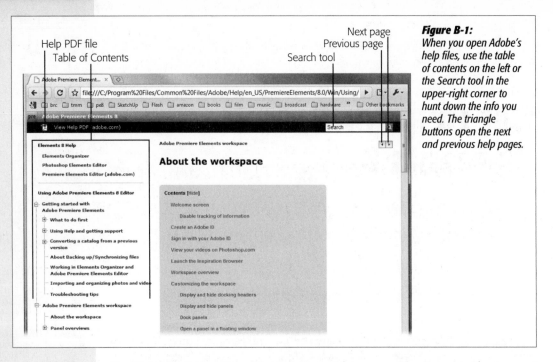

Help PDF file
Table of Contents
Next page
Previous page
Search tool

Figure B-1:
When you open Adobe's help files, use the table of contents on the left or the Search tool in the upper-right corner to hunt down the info you need. The triangle buttons open the next and previous help pages.

You'll also find a search tool in the upper-right corner. Type in a word or two and press the Enter key to see a list of pages related to the search terms. To limit your search to the Premiere Elements 8 help files, check the box labeled "This Help system only". If you don't check the box, the search includes the Adobe User Forums and other websites (provided you're connected to the Internet). Those sites have some great info about Premiere, but it's not always concise. They're great resources if you're patient and want to learn more Premiere tips and tricks, but they can be frustrating when you're on deadline and need an answer quickly.

Two triangle buttons in the upper-right corner of the Help page move you from one page to the next, as though you were thumbing through a book. The help files don't include a lot of pictures, and those they do include are very small. You can enlarge most of 'em by clicking on them.

Print Your Own Help Docs

You can print your own Adobe Premiere Elements 8 help manual, but make sure you stock your printer with plenty of paper. Check to see that you're connected to the Internet and then press F1 to open Premiere's online help files. As shown in Figure B-2, you'll see a PDF icon in the upper-left corner, next to the words "View Help PDF (adobe.com)". Click the icon to open it in your web browser or right-click it and save the file to a folder on your computer. You can open the saved file in a browser or Adobe Reader and then print it from either program.

Adobe TV's Video Tutorials

Adobe hosts a website that includes tutorials and demonstrations related to their products. Go to *http://tv.adobe.com* and then type *Premiere Elements* in the Search Videos box. As shown in Figure B-2, you see a web page that lists several videos. While you're there, you may want to check out some of the other tutorials, including the ones for Premiere Pro, the professional-level version of Premiere Elements 8. You never know what tips and video know-how you might pick up.

Figure B-2:
Adobe hosts video tutorials on their Adobe TV website. The site organizes videos by product and skill level: beginner, intermediate, and advanced.

Help from Others

Premiere Elements is a popular program, so you don't have to search far to find other videographers interested in sharing helpful info.

Muvipix.com

The muvipix.com website (*www.muvipix.com*) focuses on video and targets people who might be described as "prosumers": serious consumers or part-time professionals. There's a lot of information about Adobe products, especially Premiere Elements (Figure B-3). In fact, both muvipix founders—Chuck Engels and Steve Grisetti—have written books about Premiere Elements. In the site's forums, you'll find active bulletin boards full of knowledgeable discussions on video and Premiere Elements. You can browse the forums as a visitor or become part of the muvipix community by signing up for a free membership. If you like what you find, you can get a paid subscription, which gives you access to additional resources like more gallery space for uploading and sharing your videos, menu templates, royalty-free music, and motion backgrounds.

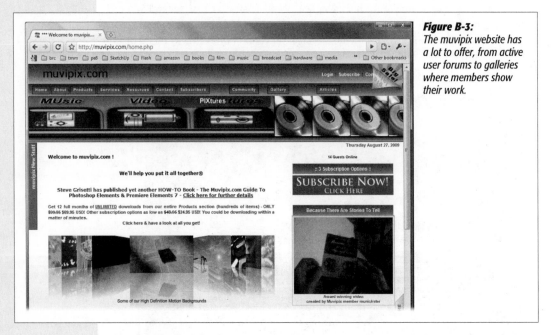

Figure B-3:
The muvipix website has a lot to offer, from active user forums to galleries where members show their work.

Lynda.com

Lynda.com (*www.lynda.com*) knows something about everything, at least when it comes to computer software (Figure B-4). A top-notch resource for educational materials, Lynda.com offers online and video-based training tutorials for almost all Adobe products, including Premiere Elements. As this book went to press, that included a great DVD for Premiere Elements 7 by Jeff Sengstack, and by the time you read this, the site may offer one for Premiere Elements 8, too. The tutorial examples are clear and the tips and instructions cut to the chase.

Elements Village

Elements Village (*www.elementsvillage.com*) is an online forum for people using Photoshop Elements and Premiere Elements. There are more Photoshop Elements users out there than Premiere Elements users, so expect the site to be weighted a little in that direction. Still, you'll find sections devoted to Premiere and making videos. As you can see from Figure B-5, the site is your typical barebones forum, but the message boards are lively and there are plenty of people willing to answer your questions. Membership is free. All you need to do is provide standard info such as a username, password, and date of birth.

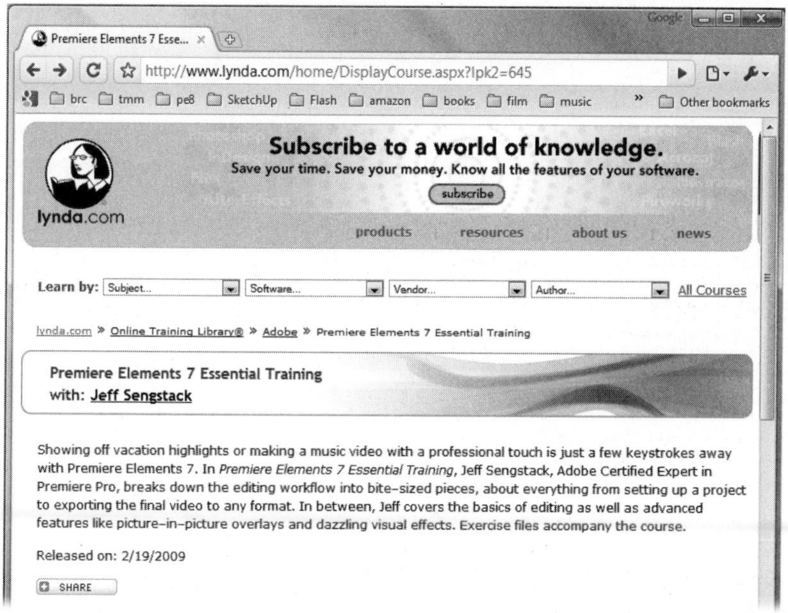

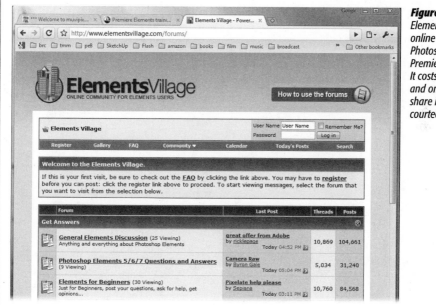

Figure B-4:
Lynda.com provides video tutorials for all different types of programs. The hosts are knowledgeable and the presentations professional.

Figure B-5:
Elements Village is an online community of Photoshop Elements and Premiere Elements users. It costs nothing to join, and once there, you'll share in some lively but courteous discussions.

Premiere Elements 8 Menu by Menu

Premiere Elements 8: The Missing Manual gives you all the details, explanations, and examples you need to create awesome movies. This appendix gives you a quick description of every command in every Premiere menu.

Note: For menu-by-menu descriptions of Elements Organizer, see page 427.

File Menu

The File menu's commands work on your Premiere projects as a whole. For example, you can create new projects and open earlier ones. It's also where you find commands for the important job of importing and exporting media.

New

This menu item opens a submenu listing what you can create in Premiere, like projects and folders.

Project (Ctrl+N)

When you start working in Premiere, you create a project file for your movie, which holds your movie's timeline and all its tracks. The project file keeps tabs on all the media clips you use in your movie, but it doesn't store the clips themselves. Instead, it uses *copies* of your original clips as you edit (called "previews") but remembers where it stored the raw clips on your computer. When it's time to create a copy of your edited movie, Premiere uses your original clips. That way, you always get the best quality video.

Folder (Ctrl+/)

Use this command to create new folders when you're in the Project panel (Windows →
Available Media). The Project panel displays all the clips you added to a project,
even if you're not currently using all those clips in your movie. You can use the
folders to organize your clips; for example, you might create a folder that holds
unused clips. You can place folders inside of folders to create subfolders.

Tip: Another way to display the Project panel is to click the Organize tab and then click the Project button.

Title (F9)

Adds a 5-second clip at the playhead position in the timeline that features a text
box and a placeholder title ("Add Text"). Premiere puts the title on its own track.
You can edit and reformat the text.

Photoshop File

This command is grayed out if you don't have Photoshop Elements installed. If
you do, use this command when you want to create or add still photos to your
project. When you select this command, your computer launches Photoshop Elements with a new, blank image file loaded and ready to go. The best part is the
image is perfectly sized for your project. You even see guidelines that show the
"video safe" and "title safe" margins.

Open Project (Ctrl+O)

Displays Premiere's Open Project window, where you can browse through your
computer's folders and open a saved project.

Open Recent Project

Click this command and you see a submenu listing the last five projects you've
opened. Click one of the project's names to open it.

Close (Ctrl+W)

Closes your project. If you have any unsaved work, Premiere prompts you to save
it. After it closes your project, Premiere is still open and ready to work on another
project.

Save (Ctrl+S)

Saves changes you made to your project. If you haven't made any changes, Premiere dims this option. If you've never saved the project before, the command
works the same way as Save As (described next).

Save As (Ctrl+Shift+S)

Saves the current project with a new name. After choosing the command, you see a standard Explorer window where you can navigate to a different folder and type in a new name. Once Premiere saves the file, the project is still open, but with a new name.

Save a Copy (Ctrl+Alt+S)

Saves a copy of the current project with a new name. Just as with the Save As command, Premiere opens an Explorer-like window where you can choose a folder and provide a filename for the copy. When you choose this command, your current project remains open, not the newly saved copy.

Revert

Discards any changes you made to a project or media file since the last time you saved it. This command is handy when you decide you've gone down the wrong path and want things the way they were before. (It works only in Premiere, though, not in real life.)

Get Media From

Click this important command to bring media clips into your project. A submenu opens where you have these choices:

- DV Camcorder

- HDV Camcorder

- DVD (Camcorder or PC DVD Drive)

- Tapeless Camcorder (Hard disk or memory)

- Digital Still Camera

- Mobile Phone and Players

- Webcam or WDM Device

- PC Files and Folders

You can also import media by clicking the Organize tab and then clicking the Get Media button. For more on importing media clips, see page 41.

Export

The Export command should be named Export Title because that's the only type of file it exports. (This changed from previous versions of Premiere Elements.)

Tip: If you want to Export a media clip, put it in the timeline, then go to Share → Personal Computer. At that point, you can choose a file format and save the media clip. For more details, see page 380.

Project Archiver

Premiere Elements' project files keep track of all the media clips you use in your project. They don't store copies of the original clips, but they know where those files are on your computer. So what if you want to store all the bits and pieces related to a movie in one place? Say you want to store all the data files on a DVD or an external hard drive. In that case, use the Project Archiver command to save your project file *and* all the media files associated with it in one location. You can choose to save only the clips in your timeline or all the clips in your project, including those that aren't in the timeline.

Get Properties For

As you work, it's often helpful to examine the properties of different media clips and files. Click this command and Premiere opens a window where you can browse through the folders on your computer and select files. Double-click a file-name and Premiere opens a Properties window that provides details such as the file's format, image or frame size, frame rate, and audio specifications.

Interpret Footage

Use this command to mix video clips shot in different formats, such as when you want to use HDV video in a Standard DV project. The Interpret Footage dialog box lets you manually change a clip's properties, such as the pixel aspect ratio and alpha channel properties. Select a clip in the Project panel before using this command.

Exit (Ctrl+Q)

Closes any open project and then closes Premiere Elements itself. If you have unsaved work in your project, Premiere prompts you to save it.

Edit Menu

The Edit menu includes the standard Copy, Cut, and Paste commands you'd expect, and a whole lot more. The last item in this menu, in classic PC tradition, lets you adjust the program's settings.

Undo (Ctrl+Z)

This command undoes the last command you applied. So if you accidentally delete a clip or commit an editing faux pas, this command can rescue you. Remember Undo for those moments when you smack your forehead and say "Oh no! Why'd I do that?" Premiere keeps track of your actions sequentially, so you can use this command several times in a row to backtrack through your recent activity.

Redo (Ctrl+Shift+Z)

This command lets you undo the Undo command. If you undo an action or a command and then decide you preferred it before the Undo, use the Redo command to get back to square one. You can use multiple Undos and Redos to move back and forth through your recent Premiere activities.

Cut (Ctrl+X)

Removes the selected media clip or item and places a copy on your computer's Clipboard (temporary memory). Once it's in the Clipboard, you can paste it to another location.

Tip: The quickest way to use the Cut, Copy, Paste, and Clear commands is often through the shortcut menu. Right-click a clip in the timeline or Project panel and these commands appear at the top of the pop-up menu.

Copy (Ctrl+C)

Copies the selected media clip or item and places it in the Clipboard. The original stays in place. Using this command to copy a clip on your timeline and paste a duplicate in another location.

Paste (Ctrl+V)

Places the item in the Clipboard in the timeline or Project panel. If you're working in the timeline, the Paste command places the clip at the playhead's position.

Tip: When you work with text like titles, the Cut, Copy, and Paste commands work just as they do in a word processor.

Paste Insert (Ctrl+Shift+V)

This version of the Paste command inserts a clip in the Clipboard into the timeline and shifts the other clips to make room.

Paste Attributes (Ctrl+Alt+V)

Use this time-saving command to paste the effects you applied to one media clip to another clip. For example, if you want to use the colorful Find Edges effect on several clips, apply it to one clip and fine-tune it. Then, copy the effect and use this command to paste the Find Edges command to your other clips.

Clear (Shift+Delete)

Removes the selected item from the timeline, media, or Project panel. Unlike the Cut command, Premiere doesn't put the item in the Clipboard, so you can't paste it elsewhere. If you make a mistake with the Clear command, you can Undo (Ctrl+Z) your action.

Delete and Close Gap (Backspace)

Removes a clip from the timeline and shifts the other clips to the left to close the gap left by the deleted clip.

Duplicate (Ctrl+Shift+/)

Used in the Project panel, this command creates a duplicate of the selected media clip in the Project panel.

Select All (Ctrl+A)

Selects all the media clips in the timeline, sceneline, media view, and Project panel.

Deselect All (Ctrl+Shift+A)

Deselects any media clips you've selected. This command works in the timeline and the Project panel.

Find (Ctrl+F)

Use this command in the Project panel to open Premiere's versatile Find panel, where you can search for clips in your project. The Find panel lets you search specific file attributes like name, description, and media type. You can limit the search results by using qualifiers such as Contains, Starts With, Ends With, or Matches Exact.

Locate Media

Premiere project files store details about your media, including file locations. If you move a media file or it's otherwise inaccessible to Premiere, the clip shows up in your project as an offline file. Use this command to locate it and reconnect it with Premiere.

Label

You can use colored labels to help organize your clips. Premiere uses the color as a background for clips in the timeline. To apply a label, select your clip then choose a color from the Label submenu.

Select Label Group

Use the Select Label Group command to select all the clips that have the same label. For example, in the timeline, click on a clip with a green label. Then choose Edit → Label → Select Label Group and Premiere highlights all the clips in the timeline that have a green label.

Edit Original (Ctrl+E)

Use this command to open a media clip in a program other than Premiere. For example, if you select a still photo and then choose Edit → Edit Original, Premiere opens the photo file in Photoshop Elements or another photo-editing program.

Keyboard Customization

If you're not happy with Premiere's keyboard shortcuts, use this command to change them. A window opens that displays every command and its current shortcut (if it has one). You can select any command and type in a new shortcut. You get a warning if you try to assign an existing shortcut.

Project Settings

When you create a new project in Premiere, you have to choose a Project preset, which defines several of the project's properties, such as the video format, frame rate, and frame size. As you work, you may want to review or change some of these settings.

General

You can view several of Premiere's General settings here, but you can't change most of them after you create a project (Premiere grays them out); examples include frame size, pixel aspect ratio, and fields. You *can* edit some other settings even after you create a project, such as the project's "title safe" margins.

Capture

Choose the type of file formats Premiere can import for this project, such DV, HDV, or WDM clips.

Video Rendering

You can view rendering file formats and compressors (codecs), but you may not be able to make changes.

Tip: When you select one of the Project Settings, such as General or Capture, a window opens that holds all the project's settings. Click the list on the left side to choose an option. The Preferences settings (discussed next) work the same way.

Preferences

Premiere gives you more than a dozen preference panels you can use to make the program work the way you want it to. You don't *have* to make any changes here. In fact, you may want to leave them alone until you learn your way around the program.

General

This panel includes preferences related to the way Premiere plays back your video. For example, you can specify a default value for transitions and set the timeline to scroll smoothly or to display one page at a time. One important option here is the Enable Background Rendering checkbox. Premiere makes temporary copies of your original media clips, and you actually edit these files as you create your movie. If you turn on the Rendering checkbox, Premiere does all the calculations necessary to play back your movie smoothly when it's not busy with other tasks. But if your computer struggles to keep up with your edits, turn off this checkbox. When you need to render a clip to see your movie play back seamlessly, you do it manually, by pressing the Enter key while you're working in the timeline or sceneline.

Audio

These preferences control your movie's audio playback and other audio features as you edit. For example, if you don't like the garbled sound when you play clips backward or at odd speeds, turn off the "Play audio while scrubbing" checkbox. This section also has settings for SmartMix, Premiere's tool for automatically balancing the volume of different sounds in your video.

Audio Hardware

Use this to specify the audio hardware you want Premiere to use. In most cases, you don't need to make changes here.

Audio Output Mapping

Use this to specify your computer's audio hardware. Again, in most cases, you don't need to change these settings.

Auto Save

Premiere automatically saves your projects. That way, if disaster strikes, you may be able to recover a good chunk of your work. These settings let you choose how frequently Premiere auto-saves your project.

Capture

Capturing video doesn't always go smoothly. If your computer can't keep up with the camcorder or other device feeding it video, it fails to capture all the frames in the video clip. These gaps are called "dropped frames." Use these settings to tell Premiere how many dropped frames you'll tolerate.

Device Control

Device control, where Premiere takes over operation of your camcorder, is described in detail on page 43. Unless you have a very old or unusual camcorder or video device, Premiere's standard settings should work well. If they don't, you can use these settings to fine-tune capture options. For a list of specific devices by brand and model number, click the Options button.

Label Colors

Don't care for the colors Premiere uses for labels? Choose this preference panel and go crazy. Click on a despised color and choose a new one from the color picker.

Label Defaults

Premiere uses specific colors for different labels it applies to your clips. For example, video clips use gray labels, while audio clips use green. Here's where you can change these colors to match your own sense of style.

Media

Premiere makes temporary copies of your media clips as you edit and stores them in a place called the Media Cache. After a while, your computer may become filled up with files you no longer need. Use the settings here to remove these temporary files by clicking the Clean button. After you do, Premiere makes a new set of temporary files as needed.

Scratch Disks

Premiere works with lots of different files, like your original media clip files and your temporary editing files. Premiere lists the different file types (captured video, captured audio, video previews, and so on) here. The Scratch Disks preferences let you choose where on your computer Premiere stores these different files. If your PC has a single drive, you don't need to make changes here. But if you have more than one internal drive, you may be able to get Premiere to work faster by choosing your fastest drive for items listed in this panel and then putting your project files on another drive. Don't use external USB drives for these options, though— they aren't fast enough for the job.

Stop Motion Capture

You can create stop-motion special effects as you capture video from a camcorder or other device (see page 53). Use these preferences to set the initial frame rate and the onion-skin settings.

Titler

Choose the letters you want to appear when Premiere displays your font options as you create movie titles. Unless you change this setting, Premiere displays an upper- and lowercase "A".

Web Sharing

Premiere's Share options include presets for Photoshop.com, YouTube, and Podbean. Premiere periodically checks for new services (unless you turn off the "Automatically Check for Services" checkbox), but you can manually check for them, too, by clicking the Refresh button.

User Interface

When you first run Premiere, the workspace background is a dark gray. This works well because images pop out from the dark, neutral background. But if gray isn't your color, change the brightness settings here—or change Premiere's colors to match those your version of Windows uses.

Clip Menu

When you work in Premiere, you're almost always working with media clips. This menu is devoted to clip-related tasks like grouping and ungrouping clips and managing clip markers.

Rename (Ctrl+H)

When you add media to your project, the clips display their filenames in the Media View and Project panel. Often it's something unhelpful like *VID00021.MP4*. You can change that to something that makes more sense, like *eagle catches salmon*. This doesn't change the original clip's filename, it only changes the name *as it appears in your project*.

Insert

Puts the selected clip at the playhead position in the timeline or sceneline. Premiere repositions other clips to accommodate the newcomer.

Overlay

Use this command to replace video in the timeline. First, select a clip in the Project panel or open it in the Preview window. Then, position the playhead where you want the new video to appear. Choose the Overlay command and the selected clip takes the place of the video in the timeline. Alternatively, you can Ctrl-drag a clip from the Project panel or the Preview window.

Enable

Enable is a toggle for clips. Initially, Premiere enables—makes active—all your clips, and a checkmark appears next to the Enable command. To disable a clip so that it won't play back in your movie and won't be included when you export the timeline, select a clip and then choose this option so the checkmark disappears. What's the advantage of this? It gives you a quick and easy way to preview different editing ideas.

Unlink Audio and Video

Most clips you import from your camcorder include audio and video tracks that play in lockstep. Occasionally, you may want to work with just the audio or just the video track. Use this command to separate the two. Then, you can use one or the other.

Group (Ctrl+G)

This command lets you group several clips together so they move around the timeline as a single clip, which can be a real timesaver. For example, you may have edited together a sequence of several clips that you wan to reposition. Use this command to move all the clips at once.

Ungroup (Ctrl+Shift+G)

Use this command to break apart clips you grouped.

Replace Footage

Replaces a clip in your Project panel with a clip that you choose from your computer's files. This process doesn't replace footage in your timeline.

Set Clip Marker

Premiere has lots of different markers. You can place markers in the timeline or within a clip. Clip In and Out points are a type of clip marker. To place markers in a clip, open the clip in Premiere's Preview monitor and then choose one of these options.

In

When you view a clip in the Preview monitor, you can set In and Out points. Then, when you drag the clip from the Preview monitor to the timeline or sceneline, Premiere adds only the frames between the In and Out points to your movie.

This command sets the In point in a clip, the beginning of a scene you want to use in your movie.

Out

This command sets a clip's Out point.

Video In

You can set a clip's video and audio In and Out points separately. This command sets the Video In point.

Video Out

This command sets the Video Out point.

Audio In

This command sets the Audio In point.

Audio Out

This command sets the Audio Out point.

Unnumbered

Inserts an unnumbered marker in the clip at the playhead's position. You can insert markers in a clip for any reason. You may want to mark the place where the Titanic sinks or Leonardo DiCaprio makes his entrance, for example.

Next Available Numbered

Inserts a numbered marker at the playhead using the next unused number.

Other Numbered

Inserts a numbered marker at the playhead. You get to choose the number.

Go to Clip Marker

Use these options to navigate to specific markers in your clip. Your options are:

- Next (Ctrl+Shift+right arrow key)
- Previous (Ctrl+Shift+left arrow key)
- In
- Out
- Video In
- Video Out
- Audio In
- Audio Out
- Numbered (Ctrl+Shift+3)

Clear Clip Marker

You can clear (remove) clip markers one at a time or in bunches.

Current (Ctrl+Shift+0)

Clears the marker at the playhead. The easiest way to position the playhead at a marker is to use one of the Go to Clip Marker commands.

All Markers (Atl+Shift+0)

Removes all the markers from a clip except for In and Out points.

In and Out

Removes In and Out markers.

In

Removes an In marker.

Out

Removes an Out marker.

Numbered

Removes all numbered markers.

Video Options

There are several clip commands that affect the video clip's appearance:

Frame Hold

You can pause a single frame in your video clip for the duration of the clip. During this time, the audio track continues to play. You have three options for choosing the frame Premiere displays: the clip's In point, its Out point, or a marker that's numbered 0.

Field Options

Video often displays a frame of film by weaving together the even-numbered lines of the frame's pixels with the odd-numbered lines. This type of playback is called "interlaced." Usually, the playback is so fast that you never notice the interlacing. However, in freeze frames, slow motion shots, or shots with text (titles) in them, you may be able to see the interlacing. Experiment with these options to fix the problem.

Frame Blend

This option can solve interlacing problems in clips played at less than full speed.

Scale to Frame Size

Resizes a clip to match the frame size of the project.

Audio Options

Premiere gives you two clip commands for audio tracks:

Audio Gain

There are two options in the Audio Gain panel. Click the Normalize button to automatically boost the gain (volume) where it's too low and to reduce the gain where it's too high. Use the number box to increase or decrease the overall input volume of the clip. Positive numbers increase the gain, negative numbers reduce it.

Render and Replace

Creates a WAV file using the audio from your clip and any effects you may have applied to it. Premiere makes sure the WAV file matches Premiere's technical settings for your project. It makes the file available in your Media View and Project panel.

Time Stretch (Ctrl+R)

Opens the Time Stretch panel to change the speed of a clip. Speed is represented as a percentage, with 100 percent representing normal speed. To play your clip in reverse, turn on the "Reverse Speed" box. For more details on Time Stretch, see page 220.

Scene Detect

Use this command to have Auto-Analyzer break a long clip into smaller parts. It looks for dramatic changes in the clip's images and splits the clip into separate scenes.

Beat Detect

This command analyzes the rhythm of an audio clip and creates beat markers in the timeline. You can use those markers to edit your video to the rhythm of the soundtrack.

Effects Mask

Use the Effect Mask command to apply an effect to only a portion of the video image.

Apply

Creates a rectangular effects mask in the monitor and adds a duplicate clip in an upper layer of the timeline. You can change the mask's size and shape by dragging the corner handles.

Edit

After you apply an effects mask and work in other parts of the timeline, you can no longer see the effects mask rectangle. Select the duplicate clip in the upper layer of the timeline and then choose this command to display the effects mask again. Once it's displayed, you can move and resize it.

Remove

Deletes the effects mask and the duplicate clip from the timeline.

Remove Effects

Sure, you can manually remove effects from a clip one by one, but that's a lot of work. Use these commands to remove more than one effect at a time. Select a clip in the timeline and then choose one of the following options from the submenu:

- Audio Effects
- Video Effects
- All Effects

Timeline Menu

This menu lets you control the way the timeline works. The options here affect things like video rendering, the timeline's appearance, and the markers.

Render Work Area (the Enter key)

Use this command to render any unrendered clips beneath the work area bar, the gray bar right below the time scale. You can resize the bar by dragging the handles at either end. Rendering your work smoothes out video playback.

Delete Rendered Files

With Premiere constantly making temporary media files as you edit, your computer can become pretty cluttered with big files. You may no longer need some of these files because you're not using the clips in your timeline. Select this command to delete all temporary files for the project currently open. Premiere will continue to render files as they're needed.

Delete Rendered Files for All Projects

Running out of disk space? Use this command to delete *all* the temporary files Premiere has created for different projects.

Split Clip (Ctrl+K)

Position the playhead where you want to break a clip into two parts and then select this command or click the scissors button in the monitor.

Smart Trim Mode

The Auto-Analyzer examines your clips and marks parts as good or bad. Use this option to run the Auto-Analyzer and remove the bad portions of clips from your timeline.

Smart Trim Options

This command lets you guide the Auto-Analyzer and the Smart Trim tool (which identifies bad portions of clips) as they work. Perhaps you don't mind shaky video or underexposed clips. Use sliders to adjust Smart Trim's sensitivity regarding clip quality and interest (or subject matter). In manual mode, Smart Trim simply marks the bad portions, and you can remove them or not. In Automatic mode, Smart Trim deletes the bad bits right away.

Zoom In (=)

Zooms in on the timeline so you see fewer frames but have a better view of individual clips and frames.

Zoom Out (–)

Zooms out from the timeline so you see more of the clips and frames in your project, but in less detail.

Tip: You can also use the timeline's slider to zoom in and out. It's faster and easier to get exactly the view you want.

Set Beat Marker

Use this command to place a beat marker at the playhead position. You use beat markets to edit a video to the rhythm of its soundtrack. If you don't want to manually set beat markers, you can have Premiere automatically detect beats by clicking the Audio Tools menu and then choosing Detect Beats.

Go to Beat Marker

This command helps you navigate from one beat marker to the next. The two submenu options are Next and Previous.

Clear Beat Marker

Move the playhead to a beat marker and then choose this command to remove the marker.

Set Timeline Marker

You use timeline markers to tag a particular point in your movie. The markers stay at the same point in time even if you resize or rearrange clips in the timeline. Timeline markers come in two flavors: unnumbered and numbered.

Unnumbered

Inserts an unnumbered marker in the timeline. You can use a dialog box to add comments and adjust the marker's settings.

Next Available Numbered

Premiere adds a marker to your timeline and gives it the next available number.

Other Numbered

Premiere adds a marker to your timeline and you can assign a number to it.

Go to Timeline Marker

This command helps you navigate from one timeline marker to the next. The three submenu options are:

• Next (Ctrl+right arrow key)

• Previous (Ctrl+left arrow key)

• Numbered (Ctrl+3)

Clear Timeline Marker

When your timeline gets overly cluttered, you can remove the markers in a number of ways:

Timeline Marker at Current Time Indicator (Ctrl+0)

Move the playhead to a timeline marker and then use this command to remove it.

All Markers (Alt+0)

Use this to remove all the markers on a timeline

Numbered

This command removes numbered timeline markers, but leaves the unnumbered ones.

Edit Timeline Marker

Use this command to open a window where you can edit a timeline marker's features. For example, you can add comments or create a web link. Some options only work with certain types of video files.

Snap (S)

Make sure this option is checked if you want clips in the timeline to snap together end-to-end as you work with them.

Apply Default Transition

If you want to have Premiere apply a transition to every cut in the timeline, use this command. How do you choose a default transition? Go to Window → Transitions to view all your options. Right-click a transition and then choose "Set Selected as Default Transition" from the shortcut menu.

Apply Default Transition Along CTI

Use the Page Up and Page Down keys to position the playhead at a cut between two clips. Then use this command to apply the default transition. Using the submenu, you can choose between an audio or video transition. CTI stands for Current Time Indicator, which this book refers to as the playhead.

Add Tracks

Most of the time, Premiere adds tracks before you need them. But you can use this command to add tracks manually or to add several tracks at once.

Delete Empty Tracks

Empty tracks don't have any effect on your project (they don't even increase the size of the project file much). But they get in the way as you edit. You can use this command to tidy up and remove any unused tracks in your project.

Disc Menu

This menu is devoted to saving your movie to a DVD or Blu-ray disc. Most of the commands here have to do with disc menus and the markers you place in the timeline to create menus. If you need more details, there's an entire chapter about creating DVD and Blu-ray discs (page 337).

Change to Auto-Play

DVD and Blu-ray discs without menus are called Auto-Play discs because they start playing as soon as you pop them in a player. Use this command to remove all the menu markers from your project—making it an Auto-Play project.

Generate Menu Marker

Use this command to automatically add scene menu markers to the timeline based on the options you choose (at the beginning of every clip or every *x* minutes). When you copy your movie to a DVD or Blu-ray disc, Premiere uses these markers to create menus.

Set Menu Marker

Use this command to manually place a menu marker at the playhead's position. The Menu Marker window opens where you can select the type of marker and name it.

Go to Menu Marker

This command helps you navigate from one menu marker to the next. The two submenu options are Next and Previous.

Clear Menu Marker

You can remove menu markers one at a time or all at once.

Marker at Current Time Indicator

Use the "Go to Menu Marker" commands to position the playhead at a menu marker, and then use this command to remove the marker.

All Markers

This option removes all the menu markers from your project.

Title Menu

You use titles to add text to your videos. Premiere comes with templates that add predesigned titles to your projects, or you can create your own. You can format and edit the title text just as you would in a word processor. Some of the different title styles include a main title (used at the beginning of a movie to display its name), credits, and lower third (used as a label to identify people and places). If you need more details on titles, check out Chapter 9.

New Title

Use this command to add new generic titles to a movie. You can choose from three different types of titles:

- **Default Still.** Static text that doesn't move.
- **Default Roll.** Text that moves vertically off the screen, often used in closing credits.

• **Default Crawl.** A band of text that moves horizontally across the screen. This is a favorite of cable news channels.

After you create a new title with this command, you can reposition it on the screen.

Font

Use this option to choose the typeface (font) for your titles. A submenu lists all the fonts installed on your computer.

Size

Choose a font size. Submenu options list appropriately large fonts, but you can choose the Other option and enter any size you want.

Type Alignment

Choose to align text to the left, right, or center.

Orientation

You can orient text horizontally or vertically.

Word Wrap

When you apply this command to your titles, if it's too long to fit on a single line, Premiere moves the excess to the next line.

Roll/Crawl Options

This command opens the Roll/Crawl Options panel, where you control how text and titles move on your screen. For example, you can make text that crawls horizontally move to the left or to the right. Or you can add extra blank space at the beginning or end of credits.

Image

When you create custom titles, you may want to add clip art or photos to dress them up. Use these commands to add and format those images:

Add Image

Use this command to add an image as an independent graphic that you can reposition on-screen. A window opens so you can find graphic files stored on your computer.

Insert Image into Text

Use this option to place an image in your text. The image's position is linked to its place in the text.

Restore Image Size

Images have bounding boxes with handles that you use to resize and reshape the image. Use this command to restore a modified image to its original size.

Restore Image Aspect Ratio

Use this command to return a distorted image to its original aspect ratio.

Transform

The different title elements appear in Premiere's monitor as graphic elements. These elements have bounding-box borders with handles that you can use to reshape and resize the titles. You can also use the following commands to adjust the items:

- Position

- Scale

- Rotation

- Opacity

Select

Use these options to navigate between the different elements that make up a single title:

- First Object Above

- Next Object Above (Ctrl+Alt+])

- Next Object Below (Ctrl+Alt+[)

- Last Object Below

Arrange

These options let you move a selected element up and down in relation to the other elements in the title layers. If you've used other Adobe software, such as Photoshop or Flash, the Arrange options, and even their shortcuts, may look familiar. Your choices are:

- Bring to Front (Ctrl+Shift+])

- Bring Forward (Ctrl+])

- Send to Back (Ctrl+Shift+[)

- Send Backward (Ctrl+[)

Position

This command helps you place title elements horizontally and vertically in the video frame. You have three options:

- Horizontal Center
- Vertical Center
- Lower Third

Align Objects

Use these options to align elements in relation to each other. For example, you could make sure several titles of different lengths are all centered in relation to each other. Your choices are:

- Horizontal Left
- Horizontal Center
- Horizontal Right
- Vertical Top
- Vertical Center
- Vertical Bottom

Distribute Objects

These commands puts an equal amount of space between different title elements:

- Horizontal Left
- Horizontal Center
- Horizontal Right
- Horizontal Even Spacing
- Vertical Top
- Vertical Center
- Vertical Bottom
- Vertical Even Spacing

View

Use the View options to show and hide different guidelines in the monitor.

Safe Title Margin

The Safe Title Margin is a rectangle that shows the boundaries for title text. Some TVs might not display text outside these boundaries.

Safe Action Margin

Similar to the Safe Title Margin, the Safe Action Margin is a little bit bigger. Objects outside the box may not show up on some TVs.

Text Baselines

The Text Baseline is a thin line that marks the bottom of text, not counting descenders in letters like "p" and "g."

Window Menu

Most of these commands open a floating window or a specific panel in the Tasks panel on the right of the Premiere workspace.

Restore Workspace

You can change Premiere's workspace by resizing the panels and undocking them so they float independently. This command puts everything back in their original positions.

Show Docking Headers

Docking headers appear above the timeline, the monitor, and the Tasks panel. When the docking header is visible, you can drag the monitor and the timeline to new positions.

Hide Docking Headers

Hides docking headers, giving you a little extra workspace.

Available Media

Displays the Project panel, where you can see all the media that's part of your project. This is the same view you see when you click the Organize tab and then the Project button.

Get Media

Displays the Get Media panel, where you can import clips from camcorders and PC files and folders. This is the same view you see when you click the Organize tab and then the Get Media Button.

Organize

Calls up the Media panel, where you can see all the media in Premiere, including media that's not part of your project. Drag any media clip to the timeline and it becomes part of your project and appears in the Project panel. This is the same view you see when you click the Organize tab and then the Media button.

Themes

Displays pre-designed themes that come with Premiere. This is the same view you see if you click the Edit tab and then the Themes button. You apply themes to your project by selecting a theme and clicking the Next button. In the following panels, you can choose which theme features to apply to your movie.

Effects

Displays the Effects panel, where you can choose video and audio effects. This is the same view you see when you click the Edit tab and then the Effects button. You apply effects by dragging them onto a clip in the timeline or onto the monitor.

Transitions

Shows available transitions in the Tasks panel. Apply transitions by dragging them to the beginning or end of a clip. This is the same view you see if you click the Edit tab and then the Transitions button.

Titles

Opens the Titles panel with its tools and settings. You can add titles to your project by dragging them onto the monitor. This is the view you see when you click the Edit panel and then click the Title button.

Disc Menus

Opens the Disc Menus tab, where you can create menus for your DVD and Blu-ray discs.

Share

Opens the Share tab, where you can export your movie to discs, websites, computer files, and handheld devices.

Monitor

Displays Premiere's monitor if you closed or hid it.

Properties

If a clip is selected, this command displays the effects applied to the clip. This is the same as right-clicking a clip and choosing Show Properties.

Disc Layout

Shows the Disc Layout monitor used to prepare movies before you copy them to a DVD or Blu-Ray disc. Disc Layout lists menu items in the monitor and gives you the option of previewing the menu system.

My Project

Displays the Sceneline/Timeline panel if you closed or hid it.

Narration

Opens the Narration panel where you can start and stop recording a voiceover.

Audio Meters

Opens the Audio Meters panel that displays the level for each audio channel in your project. Premiere usually hides this panel.

Audio Mixer

Opens the Audio Mixer panel where you can adjust the level and balance for each audio track in your project. Premiere normally hides this panel.

History

Displays the History panel, which keeps a running list of the actions you perform in Premiere. You can drag the slider button on the left side of the list to undo your actions and revert to an earlier version of your project.

Info

Opens the Info panel so you can see details about a selected object. For example, when you select a clip, the Info panel lists the type of clip, the duration, and details about its file format. If it's in the timeline, you see the clip's start and end times in relation to the timeline. If the clip is in the Project panel, the Info panel lists the In and Out points.

Events

Opens the Events panel, which displays warnings and error messages that can help you troubleshoot Premiere problems. To learn more about any of the listed events, click the Details button.

Help Menu

Adobe Premiere Elements Help (F1)

Displays Premiere's help files in a browser window. For details, see page 393.

Keyboard

Displays a list of keyboard shortcuts.

How to Use Help

Displays tips on how to use the different Premiere help tools.

Online Support

This option takes you to Adobe's website, which includes user forums and other online support tools.

About Adobe Premiere Elements

Opens the panel that lists your program's version number, legal notices, and the names of the people who developed the program.

Registration

If you didn't register your copy of Premiere when you first installed it, choose this option to do so.

Deactivate

Premiere's license lets you install the program on two computers. The activation process makes sure you don't exceed that number. (You activate the program when you first install and use Premiere.) If you upgrade to a new computer, use this command to deactivate Premiere on the old computer so you can install a legal copy on your new one.

Updates

This option runs the Adobe Updater, which checks Adobe's website to see if any of your Adobe products need to be updated. If so, this tool walks you through the process.

The "pre" Menu

At first, you might not recognize the purple "pre" icon in the upper-left corner of Premiere's screen as a menu, but it is. It offers basic controls for the Premiere workspace, commands like Minimize and Maximize that you'd find in any Windows programs.

A program window like the Premiere Elements workspace has different "states." For example, you can maximize the window so that it fills your entire screen, or you can minimize it so that it covers only part of the screen, leaving room for you to see other windows. The commands described below control these different window states.

Restore

When you minimize Premiere's window using the Minimize command described below, Premiere's screen closes and Windows creates a Premiere program icon in the Taskbar (the strip at the bottom of your screen). To get Premiere's screen back, right-click that icon and then click Restore.

Move

You can't use the Move command if you have Premiere's display set to Maximize, otherwise you can drag Premiere's top bar to put the window in a new spot. Or if you prefer, you can right-click the Premiere icon in the Taskbar, select Move from the drop-down menu, and use the arrow keys to move the window.

Size

Just as with the Move command, you can't resize a maximized window. But when the Premiere window covers only part of the screen, you can drag any edge to resize it. Or you can right-click the Premiere icon in the Taskbar, select Size from the drop-down menu, and then use the arrow keys to change window's shape and size.

Minimize

Hides an open window. Windows deselects Premiere's icon in the Taskbar.

Maximize

This command makes the Premiere window fill the entire screen.

Close (Alt+4)

This closes the Premiere window and exits the program.

Elements Organizer Menu by Menu

Adobe's Elements Organizer program is a standalone application that both Photoshop Elements (Adobe's editing program for still images) and Premiere Elements use. You install it automatically whenever you install either program.

The Organizer began life as an organizing and editing program for still photographers, so many of the commands relate only to still photos. This appendix lists those commands as "For photos" and only covers them briefly. If you need more details, check out *Photoshop Elements 8 for Windows: The Missing Manual* by Barbara Brundage.

Note: For a menu-by-menu description of Premiere Elements, see Appendix C.

File Menu

As with most programs, you use the File menu to manage documents as a whole. In the case of the Organizer, those documents may be photos, videos, or the Organizer catalog.

Get Photos and Videos

Use this command to add media (videos, audio, stills) to the Organizer catalog.

From Camera or Card Reader

Imports stills from a camera or card reader.

From Scanner

Starts your scanner software (a separate program) and imports images you scan.

From Files and Folders

Use this command to import video and audio files from your computer into the Organizer catalog.

By Searching

Searches your hard drive(s) for media files; it looks for common media-file extensions, like AVI for video and MP3 for audio.

This command simply looks for media file types, you can't limit its scope by providing part of a filename, although you *can* limit the search using a couple of check boxes:

- **Exclude System and Program Folders.** This option tells the Organizer not to search folders that are unlikely to contain media files. If you leave this box unchecked, the search turns up media files—like logos and clip art—that are part of programs you install.
- **Exclude Files Smaller Than.** Sets the minimum size for files the search reports.

After the search, the Organizer displays a list of the folders that contain media. You can select and import the contents of entire folders.

New

This command lets you create video projects and, if you have Photoshop Elements, still photos.

Photoshop Elements Image File

Starts the Photoshop Elements program and creates an empty Photoshop (.psd) file.

Premiere Elements Video Project

Starts the Premiere Elements program and creates an empty Premiere Elements (.prel) project.

Image from Clipboard

The behavior of this command varies depending on what type of file the Organizer has in its Clipboard (temporary memory). For example, if you select a still image and click the Copy command (Edit → Copy), when you use the "Image from Clipboard command", the Photoshop Elements Editor opens and creates a new document using that image. If you use this command after you select a video clip and use the Copy command, Premiere Elements opens instead.

Photomerge Group Shot

For still photos. You can put people from different photos into a single image. Zelig yourself!

Photomerge Faces

For still photos. You can combine different facial parts into a single face. Identikits anyone?

Photomerge Scene Cleaner

For still photos. Lets you remove unwanted relatives from family photos.

Photomerge Panorama

For still photos. Opens the Photoshop Elements Editor, where you can stitch several photos together into a single image.

Photomerge Exposure

For still photos. Opens the Photoshop Elements Editor, where you can make exposure adjustments by averaging the exposure of two different images.

Open Recently Edited File in Editor

Works as advertised to help you launch photos and video projects you recently worked on. This option presents two lists, one for Premiere Elements and one for Photoshop Elements.

Catalog

Elements Organizer keeps track of different media files. The file where the Organizer stores this information is called the *catalog*. This command opens the Catalog Manager. You may not need to use the commands here often, but they let you rename, move (to a new folder), and remove catalogs. If the Organizer is extremely sluggish or behaving oddly, try the Optimize or Repair buttons.

Usually, you want to have a single catalog to keep track of all your media, but you may want to have more than one. Perhaps you'd like to keep your personal media separate from your business media, for example. In that case, use this command to open the Catalog Manager, where you can work with multiple catalogs.

Burn data CD/DVD

Use this command to create copies of your media files. When you use this command with video files, you're not creating a DVD that plays in your home DVD player. Instead, you're making copies of your raw video clips as an archive.

Copy/Move to Removable Disk

If you want to move media clips to different folders or drives on your computer, use this command. The purpose of the Organizer is to keep track of your media. If, after you import a video clip or photo using the Organizer, you use Windows Explorer to move the file, the Organizer won't know where to find it.

Backup Catalog to CD, DVD or Hard Drive

Use this command to make a backup copy of your media files. It's always good to have more than one copy of important or irreplaceable files, and photos and videos often fit that description.

Restore Catalog from CD, DVD or Hard Drive

Use this command to copy (or restore) your backed-up files to your computer and catalog.

Duplicate

Select a photo or media clip and then choose this command to create a copy of it. You see two thumbnails of the clip in the Organizer and two copies on your computer.

Reconnect

If you rename folders or move files using other programs, the Organizer loses track of them. Use these commands to find missing files and reconnect them to the Organizer catalog.

Missing File

If the Organizer can't find a file you previously added to its catalog, you see a thumbnail image with a question mark. Select the thumbnail and then choose this command to find the missing file.

All Missing Files

Use this command to find and reconnect all the media in the catalog that's unaccounted for.

Watch Folders

The Organizer can "watch" folders on your computer and automatically add any media you put there to its catalog. Select this menu item to tell the program which folders you want it to keep tabs on.

Rename

Use this command to rename your media. If you use other programs, such as Windows Explorer, to rename your photos or video files after you've added them to the Organizer's catalog, the Organizer will lose track of them.

Write Keyword Tag and Properties Info to Photo

For still photos. This command lets you store keywords tags in a photo file as part of its metadata. (Metadata is info about a file that's stored with that file.)

Move

Use this command to, well, move your media. If you use other programs, such as Windows Explorer, to move your photos or video files after you've added them to the Organizer's catalog, the Organizer will lose track of them.

Export As New File(s)

Select the media files you want to export, and then select this command. A window opens where you can choose a location for the duplicate files. When you work with photos, you can choose new file formats, too. For example, you can export a Photoshop (.psd) file as a JPEG (.jpg).

Print

Use this option to print photos or the first frame of your videos.

Exit

Closes the catalog and then closes the Organizer itself. (Closing the Organizer doesn't close Premiere Elements.)

Edit Menu

The Edit menu's items help you work on individual photos and media clips.

Undo

This command undoes the last command you applied. So it can come to the rescue if you accidentally delete a clip or you commit an editing faux pas. Remember Undo for those moments when you smack your forehead and say "Oh no! Why'd I do that?" The Organizer keeps track of your actions sequentially, so you can use Undo multiple times to backtrack through your recent actions.

Redo

This command lets you undo an Undo. If you undo an action or a command and then decide that you preferred it before the Undo, use Redo to get back to square one. You can use multiple Undos and Redos to move back and forth through your recent Organizer activities.

Copy

Copies the selected media clip or other item (photo, MP3, sound file, and so on) and places the copy on the Clipboard (the original stays where it is).

Select All

Selects all the items in the Organizer's catalog.

Deselect

Deselects any items you've selected.

Delete from Catalog

Remove an item from the Organizer's catalog. (This *doesn't* delete the file from your computer.)

Rotate 90 Degrees Left

For still photos. Rotates the image 90 degrees counter-clockwise.

Rotate 90 Degrees Right

For still photos. Rotates the image 90 degrees clockwise.

Auto Smart Fix

For still photos. Applies several of Photoshop Elements' Smart Fix options to improve the photo.

Auto Red Eye Fix

For still photos. Reduces red eye caused by camera flash.

Edit with Photoshop Elements

For still photos. Opens a still image in Photoshop Elements.

Edit with Premiere Elements

Opens a movie clip in Premiere Elements. Adds the clip to the end of the timeline.

Edit with Photoshop

For still photos. Opens a still image in Photoshop.

Adjust Date and Time

The date and time the Organizer displays under catalog thumbnails don't have to match the file's Date Created or Date Modified settings. Use this command when you want to reset an item's displayed date and time. The panel that appears gives your three options:

• Change to a specified date and time.

• Change to match the file's date and time.

• Shift by a set number of hours (time zone adjust).

Add Caption

Use this command to add a caption to photos or media clips. You can then use this text to search for specific items.

Update Thumbnail

Updates the thumbnail for the selected photo or media clip. If you need to reconnect the file to the Organizer (see the Reconnect command on page 430), a search panel opens and automatically searches for the original file.

Set as Desktop Wallpaper

For still photos. Changes your Windows desktop settings to use the selected photo as your desktop's background.

Ratings

You can easily give your photos and clips a rating of from 1 to 5 stars, a great way to separate good media from so-so media. Once you apply a rating, you can filter the clips in the catalog by their rating. For more details, see page 109.

Visibility

Use these commands to show and hide media in the catalog. They're helpful when you want to reduce clutter.

Mark as Hidden/Mark as Visible

Toggles whether the selected file is hidden or visible.

Show All Files

Displays all your files, even those marked as hidden.

Show Only Hidden Files

Shows only your hidden files.

Place on Map

For still photos. Use this command to link a photo to a particular location using Yahoo! Maps.

Remove from Map

For still photos. Breaks the link between a photo and a geographical location.

Show on Map

For still photos. Displays a photo location on a Yahoo! Map.

Stack

For still photos. Used to group still photos together. Only the top photo in a stack is visible unless you expand the stack. Similar to video scenes, described below.

Version Set

For still photos. Used to keep track of different versions of an edited image.

Video Scene

Select this menu item and Premiere's Auto-Analyzer breaks the selected video clip into scenes based on changes in the image. A single clip that has several scenes displays a lighter-colored frame than continuous clips. Use this command or click the button on the right side of the thumbnail's frame to expand and collapse clips with scenes.

Run Auto-Analyzer

Starts the Auto-Analyzer, which examines the selected media. When it's done, it applies Smart Tags to the clips and may divide the clip into scenes. Smart Tags describe many clip characteristics, including overall quality, audio quality, exposure, contrast, focus, motion, shakiness, faces, and number of objects.

Color Settings

For still photos. Used to manage the color settings for photos, according to professional standards. You can choose to optimize color for computer screens or printing.

Contact Book

If you frequently send photos or clips to the same people, you can create a contact book within the Organizer to stores names, email addresses, and physical addresses. You can import vCards (electronic business cards) into the contact book.

Preferences

Use this commands to adjust the way the Organizer works. For example, if you only use Premiere Elements and not Photoshop Elements, go to Edit → Preferences → Editing and deselect "Show Photoshop Elements Options". You can also use the preferences to control how the Auto-Analyzer behaves. You can choose whether to have Auto-Analyzer automatically analyze everything in your catalog and which features it identifies. If you want, you can even have the Auto-Analyzer start working when you first turn on your computer, even when you haven't started Premiere Elements.

Find Menu

The commands on the Find menu help you hunt down needles in haystacks. As time goes on, your catalog gets bigger and bigger, so you need these tools to work quickly and efficiently. In general, the Find tools act as filters or they sort items in the catalog so you can zero in on the media you need.

Set Date Range

Opens the Set Date Range dialog box, where you can specify a Start Date and End Date so the Organizer only displays media within that range.

Clear Date Range

Removes the Date Range filter and displays all the media in your catalog.

By Caption or Note

Use this command to search for media by the text in your captions or notes.

Note: After you use one of the Find commands, click the Show All button below the menu bar to see your entire catalog again.

By Filename

Use this command to search for media by the text in their filenames. You don't have to use a complete filename—just a few characters does the trick.

All Version Sets

For still photos. Used to display all of an image's version sets (see the Version Set command on page 434).

All Stacks

For still photos. Used to display all your photo stacks (see the Stack command on page 434).

By History

The Organizer keeps track of what you do with your media. So if you remember emailing a clip to someone, you can go to By History → "E-mailed to" to hunt down the name of the file you sent. Here are the By History commands:

- Imported on
- E-mailed to
- Printed on
- Exported on
- Ordered Online
- Shared Online
- Used in Projects

By Media Type

Use this command to display a particular type of media. For example, you can view all your audio clips. The options are:

- Photos
- Video
- Audio
- Projects
- PDF
- Items with Audio Captions

By Details (Metadata)

This command lets you search the info stored with video or still files (see "Write Keyword Tag and Properties Info to Photo" on page 431). In general, still photos store a much richer set of information. However, you can search video files for certain details, like displaying all the video clips that use a frame rate greater than 15fps.

For still photos: Certain image file formats can store text info along with the image. That text is called metadata, and it may include details about the subject in the photo or the camera settings used to capture the image. Use this command to hunt down photos based on their metadata.

Items with Unknown Date or Time

Displays items that don't have a date and timestamp.

By Visual Similarity with Selected Photo(s) and Video(s)

Looks for photos or video clips that have similar colors and tonal qualities that match the selected media. The Organizer arranges your clips with the closest matches first. A percentage number in the lower-left corner of the thumbnails tells you how close the media matches the selected media.

Untagged Items

Displays catalog items that don't have any tags.

Unanalyzed Content

Displays catalog items that the Auto-Analyzer hasn't scrutinized.

Items not in any Album

Displays catalog items that aren't part of an Album.

Find People for Tagging

Finds faces in media, so you can tag the photo or video with an appropriate name.

View Menu

Use the View menu's commands to show and hide items in your catalog.

Refresh

Occasionally, the Organizer window may get a little scrambled. When that happens, choose this option to refresh the screen.

Media Types

The Media Types submenu let's you choose what the catalog displays. Interested only in video? Remove the checkmarks next to all the other options. Here are your choices:

- Photos
- Video
- Audio
- Projects
- PDF

Hidden Files

Similar to the Edit → Visibility commands, you can choose whether your catalog displays files marked Hidden. The options are:

- Hide Hidden Files
- Show All Files
- Show Only Hidden Files

Details

Displays information about a video, photo, or other media under its thumbnail. The details include the file's star rating, date and time, duration (for video), and name.

Show File Names

Shows or hides filenames in the Details list.

Show Grid Lines

Separates media thumbnails using gridlines.

Show Borders around Thumbnails

The Organizer adds a barely noticeable border around thumbnail images.

Expand All Stacks

For still photos. Expands stacked photos.

Collapse All Stacks

For still photos. Collapses all stacked photos.

Window Menu

Use these commands to show and hide different parts of the Organizer workspace.

Show/Hide Task Pane

Opens and closes the Task Pane on the right side of the Organizer.

Show Map

For still photos. Shows and hides the Yahoo! Map panel where you can link photos to specific locations.

Timeline

Shows and hides a timeline at the top of the Organizer window. Not to be confused with the timeline in Premiere Elements, the Organizer's timeline displays a bar graph representing your media by the date displayed in the Organizer. Usually this date is the same as the date you imported or last changed the file, but you can change it using the Edit → "Adjust Date and Time" command (page 433). Click on a bar to display the related photos and media clips.

Properties

Opens the Properties panel for selected media. This panel is helpful when you want to find a file's location or determine its size. The Properties panel has four tabs:

- **General.** Includes the filename, size, folder location, and date stamp.

- **Metadata.** For videos, this displays the date the file was created and modified, as well as the document type and details such as the frame rate. For photos, this displays the metadata saved with the image.

- **Keyword Tags.** Displays the keyword tags applied to the selected media.

- **History.** Displays details such as when you imported, emailed, or shared a media clip.

Help Menu

The Organizer's Help menu leads to help and support for three different programs: the Organizer, Premiere Elements, and Photoshop Elements. For more details on getting help with Premiere, see Appendix B.

Elements Organizer Help

Opens the Elements Organizer's help files in your web browser.

Key Concepts

Opens help files that explain the basics of using Elements Organizer.

Support

Photoshop Elements

Opens your web browser and then opens the Photohop Elements product support page on the Adobe web site. Once you're there, you see video tutorials, tips and online help files.

Premiere Elements

Opens your web browser and then opens the Premiere Elements product support page on the Adobe web site. Once you're there, you see video tutorials, tips and online help files.

Video Tutorials

Opens a drop-down menu where you choose either "Photoshop Elements" or "Premiere Elemens". Takes you to the Adobe TV website (*http://tv.adobe.com*) and displays a list of tutorial videos for the selected programs.

Forum

Displays the web pages for Adobe's Premiere Elements or Photoshop Elements user forums.

About Elements Organizer

Opens the panel that lists the version number for the Organizer and the names of the people who developed the program.

Patent and Legal Notices

Displays the patent numbers and legal details related to the Organizer.

System Info

Displays info about your computer and your version of the Organizer. These details can be helpful when you're troubleshooting problems.

Updates

Searches for updates to your Adobe programs.

Elements Inspiration Browser

Opens the Elements Inspiration Browser, which is another way to access Adobe's web-based resources, such as tutorials and videos.

The Organizer Window Menu

At first you might not recognize it as a menu, but the gray-and-blue lightbox icon in the upper-left corner of Premiere's screen as a menu, but it is. It offers basic controls for the Organizer workspace, commands like Minimize and Maximize, which you find in any Windows programs.

A program window like the Organizer workspace has different "states." For example, you can maximize the window so that it fills your entire screen, or you can minimize it so that it covers only part of the screen, leaving room for you to see other windows. The commands described below control these different window states.

Restore

When you minimize the Organizer window using the Minimize command described below, Windows closes the Organizer's screen and adds an Organizer icon to Taskbar (the strip at the bottom of your screen). To get the Organizer's screen back, right-click that icon and then click Restore.

Move

You can't use the Move command if you maximize the Organizer's window, but when it covers only part of the screen, you can drag the top bar to put the window in a new spot. Or right-click the Organizer icon in the Taskbar, select Move from the drop-down menu, and use arrow keys to move the window.

Size

Just as with the Move command, you can't resize a maximized window. But when the Organizer window covers only part of your screen, you can drag any edge to resize it. Or if you prefer, you can right-click the Organizer's icon in the Taskbar, select Size from the drop-down menu, and then use the arrow keys to change the window's shape and size.

Minimize

Hides an open window. Windows deselects the Organizer's icon in the Taskbar.

Maximize

This command makes the Organizer window fill your whole screen.

Close (Alt+4)

This closes the Organizer window and exits the program.

Tip: If you're working with dual monitors and have trouble getting the Elements Organizer to show itself, try this: Right-click the Organizer icon in the Windows task bar and choose Minimize. Then right-click it and choose Maximize. If you still don't see the Organizer, right-click it one more time in the Task Bar and choose Maximize a second time. It doesn't seem quite right, but it works with most dual monitor setups.

Index

G

H

I

M

Colophon

Sumita Mukherji provided quality control for *Premiere Elements 8: The Missing Manual*.

The cover of this book is based on a series design originally created by David Freedman and modified by Mike Kohnke, Karen Montgomery, and Fitch (*www.fitch.com*). Back cover design, dog illustration, and color selection by Fitch.

David Futato designed the interior layout, based on a series design by Phil Simpson. This book was converted by Abby Fox to FrameMaker 5.5.6. The text font is Adobe Minion; the heading font is Adobe Formata Condensed; and the code font is LucasFont's TheSansMonoCondensed. The illustrations that appear in the book were produced by Robert Romano using Adobe Photoshop CS4 and Illustrator CS4.

Get even more for your money.

Join the O'Reilly Community, and register the O'Reilly books you own.It's free, and you'll get:

- 40% upgrade offer on O'Reilly books
- Membership discounts on books and events
- Free lifetime updates to electronic formats of books
- Multiple ebook formats, DRM FREE
- Participation in the O'Reilly community
- Newsletters
- Account management
- 100% Satisfaction Guarantee

Signing up is easy:

1. **Go to: oreilly.com/go/register**
2. **Create an O'Reilly login.**
3. **Provide your address.**
4. **Register your books.**

Note: English-language books only

To order books online:

oreilly.com/order_new

For questions about products or an order:

orders@oreilly.com

To sign up to get topic-specific email announcements and/or news about upcoming books, conferences, special offers, and new technologies:

elists@oreilly.com

For technical questions about book content:

booktech@oreilly.com

To submit new book proposals to our editors:

proposals@oreilly.com

Many O'Reilly books are available in PDF and several ebook formats. For more information:

oreilly.com/ebooks

O'REILLY®

Spreading the knowledge of innovators   www.oreilly.com

Buy this book and get access to the online edition for 45 days—for free!

Premiere Elements 8: The Missing Manual
By Chris Grover
October 2009, $34.99
ISBN 9780596803360

With Safari Books Online, you can:

Access the contents of thousands of technology and business books

- Quickly search over 7000 books and certification guides
- Download whole books or chapters in PDF format, at no extra cost, to print or read on the go
- Copy and paste code
- Save up to 35% on O'Reilly print books
- **New!** Access mobile-friendly books directly from cell phones and mobile devices

Stay up-to-date on emerging topics before the books are published

- Get on-demand access to evolving manuscripts.
- Interact directly with authors of upcoming books

Explore thousands of hours of video on technology and design topics

- Learn from expert video tutorials
- Watch and replay recorded conference sessions

To try out Safari and the online edition of this book FREE for 45 days, go to **www.oreilly.com/go/safarienabled** and enter the coupon code NFXTOXA. To see the complete Safari Library, visit safari.oreilly.com.

Spreading the knowledge of innovators   safari.oreilly.com